*research problems
in psychology*

research problems in psychology

Pietro Badia
Bowling Green State University

Audrey Haber
Richard P. Runyon
C. W. Post College of Long Island University

Addison-Wesley Publishing Company
Reading, Massachusetts · Menlo Park, California
London · Amsterdam · Don Mills, Ontario · Sydney

ISBN 0-201-06607-6
EFGHIJKLMN-CO-798765

preface

In selecting the material for this book, the primary goal was to facilitate the training of students to become better researchers. It is our belief that this goal can be reached most effectively by providing the student with essential information in certain key areas of experimentation. Therefore, the readings which we have selected are intended primarily to provide a clearer description and understanding of some uncontrolled factors which can affect the outcome of an experiment independently of the variables deliberately manipulated.

While it is generally conceded that the scientific method is unsurpassed for the acquisition of information, the naive adoption of the experimental model used with inanimate objects in physics has at times proved troublesome to the behavioral scientists. This statement is supported by the concern shown by behavioral scientists with the difficulties experienced in attempting to replicate their own findings as well as those of others. Despite increasing technological innovation and refinement of scientific tools, failures at replication occur too frequently. It would appear, therefore, that a more careful assessment of the total experiment by the behavioral investigator is necessary.

The organization of these articles follows no rigid pattern. The student can begin with any block of readings he finds most appealing.

The primary intent of the first block of readings is to deal with some research problems relating to the experimental situation, the experimenter, and the subject. The demand characteristics of the experiment, experimenter bias, and subject characteristics are discussed in relation to the effects they may have on experimental outcomes. Other topics deal with the treatment of experimental subjects, their increasing sophistication, and the possible negative effects of using subject deception. It is our belief that emphasis on these factors will provide the student with the needed understanding of how an investigator can inadvertently allow these variables to affect his experimental outcomes.

In doing research, questions often arise as to the efficacy or appropriateness of a manipulative versus a correlational method. At other times, the question may center on the efficacy of a within-subject design as opposed to a between-subject design. The second block of readings describes the different characteristics of these methodologies and also provides guidelines for selecting the most effective technique. In addition, readings are included which caution the researcher about inferring individual performance from a function based on average data.

Training students to be better researchers can also be enhanced by providing them with information bearing on the logical issues involved in current data evaluation practices. The final block of readings brings together some of the most fundamental and enduring issues related to the statistical evaluation of research findings. Several of the readings take issue with and question the test of significance in psychological research. Considerable emphasis is placed on the controversy surrounding null hypothesis testing. Classical and Bayesian approaches to data analyses are discussed, and the difference between theory testing in physics and in psychology is described. Further empirical and theoretical effort concerning these controversies is inevitable. Students who acquaint themselves with today's issues in these areas will unquestionably be better prepared for future developments.

We are most grateful to the many authors and publishers who permitted us to use their articles.

March 1970

R. P. R.
A. H.
P. B.

contents

block 1

1. Orne, M. T. On the social psychology of the psychological experiment: with particular reference to demand characteristics and their implications. *American Psychologist*, 1962, **17,** 776–783.

2. Rosenthal, R. The volunteer subject. *Human Relations*, 1965, **18,** 389–406.

3. McGuigan, F. J. The experimenter: a neglected stimulus object. *Psychological Bulletin*, 1963, **60,** 421–428.

4. Kintz, B. L., Delprato, D. J., Mettee, D. R., Persons, C. E., and Schappe, R. H. The experimenter effect. *Psychological Bulletin*, 1965, **63,** 223–233.

5. Rosenthal, R. Experimenter outcome-orientation and the results of the psychological experiment. *Psychological Bulletin*, 1964, **51,** 405–412.

6. Kelman, H. C. Human use of human subjects: The problem of deception in social psychological experiments. *Psychological Bulletin*, 1967, **67,** 1–11.

Research problems which are typically not emphasized in courses dealing with design and statistics are included in this first block of readings. If titles were to be used for each block, the most appropriate title for the first series of papers might simply be *Research on Research*. Investigations directed toward research procedures and methods are increasing in number and the overall effect on research in the behavioral sciences cannot help but be salutary.

Problems must be identified before they can be eliminated or controlled. One such problem is bias. In these readings the point is made repeatedly that bias can, and often does, enter the research setting in many varied and subtle forms. Investigators have begun to realize more fully that there exist many unintended sources of bias that operate in behavioral research, and that relevant data identifying and assessing these biases are essential. Therefore, more investigators are devoting a greater share of their professional effort to a critical analysis of the research setting and procedure.

If the experiment proper were to be broken down into some of its component parts and analyzed critically, then separate analyses would most likely occur for the experimenter, the subject, and the experimental setting. Bias can come into contact with the experiment at any of these points, and sufficient data are presented in the first block of readings to cause concern among researchers. Experimenter bias, subject characteristics and demand characteristics of the experiment are discussed in relation to the effects they may have on experimental outcomes. Other articles deal with the ethical treatment of subjects who participate in behavioral experiments; their increasing sophistication and the possible negative effects on subjects which may result from frequent use of deception by experimenters.

Judging from the conclusions reached in the various readings of this first block, it would appear that behavioral scientists must consider more carefully the characteristics of subjects used in experiments, the use of deception in research, and the demand characteristic of the experiment.

1

on the social psychology of the psychological experiment:

with particular reference to demand characteristics and their implications[1]

Martin T. Orne[2]

It is to the highest degree probable that the subject['s] ... general attitude of mind is that of ready complacency and cheerful willingness to assist the investigator in every possible way by reporting to him those very things which he is most eager to find, and that the very questions of the experimenter ... suggest the shade of reply expected .... Indeed ... it seems too often as if the subject were now regarded as a stupid automaton ....

A. H. PIERCE, 1908[3]

From *American Psychologist*, Vol. 17, 1962, pp. 776–783. Reprinted by permission of the author and the American Psychological Association.

1. This paper was presented at the Symposium, "On the Social Psychology of the Psychological Experiment," American Psychological Association Convention, New York, 1961.

   The work reported here was supported in part by a Public Health Service Research Grant, M-3369, National Institute of Mental Health.

2. I wish to thank my associates Ronald E. Shor, Donald N. O'Connell, Ulric Neisser, Karl E. Scheibe, and Emily F. Carota for their comments and criticisms in the preparation of this paper.

3. See reference list (Pierce, 1908).

Since the time of Galileo, scientists have employed the laboratory experiment as a method of understanding natural phenomena. Generically, the experimental method consists of abstracting relevant variables from complex situations in nature and reproducing in the laboratory segments of these situations, varying the parameters involved so as to determine the effect of the experimental variables. This procedure allows generalization from the information obtained in the laboratory situation back to the original situation as it occurs in nature. The physical sciences have made striking advances through the use of this method, but in the behavioral sciences it has often been difficult to meet two necessary requirements for meaningful experimentation: reproducibility and ecological validity.[4] It has long been recognized that certain differences will exist between the types of experiments conducted in the physical sciences and those in the behavioral sciences because the former investigates a universe of inanimate objects and forces, whereas the latter deals with animate organisms, often thinking, conscious subjects. However, recognition of this distinction has not always led to appropriate changes in the traditional experimental model of physics as employed in the behavioral sciences. Rather the experimental model has been so successful as employed in physics that there has been a tendency in the behavioral sciences to follow precisely a paradigm originated for the study of inanimate objects, i.e., one which proceeds by exposing the subject to various conditions and observing the differences in reaction of the subject under different conditions. However, the use of such a model with animal or human subjects leads to the problem that the subject of the experiment is assumed, at least implicitly, to be a *passive responder* to stimuli—an assumption difficult to justify. Further, in this type of model the experimental stimuli themselves are usually rigorously defined in terms of what *is done* to the subject. In contrast, the purpose of this paper will be to focus on what the human subject *does* in the laboratory: what motivation the subject is likely to have in the experimental situation, how he usually perceives behavioral research, what the nature of the cues is that the subject is likely to pick up, etc. Stated in other terms, what factors are apt to affect the subject's reaction to the well-defined stimuli in the situation? These factors comprise what will be referred to here as the "experimental setting."

---

4. Ecological validity, in the sense that Brunswik (1947) has used the term: appropriate generalization from the laboratory to nonexperimental situations.

Since any experimental manipulation of human subjects takes place within this larger framework or setting, we should propose that the above-mentioned factors must be further elaborated and the parameters of the experimental setting more carefully defined so that adequate controls can be designed to isolate the effects of the experimental setting from the effects of the experimental variables. Later in this paper we shall propose certain possible techniques of control which have been devised in the process of our research on the nature of hypnosis.

Our initial focus here will be on some of the qualities peculiar to psychological experiments. The experimental situation is one which takes place within the context of an explicit agreement of the subject to participate in a special form of social interaction known as "taking part in an experiment." Within the context of our culture the roles of subject and experimenter are well understood and carry with them well-defined mutual role expectations. A particularly striking aspect of the typical experimenter-subject relationship is the extent to which the subject will play his role and place himself under the control of the experimenter. Once a subject has agreed to participate in a psychological experiment, he implicitly agrees to perform a very wide range of actions on request without inquiring as to their purpose, and frequently without inquiring as to their duration.

Furthermore, the subject agrees to tolerate a considerable degree of discomfort, boredom, or actual pain, if required to do so by the experimenter. Just about any request which could conceivably be asked of the subject by a reputable investigator is legitimized by the quasi-magical phrase, "This is an experiment," and the shared assumption that a legitimate purpose will be served by the subject's behavior. A somewhat trivial example of this legitimization of requests is as follows:

A number of casual acquaintances were asked whether they would do the experimenter a favor; on their acquiescence, they were asked to perform five push-ups. Their response tended to be amazement, incredulity and the question "Why?" Another similar group of individuals were asked whether they would take part in an experiment of brief duration. When they agreed to do so, they too were asked to perform five push-ups. Their typical response was "Where?"

The striking degree of control inherent in the experimental situation can also be illustrated by a set of pilot experiments which were performed in the course of designing an experiment to test whether the degree of control inherent in the *hypnotic* relationship is greater than that in a waking relationship.[5] In order to test this question, we tried to develop a set of tasks which waking subjects would refuse to do, or would do only for a short period of time. The tasks were intended to be psychologically noxious, meaningless, or boring, rather than painful or fatiguing.

For example, one task was to perform serial additions of each adjacent two numbers on sheets filled with rows of random digits. In order to complete just one sheet, the subject would be required to perform 224 additions! A stack of some 2,000 sheets was presented to each subject—clearly an impossible task to complete. After the instructions were given, the subject was deprived of his watch and told, "Continue to work; I will return eventually." Five and one-half hours later, the *experimenter* gave up! In general, subjects tended to continue this type of task for several hours, usually with little decrement in performance. Since we were trying to find a task which would be discontinued spontaneously within a brief period, we tried to create a more frustrating situation as follows:

Subjects were asked to perform the same task described above but were also told that when finished the additions on each sheet, they should pick up a card from a large pile, which would instruct them on what to do next. However, every card in the pile read,

You are to tear up the sheet of paper which you have just completed into a minimum of thirty-two pieces and go on to the next sheet of paper and continue working as you did before; when you have completed this piece of paper, pick up the next card which will instruct you further. Work as accurately and as rapidly as you can.

Our expectation was that subjects would discontinue the task as soon as they realized that the cards were worded identically, that each finished piece of work had to be destroyed, and that, in short, the task was completely meaningless.

Somewhat to our amazement, subjects tended to persist in the task for several hours with relatively little sign of overt hostility. Removal of the one-way screen did not tend to make much difference. The postexperimental inquiry helped to explain the subjects' behavior. When asked about the tasks, subjects would invariably attribute considerable meaning to their performance, viewing it as an endurance test or the like.

---

5.   These pilot studies were performed by Thomas Menaker.

Thus far, we have been singularly unsuccessful in finding an experimental task which would be discontinued, or, indeed, refused by subjects in an experimental setting.[6, 7] Not only do subjects continue to perform boring, unrewarding tasks, but they do so with few errors and little decrement in speed. It became apparent that it was extremely difficult to design an experiment to test the degree of social control in hypnosis, in view of the already *very high degree of control in the experimental situation itself.*

The quasi-experimental work reported here is highly informal and based on samples of three or four subjects in each group. It does, however, illustrate the remarkable compliance of the experimental subject. The only other situations where such a wide range of requests are carried out with little or no question are those of complete authority, such as some parent-child relationships or some doctor-patient relationships. This aspect of the experiment as a social situation will not become apparent unless one tests for it; it is, however, present in varying degrees in all experimental contexts. Not only are tasks carried out, but they are performed with care over considerable periods of time.

Our observation that subjects tend to carry out a remarkably wide range of instructions with a surprising degree of diligence reflects only one aspect of the motivation manifested by most subjects in an experimental situation. It is relevant to consider another aspect of motivation that is common to the subjects of most psychological experiments: high regard for the aims of science and experimentation.

A volunteer who participates in a psychological experiment may do so for a wide variety of reasons ranging from the need to fulfill a course requirement, to the need for money, to the unvoiced hope of altering his personal adjustment for the better, etc. Over and above these motives, however, college students tend to share (with the experimenter) the hope and expectation that the study in which they are participating will in some material way contribute to science and

---

6. Tasks which would involve the use of actual severe physical pain or exhaustion were not considered.

7. This observation is consistent with Frank's (1944) failure to obtain resistance to disagreeable or nonsensical tasks. He accounts for this "primarily by *S*'s unwillingness to break the tacit agreement he had made when he volunteered to take part in the experiment, namely, to do whatever the experiment required of him" (p. 24).

perhaps ultimately to human welfare in general. We should expect that many of the characteristics of the experimental situation derive from the peculiar role relationship which exists between subject and experimenter. Both subject and experimenter share the belief that whatever the experimental task is, it is important, and that as such no matter how much effort must be exerted or how much discomfort must be endured, it is justified by the ultimate purpose.

If we assume that much of the motivation of the subject to comply with any and all experimental instructions derives from an identification with the goals of science in general and the success of the experiment in particular,[8] it follows that the subject has a stake in the outcome of the study in which he is participating. For the volunteer subject to feel that he has made a useful contribution, it is necessary for him to assume that the experimenter is competent and that he himself is a "good subject."

The significance to the subject of successfully being a "good subject" is attested to by the frequent questions at the conclusion of an experiment, to the effect of, "Did I ruin the experiment?" What is most commonly meant by this is, "Did I perform well in my role as experimental subject?" or "Did my behavior demonstrate that which the experiment is designed to show?" Admittedly, subjects are concerned about their performance in terms of reinforcing their self-image; nonetheless, they seem even more concerned with the utility of their performances. We might well expect then that as far as the subject is able, he will behave in an experimental context in a manner designed to play the role of a "good subject" or, in other words, *to validate the experimental hypothesis.* Viewed in this way, the student volunteer is *not* merely a passive responder in an experimental situation but rather he has a very real stake in the successful outcome of the experiment. This problem is implicitly recognized in the large number of psychological studies which attempt to conceal the true purpose of the experiment from the subject in the hope of thereby obtaining more reliable data. This maneuver on the part of psychologists is so widely known in the college population that even if a psychologist is honest with the subject, more often than not he will be distrusted. As one subject pithily put it, "Psychologists always lie!" This bit of paranoia has some support in reality.

---

8. This hypothesis is subject to empirical test. We should predict that there would be measurable differences in motivation between subjects who perceive a particular experiment as "significant" and those who perceive the experiment as "unimportant."

The subject's performance in an experiment might almost be conceptualized as problem-solving behavior; that is, at some level he sees it as his task to ascertain the true purpose of the experiment and respond in a manner which will support the hypotheses being tested. Viewed in this light, the totality of cues which convey an experimental hypothesis to the subject become significant determinants of subjects' behavior. We have labeled the sum total of such cues as the "*demand characteristics of the experimental situation*" (Orne, 1959a). These cues include the rumors or campus scuttlebutt about the research, the information conveyed during the original solicitation, the person of the experimenter, and the setting of the laboratory, as well as all explicit and implicit communications during the experiment proper. A frequently overlooked, but nonetheless very significant source of cues for the subject lies in the experimental procedure itself, viewed in the light of the subject's previous knowledge and experience. For example, if a test is given twice with some intervening treatment, even the dullest college student is aware that some change is expected, particularly if the test is in some obvious way related to the treatment.

The demand characteristics perceived in any particular experiment will vary with the sophistication, intelligence, and previous experience of each experimental subject. To the extent that the demand characteristics of the experiment are clear-cut, they will be perceived uniformly by most experimental subjects. It is entirely possible to have an experimental situation with clear-cut demand characteristics for psychology undergraduates which, however, does not have the same clear-cut demand characteristics for enlisted army personnel. It is, of course, those demand characteristics which are perceived by the subject that will influence his behavior.

We should like to propose the heuristic assumption that a subject's behavior in any experimental situation will be determined by two sets of variables: (a) those which are traditionally defined as experimental variables and (b) the perceived demand characteristics of the experimental situation. The extent to which the subject's behavior is related to the demand characteristics, rather than to the experimental variable, will in large measure determine both the extent to which the experiment can be replicated with minor modification (i.e., modified demand characteristics) and the extent to which generalizations can be drawn about the effect of the experimental variables in nonexperimental contexts [the problem of ecological validity (Brunswik, 1947)].

It becomes an empirical issue to study under what circumstances, in what kind of experimental contexts, and with what kind of subject populations, demand characteristics become significant in determining the behavior of subjects in experimental situations. It should be clear that demand characteristics cannot be eliminated from experiments; all experiments will have demand characteristics, and these will always have some effect. It does become possible, however, to study the effect of demand characteristics as opposed to the effect of experimental variables. However, techniques designed to study the effect of demand characteristics need to take into account that these effects result from the subject's *active* attempt to respond appropriately to the *totality* of the experimental situation.

It is perhaps best to think of the perceived demand characteristics as a contextual variable in the experimental situation. We should like to emphasize that, at this stage, little is known about this variable. In our first study which utilized the demand characteristics concept (Orne, 1959b), we found that a particular experimental effect was present only in records of those subjects who were able to verbalize the experimenter's hypothesis. Those subjects who were unable to do so did not show the predicted phenomenon. Indeed we found that whether or not a given subject perceived the experimenter's hypothesis was a more accurate predictor of the subject's actual performance than his statement about what he thought he had done on the experimental task. It became clear from extensive interviews with subjects that response to the demand characteristics is not merely conscious compliance. When we speak of "playing the role of a good experimental subject," we use the concept analogously to the way in which Sarbin (1950) describes role playing in hypnosis: namely, largely on a nonconscious level. The demand characteristics of the situation help define the role of "good experimental subject," and the responses of the subject are a function of the role that is created.

We have a suspicion that the demand characteristics most potent in determining subjects' behavior are those which convey the purpose of the experiment effectively but not obviously. If the purpose of the experiment is not clear, or is highly ambiguous, many different hypotheses may be formed by different subjects, and the demand characteristics will not lead to clear-cut results. If, on the other hand, the demand characteristics are so obvious that the subject becomes fully conscious of the expectations of the experimenter, there is a tendency to lean over backwards to be honest. We are encountering here the effect of another facet of the college student's attitude toward science. While the student wants studies to "work," he feels he must be honest in his report; otherwise, erroneous conclusions will be drawn. Therefore, if the subject becomes acutely aware of the experimenter's expectations, there may be a tendency for biasing in the opposite direction. (This is analogous to the often observed tendency to favor individuals whom we dislike in an effort to be fair.)[9]

Delineation of the situations where demand characteristics may produce an effect ascribed to experimental variables, or where they may obscure such an effect and actually lead to systematic data in the opposite direction, as well as those experimental contexts where they do not play a major role, is an issue for further work. Recognizing the contribution to experimental results which may be made by the demand characteristics of the situation, what are some experimental techniques for the study of demand characteristics?

As we have pointed out, it is futile to imagine an experiment that could be created without demand characteristics. One of the basic characteristics of the human being is that he will ascribe purpose and meaning even in the absence of purpose and meaning. In an experiment where he knows some purpose exists, it is inconceivable for him not to form some hypothesis as to the purpose, based on some cues, no matter how meager; this will then determine the demand characteristics which will be perceived by and operate for a particular subject. Rather than eliminating this variable then, it becomes necessary to take demand characteristics into account, study their effect, and manipulate them if necessary.

One procedure to determine the demand characteristics is the systematic study of each individual subject's perception of the experimental hypothesis. If one can determine what demand characteristics are perceived by each subject, it becomes possible to determine to what extent these, rather than the experimental variables, correlate with the observed behavior. If the subject's behavior correlates better with the demand characteristics than with the experimental variables, it is probable that the demand characteristics are the major determinants of the behavior.

The most obvious technique for determining what demand characteristics are perceived is the use of postexperimental inquiry. In this regard, it is well to point out that considerable self-discipline is necessary for the experimenter to obtain a valid inquiry. A great many experimenters at least implicitly make the demand that the

9. Rosenthal (1961) in his recent work on experimenter bias, has reported a similar type of phenomenon. Biasing was maximized by ego involvement of the experimenters, but when an attempt was made to increase biasing by paying for "good results," there was a marked reduction of effect. This reversal may be ascribed to the experimenters' becoming too aware of their own wishes in the situation.

subject not perceive what is really going on. The temptation for the experimenter, in, say, a replication of an Asch group pressure experiment, is to ask the subject afterwards, "You didn't realize that the other fellows were confederates, did you?" Having obtained the required, "No," the experimenter breathes a sigh of relief and neither subject nor experimenter pursues the issue further.[10] However, even if the experimenter makes an effort to elicit the subject's perception of the hypothesis of the experiment, he may have difficulty in obtaining a valid report because the subject as well as he himself has considerable interest in appearing naive.

Most subjects are cognizant that they are not supposed to know any more about an experiment than they have been told and that excessive knowledge will disqualify them from participating, or, in the case of a postexperimental inquiry, such knowledge will invalidate their performance. As we pointed out earlier, subjects have a real stake in viewing their performance as meaningful. For this reason, it is commonplace to find a pact of ignorance resulting from the intertwining motives of both experimenter and subject, neither wishing to create a situation where the particular subject's performance needs to be excluded from the study.

For these reasons, inquiry procedures are required to push the subject for information without, however, providing in themselves cues as to what is expected. The general question which needs to be explored is the subject's perception of the experimental purpose and the specific hypotheses of the experimenter. This can best be done by an open-ended procedure starting with the very general question of, "What do you think that the experiment is about?" and only much later asking specific questions. Responses of "I don't know" should be dealt with by encouraging the subject to guess, use his imagination, and in general, by refusing to accept this response. Under these circumstances, the overwhelming majority of students will turn out to have evolved very definite hypotheses. These hypotheses can then be judged, and a correlation between them and experimental performance can be drawn.

Two objections may be made against this type of inquiry: (a) that the subject's perception of the experimenter's hypotheses is based on his own experimental behavior, and therefore a correlation between these two variables may have little to do with the determinants of behavior, and (b) that the inquiry procedure itself is subject to demand characteristics.

---

10.   Asch (1952) himself took great pains to avoid this pitfall.

A procedure which has been independently advocated by Riecken (1958) and Orne (1959a) is designed to deal with the first of these objections. This consists of an inquiry procedure which is conducted much as though the subject had actually been run in the experiment, without, however, permitting him to be given any experimental data. Instead, the precise procedure of the experiment is explained, the experimental material is shown to the subject, and he is told what he would be required to do; however, he is not permitted to make any responses. He is then given a postexperimental inquiry as though he had been a subject. Thus, one would say, "If I had asked you to do all these things, what do you think that the experiment would be about, what do you think I would be trying to prove, what would my hypothesis be?" etc. This technique, which we have termed the pre-experimental inquiry, can be extended very readily to the giving of pre-experimental tests, followed by the explanation of experimental conditions and tasks, and the administration of postexperimental tests. The subject is requested to behave on these tests as though he had been exposed to the experimental treatment that was described to him. This type of procedure is not open to the objection that the subject's own behavior has provided cues for him as to the purpose of the task. It presents him with a straight problem-solving situation and makes explicit what, for the true experimental subject, is implicit. It goes without saying that these subjects who are run on the pre-experimental inquiry conditions must be drawn from the same population as the experimental groups and may, of course, not be run subsequently in the experimental condition. This technique is one of approximation rather than of proof. However, if subjects describe behavior on the pre-inquiry conditions as similar to, or identical with, that actually given by subjects exposed to the experimental conditions, the hypothesis becomes plausible that demand characteristics may be responsible for the behavior.

It is clear that pre- and postexperimental inquiry techniques have their own demand characteristics. For these reasons, it is usually best to have the inquiry conducted by an experimenter who is not acquainted with the actual experimental behavior of the subjects. This will tend to minimize the effect of experimenter bias.

Another technique which we have utilized for approximating the effect of the demand characteristics is to attempt to hold the demand characteristics constant and eliminate the experimental variable. One way of accomplishing this purpose is through the use of simulating subjects. This is a group of subjects who are not exposed to the experimental variable to which the effect has been attributed, but who are instructed to act *as if* this were the case. In order to control for experimenter bias under these circumstances, it is advisable to utilize more than one experimenter and to have the experimenter who actually runs the subjects "blind" as to which group (simulating or real) any given individual belongs.

Our work in hypnosis (Damaser, Shor, and Orne, 1963; Orne, 1959b; Shor, 1959) is a good example of the use of simulating controls. Subjects unable to enter hypnosis are instructed to simulate entering hypnosis for another experimenter. The experimenter who runs the study sees both highly trained hypnotic subjects and simulators in random order and does not know to which group each subject belongs. Because the subjects are run "blind," the experimenter is more likely to treat the two groups of subjects identically. We have found that simulating subjects are able to perform with great effectiveness, deceiving even well-trained hypnotists. However, the simulating group is not exposed to the experimental condition (in this case, hypnosis) to which the given effect under investigation is often ascribed. Rather, it is a group faced with a problem-solving task: namely, to utilize whatever cues are made available by the experimental context and the experimenter's concrete behavior in order to behave as they think that hypnotized subjects might. Therefore, to the extent that simulating subjects are able to behave identically, it is possible that demand characteristics, rather than the altered state of consciousness, could account for the behavior of the experimental group.

The same type of technique can be utilized in other types of studies. For example, in contrast to the placebo control in a drug study, it is equally possible to instruct some subjects not to take the medication at all, but to act as if they had. It must be emphasized that this type of control is different from the placebo control. It represents an approximation. It maximally confronts the simulating subject with a problem-solving task and suggests how much of the total effect could be accounted for by the demand characteristics—assuming that the experimental group had taken full advantage of them, an assumption not necessarily correct.

All of the techniques proposed thus far share the quality that they depend upon the active cooperation of the control subjects, and in some way utilize his thinking process as an intrinsic factor. The subject does *not* just respond in these control situations but, rather, he is required *actively* to solve the problem.

The use of placebo experimental conditions is a way in which this problem can be dealt with in a more classic fashion. Psychopharmacology has used such techniques extensively, but here too they present problems. In the case of placebos and drugs, it is often the case that the physician is "blind" as to whether a drug is placebo or active, but the patient is not, despite precautions to the contrary; i.e., the patient is cognizant that he does not have the side effects which some of his fellow patients on the ward experience. By the same token, in psychological placebo treatments, it is equally important to ascertain whether the subject actually perceived the treatment to be experimental or control. Certainly the subject's perception of himself as a control subject may materially alter the situation.

A recent experiment (Orne and Scheibe, 1964) in our laboratory illustrates this type of investigation. We were interested in studying the demand characteristics of sensory deprivation experiments, independent of any actual sensory deprivation. We hypothesized that the overly cautious treatment of subjects, careful screening for mental or physical disorders, awesome release forms, and, above all, the presence of a "panic (release) button" might be more significant in producing the effects reported from sensory deprivation than the actual diminution of sensory input. A pilot study (Stare, Brown, and Orne, 1959), employing pre-inquiry techniques, supported this view. Recently, we designed an experiment to test more rigorously this hypothesis.

This experiment, which we called Meaning Deprivation, had all the *accoutrements* of sensory deprivation, including release forms and a red panic button. However, we carefully refrained from creating any sensory deprivation whatsoever. The experimental task consisted of sitting in a small experimental room which was well lighted, with two comfortable chairs, as well as ice water and a sandwich, and an optional task of adding numbers. The subject did not have a watch during this time, the room was reasonably quiet, but not soundproof, and the duration of the experiment (of which the subject was ignorant) was four hours. Before the subject was placed in the experimental room, 10 tests previously used in sensory deprivation research were administered. At the completion of the experiment, the same tasks were again administered. A microphone and a one-way screen were present in the room, and the subject was encouraged to verbalize freely.

The control group of 10 subjects was subjected to the identical treatment, except that they were told that they were control subjects for a sensory deprivation experiment. The panic button was eliminated for this group. The formal experimental treatment of these two groups of subjects was the same in terms of the objective stress—four hours of isolation. However, the demand characteristics had been purposively varied for the two groups to study the effect of demand characteristics as opposed to objective stress. Of the 14 measures which could be quantified, 13 were in the predicted direction, and 6 were significant at the selected 10% alpha level or better. A Mann-Whitney U test has been performed on the summation ranks of all measures as a convenient method for summarizing the overall differences. The one-tailed probability which emerges is $p = .001$, a clear demonstration of expected effects.

This study suggests that demand characteristics may in part account for some of the findings commonly attributed to sensory deprivation. We have found similar significant effects of demand characteristics in accounting for a great deal of the findings reported in hypnosis. It is highly probable that careful attention to this variable, or group of variables, may resolve some of the current controversies regarding a number of psychological phenomena in motivation, learning, and perception.

In summary, we have suggested that the subject must be recognized as an active participant in any experiment, and that it may be fruitful to view the psychological experiment as a very special form of social interaction. We have proposed that the subject's behavior in an experiment is a function of the totality of the situation, which includes the experimental variables being investigated and at least one other set of variables which we have subsumed under the heading, demand characteristics of the experimental situation. The study and control of demand characteristics are not simply matters of good experimental technique; rather, it is an empirical issue to determine under what circumstances demand characteristics significantly affect subjects' experimental behavior. Several empirical techniques have been proposed for this purpose. It has been suggested that control of these variables in particular may lead to greater reproducibility and ecological validity of psychological experiments. With an increasing understanding of these factors intrinsic to the experimental context, the experimental method in psychology may become a more effective tool in predicting behavior in nonexperimental contexts.

References

Asch, S. E. *Social psychology.* New York: Prentice Hall, 1952.

Brunswik, E. *Systematic and representative design of psychological experiments with results in physical and social perception.* (Syllabus Series, No. 304) Berkeley: Univer. California Press, 1947.

Damaser, Esther C., Shor, R. E., and Orne, M. T. Physiological effects during hypnotically-requested emotions. *Psychosom. Med.*, 1963, **25**, 334–343.

Frank, J. D. Experimental studies of personal pressure and resistance: I. Experimental production of resistance. *J. gen. Psychol.*, 1944, **30**, 23–41.

Orne, M. T. The demand characteristics of an experimental design and their implications. Paper read at American Psychological Association, Cincinnati, 1959. (a)

Orne, M. T. The nature of hypnosis: Artifact and essence. *J. abnorm. soc. Psychol.*, 1959, **58,** 277–299. (b)

Orne, M. T., and Scheibe, K. E. The contribution of nondeprivation factors in the production of sensory deprivation effects: The psychology of the "panic button." *J. abnorm. soc. Psychol.*, 1964, **68,** 3–12.

Pierce, A. H. The subconscious again. *J. Phil., Psychol., scient. Meth.*, 1908, **5,** 264–271.

Riecken, H. W. A program for research on experiments in social psychology. Paper read at Behavioral Sciences Conference, University of New Mexico, 1958.

Rosenthal, R. On the social psychology of the psychological experiment: With particular reference to experimenter bias. Paper read at American Psychological Association, New York, 1961.

Sarbin, T. R. Contributions to role-taking theory: I. Hypnotic behavior. *Psychol. Rev.*, 1950, **57,** 255–270.

Shor, R. E. Explorations in hypnosis: A theoretical and experimental study. Unpublished doctoral dissertation, Brandeis University, 1959.

Stare, F., Brown, J., and Orne, M. T. Demand characteristics in sensory deprivation studies. Unpublished seminar paper, Massachusetts Mental Health Center and Harvard University, 1959.

2

the volunteer subject[1]

Robert Rosenthal

Introduction

McNemar wisely said 'The existing science of human behavior is largely
the science of the behavior of sophomores' (1946, p. 333). Whether a
useful, comprehensive science of human behavior can be based upon
our knowledge of sophomores would seem to be an empirical question
of great importance. Our concern in the following pages is, however,
more narrow. Do we, in fact, have a science even of sophomores? To
a great extent we may have a science of those sophomores who are
enrolled in psychology courses and who volunteer to participate in
given psychological experiments.

The widespread practice of requiring students in various psychology courses to participate in a certain number of hours' worth of

From *Human Relations* Vol. 18, 1965, pp. 389–406. Reprinted by permission
of the author and *Human Relations*.

1.   Preparation of this paper was facilitated by research grants (G-17685,
     G-24826, and GS-177) from the Division of Social Sciences of the National
     Science Foundation. Special thanks are due to Ray C. Mulry for biblio-
     graphical assistance.

experiments may in some cases permit the generalization of research findings at least to psychology students enrolled in certain courses. In many cases, however, even this generalization may be unwarranted. Frequently the psychology student, while required to serve as *S* in psychological research, has a choice of which experiment to participate in. Do brighter (or duller) students sign up for learning experiments or at least for experiments that are labelled 'learning'? Do better (or more poorly) adjusted students sign up for experiments labelled as personality experiments? Do better (or more poorly) coordinated students sign up for motor skills studies? The answers to these types of question and, more importantly, whether they make a difference, are also empirical matters.

Psychologists have concerned themselves a good deal with the problem of the volunteer *S*. Evidence for this concern will be found in the following pages, where we will find a fair number of attempts to learn something of the act of volunteering and of the differences between volunteers and nonvolunteers. Further evidence for this concern can be found, too, in the frequent statements made with pride in the psychological literature of recent vintage that 'the subjects employed in this experiment were nonvolunteers'. The discipline of mathematical statistics, that good consultant to the discipline of psychology, has concerned itself with the volunteer problem (e.g., Cochran, Mosteller, and Tukey, 1953). Evidence for this concern can be found in the fact that we now know a good bit about the implications for statistical procedures and inference of having drawn a sample of volunteers (Bell, 1961). Generally, the concern over the volunteer problem has had as its goal the reduction of the non-representativeness of volunteer samples in order to increase the generality of research findings (e.g., Locke, 1954; Hyman and Sheatsley, 1954). The magnitude of the potential biasing effect of volunteer samples is clearly illustrated in a report[2] that, at a large university, rates of volunteering varied from 10 to 100 percent. Within the same course, different recruiters going to different sections of the course obtained volunteering rates anywhere from 50 to 100 percent.

Our special purposes here will be first to organize and conceptualize whatever may be substantively known about the act of volunteering and the more enduring personal attributes of volunteers compared with nonvolunteers. Subsequently we shall examine the implications of our analysis for the representativeness of research findings and for the possible effects on experimental outcomes.

---

2. John R. P. French, Jr., personal communication, 19 August 1963.

The act of volunteering

Offering one's services as a subject in a psychological experiment is not a random event. The act of volunteering has as great a reliability as many widely used tests of personality. Martin and Marcuse (1958), employing several experimental situations, found the reliabilities of the act of volunteering for any given experiment to range from .67 to .97.

Volunteering is not, of course, independent of either the task for which volunteering is solicited or the situation in which the request is made. Understandably enough, Staples and Walters (1961) found that *S*'s who had been threatened with electric shocks were less willing to volunteer for subsequent experiments involving the use of shock. Nor was it too surprising to find that rates of volunteering might be increased by making the alternative to volunteering rather unattractive. Conversely, rates of volunteering could be decreased by making the alternative to volunteering more attractive (Blake, Berkowitz, Bellamy and Mouton, 1956). Rates of volunteering could also be manipulated by varying the intensity of the request to participate as well as the perception of the likelihood that others in a similar situation did or would volunteer (Rosenbaum and Blake, 1955; Rosenbaum, 1956; Schachter and Hall, 1952). It would seem likely, too, that *S*'s would volunteer more readily for an *E* they knew well than for one less well or not at all known to them. At least in the area of survey research this does seem to be the case (Norman, 1948; Wallin, 1949). Norman also concluded that there was a general trend for higher prestige survey originators to obtain better participation rates.

Responding to a mail questionnaire is undoubtedly different from volunteering for participation in a psychological experiment (Bell, 1961). Yet there are likely to be phenomenological similarities. In both cases the prospective data-provider, be he 'subject' or 'respondent', is asked to make a commitment of time for the serious purposes of the data-collector. In both cases, too, there may be an explicit request for candor, and almost certainly there will be an implicit request for it. Perhaps most important, in both cases, the data-provider recognizes that his participation will make the data-collector wiser about him without making him wiser about the data-collector. Within the context of the psychological experiment, Riecken (1962) has referred to this as the 'one sided distribution of information'. On the basis of this uneven distribution of information the *S* or respondent is likely to feel an uneven distribution of *legitimate negative evaluation*. On the basis of what the *S* or respondent does or says, the data-collector may evaluate him as maladjusted, stupid, unemployed, or lower class, any of which might be enough to prevent someone from volunteering for either surveys or experiments. The data-provider, on the other hand, can, and often does, negatively evaluate the data-collector. He can call him, his task, or his questionnaire inept, stupid, banal, and the like, but hardly with any great feeling of confidence that this evaluation is really accurate; the data-collector, after all, has a plan for the use of his data, and the subject or respondent usually does not know this plan, though he is aware that a plan exists. He is, therefore, in a poor position to evaluate the data-collector's performance, and he is likely to know it.

Riecken (1962) has postulated that one of an experimental S's major aims in the experimental interaction is to 'put his best foot forward'. It follows from this and from what we have said earlier that, in both surveys and experiments, prospective respondents or S's are more likely to volunteer or respond when there is an increase in their subjective probability of being evaluated more favorably. And so it seems to be—a finding based primarily upon studies of nonresponders in survey research studies. Edgerton, Britt, and Norman (1947) found that winners of contests responded most helpfully to follow-up questionnaires, whereas losers responded least. Their interpretation of greater interest in the subject on the part of the winner group does not by itself seem entirely convincing. Contest winners have the secure assurance that they did win, and they are being asked to respond, very likely, in their winner role. Contest losers, on the other hand, have the less happy assurance that they were losers and perhaps would be further evaluated as such. These same authors (1947) convincingly demonstrated the consistency of their results by summarizing work which showed, for example, that: parents of delinquent boys were more likely to answer questionnaires about them if they had nicer things to say about them; college professors holding minor and temporary appointments were less likely to reply usefully to questionnaires; teachers who had no radios replied less promptly to questionnaires about the use of radios in the classroom than did teachers who had radios; patrons of commercial airlines more promptly returned questionnaires about airline usage than did nonpatrons; college graduates replied more often and more promptly to college follow-up questionnaires than did drop-outs. Norman (1948) cited evidence that technical and science graduates replied less promptly to questionnaires if they were unemployed, or employed outside the field in which they had been trained. Locke (1954) found married respondents more willing to be interviewed about marital adjustment than divorced respondents. None of these findings argues against the interest hypothesis advanced by Edgerton, Britt, and Norman (1947), and, indeed, they cite additional evidence, not reported here, which seems to be most simply interpreted as showing that greater interest in a topic leads to higher response rates. Nevertheless, on the basis of the empirical findings presented and on the basis of Riecken's (1962) and our own analysis, we postulate that: One major variable contributing to the decision to volunteer to participate in either an experiment or a survey is the subjective probability of subsequently being favorably evaluated by the investigator. It would seem trite but necessary to add that this formulation requires more direct empirical test.

Characteristics of volunteers

We have already considered some characteristics of those who respond more readily to a request to participate in behavioral research. These characteristics have, by and large, been specifically related to the source and nature of the request for participation and do not seem to be stable and enduring characteristics serving to differentiate volunteers from nonvolunteers. We shall now consider fairly exhaustively these potentially more stable attributes of volunteers.

Sex. In two survey research projects and in a social psychological experiment, Belson (1960), Wallin (1949), and Schachter and Hall (1952) all found no difference between men and women in their willingness to participate as S's. Two studies have dealt with characteristics of experimental S's who fail to keep their experimental appointments. Frey and Becker (1958) found no sex differences between S's who notify their E that they will be unable to keep an experimental appointment and those who do not notify their E of their impending absence. Since these workers claim that those S's who simply fail to appear can very rarely be rescheduled, their characteristics are likely to be the characteristics of nonvolunteers, and determined ones at that. Though this study argues against a sex difference in volunteering, at least indirectly, the entire experimental sample was composed of extreme scorers on a test of introversion-extraversion. Furthermore, no comparison was given of either group of no-shows with the parent population from which the experimental samples were drawn. Leipold and James (1962) compared characteristics of those S's who failed to appear for a psychological experiment with characteristics of those who did appear. Their total group of shows and no-shows was a random sample of introductory psychology students who had simply been requested to appear in order to satisfy a course requirement. Considering the no-show student again as a determined nonvolunteer, and the appearing student as volunteerlike in finding his way into an experiment, these workers confirmed Frey and Becker's finding of no sex difference associated with volunteering or nonvolunteering. A sad footnote to these results is provided by the fact that about half of Frey and Becker's no-shows notified their *E*'s of their forthcoming absence whereas only one of Leipold and James's 39 no-shows so demeaned himself.

London (1961), too, found almost identical rates of simple willingness to participate in a psychological experiment among men and women, this time in an experiment involving hypnosis. He did find, however, that among those who said they were 'very eager' to participate there were many more men than women. More men than women, too, are willing to volunteer for electric shocks (Howe, 1960), and for Kinsey-type interviews dealing with sex attitudes or behavior (Siegman, 1956; Martin and Marcuse, 1958). London interpreted his finding for the hypnosis research situation as a reflection of the girls' greater fear of loss of control. A more parsimonious interpretation, which takes London's finding into account as well as the findings of Howe, Siegman, and Martin and Marcuse, may be that being 'very eager' to be hypnotized and being willing to be Kinsey-interviewed or electrically shocked are indications of a somewhat generalized unconventionality associated culturally with males for certain types of situation. It has been shown, and will be discussed in detail later, that more unconventional students do, in fact, volunteer more for psychological research, defining unconventionality in a variety of ways. For more run-of-the-mine type experiments, this sex-linked unconventionality would not be so relevant to volunteering, an interpretation which is not too inconsistent with findings by Himelstein (1956) and Schubert (1960). Both these workers found that, for experiments unspecified for their *S*'s, females volunteered significantly more than males.

The likelihood of sex by experimental-situation interaction effects is maintained by a further finding of Martin and Marcuse (1958). To requests for volunteers for experiments in learning, personality, and hypnosis, girls tend to respond more in each case, although none of the differences could be judged statistically significant. It should be added that these authors did not ask their potential hypnosis *S*'s whether they were 'very eager'.

Finally, we need to remind ourselves of Coffin's (1941) caution that any obtained sex differences in behavioral research may be a function of the sex of *E*. Thus we may wonder, along with Coffin and Martin and Marcuse, about (i) the differential effects on volunteer rates among male and female *S*'s of being confronted with a male vs. a female Kinsey interviewer; and (ii) the differential effects on eagerness to be hypnotized of being confronted with a male vs. a female hypnotist.

Related to the sex effect on differential volunteering rates are the findings of Rosen (1951) and Schubert (1960). Both workers found males who showed greater femininity of interests to be more likely to volunteer for psychological experiments.

Birth Order. Stemming from the work of Schachter (1959) there has been increasing interest in birth order as a useful independent variable in social psychological research. Only two studies were found relating birth order to volunteering for psychological research participation, though we may predict that others will follow. Capra and Dittes (1962), working with a student sample in which first-borns were significantly over-represented, found 36 percent of first-borns volunteering for a small group experiment. Among later-borns, only 18 percent volunteered, a difference significant at the .05 level. A subsequent study by Weiss, Wolf, and Wiltsey (1963) served to restrict the generality of any association between birth order and volunteering. They found this relationship to depend upon the recruitment technique. When a ranking of preferences was employed, first-borns more often volunteered for a group experiment. However, when a simple yes-no technique was employed, first-borns volunteered relatively *less* for group than for individual or isolation experiments. Should subsequent work clarify the nature of the relationship between birth order and volunteering, Schachter's work would suggest that such a relationship might be mediated by the greater sociability of first-borns. It is this variable to which we now turn.

Sociability. London, Cooper, and Johnson (1961) found a slight tendency for more serious volunteers to be more sociable as defined by the California Psychological Inventory. Schubert (1960) also found volunteers to score as somewhat more sociable, using a different paper-and-pencil test definition of sociability (MMPI). Martin and Marcuse (1957), employing the Bernreuter, found for their female volunteers for a hypnosis experiment significantly higher sociability scores than for their nonvolunteers, but no difference on the related variable of extraversion. In general, it seems that volunteers may be a more sociable group than nonvolunteers. A possible exception to these generally consistent findings, however, is suggested by the work of Frey and Becker (1958). Among those no-show *S*'s who more closely resembled volunteers, these workers found less sociability (Guilford scale) than among those no-show subjects who seemed rather to be determined nonvolunteers. Interpretation of these findings is rendered difficult, however, by (i) the fact that theirs was not meant to be a direct study of volunteer characteristics, and (ii) the extremeness of all their subjects' scores on a sociability-relevant variable: introversion-extraversion.

Anxiety. Our understanding of the relationship between *S*s' anxiety and the volunteering response suffers not so much from lack of data as from lack of consistency. Some studies reveal volunteers to be more anxious than nonvolunteers, some suggest that they are less anxious, and still others find no differences in this respect.

There were no apparent systematic differences in the types of experiment for which participation was requested between those workers who found volunteers more anxious and those who found them less anxious.

Scheier (1959), utilizing the IPAT questionnaires, found volunteers to be less anxious than nonvolunteers; and Himelstein (1956), employing the TMAS, found a trend in the same direction, though his differences were not judged statistically significant. Heilizer (1960), Howe (1960), and Siegman (1956) found no statistically significant differences in the levels of TMAS anxiety of volunteer and nonvolunteer *S*'s. Both Rosen (1951) and Schubert (1960), however, found volunteers scoring higher on anxiety as defined by the MMPI-Pt scale. It might be tempting to summarize these findings by saying that differences in anxiety level between volunteers and nonvolunteers cancel out to no difference at all. Though this might simplify our interpretation, it would be a little like taking two relatively unlikely events on opposite ends of a continuum (say feast and famine or drought and flood) and concluding that two usual events had occurred. Two other studies are relevant here and may provide a clue to the interpretation of the inconsistent findings reported.

Leipold and James (1962) compared those *S*'s who failed to appear for an experiment with those who did appear on level of anxiety (TMAS) separately for each sex, after finding a significant interaction effect of sex and showing up for the experiment. They found no difference in anxiety level among female *S*'s, but the male *S*'s who failed to appear (the determined nonvolunteers) were significantly more anxious people than those who appeared and therefore were more representative of those males who find their way into the role of subject of a psychological experiment. Martin and Marcuse (1958) also found volunteering *S*'s to differ in anxiety level (TMAS) from nonvolunteers, this time as a function of the type of experiment for which volunteering had been requested. Their volunteers were higher in anxiety than their nonvolunteers for an experiment in personality. No differences (that held for both male and female subjects) were found between volunteers and nonvolunteers for experiments in hypnosis, learning, or attitudes about sex. However, males volunteering for a hypnosis experiment were less anxious than male nonvolunteers. This difference was not found for female S's. The Martin and Marcuse data, while providing further contradictory evidence, suggest that future studies of anxiety may resolve these contradictory findings by considering the likelihood of significant interaction effects of sex of S and type of experiment for which volunteers are solicited upon the differences in anxiety level obtained between volunteers and nonvolunteers.

Need for Social Approval. Marlowe and Crowne (1961) found S's with greater needs for social approval as measured by their social desirability scale (M-C SD) reporting greater willingness to serve again as volunteers in an excruciatingly dull task. Consistent with this finding was that of Leipold and James (1962) that males who failed to appear for their experimental appointments tended to score lower on the same social desirability scale. Crowne (1961) has described high scorers on the M-C SD scale as more intropunitive than extrapunitive, making relevant to our present discussion a finding by Riggs and Kaess (1955). These workers, using Kaess's College Situation Test, found volunteers to be more intropunitive than extrapunitive, a finding which seems to fit into our sparsely stranded nomological net relating need for social approval to the act of volunteering for a psychological experiment.

Conformity. Strickland and Crowne (1962) have shown that high scorers on M-C SD conform more in an Asch-type situation. Since scores on M-C SD correlate positively with both volunteering and conformity, we might reasonably predict a positive correlation between volunteering and Asch-type conformity. Foster (1961) found such a relationship among his male S's but not among his female S's, for whom this relationship was in fact reversed. In any case, neither of these correlations was judged statistically significant. Inconsistent, if only indirectly, with the trend found by Foster was Newman's (1957) finding that male volunteers strongly tended to be more autonomous than male nonvolunteers, and Martin and Marcuse's (1957) finding that male volunteers were more dominant as defined by the Bernreuter. Lubin, Levitt, and Zuckerman (1962) found their female respondents to differ from nonrespondents to a questionnaire. Respondents were lower in dominance and autonomy relative to their scores on deference, succorance, and abasement. The test employed here was the Edwards

Personal Preference Schedule. However, Frye and Adams (1959), employing the same instrument, found no personality difference between (male and female) volunteers and nonvolunteers for an experiment in social psychology. At least for the variety of measures of 'conformity' employed, no general conclusions about their relationship to the volunteering response seem warranted.

Age. Participants in survey research studies tend to be younger than nonparticipants, as shown by Wallin (1949). In addition, earlier compliers with a request to complete a questionnaire tend to be younger than later compliers (Abeles, Iscoe, and Brown, 1954–55). Volunteers for personality research were found to be younger than nonvolunteers by Newman (1957), who also demonstrated that, at least among females, variability of age of volunteers is a function of the type of experiment for which participation is solicited. Rosen (1951) found younger females to volunteer more than older females, but no such relationship held for male *S*'s. We may have somewhat greater confidence in summarizing the relationship of age to volunteering than is warranted for some of the other variables discussed in this section. Volunteers tend to be younger than nonvolunteers, especially among female *S*'s.

Intelligence. Here we shall include not only intelligence-test differences between volunteers and nonvolunteers, but comparisons on the related variables of motor skill, grades, education, and serious-mindedness as well. Martin and Marcuse (1957, 1958) reported that their volunteers earned higher scores on a standard test of intelligence (ACE), a finding supported by Edgerton, Britt, and Norman (1947) in their review of several survey research studies. Brower's (1948) data showed volunteers to perform a difficult motor task with greater speed and fewer errors than a group of *S*'s who were forced to participate. For simpler motor tasks, performance differences were less clear cut. Leipold and James (1962) found that those *S*'s who showed up for an experiment to which they had been assigned were earning somewhat higher grades in introductory psychology than those who did not show up. The trend they found was greater for female than for male *S*'s. Similarly, Abeles, Iscoe, and Brown (1954–55) reported higher grades earned by those who complied more promptly with a request to participate in a questionnaire study. Rosen (1951), on the other hand, did not find a difference in respect of grades earned between volunteers and nonvolunteers for psychological experiments. He did find, however, that female volunteers were more serious-minded than female nonvolunteers. If we may consider not belonging to a fraternity as a mark of serious-mindedness among college students, data obtained by Abeles *et al.* support Rosen's finding of greater serious-mindedness among volunteers. Riggs and Kaess (1955) found volunteers to show more introversive thinking (Guilford scale) than nonvolunteers. These last three findings we may interpret as differences in intellectuality of interest if not in ability. Finally, Wallin (1949) reported that participants in his survey research study were better educated than those who chose not to participate.

Overall, the evidence suggests that, in comparison with nonvolunteers, volunteers are likely to be brighter, as defined by standard tests of intelligence; to perform better in a difficult motor task; to be earning higher grades if college students; and to be somewhat better educated.

Authoritarianism. Rosen (1951) found volunteers for psychological studies to be less fascist-minded (F) than nonvolunteers; and Martin and Marcuse (1957) found volunteers for an experiment in hypnosis to score as less ethnocentric (E) than nonvolunteers. This finding was particularly true for their male subjects. Consistent with these findings was that of Wallin (1949), whose survey participants were more politically and socially liberal than the nonparticipants.

Conventionality. A number of studies have found that volunteers for a Kinsey type of personal interview tend to be more unconventional than nonvolunteers in either their sexual behavior or their attitudes (Maslow, 1942; Maslow and Sakoda, 1952; Siegman, 1956). In order to determine whether this relative unconventionality of volunteers is specific to the Kinsey-type situation, we should need to know whether these same volunteers would be more likely than nonvolunteers to participate in other types of psychological studies. Further, it would be helpful if we knew whether groups matched on sexual conventionality, but differing in other types of conventionality, showed different rates of volunteering for a Kinsey-type interview.

More general evidence for the role of conventionality in predicting volunteering comes from Rosen (1951), who found volunteers to be less conventional than nonvolunteers. Wallin (1949), however, did not find a difference in conventionality between his survey respondents and the nonrespondents. Some indirect evidence is available bearing on the question of volunteering as a function of general unconventionality. The Pd scale of the MMPI is often clinically regarded as reflecting dissatisfaction with societal conventions, and higher scorers may be regarded as less conventional than lower scorers. Both London *et al.* (1961) and Schubert (1960) found volunteers for different types of experiments to be more unconventional by this definition. These same workers further found volunteers to score higher on the F scale of the MMPI, which reflects a willingness to admit to unconventional experiences. The Lie scale of the MMPI taps primness and propriety, and high scorers may be regarded as more conventional than low scorers. Although Heilizer (1960) found no Lie-scale differences between volunteers and nonvolunteers, Schubert (1960) found volunteers to score lower.

It seems to be generally true that volunteers for a variety of psychological studies tend to be more unconventional than their nonvolunteering counterparts. Of a dozen relevant bits of evidence, ten are consistent with this formulation and only two are not. These two inconsistent bits of evidence seem less weakening of our conclusion by virtue of the fact that they find no difference between volunteers and nonvolunteers in this respect, rather than differences in the opposite direction. In general, these findings have been found to occur with both male and female *S*'s. There is, however, some evidence which should caution us to look for possible interaction effects of sex of *S* with the relationship of conventionality to volunteering. London *et al.* (1961) concluded that, at least for hypnosis experiments, girls who volunteer may be significantly more interested in the novel and the unusual, whereas for boys this relationship seems less likely. Under the heading of conformity we have already mentioned a finding that may bear out London *et al.* This was Foster's (1961) finding that the relationship between conformity and volunteering was in the opposite direction for boys as compared with girls. Although his finding did not reach statistical significance, it has theoretical significance for us here when viewed in the light of the results of London *et al.*

Arousal-seeking. Schubert (1960) postulated that volunteering is a function of a trait he called arousal-seeking. Evidence for this relationship came from the fact that his volunteers for a 'psychological experiment' reported greater coffee-drinking and caffeine pill-taking in comparison with nonvolunteers, as well as from differences in scores between volunteers and nonvolunteers on various scales of the MMPI which might be considered consistent with his hypothesis. Those MMPI characteristics he found associated with greater volunteering were generally also found by London *et al.* (1961), with one important exception. The Hypomanic (Ma) scale of the MMPI was found by Schubert to correlate positively with volunteering. Since the implied hyperactivity of high Ma scorers is consistent with the trait of arousal-seeking, this finding strengthened Schubert's hypothesis. London *et al.*, however, found a negative relationship between the

Ma-scale scores and volunteering for a hypnosis experiment, a result that appears damaging to the generality of the arousal-seeking hypothesis. Riggs and Kaess (1955) found that volunteers were more characterized by cycloid emotionality, consistent perhaps with the MMPI Ma scale. As mentioned earlier in our discussion of conventionality, London *et al.* did find a tendency that seems to be related to arousal-seeking among their female volunteers. Since scores on the Ma scale do not appear to be consistently predictive of volunteering, and since caffeine pill-taking may as easily be interpreted as an attribute of 'unconventionality' as of arousal-seeking, it would seem that it might be possible to subsume Schubert's findings under the variable of conventionality. Schubert's contribution to this area of inquiry is noteworthy for its empirically-oriented attempt to establish a specific microtheory of volunteering for psychological experiments in general.

Psychopathology and Adjustment. We shall consider here some variables that have been related to global definitions of psychological adjustment or pathology. While some of the variables with which we dealt earlier have been related to such global views of adjustment, our discussion of them was intended to carry no special implications bearing on Ss' 'adjustment'. Thus in discussing anxiety as a variable we have not meant to imply that higher anxiety was related to maladjustment; indeed, within the range of scores considered, the converse might be equally true.

Self-esteem is usually regarded as a correlate if not a definition of good adjustment. Maslow (1942) and Maslow and Sakoda (1952) reported that volunteers for interviews concerning the respondents' sex behavior showed greater self-esteem (but not greater security) as measured by Maslow's tests than did nonvolunteers. This trend tended to be reversed when students from a more advanced psychology class served as Ss. Siegman (1956), employing his own test, found no such differences at all. Newman (1957) found male volunteers to be less variable in degree of self-actualization than male nonvolunteers, whereas his female volunteers showed greater variability than his female nonvolunteers. If we can accept his self-actualization variable as a measure of adjustment, it would suggest that curvilinear and opposite relationships might exist between adjustment and volunteering for a psychological experiment as a function of sex of volunteer. Thus whereas the best and the least well adjusted males may be less likely to volunteer than moderately well adjusted males, the best and the least well adjusted females may be more likely to volunteer than the moderately well adjusted females.

London *et al.* (1961) concluded that those *S*'s who volunteered for hypnosis experiments in order to serve science (rather than for novelty) were a psychologically more stable or 'upright' group as defined by 16 Pf. Rosen (1951) found his volunteers to be more psychologically-minded (e.g., F-scale scores) and to admit more readily to feelings of anxiety and inadequacy (MMPI). It is difficult to decide whether we should therefore consider volunteers better or worse adjusted than nonvolunteers. In clinical lore these feelings are ostensibly 'bad' to have, but, on the other hand, knowing you have them gives you an adjustive edge.

In the area of medical research, Richards (1960) found projective test differences between those who volunteered to take Mescaline and those who did not. The investigator could not determine, however, which group was the better adjusted. In a sample drawn by Lasagna and von Felsinger (1954), volunteers for medical research seemed to be relatively poorly adjusted. For the area of medical research, finally, Pollin and Perlin (1958) and Perlin, Pollin, and Butler (1958) concluded that the greater the intrinsic motivation of a subject to volunteer for the role of normal control, the greater the likelihood of psychopathology. This does seem to be the clearest evidence of a relationship between volunteering and psychopathology we have yet encountered. Two circumstances should be taken into account, however, in evaluating this finding. First is the notorious unreliability of psychiatric diagnosis, and second is the fact that the medical research studies included in our discussion may differ qualitatively from the more usual psychological studies we have been considering.

On the basis of the evidence presented we may propose that the nature of the relationship between volunteering and adjustment, while essentially unknown, may be a function of the task for which volunteers are solicited, and may be differentially curvilinear as a function of sex of *S*.

Sociological Variables. Insufficient data are available to warrant much discussion of such variables as social and economic status, religious affiliation, marital status, and regional factors in the determination of volunteering behavior. Although Belson (1960) reported higher social class *S*'s to volunteer more, Rosen (1951) found the opposite relationship among his female college *S*'s. Rosen found few other sociological variables to make much difference. Wallin's (1949) data are in partial agreement except that for his survey situation he did find religious affiliation a relevant predictor variable. For a Kinsey-type interview, Siegman (1956) reported higher volunteering rates in an eastern compared with a western university, whereas Edgerton, Britt, and

Norman (1947) cite a possibly contradictory finding of rural background being associated with greater volunteering. It seems wisest to forgo discussion of these findings at this stage of our knowledge except perhaps to raise again the issue that the nature of the relationship between sociological variables and volunteering may be a function of both subject and task variables.

Overview of populations investigated

Before summarizing what it is we may know and what it is we surely do not know about differentiating characteristics of volunteers for psychological studies, we must examine the populations that we have been discussing. All the studies referred to have sampled from populations of subjects, from populations of situations, tasks, and contexts, and from populations of personal characteristics and various measures of these characteristics (Brunswik, 1956).

Subject Samples. All of the requests to participate in a psychological experiment have been made of college students. Even many of the requests to participate in a survey by answering questionnaire items have employed samples of this population. As far as the study of volunteer characteristics is concerned, McNemar's criticism that the science of human behavior is largely the science of the behavior of sophomores has excellent grounds. Those studies which sampled from other populations, such as teachers, parents, householders, and magazine subscribers, were invariably survey research studies. From the standpoint of representativeness in the design of experiments this may be undesirable, but it does no damage to our purpose here since our interest is in the college student as the human guinea pig most frequently used by psychological researchers.

Task Samples. More serious is the nonuniformity of situations, tasks, and contexts sampled by the various studies we have discussed. The tasks for which volunteering has been requested have included survey questionnaires, Kinsey-type interviews, medical control studies, and, more specifically, psychological experiments focused on group interaction, hypnosis, learning, personality, perception, and pain. Unfortunately, very few studies have employed more than one task for which to solicit volunteers, so that little is known about the effects of the specific task either on the rate of volunteering to undertake it or on the nature of the relationship between volunteering and the personal characteristics of volunteers. Newman (1957) did employ more than one task in his study. His *S*'s were asked to volunteer for both a personality and a perception experiment, but he found no systematic effect of these two tasks on the relationships between the variables he investigated and the act of volunteering. Martin and Marcuse (1958) employed four tasks for which volunteering was requested. They found greater differences between volunteers and nonvolunteers for their hypnosis experiment than were found between the two groups for experiments in learning, attitudes to sex, and personality. Of these last three experimental situations, the personality study situation tended to reveal somewhat more personality differences between volunteers and nonvolunteers than were found in the other two situations. Those differences that did emerge from the more differentiating tasks did not seem to be particularly related conceptually to the differential nature of the tasks for which volunteering had been requested. These findings should warn us, however, that any of the characteristics of volunteers we have discussed may be a function of the particular situation for which volunteering had been requested.

Since it would be desirable to be able to speak about characteristics of volunteers for a 'generalized' psychological experiment, a special effort was made to find studies wherein the request for volunteers was quite nonspecific. Several of the studies discussed met this specification (e.g., Himelstein, 1956; Leipold and James, 1962; Schubert, 1960). In these studies, requests were simply for participation in an unspecified psychological experiment. Comparison of the characteristics of volunteers for this more general situation with differentiating characteristics obtained for other task requests again revealed no systematic differences.

Attribute Samples. We have discussed virtually all the attributes of volunteers for psychological experiments which differentiate them from nonvolunteers of which we are aware. For organizational and heuristic purposes, however, we have grouped these together under a smaller number of headings. Decisions to group any variables under a given heading were made on the basis of empirically established and/or conceptually meaningful relationships.

It should be further noted that, within any heading, such as *anxiety*, several different operational definitions may have been employed. Thus we have discussed anxiety as defined by the Taylor Manifest Anxiety Scale as well as by the Pt scale of the MMPI. Intelligence has been defined by several tests of intellectual ability. This practice has been necessary to our discussion in view of the limited number of studies employing identical operational definitions of any variables excepting age, birth, order, and sex. This necessity, however, is not unmixed with virtue. If, in spite of differences of operational definition, the variables serve to predict the act of volunteering, we can feel greater confidence in the construct underlying the varying definitions and in its relevance to the predictive and conceptual task at hand.

**Summary of
volunteer characteristics**

For the purpose of summarizing our analysis of the data bearing on characteristics that differentiate volunteers from nonvolunteers for psychological studies, we have placed each characteristic or attribute into one of two groups. One of these groups contains those variables in respect of which we have some confidence that they are indeed relevant to the act of volunteering. To the second group we have allocated the variables in respect of which such confidence is lacking. Our confidence is operationally inspired by three or more supporting findings and the absence of any completely contradictory findings. Our summary is in the form of statements of relationships, comparing volunteers with nonvolunteers, in roughly descending order of confidence within each group.

I. *Statements Warranting Some Confidence*

1. Volunteers tend to manifest greater intellectual ability, intellectual interest, and intellectual motivation.
2. Volunteers tend to be more unconventional.
3. Volunteers, particularly females, tend to be younger.
4. Volunteers tend to be less authoritarian.
5. Volunteers tend to manifest greater need for social approval.
6. Volunteers tend to be more sociable.

II. *Statements Warranting Little Confidence*

7. Volunteers tend to be more feminine in interests when the experiment is routine, but more masculine when the experiment is unusual.
8. Volunteers tend to have a greater need for arousal.
9. Volunteers tend more often to be first-born children.
10. Volunteers tend to be less anxious when male but more anxious when female.

11. Volunteers tend more often to be moderately well or poorly adjusted when male, and better or worse than moderately well adjusted when female.

12. Volunteers tend to be less conforming when male but more conforming when female.

Obviously the variables listed need further investigation, particularly those in our second group. The situation would seem especially to call for the use of factor-analytic and multiple-regression techniques. One particularly troublesome question arises from examination of the internal consistency of the variables listed in Group I. There we see that volunteers tend to be more unconventional than nonvolunteers, yet to manifest a greater need for approval. On the basis of Crowne's (1961) discussion of the need for approval variable, this is quite unexpected and nomologically nettling.

Implications of volunteer characteristics

For Representativeness. One conclusion seems eminently tenable from our analysis. In any given psychological experiment the chances are very good indeed that a sample of volunteer S's will differ appreciably from the unsampled nonvolunteers. Let us examine some of the implications of this conclusion. One that is rather well known is the limitation placed on subsequent statistical procedures and inference by the violation of the requirement of random sampling. This problem is discussed in basic texts in sampling theory and is mentioned by some of the workers we have had occasion to cite earlier (Cochran, Mosteller, and Tukey, 1953).

Granted that volunteers are never a random sample of the population from which they were recruited, and further granting that a given sample of volunteers differs on a number of important dimensions from a sample of nonvolunteers, we still do not know whether volunteer status actually makes a difference or not. It is entirely possible that in a given experiment the performance of the volunteer S's would not differ at all from the performance of the unsampled nonvolunteers if these had actually been recruited for the experiment (Lasagna and von Felsinger, 1954). The point is that substantively we have little idea of the effect of using volunteer S's. Needed are series of investigations, covering a variety of tasks and situations, for which volunteers are solicited but both volunteers and nonvolunteers are actually used, in order to determine in what type of study the use of volunteers actually makes a difference, what kind of difference, and how much of a difference. Once we know something about these questions, we can enjoy the convenience of volunteer S's with better scientific conscience. In the meantime the best we can do is to hypothesize what the effects of volunteer characteristics might be on any given line of inquiry.

As an example of this kind of hypothesizing we can take the much analyzed Kinsey-type study of sexual behavior. We have already seen how volunteers for this type of study tend to have unconventional attitudes about sexuality and may in addition behave in sexually unconventional ways. This tendency, as has been frequently pointed out, may have had grave effects on the outcome of Kinsey-type studies, leading to population estimates of sexual behavior seriously biased in the unconventional direction. The extent of this type of bias could probably be partially assessed over a population of college students among whom the nonvolunteers could be turned into 'volunteers' in order to estimate the effect on data outcome of initial volunteering vs. nonvolunteering. Clearly, such a study would be less feasible among a population of householders who stood to gain no course credit or instructor's approval from changing their status of nonvolunteer to volunteer.

Far fewer data are available for most other areas of psychological inquiry. Greene (1937) showed that precision in discrimination tasks was related to the nature of S's type of personal adjustment and to his intelligence. Since volunteers may differ from nonvolunteers in adjustment and, even more likely, in intelligence, experiments utilizing discrimination tasks might well be affected by volunteer characteristics. One might speculate, too, about the effect on the standardization of a new intelligence test where the normative sample volunteered for the task, in view of our rather consistent finding that volunteers are brighter than nonvolunteers.

For Experimental Outcomes. For the situations described, the effect of using volunteer samples would be to change the average performance obtained from a sample of S's. In most psychological studies that manipulate an independent variable, interest is not centered on such statistics as the mean but rather on the significance of a difference between means which can be attributed to the operation of the independent variable. If a sample of volunteers is drawn and divided into an experimental and a control group for differential treatment, can the fact of their volunteer status serve to alter the significance of any obtained difference between the means of the two groups? Unfortunately we have no definite empirical answer to this question but we can readily envision an affirmative response.[3] Consider an experiment to test the effects of an independent variable on gregariousness. If volunteers are indeed more sociable than nonvolunteers, the untreated control *S*'s may show a high enough level of gregariousness to result in the treatment's being adjudged ineffective when, with a less restricted range of sociability of *S*'s, the treatment might well have been judged as leading to a statistically significant difference between the means. To cite an example leading to the opposite type of error, let us consider an experiment using female *S*'s in which some dependent variable is observed as a function of good and poor psychological adjustment. If female volunteers are more variable than nonvolunteers on the dimension of adjustment, comparing *S*'s in the top and bottom 27 percent for adjustment level on the dependent variable might lead to a greater 'treatment' effect than would have been obtained with a sample of nonvolunteers.

General summary and conclusions

To McNemar's statement that ours is a science of sophomores, we have added the question of whether we might not lack even this degree of generality in our science. The volunteer status of many who serve as *S*'s in psychological research is a fact of life to be reckoned with. Our purpose here has been to organize and conceptualize our substantive knowledge about the act of volunteering and the more stable characteristics of those more likely to find their way into the role of *S* in psychological research.

The act of volunteering was viewed as a nonrandom event, determined in part by more general situational variables and in part by more specific personal attributes of the person asked to participate in psychological research as *S*. More general situational variables postulated as increasing the likelihood of volunteering responses included the following:

1. Having only a relatively less attractive alternative to volunteering.

2. Increasing the intensity of the request to volunteer.

3. Increasing the perception that others in a similar situation would volunteer.

---

3. Dittes's (1961) finding that lessened acceptance by peers affected first-borns' but not later-borns' behavior is a most relevant example to the extent that we can be sure that first-borns find their way into group experiments reliably more often than later-borns.

4. Increasing acquaintanceship with, the perceived prestige of, and liking for, the experimenter.

5. Having greater intrinsic interest in the subject-matter being investigated.

6. Increasing the subjective probability of subsequently being favorably evaluated or not unfavorably evaluated by the experimenter.

Primarily on the basis of studies conducted with college student populations in a variety of experimental situations, it was postulated that those personal attributes likely to be associated with a greater degree of volunteering included the following:

1. Greater intellectual ability, interest, and motivation.

2. Greater unconventionality.

3. Lower age.

4. Less authoritarianism.

5. Greater need for social approval.

6. Greater sociability.

Personal attributes investigated but resulting in only equivocal relationships to the likelihood of volunteering included the variables of sex, birth order, need for arousal, anxiety, adjustment, conformity, and various sociological variables. For all the personal attributes investigated, but particularly for those related more equivocally to the likelihood of volunteering, the direction of the relationship may often be a function of recruitment-situational variables.

The implications of characteristics differentially associated with volunteering and nonvolunteering were considered from the frequently discussed standpoint of nonrepresentativeness and from the less frequently discussed standpoint of implications for experimental outcomes in terms of inferential errors of the first and of the second kind.

References

Abeles, N., Iscoe, I., and Brown, W. F. (1954–55). Some factors influencing the random sampling of college students. *Publ. Opin. Quart.* **18,** 419–423.

Bell, C. R. (1961). Psychological versus sociological variables in studies of volunteer bias in surveys. *J. appl. Psychol.* **45,** 80–85.

Belson, W. A. (1960). Volunteer bias in test room groups. *Publ. Opin. Quart.* **24,** 115–126.

Blake, R. R., Berkowitz, H., Bellamy, R. Q., and Mouton, Jane S. (1956). Volunteering as an avoidance act. *J. abnorm. soc. Psychol.* **53**, 154–156.

Brower, D. (1948). The role of incentive in psychological research. *J. gen. Psychol.* **39**, 145–147.

Brunswik, E. (1956). *Perception and the representative design of psychological experiments.* Berkeley, Calif.: University of California Press.

Capra, P. C. and Dittes, J. E. (1962). Birth order as a selective factor among volunteer subjects. *J. abnorm. soc. Psychol.* **64**, 302.

Cochran, W. G., Mosteller, F., and Tukey, J. W. (1953). Statistical problems of the Kinsey report. *J. Amer. Statist. Assoc.* **48**, 673–716.

Coffin, T. E. (1941). Some conditions of suggestion and suggestibility. *Psychol. Monogr.* **53**, No. 4 (Whole No. 241).

Crowne, D. P. (1961). The motive for approval: studies in the dynamics of influencibility and stereotypical self-acceptability. Unpublished manuscript, Ohio State University.

Dittes, J. E. (1961). Birth order and vulnerability to differences in acceptance. *Amer. Psychologist* **16**, 358 (abstract).

Edgerton, H. A., Britt, S. H., and Norman, R. D. (1947). Objective differences among various types of respondents to a mailed questionnaire. *Amer. Sociol. Rev.* **4**, 434–444.

Foster, R. J. (1961). Acquiescent response set as a measure of acquiescence. *J. abnorm. soc. Psychol.* **63**, 155–160.

Frey, A. H. and Becker, W. C. (1958). Some personality correlates of subjects who fail to appear for experimental appointments. *J. consult. Psychol.* **22**, 164.

Frye, R. L. and Adams, H. E. (1959). Effect of the volunteer variable on leaderless group discussion experiments. *Psychol. Rep.* **5**, 184.

Greene, E. B. (1937). Abnormal adjustments to experimental situations. *Psychol. Bull.* **34**, 747–748 (abstract).

Heilizer, F. (1960). An exploration of the relationship between hypnotizability and anxiety and/or neuroticism. *J. consult. Psychol.* **24**, 432–436.

Himelstein, P. (1956). Taylor scale characteristics of volunteers and nonvolunteers for psychological experiments. *J. abnorm. soc. Psychol.* **52**, 138–139.

Howe, E. S. (1960). Quantitative motivational differences between volunteers and nonvolunteers for a psychological experiment. *J. appl. Psychol.* **44**, 115–120.

Hyman, H. and Sheatsley, P. B. (1954). The scientific method. In D. P. Geddes (Ed.), *An analysis of the Kinsey reports.* New York: New American Library. Pp. 93–118.

Lasagna, L. and von Felsinger, J. M. (1954). The volunteer subject in research. *Science* **120**, 359–361.

Leipold, W. D. and James, R. L. (1962). Characteristics of shows and no-shows in a psychological experiment. *Psychol. Rep.* **11,** 171–174.

Locke, H. J. (1954). Are volunteer interviewees representative? *Soc. Probl.* **1,** 143–146.

London, P. (1961). Subject characteristics in hypnosis research: Part I. A survey of experience, interest, and opinion. *Int. J. clin. exper. Hypnosis* **9,** 151–161.

London, P., Cooper, L. M., and Johnson, H. J. (1961). Subject characteristics in hypnosis research. II: Attitudes towards hypnosis, volunteer status, and personality measures. III: Some correlates of hypnotic susceptibility. Unpublished manuscript, University of Illinois.

Lubin, B., Levitt, E. E., and Zuckerman, M. (1962). Some personality differences between responders and nonresponders to a survey questionnaire. *J. consult. Psychol.* **26,** 192.

McNemar, Q. (1946). Opinion-attitude methodology. *Psychol. Bull.* **43,** 289–374.

Marlowe, D. and Crowne, D. P. (1961). Social desirability and response to perceived situational demands. *J. consult. Psychol.* **25,** 109–115.

Martin, R. M. and Marcuse, F. L. (1957). Characteristics of volunteers and nonvolunteers for hypnosis. *J. clin. exper. Hypnosis* **5,** 176–180.

Martin, R. M. and Marcuse, F. L. (1958). Characteristics of volunteers and non-volunteers in psychological experimentation. *J. consult. Psychol.* **22,** 475–479.

Maslow, A. H. (1942). Self-esteem (dominance feelings) and sexuality in women. *J. soc. Psychol.* **16,** 259–293.

Maslow, A. H. and Sakoda, J. M. (1952). Volunteer error in the Kinsey study. *J. abnorm. soc. Psychol.* **47,** 259–262.

Newman, M. (1957). Personality differences between volunteers and non-volunteers for psychological investigation: self-actualization of volunteers and nonvolunteers for research in personality and perception. *Dissert. Abstr.* **17,** 684 (abstract).

Norman, R. D. (1948). A review of some problems related to the mail questionnaire technique. *Educ. psychol. Measmt.* **8,** 235–247.

Perlin, S., Pollin, W., and Butler, R. N. (1958). The experimental subject: 1. The psychiatric evaluation and selection of a volunteer population. *A.M.A. Arch. Neurol. Psychiat.* **80,** 65–70.

Pollin, W. and Perlin, S. (1958). Psychiatric evaluation of 'normal control' volunteers. *Amer. J. Psychiat.* **115,** 129–133.

Richards, T. W. (1960). Personality of subjects who volunteer for research on a drug (mescaline). *J. Proj. Tech.* **24,** 424–428.

Riecken, H. W. (1962). A program for research on experiments in social psychology. In Washburne, N. F. (Ed.), *Decisions, values and groups*, Vol. II. New York: Pergamon Press. Pp. 25–41.

Riggs, Margaret M. and Kaess, W. (1955). Personality differences between volunteers and nonvolunteers. *J. Psychol.* **40,** 229–245.

Rosen, E. (1951). Differences between volunteers and nonvolunteers for psychological studies. *J. appl. Psychol.* **35,** 185–193.

Rosenbaum, M. E. (1956). The effect of stimulus background factors on the volunteering response. *J. abnorm. soc. Psychol.* **53,** 118–121.

Rosenbaum, M. E. and Blake, R. R. (1955). Volunteering as a function of field structure. *J. abnorm. soc. Psychol.* **50,** 193–196.

Schachter, S. (1959). *The psychology of affiliation.* Stanford, Calif.: Stanford University Press; London: Tavistock Publications, 1961.

Schachter, S. and Hall, R. (1952). Group-derived restraints and audience persuasion. *Hum. Relat.* **5,** 397–406.

Scheier, I. H. (1959). To be or not to be a guinea pig: preliminary data on anxiety and the volunteer for experiment. *Psychol. Rep.* **5,** 239–240.

Schubert, D. S. P. (1960). Volunteering as arousal seeking. *Amer. Psychol.* **15,** 413 (abstract). (Extended report available.)

Siegman, A. (1956). Responses to a personality questionnaire by volunteers and nonvolunteers to a Kinsey interview. *J. abnorm. soc. Psychol.* **52,** 280–281.

Staples, F. R. and Walters, R. H. (1961). Anxiety, birth order and susceptibility to social influence. *J. abnorm. soc. Psychol.* **62,** 716–719.

Strickland, Bonnie R. and Crowne, D. P. (1962). Conformity under conditions of simulated group pressure as a function of the need for social approval. *J. soc. Psychol.* **58,** 171–182.

Wallin, P. (1949). Volunteer subjects as a source of sampling bias. *Amer. J. Sociol.* **54,** 539–544.

Weiss, J. M., Wolf, A., and Wiltsey, R. G. (1963). Birth order, recruitment conditions, and preferences for participation in group versus nongroup experiments. *Amer. Psychol.* **18,** 356 (abstract).

3

the experimenter:

a neglected stimulus object[1]

F. J. McGuigan[2]

To say that behavior is a function of a fantastically large number of stimulus variables is to understate the immensity of the problem facing the psychologist. Clearly, the sustained laboratory dissection of our environment has produced considerable information about the relationship between behavior and a number of classes of stimulus variables, but just as clearly much more remains to be accomplished. In assessing our status, it is well to emphasize the presence of one particular stimulus object of the complex environment in which we immerse subjects—the experimenter himself. While we have traditionally recognized that the characteristics of an experimenter may indeed influence behavior, it is important to observe that we have not seriously attempted to study him as an independent variable. Rather,

From *Psychological Bulletin*, Vol. 60, 1963, pp. 421–428. Copyright 1963 by The American Psychological Association. Reproduced by permission.

1. Modification of a paper presented at the American Psychological Association meetings, 1961, in a symposium entitled "The Social Psychology of the Psychological Experiment."

2. The author expresses appreciation to Sherman Ross for his valuable suggestions concerning the presentation of this paper.

Table 1
Number of possible data collectors in a sample of
articles from the Journal of Experimental Psychology

No. of Authors	No. of Articles	No. of Possible Data Collectors			
		1	2	3	4
1	16	10	3	1	2
2	17	0	14	2	1
3	4	0	0	4	0
Total	37	10	17	7	3

we have typically regarded the experimenter as necessary, but undesirable, for the conduct of an experiment. Accordingly, in introductory textbooks on experimental psychology we provide prescriptions for controlling this extraneous variable; but seldom do we consider the experimenter variable further, and the extent to which we actually control it in our experimentation can be seriously questioned. As documentation for this statement, consider some findings based on an analysis of 37 usable articles from three recent issues (selected at random) of the *Journal of Experimental Psychology*. These articles were classified according to the number of possible data collectors and number of authors. In Table 1 we can see that 10 of the 37 articles had only one possible data collector. It is reasonable to assume that at least a majority of the other 27 experiments employed more than one data collector. In no article was any mention made of techniques of controlling the experimenter variable and in only one of the articles was the number of data collectors actually specified. Furthermore, in no article was a statistical analysis of results as a function of experimenters reported. It seems quite clear that we are deficient in the write-up and analysis, if not in the design of our experiments as far as the experimenter variable is concerned. The possibility is alarming that in multidata collector experiments adequate control is not exercised. Especially is this so for those psychologists who have witnessed in amazement the conduct of experiments by some of their colleagues in which one experimenter collects data for a while, after which he is relieved by another experimenter, with no plan for balancing the subjects in the groups over the experimenters. Such an experiment is totally indefensible. But it is, optimistically, assumed to be relatively rare. Where pains *have* been taken to control the experimenter variable in multiexperimenter experiments, it is unreasonable to request that results be presented as a function of experimenters. This request has three bases:

(a) it will justify the control procedures used, (b) it will help indicate the extent to which the results are generalizable to a population of experimenters, and (c) it will provide much needed information on the extent and nature of the experimenter's influence on the subjects. Point a needs no further elaboration. But Points b and c can profitably be developed.

Sampling from a population of experimenters

Assume that in a given experiment it was possible to control the experimenter variable in a completely adequate fashion by holding that variable constant. This means that the numerous stimuli emanating from the experimenter-stimulus object have assumed the same constant, but unspecified, value for all the subjects throughout the experiment. Whatever the intensity and other values of these experiment-produced stimuli, we are assuming that they have not differentially affected the behavior of the subjects.

Clearly such a technique of controlling the experimenter variable is not practical. But that is not the worst of it. For controlling any variable by holding it constant is only defensible in the long run if the one experiment concerned exhausts the universe of investigations on the problem posed. And never would a universe of experiments be limited to one. Hence, let us consider that our hypothetical experiment in which the experimenter variable is held constant is repeated by another experimenter, one who takes pains to duplicate all of the conditions of our experiment that have been specified. And there is the rub. In the original experiment we have held the experimenter variable constant, but it simply was not possible to specify the intensity and other values of that complex variable. While in the replication of our hypothetical experiment we may assume that the experimenter variable was similarly held constant, it is also safe to assume that it was held constant at different values than obtained in our original experiment.

Let us take a particular, measurable, characteristic of the experimenter as an illustration. Suppose that the experimenter in one experiment manifests what we call a high degree of anxiety, whereas the second experimenter has a low degree of anxiety. We can well expect that the stimuli emitted by these two experimenters will either be different in nature, or in value. Will these two classes of stimuli differentially affect the dependent variable measures of the subjects in the two experiments? This question gives us the opportunity to make sure that we are in agreement with respect to the place of the experimenter variable in psychological research.

The problems arising in the sampling of subjects for experimentation have received considerable attention—the undergraduate psychology major who is not aware of the mechanics of obtaining a random sample from a well-defined population of subjects is probably a rare specimen. While the way was paved some years ago, particularly by Brunswik (e.g., 1947), however, the same cannot be said with regard to other populations relevant to experimentation. Brunswik emphasized the importance of sampling stimulus populations, but rarely are such populations actually systematically sampled in psychology today—especially is this true of the subclass of stimulus variables emitted by the experimenter who faces the subjects. On any given problem, we could define a population of experimenters, although admittedly not easily in an unambiguous fashion. In our conduct of an experiment on that problem, then, strictly speaking we should employ a design (such as a complete factorial design) that allows us to vary experimenters—we should randomly sample from a population of experimenters and replicate the experiment for each experimenter used.

Now let us return to our question: does the fact that two experimenters who differ only in regard to a single characteristic affect the performance of subjects in two otherwise identical experiments? There are three general answers possible.

Case 1. First, the stimulus characteristic in question is totally unrelated to the dependent variable being measured. In this event essentially the same scores would be obtained by both experimenters. Clearly in this case, we need not be concerned in the slightest as to whether or not experimenters in our hypothetical population differ—their respective characteristics have no differential effects on the dependent variable. There is but one remaining point: we could not possibly know this unless we had designed and analyzed our experiment to find it out.

Case 2. The second general possibility is that the variable for which the two experimenters differ does affect the dependent variable, but it affects all subjects in the same way, regardless of the experimental condition to which those subjects were assigned. For example, we might suppose that subjects assigned to the anxious experimenter perform at a higher level on the average, than do those assigned to the nonanxious experimenter.

Typically, we are interested in whether or not one group of subjects performs higher or lower than a second group on a given dependent variable measure. Since in this second case we are able to reach the same conclusion with regard to our hypothesis regardless of which experimenter conducted the experiment, we are not immediately interested in the experimenter difference. As an adjunct to this experiment, however, we note that a particular kind of behavior *is* influenced by this experimenter characteristic, information that is potentially valuable.

Case 3. The first two possible answers to our question do not greatly concern us. The third, however, can be rather important. To take an extreme case, let us say that the performance of an experimental group is superior to that of a control group for the anxious experimenter, but that the reverse is true for the nonanxious experimenter. In short, suppose that there is an interaction between the characteristics with which the experimenters differ and the independent variable of the experiment.

As an example of a Case 3 experiment, briefly consider an interaction reported by Kanfer (1958). Two experimenters who had "minimal gross differences" participated in a verbal conditioning experiment. The subjects were required to say words continually and the verbs that they emitted were reinforced by flashing a light according to one of three reinforcement schedules. The experimenter's task was simple—to discriminate between verbs and nonverbs, and flash a light. The results indicated a significant Method × Experimenter interaction —there was more frequent reinforcement of words for one schedule than for the others, the frequency varying for the experimenters. The experimenters evidently differed from each other in their ability to perceive verbs as a function of reinforcement schedule. The reason for this seems obscure, but the lesson to the investigator is again driven home—if our results are a function of experimenter characteristics, then they are highly specific and cannot be generalized.

It should be emphasized that interactions involving experimenters may not only be unexpected, but quite obscure. In general we simply have not had enough experience with experimenter interactions to know where to look for them. To further emphasize the obscurity of this type of interaction, consider some results from a study involving four methods of learning and nine experimenters (McGuigan, 1960). The analysis of variance indicated that there was a significant difference among methods but that experimenters did not differ, and particularly that the methods by experimenter interaction was not significant. According to our normal procedure, we would conclude that the results with regard to methods is not a function of experimenters. But now let us study the interexperimenter variability more closely. We can note that there is considerable variability among experimenters for Methods P and VIW in Figure 1, but that there is relatively little

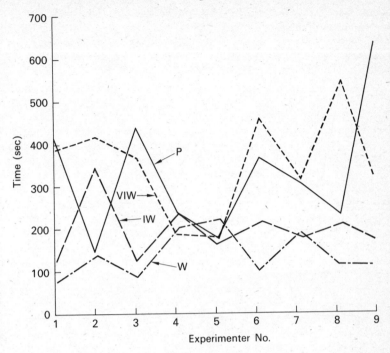

Fig. 1
Dependent variable scores for four methods plotted as a function of experimenters (after McGuigan, 1960).

interexperimenter variability for Methods IW and W. The variance for each method was computed and it was found that they differ significantly. Furthermore, the variability among the experimenters is a function of methods when methods are ordered from P to VIW to IW and to W.

In Figure 1 we arranged the experimenters on the horizontal axis in a random fashion. Lines of best fit are approximately parallel. In Figure 2, however, we have arranged the experimenters according to intraexperimenter variability. Now lines of best fit appear to deviate rather markedly from being parallel. Particularly note that the relative proficiency due to the various methods is a function of the experimenters. Here we have a single experiment replicated nine times. Suppose that we had conducted the experiment only once using, say, Experimenter Number 9. This experimenter yielded a clear set of results due to methods. But had we chosen Experimenter Number 8,

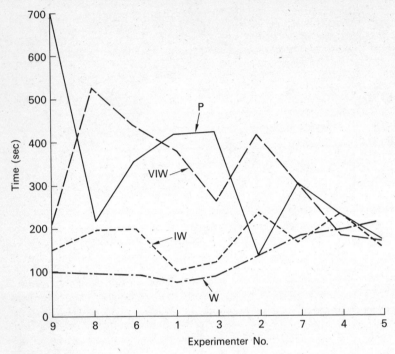

Fig. 2
The data points of Figure 1 ordered according to intraexperimenter variability.

a different set of results would have obtained. And contrast these results with those obtained by Experimenter Number 4 where no significant differences among methods appear. The problem posed by Figure 2 is: What are the characteristics of the experimenters that cause them to be ordered along the horizontal axis in this particular fashion? There are two possible answers: First, that the experimenters varied in their techniques of administering the independent variables and recording the dependent variable. In this case the solution is quite clear and we have long been aware of the problem—precise adherence to experimental procedure as we report it in detail in our publications. That this principle is not strictly adhered to can be made manifestly clear by conducting interexperimenter analyses. The recent work of Azrin, Holz, Ulrich, and Goldiamond (1961) on operant conditioning of conversations by student experimenters indicated considerable variation in reinforcement techniques as well as downright distortion.

Table 2
r's between personality characteristics of nine
experimenters and dependent variable scores
(*time to perform a task*) of their subjects

Bernreuter		Bell	Manifest Anxiety
B1-N:	.35	A: .15	.04
B2-S:	.19	B: .15	
B3-I:	.24	C: .09	
B4-D:	.14	D: .08	
F1-C:	.16		
F2-S:	.23		

Stories of violation of proper data collection procedures by graduate assistants are legion, if somewhat suppressed. Analyses to determine differences among experimenters on dependent variable scores can serve to at least stimulate investigation of procedural problems in a given experiment. The second possible difference among experimenters in Figure 2 concerns what we might call personality characteristics of the experimenters—we have a possible ordering of experimenters along some personality dimension. The only question is what is it and how might we discover it? One thing we could do when we find this sort of interaction is to administer a battery of personality tests to our experimenters, in an effort to determine personality differences that differentially influenced a given dependent variable. Hints can thus be obtained that can lead to additional experiments in which characteristics of the experimenters are varied in an effort to better understand the nature of these interactions that concern us. We actually did this for the experimenters of Figure 2. Table 2 shows a sample of the correlations between trait scores of the experimenters and dependent variable scores of their subjects. None of the correlations was significant, but several were high enough to be somewhat suggestive even without significant differences among experimenters, and with such a limited sample. As an illustration: the more neurotic (B1-N scale of the Bernreuter) the experimenter the poorer the performance of the subject.

Experiments in which experimenters with different personality characteristics were deliberately used are few in number. One such study was a verbal conditioning experiment using the response class of hostile words emitted in sentences (Binder, McConnell, and Sjoholm, 1957). Whenever the subject used a hostile word in a sentence the experimenter reinforced that response by saying "good." Two

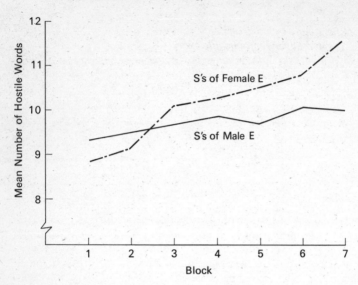

Fig. 3
Learning curves for two groups treated the same except for experimenters.
(The steeper slope for the subjects of the female experimenter illustrates
an interaction involving experimenters—after Binder et al., 1957.)

groups were used, a different experimenter for each group. The two
experimenters differed in gender, height, weight, age, appearance, and
personality:

The first ... was ... an attractive, soft-spoken, reserved young lady ...
$5'\frac{1}{2}''$ in height, and 90 pounds in weight. The ... second ... was very
masculine, 6'5" tall, 220 pounds in weight, and had many of the unre-
strained personality characteristics which might be expected of a former
marine captain—perhaps more important than their actual age difference
of about 12 years was the difference in their age appearance: the young
lady could have passed for a high school sophomore while the male
experimenter was often mistaken for a faculty member (Binder et al.,
1957, p. 309).

The results of this experiment are shown in Figure 3. We can see
that the rate of emitting hostile words increases with trials for both
groups—saying "good" reinforced the response for both experimenters.

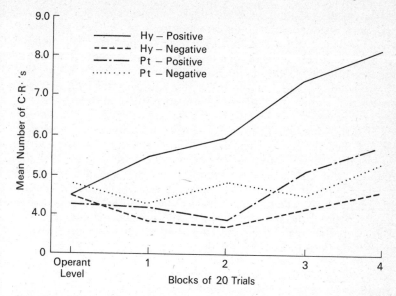

Fig. 4
Learning curves for four conditions. (The marked departure of the Hy-positive-set group—solid line—illustrates an interaction between set for the experimenter and personality characteristics of the subjects—after Spires, 1960.)

But of particular significance to us now is the fact that the rates of learning for the two groups differed significantly—the slope is steeper for the female experimenter's group. Clearly the differences between the two experimenters are numerous, so it is difficult to specify just what experimenter characteristic or combination of characteristics is responsible for this difference in learning rate of the two groups. But this research is a promising start. A follow-up of it might be aimed at testing the authors' speculation as to the important difference: that the female experimenter "provided a less threatening environment, and the *S*'s consequently were less inhibited in the tendency to increase their frequency of usage of hostile words" (Binder *et al.*, 1957, p. 313).

An interesting experiment by Spires (1960) is illustrative of how characteristics of the subjects can interact with perceived characteristics of the experimenter. Spires selected a group of subjects high on the *Hy* scale of the MMPI and a second high on the *Pt* scale. The subjects entered the experimental situation with one of two sets: the positive set was where the subject was told that the experimenter was a "warm, friendly person, and you should get along very well"; the negative set was where the subject was told that the experimenter may "irritate him a bit, that he's not very friendly, in fact kind of cold." This was a verbal conditioning study in which a class of pronouns was reinforced by saying "good." An analysis of variance for Spire's results indicated that there was a significant difference between positive and negative sets for the experimenters (the positive set leading to better conditioning), and that the interaction between set for the experimenter and MMPI score of the subject was significant. This interaction is illustrated by the learning curves shown in Figure 4. There we can see that the hysterics, who had a positive set for their experimenter, condition remarkably better than the other three groups. While apparently this is the only study which shows that a rather well defined personality characteristic of the subjects interacts with a perceived characteristic of the experimenter, further investigation would undoubtedly yield additional interactions of this nature.

Conclusions

1.   Where one data collector is used in an experiment, the best that can be done is to attempt to hold his influence on the subjects constant. The results, in this instance, cannot strictly speaking be generalized to the relevant population of experimenters—if they are, the generalization must be extended exceedingly cautiously, at best. While it is not possible to adequately specify the experimenter's characteristics in the report of the experiment, it should be recognized that this inability does not remove the problem—it persists and for a worker in a particular area the question of generalization from a single experimenter experiment can assume nightmarish proportions.

2.   Where more than one data collector has been used (a) techniques of control should be specified, (b) the data should be analyzed and reported as a function of experimenters, and (c) interactions between experimenters and treatments should be tested. Should the results indicate that the experiment is an instance of Cases I or II, the results are generalizable to a population of experimenters to the extent to which such a population has been sampled. Granted that completely satisfactory sampling can seldom occur, at least some sampling is better than none. And it is beneficial to *know* and to be able to *state* that, within those limitations, the results appear to be instances of Cases I or II. If the experiment turns out to be an instance of Case III, the extent to which the results can be generalized is sharply limited.

One can only say, for instance, that Method A will be superior to Method B when experimenters similar to Experimenter Number 1 are used, but that the reverse is the case when experimenters similar to Experimenter Number 2 are used. This knowledge is of course valuable, but only in a negative sense since we do not know what the characteristics of the two experimenters are—to understate the matter, the interaction tells us to proceed with considerable caution.

3. It is important to contribute to our general fund of knowledge of the experimenter variable, for it is indeed small at this time. That this request to collect relevant data will not excessively burden us is indicated by the frequency with which more than one experimenter already participates in an experiment (see Table 1; further, note that in a sample of 722 articles from journals concerned primarily with experiments, 48% had two or more authors [Woods, 1961]). Quite clearly we already have enough information to safely assert that interactions between experimenters and treatments do occur. But there is a paucity of data about their frequency of occurrence as a function of type of experimental situation. By designing more experiments to test for differences between experimenters and for interactions involving experimenters we may eventually be able to handle the problems indicated in Number 1 above and by instances of Case III.

As with all other variables with which we are concerned, determining the effects of the experimenter variable is a long, energy consuming project. But we must face up to our task. Recognizing the enormity of this project, one can well ask whether or not there is a more efficient approach. The only other possibility that occurs at present is to eliminate the experimenter from the experiment. For some problems that we study, this would be relatively easy, but it is hard to visualize how this could be accomplished in other experiments. For instance, a number of completely automated devices have been developed and successfully used in running rats—the subjects are never exposed to a human experimenter. Automation has also entered psychology at the human level, but in neither case is automation very general, and certainly it is not standardized. In a number of experiments it seems reasonable to have the subject enter the experimental room and be directed completely by taped instructions, thus removing all visual cues, olfactory stimuli, etc., emitted by the experimenter. If eventually the human experimenter is replaced by devices which automatically run the subject through his routine, we must be careful not to select values of stimuli emanating from these devices that themselves interact with the treatments that we are studying.

References

Azrin, N. H., Holz, W., Ulrich, R., and Goldiamond, J. The control of conversation through reinforcement. *J. exp. anal. Behav.,* 1961, **4,** 25–30.

Binder, A., McConnell, D., and Sjoholm, N. A. Verbal conditioning as a function of experimenter characteristics. *J. abnorm. soc. Psychol.,* 1957, **55,** 309–314.

Brunswik, E. *Systematic and representative design of psychological experiments.* Berkeley: Univer. California Press, 1947.

Kanfer, F. H. Verbal conditioning: Reinforcement schedules and experimenter influence. *Psychol. Rep.,* 1958, **4,** 443–452.

McGuigan, F. J. Variation of whole-part methods of learning. *J. educ. Psychol.,* 1960, **51,** 213–216.

Spires, A. M. Subject-experimenter interaction in verbal conditioning. Unpublished doctoral dissertation, New York University, 1960.

Woods, P. J. Some characteristics of journals and authors. *Amer. Psychologist,* 1961, **16,** 699–701.

4

the experimenter effect

B. L. Kintz
D. J. Delprato
D. R. Mettee
C. E. Persons
R. H. Schappe

It is significant that a problem which perplexed some of the most influential scientists of Germany in 1904 was resolved at that time, yet should contaminate psychology investigations of the present day, that is, the experimenter's influence on his subjects. The amazing horse of Mr. von Osten caused an uproar throughout all of Germany which Professor Stumpf and his co-workers, through meticulous investigation, demonstrated to be the result of the questioners' unintentional, involuntary cues utilized by the animal. This incident dramatically emphasized the stimulus value of "unconscious" cues emitted by an experimenter to his animal subjects. Even though questioners of "Hans" were aware that this might be the explanation for his feats and were most careful in attempting to refrain from allowing him this advantage, the unconscious cues were still emitted until the situation was carefully analyzed and the specific variables controlled (Pfungst, 1911).

From *Psychological Bulletin*, Vol. 63, (No. 4), 1965, pp. 223–232. Copyright 1965 by the American Psychological Association. Reproduced by permission.

McGuigan (1963) states:

While we have traditionally recognized that the characteristics of an experimenter may indeed influence behavior, it is important to observe that we have not seriously attempted to study him as an independent variable [p. 421].

However, Stumpf with his careful, detailed measurements of questioners' cues began the study of the experimenter as an independent variable in 1904, but not until recently has this problem been considered by experimental psychologists for study (Cordaro and Ison, 1963; McGuigan, 1963; Rosenthal and Halas, 1962). Clinical psychologists have long led the way in this aspect of investigation. The personal effect of examiners upon patients' performance in clinical tests was initiated as an object of study 35 years ago (Marine, 1929). Yet, psychologists working in the laboratory have not been completely unaware of the implications of experimenter influence upon subjects.

Ebbinghaus (1913) in discussing the effects of early data returns upon psychological research stated:

It is unavoidable that, after the observation of the numerical results, suppositions should arise as to general principles which are concealed in them and which occasionally give hints as to their presence. As the investigations are carried further, these suppositions, as well as those present at the beginning, constitute a complicating factor which probably has a definite influence upon the subsequent results [pp. 28–29].

Pavlov, noting the apparent increase in learning ability of successive generations of mice in experiments on the inheritance of acquired characteristics, suggested that an increase in the teaching ability of experimenters may have, in fact, constituted the critical variable (Gruenberg, 1929, p. 327).

The foregoing yields some indication of the scope inherent in this phenomenon. However, response-induced bias is not the only data-affected result. A study in which experimenters (E's) recorded the frequency of contractions and head turns of planaria demonstrated that E's expectancy can dramatically influence the data obtained in this type of situation (Cordaro and Ison, 1963). In this case subject's (S's) responses were not affected, but highly statistically significant differences in number of reported responses were obtained for E's expecting a low frequency of response and for E's expecting a high frequency of response. In other words, E's saw (reported) what they expected to see.

Thus far we have seen that *E* may not only bias *S*'s responses but also that this interpretation of *S*'s responses may be biased. Because these effects are dependent upon *E*'s knowledge of the hypothesis to be tested or his expectancy, one can readily propose that the solution to this problem would be, as is often the case, a simple matter of having research assistants (*A*'s) who are unaware of the hypothesis collect the data for *E*. In testing this suggestion, it was found that "a subtle transfer of cognitive events" existed, resulting in response bias (Rosenthal, Persinger, Vikan-Kline, and Mulray, 1963, p. 313). The authors state:

Our finding of a subtle transmission of E*'s bias to their* A*'s forces us to retract an earlier suggestion for the reduction of* E *bias (Rosenthal, 1963c). Our recommendation had been to have* E *employ a surrogate data collector who was to be kept ignorant of the hypothesis under test. The implication of the suggestion was simply not to have* E *tell* A *the hypothesis. It now appears that* E*'s simply not telling* A *the hypothesis may not insure* A*'s ignorance of that hypothesis [pp. 332–333].*

It is the present authors' contention that wherever an experimenter-subject relationship exists, the possibility also exists for *E* to contaminate his data by one or more of a multitude of conveyances. It appears that experimental psychology has too long neglected the experimenter as an independent variable. By relating some of the findings of clinical and social psychologists, as well as the few experimental studies to date, it is hoped that experimental psychologists will no longer accept on faith that the experimenter is necessary but harmless. Implications for experimental, counseling, and testing psychology will also be considered.

Research findings

Nondifferentiated effects

Research studies have been, on the whole, minimal in reporting differential results with regard to individual *E*'s. In particular, this is true concerning careful discussion of the possible reasons for the differing data. It is, however, illustrative of the pervasiveness of experimenter effect to examine several of the studies which have shown a nondifferentiated experimenter influence.

Lord (1950) was interested in examining Rorschach responses in three different types of situations. Thirty-six *S*'s took the Rorschach three times—once from each of three different female examiners. Of the Rorschach responses being considered for differences within

S's, Lord found 48 to yield *t* tests significant at the .10 level. Of these, 27 were due to examiner differences.

In an interesting study on learning without awareness (Postman and Jarrett, 1952), 30 different *E*'s—all students in advanced experimental psychology classes—were employed. The *S*'s responded to 240 stimulus words with another word which came to mind. Half the *S*'s were instructed to guess, and half were told, the "correct" principle of answering, which was to give common associations as found in speaking and writing. Differences among *E*'s were highly significant sources of data variance. Postman and Jarrett suggest that since complete universal uniformity of experimenter behavior is apparently impossible, the difficulty experienced in attempting to replicate results of other investigators is to be expected.

Using a verbal conditioning paradigm, Kanfer (1958) reinforced verb responses with a flashing light, under three different reinforcement schedules. Two *E*'s were employed, with apparently little difference between them. In reinforcing *S*'s, *E* simply was required to distinguish between verbs and nonverbs. A significant interaction was found between *E* and method. There was more frequent reinforcement of words for one schedule than for the others, the frequency varying with the *E*. Apparently, even the ability of an *E* to perform such a relatively elementary, objective task as judging whether a word is, or is not, a verb, is highly subject to individual differences.

A recent experiment (Severin and Rigby, 1963) investigated different patterns of digit grouping. An incidental finding from this study is pertinent here. In analyzing the variance of perfect memorizing, an *E* effect was found, significant at the .01 level. Further, this effect was largely due to only one of the four *E*'s, since repetition of the analysis without this *E*'s data yielded no significant *E* difference.

An avoidance study using rats (Harris, Piccolino, Roback, and Sommer, 1964) was primarily concerned with the effects of alcohol on learning the avoidance response in a Miller-Mowrer shuttle box. Two teams, of two *E*'s each, were employed. The alcohol did not produce differential results, but the different *E* teams did. It is likely that this outcome is due to differences in the handling of the animals by *E*'s.

Personality

In discussing the differential effect of *E* upon *S*, Masling (1960) was writing with particular attention to projective testing. However, it seems logical to postulate that if sex and aspects of the examiner's personality (such as warmth or coldness) are causative of differential

results in projective testing, the influence of these personal variables may also be felt in other, even objective, situations.

In attempting to assess effects of personality factors of experimenters in the experimental situation, McGuigan (1960) compared trait scores of *E*'s on personality tests with dependent variable scores of *S*'s. He did not obtain any significant correlations, but noted several quite high ones that may indicate directional influences. For example, the more neurotic (Bl-N scale of the Bernreuter) the *E*, the poorer the performance of *S*.

The effect of *E*'s personality upon *Ss*' performances had been investigated earlier (Sanders and Cleveland, 1953) using projective techniques. Nine *E*'s took the Rorschach, which was scored blindly by two experienced clinical psychologists. The *E*'s were then trained in administering the Rorschach, and each *E* gave it to 30 *S*'s. An attempt was made to deliberately standardize the questioning procedures used. After taking the Rorschach, each *S* filled out a questionnaire designed to elicit his attitudes about the particular *E*. Sanders and Cleveland found that overtly anxious *E*'s (as indicated by their own Rorschach responses) tended to elicit more subject flexibility and responsiveness, while overtly hostile *E*'s (again measured by their Rorschach responses) drew more passive and stereotyped responses and less of the hostile responses. The *Ss*' questionnaires indicated that *E*'s who were most liked were those who had been rated low on anxiety and hostility.

The research just mentioned has been primarily interested in the effect of the personality of *E*, *per se*, on *Ss*' performances. One further study is especially interesting, as it tries to answer the pertinent question of whether *E*'s personality and personal bias can interact. Rosenthal, Persinger, and Fode (1962) used 10 naive *E*'s, who were biased to expect certain results. They found that agreement of final data and *E* bias were related to *Es*' scores on the MMPI scales, *L*, *K*, and *Pt*, but not to age or grade-point average.

The *S-E* personality interaction is dependent, of course, not only on the personality of *E*, but also to some degree on that of *S*. In one of the few studies designed to investigate this interaction, Spires (1960; cited in McGuigan, 1963) used a 2 × 2 design in a verbal conditioning paradigm, reinforcing a particular class of pronouns with the word "good." The *S*'s were divided into two groups, one of which had scored high on the *Hy* scale of the MMPI and one of which had scored high on the *Pt* scale. Each group was subdivided in half, receiving either a positive or a negative "set" ("this experimenter is warm and friendly" or "this experimenter is cold and unfriendly"). The high *Hy*-positive set group far surpassed the other three groups. The high

Hy-negative set group performed the poorest. Thus, not only *E*'s personality, but *Ss*' perception of this personality, can contribute to the *E* effect.

Investigation of *Ss*' perception of *E* has been undertaken by two related studies (Rosenthal, Fode, Friedman, and Vikan-Kline, 1960; Rosenthal and Persinger, 1962). In the first experiment, *S*'s were asked to rate *E* on a number of variables. In the second study, the experiment was not actually conducted, but only described, and *S*'s were requested to imaginatively rate their imaginary *E*. Yet a correlation which was calculated between the ratings of the first and second studies yielded an *r* of .81. This would appear to support the hypothesis that naive *S*'s, in particular, may have a kind of predetermined "set" about what a "typical" *E* is like—scientific, intelligent, etc.

Experience

Investigators with widely variant amounts of experience are busily conducting studies every day. Cantril (1944) stated that interviewers who are highly experienced show as much bias as those who are less experienced. In an experimental investigation, however, Brogden (1962) came to a different conclusion. Four *E*'s each trained a group of rabbits and recorded the acquisition speed of a conditioned shock-avoidance response. The rabbits of the three experienced *E*'s reached the learning criterion faster than the naive *E*'s rabbits. To further study this result, the naive *E* was required to run another group of rabbits to see whether his practice would produce more rapid conditioning in the second group. Another experienced *E* trained another group of *S*'s to serve as a control measure. The data show both a significant *E* practice effect (for the naive *E* only) and a significant difference between *E*'s.

Sex

Several studies have been concerned with investigating the manner in which results are influenced by *E* differences in sex. In a verbal conditioning study (Binder, McConnell, and Sjoholm, 1957), *S*'s were reinforced for saying hostile words. Two clearly distinguishable *E*'s were employed: one—a young, petite feminine girl; the other—a mature, large masculine male. Significantly more hostile words were emitted in the presence of the female *E*. It is conceivable that *S*'s perceived the male *E* as being more hostile than the female *E*, in which case the results confirm Sanders and Cleveland's (1953) findings that hostile *E*'s elicit fewer hostile responses from their *S*'s than do other *E*'s.

Sarason and Minard (1963) also found that sex and hostility significantly influenced Ss' performances. Degree of contact between S and E and E's prestige value (as perceived by S) also contributed significant effects. Sarason and Minard warn that ignoring these situational variables is hazardous research methodology.

In a very recent experiment investigating the sex variable, Stevenson and Allen (1964) show what is perhaps the most clear-cut demonstration of S-E interaction. Eight male and eight female E's each tested eight male and eight female S's in a simple sorting task. The mean number of responses was recorded at 30-second intervals. With either male or female E's, female S's made more responses than did male S's. However, all S's performed relatively better under an opposite-sexed E.

Expectancy effect

Perhaps the component of experimenter effect which is the cause of greatest concern is that by which the E in some way influences his S's to perform as he has hypothesized. The reasons for concern about expectancy effect are that so little is known about it and so little research has been devoted to it. Only recently have systematic studies been conducted in this area.

Rosenthal and Fode (1963a) demonstrated the problem clearly in an experiment with two groups of randomly assigned animals. One group of six E's was instructed that its group of rats was "maze-bright" and a second group of six E's was instructed that its group of rats was "maze-dull." In a simple $\top$ maze, the maze-bright rats performed significantly better than the maze-dull rats.

In a similar study (Rosenthal and Lawson, in press) investigators divided 38 E's into 14 research teams, each of which had one rat randomly assigned to it. Six of the teams were told that their rats were bred for dullness and the other eight were told that their rats had been bred for brightness. Seven experiments, including such tasks as operant acquisition, stimulus discrimination, and chaining of responses, were conducted. In seven out of eight comparisons (overall $P = .02$), difference in performance again favored E's who believed their S's to be bred for brightness. A factor which may have prompted the difference was that E's who believed their rats were bred for brightness handled them more than E's who believed their rats were bred for dullness.

In both experiments cited, the question arises as to the sensitivity of the animals to attitudinal differences in E's transmitted through the tactual and sensory modalities. Further research is required to clarify the issue.

Modeling effect

Modeling effect is defined (Rosenthal, 1963b) as a significant correlation between E's performance and the performance of randomly assigned S's on the same task.

Graham (1960) divided 10 psychotherapists into two groups on the basis of their perception of movement in Rorschach inkblots. In the ensuing psychotherapeutic sessions, patients of the group of psychotherapists that perceived more movement in the inkblots saw a significantly greater amount of movement than the patients of the group of psychotherapists that had perceived less movement.

In the area of survey research the phenomenon of modeling has been reported in studies by Cantril (1944) and Blankenship (1940) who have found that interviewers elicit from their interviewees, at a probability greater than chance, responses which reflect the interviewers' own beliefs.

Rosenthal (1963b) reported eight experiments conducted to assess the existence and magnitude of experimenter modeling effect by employing the task of Ss' rating a series of photographs of people on a scale of apparent successfulness and unsuccessfulness ranging from -10 to $+10$. Prior to each experiment, E's had rated the photos which were selected because in earlier ratings on the same scale they had yielded a mean value of zero. The resulting eight rank-order correlations between E's ratings and their Ss' ratings ranged from $-.49$ to $+.65$. Only the rho of $+.65$ was significantly different from 0 ($p < .001$), but the hypothesis of equality among the eight rhos was rejected using a chi-square test ($p < .005$).

Hammer and Piotrowski (1953) had three clinical psychologists and three interns rate 400 House-Tree-Person drawings on a 3-point scale of aggression. The degree of hostility which clinicians saw in the drawings correlated .94 with the evaluations of their personal hostility made by one of the investigators.

Early data returns effect

Early data returns effect is the problem of the experimenter who is receiving feedback from his experiment through early data returns and who contaminates the subsequent data. The reasons why this occurs are unclear but some suggestions are that *E*'s mood may change if the data are contrary to his expectations, or if the data are in agreement with his expectations, there is the possibility of heightening an existing bias. There is evidence (Rosenthal, Persinger, Vikan-Kline, and Fode, 1963) that this mood change in *E*, brought about by "good results," may lead him to be perceived by the *S*'s as more "likable," "personal," and more "interested" in their work and thereby influence their performance.

In the study by Rosenthal, Persinger, Vikan-Kline, and Fode (1963), three groups of four *E*'s each had three groups of *S*'s rate the apparent success of people in photographs on a scale ranging from −10 to +10. The *E*'s were instructed that *Ss*' mean rating would be about +5. In each of two experimental groups, two *S*'s were confederates of the investigator while in a control group all of the *S*'s were naive. One of the confederate pairs was instructed to give "good data" (in accord with *E*'s expectations) and the other pair was instructed to give "bad data" (contrary to *E*'s expectations). Ratings of all *S*'s were learned after several trials. It was hypothesized that the experience of having obtained good data would lead those *E*'s to obtain "better" subsequent data while the experience of having obtained bad data would lead those *E*'s to obtain "worse" data in relation to the control. Although neither experimental group differed significantly from the control group, the experimental groups were significantly different from each other. There was a further tendency for the effect of early returns to become more pronounced in the later stages of data gathering.

Griffith (1961) states clearly the effect of early data returns in an autobiographical documentary:

Each record declared itself for or against . . . (me) . . . (and) . . . (my) . . . spirit rose and fell almost as wildly as does the gambler whose luck supposedly expresses to him a higher love or reflection [p. 309].

Overview of cues and their transmission

After discussing at some length the various experimenter effects, the question must certainly arise as to how the experimenter contaminates his data. What are these cues and how are they transmitted? Some suggestions have been made but it is necessary to look at evidence dealing directly with the problem. It was suggested earlier that in the case of laboratory animals it might be due to tactual and kinesthetic cues, but probably also involved are all of the sensory processes of the organism so that E inadvertently transmits cues by nearly everything that he does.

In dealing with humans, because of the probable lack of bodily contact, cues are transmitted verbally and/or visually. But "verbally" implies not only the words, but also the inflectional and dynamic processes of speaking.

The transmission of verbal cues was first dramatically demonstrated by Greenspoon (1955) who, by reinforcing plural nouns with "mmm-hmmm," was able to increase the frequency of emission of such words.

In a similar experiment, Verplanck (1955) was able to control the content of Ss' conversation by agreeing with some opinions and disagreeing with others. The results showed that every S increased in his rate of speaking opinions with reinforcement by agreement, and 21 out of the 24 S's decreased their rate of opinion statements with nonreinforcement.

Rosenthal and Fode (1963b) conducted two experiments specifically designed to investigate the transmission of cues from E to his human S's. The S's were to rate the apparent success or failure of persons in photographs on a scale ranging from -10 to $+10$. All E's received identical instructions except that five of them were told that their S's would probably rate the pictures at about $+5$ while the remaining E's were told their S's would probably rate the pictures at about -5. Further, prior to the experiment, each E rated the pictures on the same scale as the S's. Results showed that S's for high-biased ($+5$) E's obtained significantly higher mean ratings than S's of low-biased (-5) E's. Since E's were not permitted to say anything to S's other than what was on the instruction sheet, the communication of bias must have been done by tone, manner, gesture, or facial expression. The second experiment designed to investigate this nonverbal transmission of cues was conducted in the same manner as the first with the exception that now, instead of E showing each photo to his S's, each set of 10 photos was mounted on cardboard and labeled so that S could give his rating without Es' handling the photos. The results showed that elimination of visual cues from E to S did significantly reduce the effect of E's bias. It can be hypothesized then that visual cues play an important part in the phenomenon of E bias, but probably to a lesser degree than verbal cues.

Wickes (1956) also showed the import of visual cues by effectively using nodding, smiling, and leaning forward in his chair as reinforcement for certain responses given to inkblots by clients in psychotherapy sessions.

Considerable research is required to learn what the cues are, how they are transmitted, and how they can be controlled.

**Implications of the
experimenter effect**

The preceding survey of the literature has revealed the existence of the experimenter effect in all aspects of psychology. Although the experimenter effect is generally recognized and perhaps paid lip service, it tends to be a forgotten skeleton in the research psychologist's closet. Comparison of a study by Postman and Jarrett (1952) with one by Spence (1964) provides an example.

Postman and Jarrett (1952) commented:

We have paid too little attention to the contributions made by variations in Es' behavior to the experimental results. The difficulty which many psychologists experience in repeating the results of other investigators may be due to our failure to attack systematically the role of differences among E's [*p. 253*].

Spence (1964), after examining various aspects of variability occurring in experiments using the Taylor Manifest Anxiety scale, says the following in concluding his discussion of the experimenter-subject interaction:

This is, nevertheless, a potentially important variable and should be investigated further, possibly by deliberately manipulating the behavior of E [*p. 136*].

It is clear from a comparison of these two statements that during the past 12 years the progress in examining and controlling the experimenter effect has been something less than spectacular. Thus, the objective of this portion of the present paper is to attempt to alter further research procedure by emphasizing the implications of the experimenter effect as it relates to the individual psychologist engaged in his varied activities.

Clinical implications

Clinicians have long recognized the influence of the experimenter (therapist) upon the behavior of a subject (client). In fact, the differing views existing in the clinical realm as to the most effective therapeutic procedure to utilize seem to have their origin in the clinician's conception of the role of the therapist in the therapeutic situation. For example, the psychoanalyst believes transference is essential if the client is to be led to adjustment, whereas the nondirective therapist strives to accompany the patient along the road to adjustment rather than to lead.

Even though clinicians not only recognize but argue over the implementation of the experimenter influence, they are not exempt from a thorough evaluation of the implications (some of which are discussed below) that the experimenter variable holds for the clinical field.

Perhaps a reevaluation of the experimenter variable will reveal that pseudodifferences exist among the effect of various psychotherapeutic techniques. Goldstein (1962) showed that clients who are rehabilitated by a particular technique may be more products of perceived therapist expectancies than of therapeutic techniques. An essentially different technique employed by a therapist expecting good results with his procedure can rehabilitate the client just as completely.

Considering the present state of sophistication in the clinical realm, it is not unreasonable to assume that therapist expectancies are likely to play a large part in client rehabilitation. Thus, the pseudo-problem may tend to thwart intensive searches for valid, operationally defined therapeutic procedures.

Other more specific clinical areas affected by *E-S* interaction would include the effect upon patients' Rorschach scores as a function of experimenter differences (Lord, 1950), the once-removed influence of the experienced clinician's effect upon a neophyte therapist's prognosis of a patient (Rosenthal, 1963c), the possibility that the therapist may be a contributing factor to the patient's failure to recover as the result of perceived negative therapist expectancy (Sanders and Cleveland, 1953), and the not-so-alluring possibility that patients receiving the stamp of rehabilitation have only adjusted to the wishes of the therapist and not necessarily to the emotional problems which brought them to the therapist originally (Verplanck, 1955).

These are important problems for practicing clinicians, and it is to their credit that they have recognized this, as evidenced by the increasing use of the team approach in diagnosing clients. Utilization of the team approach may be extended to therapy in order to reduce the negative aspects of the clinician-client interaction.

Such a team approach might involve the objective assignment of patients to therapists by means of a large-scale correlational determination of what therapist-patient "personality types" interact most effectively in the therapeutic situation. Of course, the determination of personality types still leaves us with all the previously mentioned *E-S* interaction problems, but nonetheless attempts at improvement can be made even if imperfect tools must be used.

Implications for the field of testing

The general field of testing which would include IQ tests, placement tests, reading readiness tests, aptitude tests, etc., is also beset with the problem of the experimenter variable. Even though there have been rigorous attempts at standardization of test items and procedures in this area, *E* or administrator of the test still influences the test taker in other subtle ways (Kanfer, 1958; Rosenthal, 1963a).

The implications of the experimenter effect in the testing area have many ramifications. It is questionable whether many tests have been proven sufficiently reliable and valid in their own right, and this problem is further complicated by the experimenter variable. Judgment of an individual's score on special abilities and IQ tests, etc., must not only be viewed in light of which test was used, but must also take into consideration the previously ignored variable of the specific administrator. In addition to knowing that a person achieved an IQ score of 105 on the Stanford-Binet and not the Wechsler, it is also necessary to know whether or not *E* was threatening, docile, friendly, anxious, or expected the test taker to be smart, dumb, score well, etc. (Binder, McConnell, and Sjoholm, 1957; McGuigan, 1963; Rosenthal, 1963a).

The administrator contamination problem may eventually be resolved by the application of machines to the administration of tests. At this time a more judicious selection of the hundreds of available tests on the part of administrators, using test results to guide their decision-making process, is essential. In addition, test results should be viewed with a more sophisticated, critical eye, with IQ and aptitude scores being considered as but some of many indices of performance. All persons using test scores must recognize the strong influence of *E* and make decisions accordingly.

Experimental implications

The psychologist engaged in controlled experimentation should realize that he has failed to provide a control for himself. That this variable is disregarded is evidenced by Woods' (1961) investigation of 1,737 published experiments, of which 42%–45% involved multiple authorship. None of these ran an analysis of experimenter interaction.

One particular aspect of controlled experimental endeavor which has neglected the experimenter effect is learning-theory research. Much energy is expended on "crucial" experiments which ostensibly attempt to determine which of the conflicting theories of Hull, Tolmon, Guthrie, and others are correct. At the present time these crucial experiments have produced results which are generally inconclusive, except for establishing a high correlation between the theory an E's results support and his theoretical position.

The experiments already reviewed provide a speculative base for partially explaining the conflicting results obtained by the supporters of various learning theories. As Rosenthal (1963c) has shown, experimenter bias is a powerful influence in the experimental situation. The E has many opportunities to influence, unintentionally, S's who have been brought into a very strange, highly structured situation. In view of this, it is not surprising—it should be expected—that E's favoring a particular learning theory would tend to obtain results favoring this same theory.

Results reported recently (Cordaro and Ison, 1963; Rosenthal and Fode, 1963a; Rosenthal and Halas, 1962) indicate that E's also affect the results of studies using nonhuman S's. These findings further emphasize the possibility that the overlooked experimenter variable may have contaminated many crucial learning experiments.

This is not to suggest that being able to replicate studies and/or controlling the experimenter variable is the panacea for psychology's problems. But it can not be overemphasized that at the present time E is a powerful, yet much ignored, variable. It is a strange paradox that even many of the most adamantly scientific of psychologists have failed to control for the experimenter variable.

Conclusions

Future experimentation might prove more profitable if more rigorous communication could be established between researchers of differing points of view and theoretical orientations so that a system of research exchange might be established. This suggestion admittedly presents a multitude of problems, not the least of which would be that of authorship credit. Although this and many other problems would arise, they would not be insurmountable.

If research exchange were implemented, it might prove an effective means of controlling the experimenter effect and, in addition, bring scientific communication into the prepublication stage of research. This in itself might prove to be the most important contribution of all.

Other suggestions for control of the experimenter variable have been given previously by Rosenthal (1963c) and McGuigan (1963).

These suggestions included counterbalancing of *E*'s and the use of factorial designs which include the experimenter as a major independent variable. Fode (1960; cited in Rosenthal, 1963), as reported by Rosenthal (1963c), found that both visual and auditory cues influenced the behavior of *S*'s. Thus, another suggestion involves the elimination of verbal and visual cues, including inflections of the voice, speaking peculiarities, gestures, etc., as transmitted to *S*'s during the reading of instructions.

This paper, which began with a discussion of a horse and the subtlety of experimenter cues, has ranged far afield. We have seen that the experimenter effect exerts an insidious influence upon the relationship between counselor and client. Indeed, the more objective and nondirective the counselor, the greater the potential hidden effect. To be unaware of the relationship between counselor and client expectations is to lose much of the control that a counselor must maintain over the counseling situation. In the same way teachers must be aware that objective appraisal by their students is affected by the goals which the students believe their teachers have. And finally, but probably most important at this time, directors of laboratory research who use student *E*'s, must be aware of the extremely great effect of their personal biases which can be perceived by the student *E*'s and translated into practically any significant experimental effect.

References

Binder, A., McConnell, D., and Sjoholm, N. A. Verbal conditioning as a function of experimenter characteristics. *Journal of Abnormal and Social Psychology*, 1957, **55**, 309–314.

Blankenship, A. B. The effect of the interviewer upon the response in a public opinion poll. *Journal of Consulting Psychology*, 1940, **4**, 134–136.

Brogden, W. J. The experimenter as a factor in animal conditioning. *Psychological Reports*, 1962, **11**, 239–242.

Cantril, H. and Research Associates. *Gauging public opinion*. Princeton, N.J.: Princeton Univer. Press, 1944.

Cordaro, L. and Ison, J. R. Psychology of the scientist: X. Observer bias in classical conditioning of the planarian. *Psychological Reports*, 1963, **13**, 787–789.

Ebbinghaus, H. *Memory: A contribution to experimental psychology*. (Orig. publ. 1885; trans. by H. A. Ruger and Clara E. Bussenius) New York: Teachers College, Columbia University, 1913.

Fode, K. L. The effect of non-visual and non-verbal interaction on experimenter bias. Unpublished master's thesis, University of North Dakota, 1960.

Goldstein, A. P. *Therapist-patient expectancies in psychotherapy.* New York: Pergamon Press, 1962.

Graham, S. R. The influence of therapist character structure upon Rorschach changes in the course of psychotherapy. *American Psychologist,* 1960, **15,** 415.

Greenspoon, J. The reinforcing effect of two spoken sounds on the frequency of two responses. *American Journal of Psychology,* 1955, **68,** 409–416.

Griffith, R. M. Rorschach water precepts: A study in conflicting results. *American Psychologist,* 1961, **16,** 307–311.

Gruenberg, B. C. *The story of evolution.* New York: Van Nostrand, 1929.

Hammer, E. F. and Piotrowski, Z. A. Hostility as a factor in the clinician's personality as it affects his interpretation of projective drawings. *Journal of Projective Techniques,* 1953, **17,** 210–216.

Harris, H. E., Piccolino, E. B., Roback, H. B., and Sommer, D. K. The effects of alcohol on counter conditioning of an avoidance response. *Quarterly Journal of Alcoholic Studies,* 1964, **25,** 490–497.

Kanfer, F. H. Verbal conditioning: Reinforcement schedules and experimental influence. *Psychological Reports,* 1958, **4,** 443–452.

Lord, E. Experimentally induced variations in Rorschach performance. *Psychological Monographs,* 1950, **64**(10, Whole No. 316).

McGuigan, F. J. Variation of whole-part methods of learning. *Journal of Educational Psychology,* 1960, **51,** 213–216.

McGuigan, F. J. The experimenter: A neglected stimulus object. *Psychological Bulletin,* 1963, **60,** 421–428.

Marine, Edith L. The effect of familiarity with the examiner upon Stanford-Binet test performance. *Teachers College Contributions in Education,* 1929, **381,** 42.

Masling, J. The influence of situational and interpersonal variables in projective testing. *Psychological Bulletin,* 1960, **57,** 65–85.

Pfungst, O. *Der Kluge Hans.* (Orig. publ. 1905; trans. by C. L. Rahn) New York: Holt, 1911.

Postman, L. and Jarrett, R. F. An experimental analysis of learning without awareness. *American Journal of Psychology,* 1952, **65,** 244–255.

Rosenthal, R. Experimenter attributes as determinants of subjects' responses. *Journal of Projective Techniques,* 1963, **27,** 324–331. (a)

Rosenthal, R. Experimenter modeling effects as determinants of subjects' responses. *Journal of Projective Techniques,* 1963, **27,** 467–471. (b)

Rosenthal, R. On the social psychology of the psychological experiment: The experimenter's hypothesis as unintended determinant of experimental results. *American Scientist*, 1963, **51**, 268–283. (c)

Rosenthal, R. and Fode, K. L. The effect of experimenter bias on the performance of the albino rat. *Behavioral Science*, 1963, **8**, 183–189. (a)

Rosenthal, R. and Fode, K. L. Psychology of the scientist: V. Three experiments in experimenter bias. *Psychological Reports*, 1963, **12**, 491–511. (b)

Rosenthal, R., Fode, K. L., Friedman, C. J., and Vikan-Kline, L. L. Subjects' perception of their experimenter under conditions of experimenter bias. *Perceptual and Motor Skills*, 1960, **11**, 325–331.

Rosenthal, R. and Halas, E. S. Experimenter effect in the study of invertebrate behavior. *Psychological Reports*, 1962, **11**, 251–256.

Rosenthal, R. and Lawson, R. A longitudinal study of experimenter bias on the operant learning of laboratory rats. *Journal of Psychiatric Research*, in press.

Rosenthal, R. and Persinger, G. W. Let's pretend: Subjects' perception of imaginary experimenters. *Perceptual and Motor Skills*, 1962, **14**, 407–409.

Rosenthal, R., Persinger, G. H., and Fode, K. L. Experimenter bias, anxiety, and social desirability. *Perceptual and Motor Skills*, 1962, **15**, 73–74.

Rosenthal, R., Persinger, G. W., Vikan-Kline, Linda, L., and Fode, K. L. The effect of early data returns on data subsequently obtained by outcomebiased experimenters. *Sociometry*, 1963, **4**, 487–498.

Rosenthal, R., Persinger, G. W., Vikan-Kline, Linda L., and Mulray, R. C. The role of the research assistant in the mediation of experimenter bias. *Journal of Personality*, 1963, **31**, 313–335.

Sanders, R. and Cleveland, S. E. The relation between certain experimenter personality variables and subjects' Rorschach scores. *Journal of Projective Techniques*, 1953, **17**, 34–50.

Sarason, I. G. and Minard, J. Interrelationships among subjects, experimenters, and situational variables. *Journal of Abnormal and Social Psychology*, 1963, **67**, 87–91.

Severin, F. T. and Rigby, M. K. Influences of digit grouping on memory for telephone numbers. *Journal of Applied Psychology*, 1963, **47**, 117–119.

Spence, K. W. Anxiety (drive) level and performance in eyelid conditioning. *Psychological Bulletin*, 1964, **61**, 129–140.

Spires, A. M. Subject-experimenter interaction in verbal conditioning. Unpublished doctoral dissertation, New York University, 1960.

Stevenson, H. W. and Allen, Sara. Adult performance as a function of sex of experimenter and sex of subject. *Journal of Abnormal and Social Psychology*, 1964, **68**, 214–216.

Verplanck, W. S. The control of the content of conversation. *Journal of Abnormal and Social Psychology*, 1955, **51**, 668–676.

Wickes, T. H. Examiner difference in a test situation. *Journal of Consulting Psychology*, 1956, **20**, 23–26.

Woods, P. J. Some characteristics of journals and authors. *American Psychologist*, 1961, **16**, 699–701.

5

experimenter outcome-orientation and the results of the psychological experiment[1]

Robert Rosenthal

In any science, experimenters have some orientation towards the outcome or results of their research. Rarely is this orientation one of truly dispassionate disinterest. Variables are not chosen for inclusion in research by using tables of random numbers. They are, rather, chosen because the experimenter has certain expectations about the relationship or lack of relationship between the selected variables and certain other variables. A superficial exception to this might be seen in so-called heuristic hunts for relationships, which are perhaps more common to the behavioral sciences. Even here, however, the inclusion of variables is not on a random basis, and certain relationships appear more likely to be found than others.

Experimenters then often, if not always, have some sort of expectations about how the data will fall. Also often, if not always, they care about how these data fall. Some outcomes may be expected more than others; some outcomes may be desired more than others. Our

From *Psychological Bulletin*, Vol. 61, (No. 6), 1964, pp. 405–412. Copyright 1964 by the American Psychological Association. Reproduced by permission.

1. Preparation of this paper was facilitated by a grant, G-24826, from the Division of Social Sciences of the National Science Foundation.

purpose here is to discuss the question of whether experimenter's orientation (expectations and wishes) can affect the data actually obtained in his research. We are not so much concerned here with the problem of choice of experimental design or procedure and the fact that certain designs and procedures may unintentionally be more or less favorable to obtaining expected or unexpected data. Neither are we concerned with the problems of statistical tests of hypotheses and the fact that uniquely most powerful statistics may unintentionally be employed when the expectation is to be able to reject the null hypothesis, while less powerful statistics may be employed when the expectation is to be unable to reject the null hypothesis. These are interesting questions but will not be considered here. Our usage of "results" or "outcome" will be restricted to the raw data obtained by experimenters from their subjects.

The effects of experimenter's outcome orientation, or bias, were seriously considered by Wilson (1952), the physical scientist. Wilson felt that positive or expected data might too often occur because of researchers' interest in the outcome of their experiments. Their expectancies about data might determine in part the data obtained. This notion seems most related to Merton's (1948) concept of self-fulfilling prophecy. One prophesies an event and the expectation of the event, then changes the prophet's behavior in such a way as to make the predicted event more likely. Related, too, is Heider's (1958) concept of "personal causality" and his discussion of the fulfillment of personal expectancies.

Outcome-orientation effects in everyday life

The way a man golfs or bowls may be determined by his expectancy of his performance. Of greater interest here is the notion that how one person expects another to perform these activities can determine in part how he actually does perform. In an intensive study of a social group of young men, Whyte (1943) found that the group, and especially its leaders, "knew how well a man should bowl." This "knowledge" or expectancy probably did partially determine that man's actual performance. Perhaps the morale-building banter offered the one expected to do well helped him to do well. Similarly, the communicated expectancy to another that he would do poorly "shook him up" sufficiently to interfere with his performance (see also Back, 1951).

Fascinating data collected at the Bank Street College of Education suggest that in the schoolroom as in the bowling lanes, expectancies may be powerful forces determining others' behavior. Data described by John Niemeyer,[2] President of the College, lend support to the hypothesis that lower-class, minority-group children are low achievers, at least partly because of their teachers' expectation that these students are really not educable.

Outcome-orientation effects in clinical practice

As highly skilled a clinician as Fromm-Reichmann (1950) was impressed by the effects of the self-fulfilling prophecy, although she did not use that term. She spoke rather, as other clinicians have, of iatrogenic psychiatric incurabilities. The therapist's expectancy, she felt, might determine whether given symptoms might be relieved or cured. This clinical impression is somewhat supported by the work of Heine and Trosman (1960) who felt that the variable significant for a patient's continuance in psychotherapy was that of mutuality of expectation between therapist and patient. Goldstein (1960) found no client-perceived personality change due to psychotherapy related to therapist's expectancy of such change. However, therapist's expectancy was related to duration of psychotherapy. Additionally, Heller and Goldstein (1961) found therapist's expectation of client improvement significantly correlated (.62) with change in client's attraction to therapist. These workers also found that after 15 sessions, clients' behavior was no more independent than before, but their self-descriptions were of more independent behavior. The therapists generally were favorable to increased independence and tended to expect successful cases to show this decrease in dependency. Clients may well have learned from their therapists that independent-sounding verbalizations were desired and thereby served to fulfill their therapist's expectancy. The role of expectancy in the psychotherapeutic situation has been most fully discussed and reviewed by Goldstein (1962).

But psychotherapy is not the only realm of clinical practice in which expectancy effects may determine outcomes. The fatality rates of delirium tremens have recently not exceeded about 15%. However, from time to time new treatments of greatly varying sorts are reported to reduce this figure almost to zero. Gunne's (1958) work in Sweden summarized by the *Quarterly Journal of Studies on Alcohol* Editorial Staff (1959) showed that any change in therapy led to a drop in mortality rate. One interpretation of this finding is that the innovator of the new treatment expects a decrease in mortality rate, an expectancy which leads to subtle differential patient care over and above the specific

---

2. Personal communication, 1961.

treatment under investigation. A prophecy again may have been self-fulfilled.

In the practice of medicine in general, the role of physician expectancy looms large. In a very comprehensive paper dealing with placebo effects, Shapiro (1960) cites the well-known admonition: "You should treat as many patients as possible with the new drugs while they still have the power to heal [*p.* 114]." The wisdom of this statement may have its basis in the concept of the physician's faith in the power of the drug. This "faith" may have at its core expectancy as we are discussing it. The physician's expectancy about the efficacy of a treatment may be subtly communicated to the patient with resulting influence on the patient's psychobiological response.

Outcome-orientation effects in survey research

Perhaps the classic work in this area was that of Rice (1929). A sample of 2,000 applicants for charity was interviewed by a group of 12 skilled interviewers. Interviewers talked individually with their respondents who had been assigned in a wholly nonselected manner. Respondents ascribed their dependent status to factors predictable from a knowledge of the interviewers' outcome orientations. Thus, one of the interviewers who was a staunch prohibitionist obtained three times as many responses blaming alcohol as did another interviewer regarded as a socialist, who in turn obtained half again as many responses blaming industrial factors as did the prohibitionist interviewer. Rice concluded that the outcome orientation or bias of the interviewer was somehow communicated to the respondent who then replied as expected. Hyman, Cobb, Feldman, Hart, and Stember (1954) took vigorous exception to Rice's interpretation and preferred to ascribe his remarkable results to errors of recording or interpretation. The plain fact, of course, is that we cannot say whether these effects were ones which actually changed respondents' replies or not. There is no question in either case that the results of the research were affected by the investigators' outcome orientation.

One of the earliest studies deliberately creating differential expectancies in interviewers was that conducted by Harvey (1938). Each of six boys was interviewed by each of five young post-graduates. The boys were to report to the interviewers on a story they had been given to read. Interviewers were to use these reports to form impressions of the boys' character. Each interviewer was given some contrived information about the boys' reliability, sociability, and stability, but told not to regard these data in assessing the boys. Standardized questions asked of the interviewers at the conclusion of the study suggested that biases of assessment occurred even without interviewers' awareness and despite conscious resistance to bias. Harvey felt that the interviewers' bias evoked a certain attitude towards the boys which in turn determined the behavior to be expected and then the interpretation given. Note how neatly this formulation fits the model put forth by Merton. Again, we cannot be sure that subjects' responses were actually altered by interviewer expectancies. The possibility, however, is too provocative to overlook.

More recent evidence for an expectancy (outcome orientation) bias comes from the work of Hanson and Marks (1958). The most thorough discussion of this problem for the survey research literature is that by Hyman *et al.* (1954), which also carries an extensive bibliography.

Outcome-orientation effects in experimental research

It is well known that a great many studies have been conducted to establish the validity or invalidity of the Rorschach technique of personality assessment. A systematic study of 168 of these studies was undertaken by Levy and Orr (1959) who categorized each study on each of the following dimensions: the academic versus nonacademic affiliation of the author, whether the study was designed to assess construct versus criterion validity, and whether the outcome of the study was favorable or unfavorable to the hypothesis of Rorschach validity. Results showed that academicians were more interested in construct validity and that their outcomes were relatively more favorable to construct validation and less favorable to criterion validation. On the basis of their findings, these workers called for more intensive study of the researcher himself. "For, intentionally or not, he seems to exercise greater control over human behavior than is generally thought [p. 83]." We cannot safely conclude that the findings reported were a case of the effect of outcome orientation or bias. It might have been that the choice of specific hypotheses for testing, or that the choice of manner of testing them determined the apparently biased outcomes. At the very least, however, this study accomplished its task of calling attention to potential biasing effects of experimenters.

Perhaps the earliest study which employed a straightforward experimental task and actually manipulated an outcome-orientation variable was that of Stanton and Baker (1942). In their study, 12 nonsense geometric figures were presented to a group of 200 undergraduate subjects. After several days, retention of these figures was measured by five experienced workers. Experimenters were supplied with a key of "correct" responses, some of which were actually correct but some of which were incorrect. All experimenters were explicitly warned to guard against any bias associated with their having the keys before them and therefore influencing their subjects to guess correctly. Results showed that the experimenter obtained outcomes in accordance with his expectations. When the item on the key was correct, the subject's response was more likely to be correct than when the key was incorrect. In a careful replication of this study, Lindzey (1951) emphasized to his experimenters the importance of keeping the keys out of the subjects' view. This study failed to confirm the Stanton and Baker findings. The 85 subjects of Lindzey's study were much more of a volunteer population than were the subjects of the original study. We simply cannot say whether this fact might have accounted (in whole or in part) for the difference. Another replication by Friedman (1942) also failed to obtain the significance levels obtained in the original. Still, significant results of this sort, even occurring only in one out of three experiments, cannot be dismissed lightly. Stanton (1942, see pp. 16–17) himself presented further evidence which strengthened his conclusions. He employed a set of nonsense materials, 10 of which had been presented to subjects and 10 of which had not. Experimenters were divided into three groups. One group was correctly informed as to which 10 materials had been exposed, another group was incorrectly informed, while the third group was told nothing. The results of this study also indicated that the materials which experimenters expected to be more often chosen were, in fact, more often chosen.

An experiment analogous to those just described was conducted in a psychophysical laboratory by workers (Warner and Raible, 1937) who interpreted their study within the framework of parapsychological phenomena. The study involved the judgment of weights by subjects who could not see their experimenter. The latter kept his lips tightly closed to prevent unconscious whispering (Kennedy, 1938). In half the experimental trials, the experimenter knew the correct response from a key. Of the 17 subjects, 6 showed a standard error of 1.0 or more from a 50-50 distribution of errors. All 6 of these subjects made fewer errors on trials on which the experimenter knew which weight was lighter or heavier. At least for those subjects who were somewhat affected by the experimenter's knowledge of the correct response, the authors' conclusion seems justified. As an alternative to the interpretation of these results as extrasensory perception (ESP) phenomena, they suggested the possibility of some form of auditory cue transmission to the subjects.

Among the most recent studies in the area of ESP are those by Schmeidler and McConnell (1958). These workers found that subjects who believed ESP possible ("sheep") performed better at ESP tasks than did subjects who did not believe ESP possible ("goats"). These workers suggested that an experimenter by his presentation, might affect subjects' self-classification, thereby increasing or decreasing the likelihood of successful ESP performance. Similarly, Anderson and White (1958) found that teachers' and students' attitudes toward each other might influence performance in classroom ESP experiments. The mechanism operating here might also have been one of certain teachers' expectancies which were communicated to the children whose self-classification as sheep or goats might thereby be affected. The role of the experimenter in the results of ESP research has been discussed by Crumbaugh (1959) as a source of evidence against the existence of the phenomenon. We file no brief here for or against ESP, but suggest that if, in carefully done experiments, certain types of experimenters obtain certain types of ESP performances in a predictable manner (as suggested by the studies cited), that further evidence for the effects of experimenter outcome-orientation will have been adduced (Rhine, 1959).

In a more traditional area of psychological research—memory— Ebbinghaus (1913) called attention to similar experimenter effects. In his own research he noted that his expectancy of what data he would obtain affected the data he subsequently did obtain. He pointed out, furthermore, that the experimenter's knowledge of this expectancy was not sufficient to control the phenomenon. This finding has been unfortunately neglected by many subsequent researchers in the area.

Another possible case has been described by Stevens (1961). He discussed the controversy between Fechner and Plateau over the results of bisection experiments to determine the nature of the function describing the operating characteristics of a sensory system. Plateau held that it was a power rather than a log function. Delboeuf carried out experiments for Plateau, but obtained data approximating the Fechnerian prediction of a log function. Stevens puzzled over these results which may be interpreted within the notion of experimenter outcome-orientation. Either by implicitly expecting the Fechnerian outcomes or by attempting to guard against an anti-Fechnerian bias, Delboeuf may have influenced the outcome of his studies.

It would appear that Pavlov was aware of the possibility that experimenter outcome-orientation might affect the results of experiments. In an exchange of letters in *Science*, Zirkle (1958) and Razran (1959) in discussing Pavlov's attitude toward the notion of the inheritance of acquired characteristics, gave credence to a statement by Gruenberg (1929):

In an informal statement made at the time of the Thirteenth International Physiological Congress, Boston, August, 1929, Pavlov explained that in checking up these experiments, it was found that the apparent improve-

ment in the ability to learn, on the part of successive generations of mice, was really due to an improvement in the ability to teach, on the part of the experimenter! And so this "proof" of the transmission of modifications drops out of the picture, at least for the present [p. 327].

Wherry[3] has told of an experiment in which rats were able to discriminate colors, but only when the experimenter was in the room. Christie's (1951) interpretation of some differences between Iowa and Berkeley rats also suggests the possibility of experimenter effects associated with his outcome orientation.

But perhaps the best-known and most instructive case illustrating the effects of outcome-orientation is that of Clever Hans (Pfungst, 1911). By means of tapping his hoof, the horse of von Osten was able to spell, read, and solve problems of arithmetic and musical harmony. Unlike the owners of other performing animals, Hans' owner did not profit from his animal's talent, and permitted any serious investigator to test Hans even in von Osten's absence. Pfungst, and his colleague Stumpf, undertook to discover the secret of Hans' talents.

A series of brilliant and painstaking experiments revealed that Hans' questioners cued him unintentionally. A forward inclination of the questioner's head served as signal to Hans to begin his hoof tapping. A slight upward motion of the questioner's head or eyebrows served as signal for Hans to stop his tapping. Hans' amazing talents, then, may be viewed as an illustration of the power of the self-fulfilling prophecy. Questioners, even skeptical ones, expected Hans to know the correct answers to their queries. Their expectation was reflected in their signal to Hans that they awaited the cessation of his tapping. This signal brought on the expected cessation and Hans was correct again.

Pfungst aptly summarized the difficulties in uncovering the nature of Clever Hans' talents by speaking of "looking for, in the horse, what should have been sought in the man."

Turning to a more recent example of possible outcome-orientation effects, we will describe an experiment dealing with the Freudian defense mechanism of projection (Rosenthal, 1956). A total of 108 subjects was randomly divided into three groups each receiving success, failure, or neutral experience on a task structured as and simulating a standardized test of intelligence. Before the subjects' experimental-treatment condition was imposed, they were asked to rate the degree of success or failure of persons pictured in photographs. Immediately after the experimental manipulation, the subjects were asked to rate an equivalent set of photos on their degree of success

---

3.   Personal communication, 1960.

or failure. The dependent variable was the magnitude of the difference scores from pre- to postratings of the photographs. It was hypothesized that the success-treatment condition would lead to greater subsequent perception of other people's success, while the failure-treatment condition would lead to greater subsequent perception of other people's failure as measured by the pre-post difference scores.

An analysis (which was essentially unnecessary to the main purpose of the study) was performed which compared the mean preratings of the three experimental-treatment conditions. Preratings by subjects in the success-treatment group were significantly lower and less extreme than the prerating by subjects in the other conditions. In terms of the hypothesis under test, a lower prerating by this group would tend to lead to significantly different difference scores if the postratings were similar for all treatment conditions. Without the investigator's awareness, the cards had been stacked in favor of obtaining results confirming the hypothesis under test. It should be emphasized that the success and failure groups' instructions had been verbally identical during the prerating phase of the experiment.

The investigator, however, was aware for each subject which experimental treatment the subject would subsequently be administered.

The implication is that in some subtle manner, perhaps by tone, or manner, or gestures, or general atmosphere, the experimenter, although formally treating the success and failure groups in an identical way, influenced the success S's to make lower initial ratings and thus increase the experimenter's probability of verifying his hypothesis [*Rosenthal, 1956, p. 44*].

Reports of the findings of the sort just presented are not numerous and virtually never published. Nevertheless, their occurrence can be documented.[4] Allusions to the effects of the experimenter's outcome orientation[5] in general have been made by Edwards (1950); Feldman (1956); Foster (1923); Riecken (1962); Cohen, Silverman, Bressler, and Shmavonian (1961); and half facetiously by Ammons and Ammons (1957); and Rotter.[6]

---

4. O. Gardebring, 1962; J. Gengerelli, 1956; G. Mount, 1956; and G. Rosenwald, 1963; personal communications.

5. A series of experiments specifically designed to investigate the occurrence and nature of the effects of the experimenter's outcome-orientation has recently been summarized elsewhere (Rosenthal, 1963).

6. Personal communication, 1961.

References

Ammons, R. B. and Ammons, Carol H. ESP and PK: A way out? *N. Dak. Quart.*, 1957, **25**, 119–121.

Anderson, Margaret and White, Rhea. A survey of work on ESP and teacher-pupil attitudes. *J. Parapsychol.*, 1958, **22**, 246–268.

Back, K. W. Influence through social communication. *J. abnorm. soc. Psychol.*, 1951, **46**, 9–23.

Christie, R. Experimental naivete and experiential naivete. *Psychol. Bull.*, 1951, **48**, 327–339.

Cohen, S. I., Silverman, A. J., Bressler, B., and Shmavonian, B. Problems in isolation studies. In P. K. Solomon, P. E. Kubzansky, P. H. Leiderman, J. H. Mendelson, R. Trumbull, and D. Wexler (Eds.), *Sensory deprivation.* Cambridge: Harvard Univer. Press, 1961.

Crumbaugh, J. D. ESP and flying saucers: A challenge to parapsychologists. *Amer. Psychologist*, 1959, **14**, 604–606.

Ebbinghaus, H. *Memory: A contribution to experimental psychology.* (Orig. publ. 1885; trans. by H. A. Ruger and Clara E. Bussenius) New York: Teachers College, Columbia University, Bureau of Publications, 1913.

Edwards, A. L. *Experimental design in psychological research.* New York: Rinehart, 1950.

Feldman, P. E. The personal element in psychiatric research. *Amer. J. Psychiat.*, 1956, **113**, 52–54.

Foster, W. S. Experiments on rod-divining. *J. appl. Psychol.*, 1923, **7**, 303–311.

Friedman, Pearl. A second experiment on interviewer bias. *Sociometry*, 1942, **5**, 378–379.

Fromm-Reichmann, Frieda. *Principles of intensive psychotherapy.* Chicago: Univ. Chicago Press, 1950.

Goldstein, A. P. Therapist and client expectation of personality change in psychotherapy. *J. counsel. Psychol.*, 1960, **7**, 180–184.

Goldstein, A. P. *Therapist-patient expectancies in psychotherapy.* New York: Pergamon Press, 1962.

Gruenberg, B. C. *The story of evolution.* New York: Van Nostrand, 1929.

Gunne, L. M. Mortaliteten vid delirium tremens. [Mortality in delirium tremens.] *Nord. Med.*, 1958, **60**, 1021–1024.

Hanson, R. H. and Marks, E. S. Influence of the interviewer on the accuracy of survey results. *J. Amer. Statist. Ass.*, 1958, **53**, 635–655.

Harvey, S. M. A preliminary investigation of the interview. *Brit. J. Psychol.*, 1938, **28**, 263–287.

Heider, F. *The psychology of interpersonal relations.* New York: Wiley, 1958.

Heine, R. W. and Trosman, H. Initial expectations of the doctor-patient interaction as a factor in continuance in psychotherapy. *Psychiatry,* 1960, **23,** 275–278.

Heller, K. and Goldstein, A. P. Client dependency and therapist expectancy as relationship maintaining variables in psychotherapy. *J. consult. Psychol.,* 1961, **25,** 371–375.

Hyman, H. H., Cobb, W. J., Feldman, J. J., Hart, C. W., and Stember, C. H. *Interviewing in social research.* Chicago: Univer. Chicago Press, 1954.

Kennedy, J. L. Experiments on "unconscious whispering." *Psychol. Bull.,* 1938, **35,** 526. (Abstract)

Levy, L. H. and Orr, T. B. The social psychology of Rorschach validity research. *J. abnorm. soc. Psychol.,* 1959, **58,** 79–83.

Lindzey, G. A note on interviewer bias. *J. appl. Psychol.,* 1951, **35,** 182–184.

Merton, R. K. The self-fulfilling prophecy. *Antioch Rev.,* 1948, **8,** 193–210.

Pfungst, O. *Clever Hans (the horse of Mr. von Osten): A contribution to experimental, animal, and human psychology.* (Trans. by C. L. Rahn) New York: Holt, 1911.

Quarterly Journal of Studies on Alcohol Editorial Staff. Mortality in delirium tremens. *N. Dak. Rev. Alcoholism,* 1959, **4,** 3. (Abstract)

Razran, G. Pavlov the empiricist. *Science,* 1959, **130,** 916.

Rhine, J. B. How does one decide about ESP? *Amer. Psychologist,* 1959, **14,** 606–608.

Rice, S. A. Contagious bias in the interview: A methodological note. *Amer. J. Sociol.,* 1929, **35,** 420–423.

Riecken, H. W. A program for research on experiments in social psychology. In N. F. Washburne (Ed.), *Decisions, values and groups.* Vol. 2. New York: Pergamon Press, 1962. Pp. 25–41.

Rosenthal, R. An attempt at the experimental induction of the defense mechanism of projection. Unpublished doctoral dissertation, University of California, Los Angeles, 1956.

Rosenthal, R. On the social psychology of the psychological experiment: The experimenter's hypothesis as unintended determinant of experimental results. *Amer. Scientist,* 1963, **51,** 268–283.

Schmeidler, Gertrude and McConnell, R. A. *ESP and personality patterns.* New Haven: Yale Univer. Press, 1958.

Shapiro, A. K. A contribution to a history of the placebo effect. *Behav. Sci.,* 1960, **5,** 109–135.

Stanton, F. Further contributions, twentieth anniversary of the Psychological Corporation and to honor its founder, James McKeen Cattel. *J. appl. Psychol.,* 1942, **26,** 8–23.

Stanton, F. and Baker, K. H. Interviewer bias and the recall of incompletely learned materials. *Sociometry,* 1942, **5,** 123–134.

Stevens, S. S. To honor Fechner and repeal his law. *Science,* 1961, **133,** 80–86.

Warner, L. and Raible, Mildred. Telepathy in the psychophysical laboratory. *J. Parapsychol.,* 1937, **1,** 44–51.

Whyte, W. F. *Street corner society.* Chicago: Univer. Chicago Press, 1943.

Wilson, E. B. *An introduction to scientific research.* New York: McGraw-Hill, 1952.

Zirkle, C. Pavlov's beliefs. *Science,* 1958, **128,** 1476.

6

human use of human subjects:

the problem of deception in social psychological experiments[1]

Herbert C. Kelman

In 1954, in the pages of the *American Psychologist*, Edgar Vinacke raised a series of questions about experiments—particularly in the area of small groups—in which "the psychologist conceals the true purpose and conditions of the experiment, or positively misinforms the subjects, or exposes them to painful, embarrassing, or worse, experiences, without the subjects' knowledge of what is going on [p. 155]." He summed up his concerns by asking, "What ... is the proper balance between the interests of science and the thoughtful treatment of the persons who, innocently, supply the data? [p. 155]." Little effort has been made in the intervening years to seek answers to the questions he raised. During these same years, however, the problem of

From *Psychological Bulletin*, Vol. 67, (No. 1), 1967, pp. 1–11. Copyright 1967 by the American Psychological Association. Reproduced by permission.
1. Paper read at the symposium on "Ethical and Methodological Problems in Social Psychological Experiments," held at the meetings of the American Psychological Association in Chicago, September 3, 1965. This paper is a product of a research program on social influence and behavior change supported by United States Public Health Service Research Grant MH-07280 from the National Institute of Mental Health.

deception in social psychological experiments has taken on increasingly serious proportions.[2]

The problem is actually broader, extending beyond the walls of the laboratory. It arises, for example, in various field studies in which investigators enroll as members of a group that has special interest for them so that they can observe its operations from the inside. The pervasiveness of the problem becomes even more apparent when we consider that deception is built into most of our measurement devices, since it is important to keep the respondent unaware of the personality or attitude dimension that we wish to explore. For the present purposes, however, primarily the problem of deception in the context of the social psychological experiment will be discussed.

The use of deception has become more and more extensive, and it is now a commonplace and almost standard feature of social psychological experiments. Deception has been turned into a game, often played with great skill and virtuosity. A considerable amount of the creativity and ingenuity of social psychologists is invested in the development of increasingly elaborate deception situations. Within a single experiment, deception may be built upon deception in a delicately complex structure. The literature now contains a fair number of studies in which second- or even third-order deception was employed.

One well-known experiment (Festinger and Carlsmith, 1959), for example, involved a whole progression of deceptions. After the subjects had gone through an experimental task, the investigator made it clear—through word and gesture—that the experiment was over and that he would now "like to explain what this has been all about so you'll have some idea of why you were doing this [p. 205]." This explanation was false, however, and was designed to serve as a basis for the true experimental manipulation. The manipulation itself involved asking subjects to serve as the experimenter's accomplices. The task of the "accomplice" was to tell the next "subject" that the experiment in which he had just participated (which was in fact a rather boring experience) had been interesting and enjoyable. He was also asked to be on call for unspecified future occasions on which his services as accomplice might be needed because "the regular fellow couldn't

2.   In focusing on deception in *social* psychological experiments, I do not wish to give the impression that there is no serious problem elsewhere. Deception is widely used in most studies involving human subjects and gives rise to issues similar to those discussed in this paper. Some examples of the use of deception in other areas of psychological experimentation will be presented later in this paper.

make it, and we had a subject scheduled [p. 205]." These newly recruited "accomplices," of course, were the true subjects, while the "subjects" were the experimenter's true accomplices. For their presumed services as "accomplices," the true subjects were paid in advance —half of them receiving $1, and half $20. When they completed their service, however, the investigators added injury to insult by asking them to return their hard-earned cash. Thus, in this one study, in addition to receiving the usual misinformation about the purpose of the experiment, the subject was given feedback that was really an experimental manipulation, was asked to be an accomplice who was really a subject, and was given a $20 bill that was really a will-o'-the-wisp. One wonders how much further in this direction we can go. Where will it all end?

It is easy to view this problem with alarm, but it is much more difficult to formulate an unambiguous position on the problem. As a working experimental social psychologist, I cannot conceive the issue in absolutist terms. I am too well aware of the fact that there are good reasons for using deception in many experiments. There are many significant problems that probably cannot be investigated without the use of deception, at least not at the present level of development of our experimental methodology. Thus, we are always confronted with a conflict of values. If we regard the acquisition of scientific knowledge about human behavior as a positive value, and if an experiment using deception constitutes a significant contribution to such knowledge which could not very well be achieved by other means, then we cannot unequivocally rule out this experiment. The question for us is not simply whether it does or does not use deception, but whether the amount and type of deception are justified by the significance of the study and the unavailability of alternative (that is, deception-free) procedures.

I have expressed special concern about second-order deceptions, for example, the procedure of letting a person believe that he is acting as experimenter or as the experimenter's accomplice when he is in fact serving as the subject. Such a procedure undermines the relationship between experimenter and subject even further than simple misinformation about the purposes of the experiment; deception does not merely take place *within* the experiment, but encompasses the whole definition of the relationship between the parties involved. Deception that takes place while the person is within the role of subject for which he has contracted can, to some degree, be isolated, but deception about the very nature of the contract itself is more likely to suffuse the experimenter-subject relationship as a whole and to remove the possibility of mutual trust. Thus, I would be inclined to take a more absolutist stand with regard to such second-order deceptions—but even here the issue turns out to be more complicated. I am stopped short when I think, for example of the ingenious studies on experimenter bias by Rosenthal and his associates (e.g., Rosenthal and Fode, 1963; Rosenthal, Persinger, Vikan-Kline, and Fode, 1963; Rosenthal, Persinger, Vikan-Kline, and Mulry, 1963). These experiments employed second-order deception in that subjects were led to believe that they were the experimenters. Since these were experiments about experiments, however, it is very hard to conceive of any alternative procedures that the investigators might have used. There is no question in my mind that these are significant studies; they provide fundamental inputs to present efforts at reexamining the social psychology of the experiment. These studies, then, help to underline even further the point that we are confronted with a conflict of values that cannot be resolved by fiat.

I hope it is clear from these remarks that my purpose in focusing on this problem is not to single out specific studies performed by some of my colleagues and to point a finger at them. Indeed, the finger points at me as well. I too have used deception, and have known the joys of applying my skills and ingenuity to the creation of elaborate experimental situations that the subjects would not be able to decode. I am now making active attempts to find alternatives to deception, but still I have not forsworn the use of deception under any and all circumstances. The questions I am raising, then, are addressed to myself as well as to my colleagues. They are questions with which all of us who are committed to social psychology must come to grips, lest we leave their resolution to others who have no understanding of what we are trying to accomplish.

What concerns me most is not so much that deception is used, but precisely that it is used without question. It has now become standard operating procedure in the social psychologist's laboratory. I sometimes feel that we are training a generation of students who do not know that there is any other way of doing experiments in our field—who feel that deception is as much de rigueur as significance at the .05 level. Too often deception is used not as a last resort, but as a matter of course. Our attitude seems to be that if you can deceive, why tell the truth? It is this unquestioning acceptance, this routinization of deception, that really concerns me.

I would like to turn now to a review of the bases for my concern with the problem of deception, and then suggest some possible approaches for dealing with it.

**Implications of the use of deception
in social psychological experiments**

My concern about the use of deception is based on three considerations: the ethical implications of such procedures, their methodological implications, and their implications for the future of social psychology.

1. Ethical implications

Ethical problems of a rather obvious nature arise in the experiments in which deception has potentially harmful consequences for the subject. Take, for example, the brilliant experiment by Mulder and Stemerding (1963) on the effects of threat on attraction to the group and need for strong leadership. In this study—one of the very rare examples of an experiment conducted in a natural setting—independent food merchants in a number of Dutch towns were brought together for group meetings, in the course of which they were informed that a large organization was planning to open up a series of supermarkets in the Netherlands. In the High Threat condition, subjects were told that there was a high probability that their town would be selected as a site for such markets, and that the advent of these markets would cause a considerable drop in their business. On the advice of the executives of the shopkeepers' organizations, who had helped to arrange the group meetings, the investigators did not reveal the experimental manipulations to their subjects. I have been worried about these Dutch merchants ever since I heard about this study for the first time. Did some of them go out of business in anticipation of the heavy competition? Do some of them have an anxiety reaction every time they see a bulldozer? Chances are that they soon forgot about this threat (unless, of course, supermarkets actually did move into town) and that it became just one of the many little moments of anxiety that must occur in every shopkeeper's life. Do we have a right, however, to add to life's little anxieties and to risk the possibility of more extensive anxiety purely for the purposes of our experiments, particularly since deception deprives the subject of the opportunity to choose whether or not he wishes to expose himself to the risks that might be entailed?

The studies by Bramel (1962, 1963) and Bergin (1962) provide examples of another type of potentially harmful effects arising from the use of deception. In the Bramel studies, male undergraduates were led to believe that they were homosexually aroused by photographs of men. In the Bergin study, subjects of both sexes were given discrepant information about their level of masculinity or femininity; in one experimental condition, this information was presumably based on an elaborate series of psychological tests in which the subjects had participated. In all of these studies, the deception was explained to the subject at the end of the experiment. One wonders, however, whether such explanation removes the possibility of harmful effects. For many persons in this age group, sexual identity is still a live and sensitive issue, and the self-doubts generated by the laboratory experience may take on a life of their own and linger on for some time to come.

Yet another illustration of potentially harmful effects of deception can be found in Milgram's (1963, 1965) studies of obedience. In these experiments, the subject was led to believe that he was participating in a learning study and was instructed to administer increasingly severe shocks to another person who after a while began to protest vehemently. In fact, of course, the victim was an accomplice of the experimenter and did not receive any shocks. Depending on the conditions, sizable proportions of the subjects obeyed the experimenter's instructions and continued to shock the other person up to the maximum level, which they believed to be extremely painful. Both obedient and defiant subjects exhibited a great deal of stress in this situation. The complexities of the issues surrounding the use of deception become quite apparent when one reads the exchange between Baumrind (1964) and Milgram (1964) about the ethical implications of the obedience research. There is clearly room for disagreement, among honorable people, about the evaluation of this research from an ethical point of view. Yet, there is good reason to believe that at least some of the obedient subjects came away from this experience with a lower self-esteem, having to live with the realization that they were willing to yield to destructive authority to the point of inflicting extreme pain on a fellow human being. The fact that this may have provided, in Milgram's (1964) words, "an opportunity to learn something of importance about themselves, and more generally, about the conditions of human action [p. 850]" is beside the point. If this were a lesson from life, it would indeed constitute an instructive confrontation and provide a valuable insight. But do we, for the purpose of experimentation, have the right to provide such potentially disturbing insights to subjects who do not know that this is what they are coming for? A similar question can be raised about the Asch (1951) experiments on group pressure, although the stressfulness of the situation and the implications for the person's self-concept were less intense in that context.

While the present paper is specifically focused on social psychological experiments, the problem of deception and its possibly harmful effects arises in other areas of psychological experimentation as well. Dramatic illustrations are provided by two studies in which subjects were exposed, for experimental purposes, to extremely stressful conditions. In an experiment designed to study the establishment of a conditioned response in a situation that is traumatic but not painful, Campbell, Sanderson, and Laverty (1964) induced—through the use of a drug—a temporary interruption of respiration in their subjects. "This has no permanently harmful physical consequences but is nonetheless a severe stress which is not in itself painful . . . [p. 628]." The subjects' reports confirmed that this was a "horrific" experience for them. "All the subjects in the standard series said that they thought they were dying [p. 631]." Of course the subjects, "male alcoholic patients who volunteered for the experiment when they were told that it was connected with a possible therapy for alcoholism [p. 629]," were not warned in advance about the effect of the drug, since this information would have reduced the traumatic impact of the experience.[3] In a series of studies on the effects of psychological stress, Berkun, Bialek, Kern, and Yagi (1962) devised a number of ingenious experimental situations designed to convince the subject that his life was actually in danger. In one situation, the subjects, a group of Army recruits, were actually "passengers aboard an apparently stricken plane which was being forced to 'ditch' or crash-land [p. 4]." In another experiment, an isolated subject in a desolate area learned that a sudden emergency had arisen (accidental nuclear radiation in the area, or a sudden forest fire, or misdirected artillery shells—depending on the experimental condition) and that he could be rescued only if he reported his position over his radio transmitter, "which has quite suddenly failed [p. 7]." In yet another situation, the subject was led to believe that he was responsible for an explosion that seriously injured another soldier. As the authors pointed out, reactions in these situations are more likely to approximate reactions to combat experiences or to naturally occurring disasters than are reactions to various laboratory stresses, but is the experimenter justified in exposing his subjects to such extreme threats?

So far, I have been speaking of experiments in which deception has potentially harmful consequences. I am equally concerned, however, about the less obvious cases, in which there is little danger of harmful effects, at least in the conventional sense of the term. Serious ethical issues are raised by deception *per se* and the kind of use of human

---

3. The authors reported, however, that some of their other subjects were physicians familiar with the drug; "they did not suppose they were dying but, even though they knew in a general way what to expect, they too said that the experience was extremely harrowing [p. 632]." Thus, conceivably, the purposes of the experiment might have been achieved if the subjects had been told to expect the temporary interruption of breathing.

beings that it implies. In our other interhuman relationships, most of us would never think of doing the kinds of things that we do to our subjects—exposing others to lies and tricks, deliberately misleading them about the purposes of the interaction or withholding pertinent information, making promises or giving assurances that we intend to disregard. We would view such behavior as a violation of the respect to which all fellow humans are entitled and of the whole basis of our relationship with them. Yet we seem to forget that the experimenter-subject relationship—whatever else it is—is a *real* interhuman relationship, in which we have responsibility toward the subject as another human being whose dignity we must preserve. The discontinuity between the experimenter's behavior in everyday life and his behavior in the laboratory is so marked that one wonders why there has been so little concern with this problem, and what mechanisms have allowed us to ignore it to such an extent. I am reminded, in this connection, of the intriguing phenomenon of the "holiness of sin," which characterizes certain messianic movements as well as other movements of the true-believer variety. Behavior that would normally be unacceptable actually takes on an aura of virtue in such movements through a redefinition of the situation in which the behavior takes place and thus of the context for evaluating it. A similar mechanism seems to be involved in our attitude toward the psychological experiment. We tend to regard it as a situation that is not quite real, that can be isolated from the rest of life like a play performed on stage, and to which, therefore, the usual criteria for ethical interpersonal conduct become irrelevant. Behavior is judged entirely in the context of the experiment's scientific contribution and, in this context, deception—which is normally unacceptable—can indeed be seen as a positive good.

The broader ethical problem brought into play by the very use of deception becomes even more important when we view it in the light of present historical forces. We are living in an age of mass societies in which the transformation of man into an object to be manipulated at will occurs "on a mass scale, in a systematic way, and under the aegis of specialized institutions deliberately assigned to this task [Kelman, 1965]." In institutionalizing the use of deception in psychological experiments, we are, then, contributing to a historical trend that threatens values most of us cherish.

2. Methodological implications

A second source of my concern about the use of deception is my increasing doubt about its adequacy as a methodology for social psychology.

A basic assumption in the use of deception is that a subject's awareness of the conditions that we are trying to create and of the phenomena that we wish to study would affect his behavior in such a way that we could not draw valid conclusions from it. For example, if we are interested in studying the effects of failure on conformity, we must create a situation in which the subjects actually feel that they have failed, and in which they can be kept unaware of our interest in observing conformity. In short, it is important to keep our subjects naive about the purposes of the experiment so that they can respond to the experimental inductions spontaneously.

How long, however, will it be possible for us to find naive subjects? Among college students, it is already very difficult. They may not know the exact purpose of the particular experiment in which they are participating, but at least they know, typically, that it is *not* what the experimenter says it is. Orne (1962) pointed out that the use of deception "on the part of psychologists is so widely known in the college population that even if a psychologist is honest with the subject, more often than not he will be distrusted." As one subject pithily put it, " 'Psychologists always lie!' " Orne added that "This bit of paranoia has some support in reality [pp. 778–779]." There are, of course, other sources of human subjects that have not been tapped, and we could turn to them in our quest for naiveté. But even there it is only a matter of time. As word about psychological experiments gets around in whatever network we happen to be using, sophistication is bound to increase. I wonder, therefore, whether there is any future in the use of deception.

If the subject in a deception experiment knows what the experimenter is trying to conceal from him and what he is really after in the study, the value of the deception is obviously nullified. Generally, however, even the relatively sophisticated subject does not know the exact purpose of the experiment; he only has suspicions, which may approximate the true purpose of the experiment to a greater or lesser degree. Whether or not he knows the *true* purpose of the experiment, he is likely to make an effort to figure out its purpose, since he does not believe what the experimenter tells him, and therefore he is likely to operate in the situation in terms of his own hypothesis of what is involved. This may, in line with Orne's (1962) analysis, lead him to do what he thinks the experimenter wants him to do. Conversely, if he resents the experimenter's attempt to deceive him, he may try to throw a monkey wrench into the works; I would not be surprised if this kind of Schweikian game among subjects became a fairly well-established part of the culture of sophisticated campuses. Whichever course the subject uses, however, he is operating in terms of his own conception of the nature of the situation, rather than in terms of the conception that the experimenter is trying to induce. In short, the experimenter can no longer assume that the conditions that he is trying to create are the ones that actually define the situation for the subject. Thus, the use of deception, while it is designed to give the experimenter control over the subject's perceptions and motivations, may actually produce an unspecifiable mixture of intended and unintended stimuli that make it difficult to know just what the subject is responding to.

The tendency for subjects to react to unintended cues—to features of the situation that are not part of the experimenter's design—is by no means restricted to experiments that involve deception. This problem has concerned students of the interview situation for some time, and more recently it has been analyzed in detail in the writings and research of Riecken, Rosenthal, Orne, and Mills. Subjects enter the experiment with their own aims, including attainment of certain rewards, divination of the experimenter's true purposes, and favorable self-presentation (Riecken, 1962). They are therefore responsive to demand characteristics of the situation (Orne, 1962), to unintended communications of the experimenter's expectations (Rosenthal, 1963), and to the role of the experimenter within the social system that experimenter and subject jointly constitute (Mills, 1962). In any experiment, then, the subject goes beyond the description of the situation and the experimental manipulation introduced by the investigator, makes his own interpretation of the situation, and acts accordingly.

For several reasons, however, the use of deception especially encourages the subject to dismiss the stated purposes of the experiment and to search for alternative interpretations of his own. First, the continued use of deception establishes the reputation of psychologists as people who cannot be believed. Thus, the desire "to penetrate the experimenter's inscrutability and discover the rationale of the experiment [Riecken, 1962, p. 34]" becomes especially strong. Generally, these efforts are motivated by the subject's desire to meet the expectations of the experimenter and of the situation. They may also be motivated, however, as I have already mentioned, by a desire to outwit the experimenter and to beat him at his own game, in a spirit of genuine hostility or playful one-upmanship. Second, a situation involving the use of deception is inevitably highly ambiguous since a great deal of information relevant to understanding the structure of the situation must be withheld from the subject. Thus, the subject is especially motivated to try to figure things out and likely to develop idiosyncratic interpretations. Third, the use of deception, by its very nature, causes the experimenter to transmit contradictory messages to the subject. In his verbal instructions and explanations he says one thing about the purposes of the experiment; but in the experimental situations that he has created, in the manipulations that he has introduced, and probably in covert cues that he emits, he says another thing. This again makes it imperative for the subject to seek his own interpretation of the situation.

I would argue, then, that deception increases the subject's tendency to operate in terms of his private definition of the situation, differing (in random or systematic fashion) from the definition that the experimenter is trying to impose; moreover, it makes it more difficult to evaluate or minimize the effects of this tendency. Whether or not I am right in this judgement, it can, at the very least, be said that the use of deception does not resolve or reduce the unintended effects of the experiment as a social situation in which the subject pursues his private aims. Since the assumptions that the subject is naive and that he sees the situation as the experimenter wishes him to see it are unwarranted, the use of deception no longer has any special obvious advantages over other experimental approaches. I am not suggesting that there may not be occasions when deception may still be the most effective procedure to use from a methodological point of view. But since it raises at least as many methodological problems as any other type of procedure does, we have every reason to explore alternative approaches and to extend our methodological inquiries to the question of the effects of using deception.

3. Implications for the future of social psychology

My third concern about the use of deception is based on its long-run implications for our discipline and combines both the ethical and methodological considerations that I have already raised. There is something disturbing about the idea of relying on massive deception as the basis for developing a field of inquiry. Can one really build a discipline on a foundation of such research?

From a long-range point of view, there is obviously something self-defeating about the use of deception. As we continue to carry out research of this kind, our potential subjects become more and more sophisticated, and we become less and less able to meet the conditions that our experimental procedures require. Moreover, as we continue to carry out research of this kind, our potential subjects become increasingly distrustful of us, and our future relations with them are likely to be undermined. Thus, we are confronted with the anomalous circumstance that the more research we do, the more difficult and questionable it becomes.

The use of deception also involves a contradiction between our experimental procedures and our long-range aims as scientists and teachers. In order to be able to carry out our experiments, we are concerned with maintaining the naiveté of the population from which we hope to draw our subjects. We are all familiar with the experimenter's anxious concern that the introductory course might cover the autokinetic phenomenon, need achievement, or the Asch situation before he has had a chance to complete his experimental runs. This perfectly understandable desire to keep procedures secret goes counter to the traditional desire of the scientist and teacher to inform and enlighten the public. To be sure, experimenters are interested only in temporary secrecy, but it is not inconceivable that at some time in the future they might be using certain procedures on a regular basis with large segments of the population and thus prefer to keep the public permanently naive. It is perhaps not too fanciful to imagine, for the long run, the possible emergence of a special class, in possession of secret knowledge—a possibility that is clearly antagonistic to the principle of open communication to which we, as scientists and intellectuals, are so fervently committed.

**Dealing with the problem of deception
in social psychological experiments**

If my concerns about the use of deception are justified, what are some of the ways in which we, as experimental social psychologists, can deal with them? I would like to suggest three steps that we can take: increase our active awareness of the problem, explore ways of counteracting and minimizing the negative effects of deception, and give careful attention to the development of new experimental techniques that dispense with the use of deception.

*1. Active awareness of
the problem*

I have already stressed that I would not propose the complete elimination of deception under all circumstances, in view of the genuine conflict of values with which the experimenter is confronted. What is crucial, however, is that we always ask ourselves the question whether deception, in the given case, is necessary and justified. How we answer the question is less important than the fact that we ask it. What we must be wary of is the tendency to dismiss the question as irrelevant and to accept deception as a matter of course. Active awareness of the problem is thus in itself part of the solution, for it makes the use of deception a matter for discussion, deliberation, investigation, and choice. Active awareness means that, in any given case, we will try to balance the value of an experiment that uses deception against its questionable or potentially harmful effects. If we engage in this process honestly, we are likely to find that there are many occasions when we or our students can forego the use of deception—either because deception is not necessary (that is, alternative procedures that are equally good or better are available), because the importance of the study does not warrant the use of an ethically questionable procedure, or because the type of deception involved is too extreme (in terms of the possibility of harmful effects or of seriously undermining the experimenter-subject relationship).

2. Counteracting and minimizing the negative effects of deception

If we do use deception, it is essential that we find ways of counteracting and minimizing its negative effects. Sensitizing the apprentice researcher to this necessity is at least as fundamental as any other part of research training.

In those experiments in which deception carries the potential of harmful effects (in the more usual sense of the term), there is an obvious requirement to build protections into every phase of the process. Subjects must be selected in a way that will exclude individuals who are especially vulnerable; the potentially harmful manipulation (such as the induction of stress) must be kept at a moderate level of intensity; the experimenter must be sensitive to danger signals in the reactions of his subjects and be prepared to deal with crises when they arise; and, at the conclusion of the session, the experimenter must take time not only to reassure the subject, but also to help him work through his feelings about the experience to whatever degree may be required. In general, the principle that a subject ought not to leave the laboratory with greater anxiety or lower self-esteem than he came with is a good one to follow. I would go beyond it to argue that the subject should in some positive way be enriched by the experience, that is, he should come away from it with the feeling that he has learned something, understood something, or grown in some way. This, of course, adds special importance to the kind of feedback that is given to the subject at the end of the experimental session.

Postexperimental feedback is, of course, the primary way of counteracting negative effects in those experiments in which the issue is deception as such, rather than possible threats to the subject's well-being. If we do deceive the subject, then it is our obligation to give him a full and detailed explanation of what we have done and of our reasons for using this type of procedure. I do not want to be absolutist about this, but I would suggest this as a good rule of thumb to follow: Think very carefully before undertaking an experiment whose purposes you feel unable to reveal to the subjects even after they have completed the experimental session. It is, of course, not enough to give the subject a perfunctory feedback, just to do one's duty. Postexperimental explanations should be worked out with as much detail as other aspects of the procedure and, in general, some thought ought to be given to ways of making them meaningful and instructive for the subject and helpful for rebuilding his relationship with the experimenter. I feel very strongly that to accomplish these purposes, we must keep the feedback itself inviolate and under no circumstance give the subject false feedback or pretend to be giving him feedback while we are in fact introducing another experimental manipulation. If we hope to maintain any kind of trust in our relationship with potential subjects, there must be no ambiguity that the statement "The experiment is over and I shall explain to you what it was all about" means precisely that and nothing else. If subjects have reason to suspect even that statement, then we have lost the whole basis for a decent human relationship with our subjects and all hope for future cooperation from them.

3. Development of new experimental techniques

My third and final suggestion is that we invest some of the creativity and ingenuity, now devoted to the construction of elaborate deceptions, in the search for alternative experimental techniques that do not rely on the use of deception. The kind of techniques that I have in mind would be based on the principle of eliciting the subject's positive motivations to contribute to the experimental enterprise. They would draw on the subject's active participation and involvement in the proceedings and encourage him to cooperate in making the experiment a success—not by giving the results he thinks the experimenter wants, but by conscientiously taking the roles and carrying out the tasks that the experimenter assigns to him. In short, the kind of techniques I have in mind would be designed to involve the subject as an active participant in a joint effort with the experimenter.

Perhaps the most promising source of alternative experimental approaches are procedures using some sort of role playing. I have been impressed, for example, with the role playing that I have observed in the context of the Inter-Nation Simulation (Guetzkow, Alger,

Brody, Noel, and Snyder, 1963), a laboratory procedure involving a simulated world in which the subjects take the roles of decision-makers of various nations. This situation seems to create a high level of emotional involvement and to elicit motivations that have a real-life quality to them. Moreover, within this situation—which is highly complex and generally permits only gross experimental manipulations —it is possible to test specific theoretical hypotheses by using data based on repeated measurements as interaction between the simulated nations develops. Thus, a study carried out at the Western Behavioral Sciences Institute provided, as an extra, some interesting opportunities for testing hypotheses derived from balance theory, by the use of mutual ratings made by decision-makers of Nations A, B, and C, before and after A shifted from an alliance with B to an alliance with C.

A completely different type of role playing was used effectively by Rosenberg and Abelson (1960) in their studies of cognitive dilemmas. In my own research program, we have been exploring different kinds of role-playing procedures with varying degrees of success. In one study, the major manipulation consisted in informing subjects that the experiment to which they had just committed themselves would require them (depending on the condition) either to receive shocks from a fellow subject, or to administer shocks to a fellow subject. We used a regular deception procedure, but with a difference: We told the subjects before the session started that what was to follow was make-believe, but that we wanted them to react as if they really found themselves in this situation. I might mention that some subjects, not surprisingly, did not accept as true the information that this was all make-believe and wanted to know when they should show up for the shock experiment to which they had committed themselves. I have some question about the effectiveness of this particular procedure. It did not do enough to create a high level of involvement, and it turned out be be very complex since it asked subjects to role-play subjects, not people. In this sense, it might have given us the worst of both worlds, but I still think it is worth some further exploration. In another experiment, we were interested in creating differently structured attitudes about an organization by feeding different kinds of information to two groups of subjects. These groups were then asked to take specific actions in support of the organization, and we measured attitude changes resulting from these actions. In the first part of the experiment, the subjects were clearly informed that the organization and the information that we were feeding to them were fictitious, and that we were simply trying to simulate the conditions under which attitudes about new organizations are typically formed. In the second part of the experiment, the subjects were told that we were interested in studying the effects of action in support of an organization on attitudes toward it, and they were asked (in groups of five) to role-play a strategy meeting of leaders of the fictitious organization. The results of this study were very encouraging. While there is obviously a great deal that we need to know about the meaning of this situation to the subjects, they did react differentially to the experimental manipulations and these reactions followed an orderly pattern, despite the fact that they knew it was all make-believe.

There are other types of procedures, in addition to role playing, that are worth exploring. For example, one might design field experiments in which, with the full cooperation of the subjects, specific experimental variations are introduced. The advantages of dealing with motivations at a real-life level of intensity might well outweigh the disadvantages of subjects' knowing the general purpose of the experiment. At the other extreme of ambitiousness, one might explore the effects of modifying standard experimental procedures slightly by informing the subject at the beginning of the experiment that he will not be receiving full information about what is going on, but asking him to suspend judgment until the experiment is over.

Whatever alternative approach we try, there is no doubt that it will have its own problems and complexities. Procedures effective for some purposes may be quite ineffective for others, and it may well turn out that for certain kinds of problems there is no adequate substitute for the use of deception. But there *are* alternative procedures that, for many purposes, may be as effective or even more effective than procedures built on deception. These approaches often involve a radically different set of assumptions about the role of the subject in the experiment: They require us to *use* the subject's motivation to cooperate rather than to bypass it; they may even call for increasing the sophistication of potential subjects, rather than maintaining their naiveté. My only plea is that we devote some of our energies to active exploration of these alternative approaches.

References

Asch, S. E. Effects of group pressure upon the modification and distortion of judgments, In H. Guetzkow (Ed.), *Groups, leadership, and men.* Pittsburg: Carnegie Press, 1951. Pp. 177–190.

Baumrind, D. Some thoughts on ethics of research: After reading Milgram's "Behavioral Study of Obedience." *American Psychologist*, 1964, **19**, 421–423.

Bergin, A. E. The effect of dissonant persuasive communications upon changes in a self-referring attitude. *Journal of Personality*, 1962, **30**, 423–438.

Berkun, M. M., Bialek, H. M., Kern, R. P., and Yagi, K. Experimental studies of psychological stress in man. *Psychological Monographs*, 1962, **76** (15, Whole No. 534).

Bramel, D. A dissonance theory approach to defensive projection. *Journal of Abnormal and Social Psychology*, 1962, **64**, 121–129.

Bramel, D. Selection of a target for defensive projection. *Journal of Abnormal and Social Psychology*, 1963, **66**, 318–324.

Campbell, D., Sanderson, R. E., and Laverty, S. G. Characteristics of a conditioned response in human subjects during extinction trials following a single traumatic conditioning trial. *Journal of Abnormal and Social Psychology*, 1964, **68**, 627–639.

Festinger, L. and Carlsmith, J. M. Cognitive consequences of forced compliance. *Journal of Abnormal and Social Psychology*, 1959, **58**, 203–210.

Guetzkow, H., Alger, C. F., Brody, R. A., Noel, R. C., and Snyder, R. C. *Simulation in international relations.* Englewood Cliffs, N. J.: Prentice-Hall, 1963.

Kelman, H. C. Manipulation of human behavior: An ethical dilemma for the social scientist. *Journal of Social Issues*, 1965, **21**(2), 31–46.

Milgram, S. Behavioral study of obedience. *Journal of Abnormal and Social Psychology*, 1963, **67**, 371–378.

Milgram, S. Issues in the study of obedience: A reply to Baumrind. *American Psychologist*, 1964, **19**, 848–852.

Milgram, S. Some conditions of obedience and disobedience to authority. *Human Relations*, 1965, **18**, 57–76.

Mills, T. M. A sleeper variable in small groups research: The experimenter. *Pacific Sociological Review*, 1962, **5**, 21–28.

Mulder, M. and Stemerding, A. Threat, attraction to group, and need for strong leadership. *Human Relations*, 1963, **16**, 317–334.

Orne, M. T. On the social psychology of the psychological experiment: With particular reference to demand characteristics and their implications. *American Psychologist*, 1962, **17**, 776–783.

Riecken, H. W. A program for research on experiments in social psychology. In N. F. Washburne (Ed.), *Decisions, values and groups.* Vol. 2. New York: Pergamon Press, 1962. Pp. 25–41.

Rosenberg, M. J. and Abelson, R. P. An analysis of cognitive balancing. In M. J. Rosenberg *et al., Attitude organization and change.* New Haven: Yale University Press, 1960. Pp. 112–163.

Rosenthal, R. On the social psychology of the psychological experiment: The experimenter's hypothesis as unintended determinant of experimental results. *American Scientist*, 1963, **51**, 268–283.

Rosenthal, R. and Fode, K. L. Psychology of the scientist: V. Three experiments in experimenter bias. *Psychological Reports*, 1963, **12,** 491–511. (Monogr. Suppl. 3-V12)

Rosenthal, R., Persinger, G. W., Vikan-Kline, L., and Fode, K. L. The effect of early data returns on data subsequently obtained by outcome-biased experimenters. *Sociometry*, 1963, **26,** 487–498.

Rosenthal, R., Persinger, G. W., Vikan-Kline, L., and Mulry, R. C. The role of the research assistant in the mediation of experimenter bias. *Journal of Personality*, 1963, **31,** 313–335.

Vinacke, W. E. Deceiving experimental subjects. *American Psychologist*, 1954, **9,** 155.

block 2

7. Cronbach, L. J. The two disciplines of scientific psychology. *American Psychologist*, 1957, **12,** 671–684.

8. Feldt, L. S. The use of extreme groups to test for the presence of a relationship. *Psychometrika*, 1961, **26,** 307–316.

9. Grice, G. R. Dependence of empirical laws upon the source of experimental variation. *Psychological Bulletin*, 1966, **66,** 488–498.

10. Sidman, M. A note on functional relations obtained from group data. *Psychological Bulletin*, 1952, **49,** 263–269.

11. Estes, W. K. The problem of inference from curves based on group data. *Psychological Bulletin*, 1956, **53,** 134–140.

12. Dukes, W. F. *N = 1*. *Psychological Bulletin*, 1965, **64,** 74–80.

To a certain extent, all the readings in this block deal with both individual differences and with the assessment of experimental treatment effects. The selections are intended to broaden the student's knowledge of several different methods which are available and of some of the problems attending them. Cronbach's article has become somewhat of a classic, and it contains descriptions of what Cronbach calls the two disciplines in psychology: experimental psychology and correlational psychology. Related to these two disciplines is a design called the extreme groups design. Investigations using extreme groups, often chosen on the basis of personality characteristics, appear to have increased in frequency. Feldt's article provides some much needed and helpful guidelines in the use of such designs. Guidelines are provided which aid the investigator in (1) selecting what percentage of the available population should be used to define the extremes, and (2) deciding whether a correlational coefficient should be computed or whether extreme group differences should be compared. Feldt compares the two approaches and concludes that under certain conditions the correlational approach is more powerful while under other conditions the extreme group approach is more powerful.

An interesting and informative paper by Grice compares the within-subjects design with the between-subjects design. The general point which Grice makes is reflected by the title of his article. Essentially, he concludes that the kind of relationship one obtains between variables may be dependent upon the particular experimental design that is used. The second part of Grice's paper is devoted to the question of whether two different measures of behavior can be considered as measures of the same theoretical variable. Both within–group and between–group correlations are discussed as they relate to the general problem.

Selections 10 and 11 deal with the problem of functional relations and the accuracy of these relations when based upon individual versus group data. Sidman's paper describes several problems associated with each technique and is critical of functional relationships based upon group-averaged data. His general conclusion is that the mean curve does not reflect the form of individual curves. The paper by Estes (Selection 12) examines the problem further and comes to a somewhat different conclusion. Estes believes that curves based upon averaged data are valuable for the analysis of behavior. He concludes that the major problem has not been with averaged curves but with our interpretations of them.

Article 12, entitled $N = 1$, focuses on the behavior of one individual, and a case is made for the importance of $N = 1$ studies. A description is given of the conditions under which an N of 1 is appropriate and a case is made for the generalizability of data based on one individual.

7

the two disciplines of scientific psychology[1]

Lee J. Cronbach

No man can be acquainted with all of psychology today, as our convention program proves. The scene resembles that of a circus, but a circus grander and more bustling than any Barnum ever envisioned—a veritable week-long diet of excitement and pink lemonade. Three days of smartly paced performance are required just to display the new tricks the animal trainers have taught their charges. We admire the agile paper-readers swinging high above us in the theoretical blue, saved from disaster by only a few gossamer threads of fact, and we gasp as one symposiast thrusts his head bravely between another's sharp toothed jaws. This 18-ring display of energies and talents gives plentiful evidence that psychology is going places. But whither?

In the simpler days of psychology, the presidential address provided a summing-up and a statement of destination. The President called the roll of the branches of psychology—praising the growth of some youngsters, tut-tutting patriarchally over the delinquent

From *American Psychologist*, Vol. 12, 1957, pp. 671–684. Copyright 1957 by the American Psychological Association. Reproduced by permission.

1. Address of the President at the Sixty-Fifth Annual Convention of the American Psychological Association, New York, New York, September 2, 1957.

tendencies of others—and showed each to his proper place at the family table. My own title is reminiscent of those grand surveys, but the last speaker who could securely bring the whole of psychology within one perspective was Dashiell, with his 1938 address on "Rapprochements in Contemporary Psychology" [15]. My scope must be far more restricted.

I shall discuss the past and future place within psychology of two historic streams of method, thought, and affiliation which run through the last century of our science. One stream is *experimental psychology;* the other, *correlational psychology*. Dashiell optimistically forecast a confluence of these two streams, but that confluence is still in the making. Psychology continues to this day to be limited by the dedication of its investigators to one or the other method of inquiry rather than to scientific psychology as a whole.

A stream of thought is identified by many features: philosophical underpinnings, methods of inquiry, topical interests, and loci of application. The experimental and correlational streams have all these aspects, but I am concerned with them as disciplines within scientific psychology. The job of science is to ask questions of Nature. A discipline is a method of asking questions and of testing answers to determine whether they are sound. Scientific psychology is still young, and there is rapid turnover in our interests, our experimental apparatus and our tests, and our theoretical concepts. But our methods of inquiry have become increasingly stable, and it is these methods which qualify us as scientists rather than philosophers or artists.

The separation of the disciplines

The experimental method—where the scientist changes conditions in order to observe their consequences—is much the more coherent of our two disciplines. Everyone knows what experimental psychology is and who the experimental psychologists are. Correlational psychology, though fully as old as experimentation, was slower to mature. It qualifies equally as a discipline, however, because it asks a distinctive type of question and has technical methods of examining whether the question has been properly put and the data properly interpreted.

In contrast to the Tight Little Island of the experimental discipline, correlational psychology is a sort of Holy Roman Empire whose citizens identify mainly with their own principalities. The discipline, the common service in which the principalities are united, is the study of correlations presented by Nature. While the experimenter is interested only in the variation he himself creates, the correlator finds his interest in the already existing variation between individuals, social groups, and species. By "correlational psychology" I do not refer to studies which rely on one statistical procedure. Factor analysis is correlational, to be sure, but so is the study of Ford and Beach [23] relating sexual behavior to differences along the phylogenetic scale and across the cultural spectrum.

The well-known virtue of the experimental method is that it brings situational variables under tight control. It thus permits rigorous tests of hypotheses and confident statements about causation. The correlation method, for its part, can study what man has not learned to control or can never hope to control. Nature has been experimenting since the beginning of time, with a boldness and complexity far beyond the resources of science. The correlator's mission is to observe and organize the data from Nature's experiments. As a minimum outcome, such correlations improve immediate decisions and guide experimentation. At the best, a Newton, a Lyell, or a Darwin can align the correlations into a substantial theory.

During our century of scientific psychology, the correlators have marched under many flags. In perhaps the first modern discussion of scientific method in psychology (1874), Wundt [54] showed how "experimental psychology" and "ethnic psychology" (i.e., cross-cultural correlations) supplement each other. In one of the most recent (1953), Bindra and Scheier [4] speak of the interplay of "experimental" and "psychometric" method. At the turn of the century, the brand names were "experimental" and "genetic" psychology, although experimenters were also beginning to contrast their "general psychology" with the "individual psychology" of Stern and Binet.

In 1913, Yerkes made the fundamental point that all the correlational psychologies are one. His name for this branch was "comparative psychology."

Although comparative psychology in its completeness necessarily deals with the materials of the psychology of infant, child, adult, whether the being be human or infra-human; of animal or plant [!]—of normal and abnormal individuals; of social groups and of civilizations, there is no reason why specialists in the use of the comparative method should not be so distinguished, and, if it seems necessary, labelled [55].

Even in advocating research on animals [56], Yerkes is emphatic in defining the goal as correlation across species. In France, *la psychologie comparée* continues to include all of differential psychology; but in America, as Beach [2] has lamented, comparative psychology degenerated into the experimental psychology of the white rat and thereby lost the power of the correlational discipline.

Except for the defection of animal psychologists, the correlational psychologists have remained loosely federated. Developmental psychologists, personality psychologists, and differential psychologists have been well acquainted both personally and intellectually. They study the same courses, they draw on the same literature, they join the same divisions of APA.

Experimental and correlational psychologists, however, grew far apart in their training and interests. It is now commonplace for a student to get his PhD in experimental psychology without graduate training in test theory or developmental psychology, and the student of correlational branches can avoid experimental psychology only a little less completely. The journals of one discipline have small influence on the journals of the other [14]. Boring even dares to say [5, p. 578] that there is a personality difference between the fields: the distinction being that correlational psychologists like people!

Certainly the scientific values of psychologists are sharply divided. Thorndike [9, 44] recently asked American psychologists to rate various historic personages by indicating, on a forced-choice questionnaire, which have made the greatest contributions to psychology. A factor analysis of the ratings shows two distinct factors (Figure 1). One bipolar factor (irrelevant to our present discussion) ranges from verbal to quantitative psychologists. The other factor has at one pole the laboratory experimenters like Stevens, Dodge, and Ebbinghaus, and at the opposite pole those like Binet, May, and Goodenough who collect and correlate field data. A psychologist's esteem for the experimenters is correlated $-.80$ (-1.00, corrected for attenuation) with his esteem for scientists who use correlational methods.

There was no such schism in 1913 when Yerkes stated the program of correlational psychology. Genetic psychology and experimental psychology were hard at work on the same problems. Terman demonstrated in his 1923 presidential address [43] that the mental test was within the tradition of experimental, fundamental research in psychology, and had quotations to show that the contemporary experimentalists agreed with him. Wells and Goddard, in 1913, had been asked to lecture on mental tests within the Holy Temple itself, the Society of Experimental Psychologists. And, in 1910, the High Priest Titchener had said:

Individual psychology is one of the chief witnesses to the value of experiment. It furnishes the key to many, otherwise inexplicable differences of result, and it promises to allay many of the outstanding controversies . . . . There can be no doubt that it will play a part of steadily increasing importance [46].

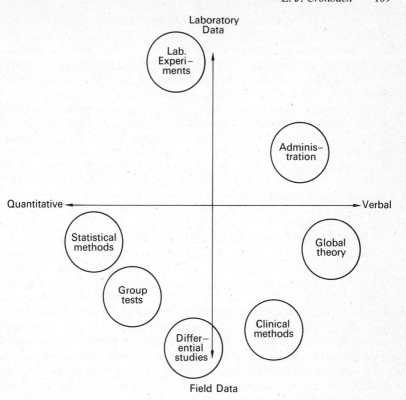

Fig. 1
Factors accounting for esteem of leaders in psychology by American psychologists (based on correlations presented by Thorndike, 44, corrected for attenuation and refactored).

But when Terman spoke in 1923, the common front had already been fatally breached. Watson had announced that experimental treatment could make and unmake individual differences at will, thus stripping them of scientific importance. Thurstone had taken the first firm stride in the opposite direction:

I suggest that we dethrone the stimulus. He is only nominally the ruler of psychology. The real ruler of the domain which psychology studies is the individual and his motives, desires, wants, ambitions, cravings, aspirations. The stimulus is merely the more or less accidental fact . . . [45, p. 364].

The personality, social, and child psychologists went one way; the perception and learning psychologists went the other; and the country between turned into desert.

During the estrangement of correlational and experimental psychology, antagonism has been notably absent. Disparagement has been pretty well confined to playful remarks like Cattell's accusation that the experimental psychologist's "regard for the body of nature becomes that of the anatomist rather than that of the lover" [7, p. 152], or the experimentalist Bartlett's [1, p. 210] satire on the testers emerging from World War I, "chanting in unaccustomed harmony the words of the old jingle

'God has a plan for every man
And He has one for you.' "

Most correlationists have done a little experimenting in the narrow sense, and experimenters have contributed proudly to testing work under war-time necessity. But these are temporary sojourns in a foreign land. (For clear expressions of this attitude, see [5, pp. 570–578 and 52, p. 24].)

A true federation of the disciplines is required. Kept independent, they can give only wrong answers or no answers at all regarding certain important problems. It is shortsighted to argue for one science to discover the general laws of mind or behavior and for a separate enterprise concerned with individual minds, or for a one-way dependence of personality theory upon learning theory. Consider the physical sciences as a parallel. Physics for centuries was the study of general laws applying to all solids or all gases, whereas alchemy and chemistry studied the properties and reactions of individual substances. Chemistry was once only a descriptive catalogue of substances and analytic techniques. It became a systematic science when organized quantitative studies yielded principles to explain differences between substances and to predict the outcomes of reactions. In consequence, Mendeleev the chemist paved the way for Bohr the physicist, and Fermi's physics contributes to Lawrence's chemistry; the boundary between chemistry and physics has become almost invisible.

The tide of separation in psychology has already turned. The perceiver has reappeared in perceptual psychology. Tested intelligence and anxiety appear as independent variables in many of the current learning experiments. Factor analytic studies have gained a fresh vitality from crossbreeding with classical learning experiments [e.g., 18, 22]. Harlow, Hebb, Hess, and others are creating a truly experimental psychology of development. And students of personality have been designing subtle combinations of experimental and correlational method [see, for example, 29] which may ultimately prove to be our parallel to the emergence of physical chemistry.

Characterization of the disciplines

In the beginning, experimental psychology was a substitute for purely naturalistic observation of man-in-habitat. The experimenter placed man in an artificial, simplified environment and made quantitative observations of his performance. The initial problem was one of describing accurately what man felt, thought, or did in a defined situation. Standardization of tasks and conditions was required to get reproducible descriptions. All experimental procedures were tests, all tests were experiments. Kraepelin's continuous-work procedure served equally the general study of fatigue and the diagnosis of individuals. Reaction time was important equally to Wundt and to Cattell.

The distinctive characteristic of modern experimentation, the statistical comparison of treatments, appeared only around 1900 in such studies as that of Thorndike and Woodworth on transfer. The experimenter, following the path of Ebbinghaus, shifted from measurement of the average mind to measuring the effect of environmental change upon success in a task [51]. Inference replaced estimation: the mean and its probable error gave way to the critical ratio. The standardized conditions and the standardized instruments remained, but the focus shifted to the single manipulated variable, and later, following Fisher, to multivariate manipulation. The experiment thus came to be concerned with between-treatments variance. I use the word "treatment" in a general sense; educational and therapeutic treatments are but one type. Treatment differences are equally involved in comparing rats given different schedules of reinforcement, chicks who have worn different distorting lenses, or social groups arranged with different communication networks.

The second great development in American experimental psychology has been its concern with formal theory. At the turn of the century, theory ranged far ahead of experiment and made no demand that propositions be testable. Experiment, for its part, was willing to observe any phenomenon, whether or not the data bore on theoretical issues. Today, the majority of experimenters derive their hypotheses explicitly from theoretical premises and try to nail their results into a theoretical structure. This deductive style has its undeniable defects, but one can not question the net gains from the accompanying theoretical sophistication. Discussions of the logic of operationism, intervening variables, and mathematical models have sharpened both the formulation of hypotheses and the interpretation of results.

Individual differences have been an annoyance rather than a challenge to the experimenter. His goal is to control behavior, and variation within treatments is proof that he has not succeeded. Individual variation is cast into that outer darkness known as "error variance." For reasons both statistical and philosophical, error variance is to be reduced by any possible device. You turn to animals of a cheap and short-lived species, so that you can use subjects with controlled heredity and controlled experience. You select human subjects from a narrow subculture. You decorticate your subject by cutting neurons or by giving him an environment so meaningless that his unique responses disappear [cf. 25]. You increase the number of cases to obtain stable averages, or you reduce N to 1, as Skinner does. But whatever your device, your goal in the experimental tradition is to get those embarrassing differential variables out of sight.

The correlational psychologist is in love with just those variables the experimenter left home to forget. He regards individual and group variations as important effects of biological and social causes. All organisms adapt to their environments, but not equally well. His question is: what present characteristics of the organism determine its mode and degree of adaptation?

Just as individual variation is a source of embarrassment to the experimenter, so treatment variation attenuates the results of the correlator. His goal is to predict variation within a treatment. His experimental designs demand uniform treatment for every case contributing to a correlation, and treatment variance means only error variance to him.

Differential psychology, like experimental, began with a purely descriptive phase. Cattell at Hopkins, Galton at South Kensington, were simply asking how much people varied. They were, we might say, estimating the standard deviation while the general psychologists were estimating the central tendency.

The correlation coefficient, invented for the study of hereditary resemblance, transformed descriptive differential research into the study of mental organization. What began as a mere summary statistic quickly became the center of a whole theory of data analysis. Murphy's words, written in 1928, recall the excitement that attended this development:

The relation between two variables has actually been found to be statable in other terms than those of experiment . . . [Moreover,] Yule's method of "partial correlation" has made possible the mathematical "isolation" of variables which cannot be isolated experimentally . . . . [Despite the limitations of correlational methods,] what they have already yielded to psychology . . . is nevertheless of such major importance as to lead the writer to the opinion that the only twentieth-century discovery comparable in importance to the conditioned-response method is the method of partial correlations [35, p. 410].

Today's students who meet partial correlation only as a momentary digression from their main work in statistics may find this excitement hard to comprehend. But partial correlation is the starting place for all of factor analysis.

Factor analysis is rapidly being perfected into a rigorous method of clarifying multivariate relationships. Fisher made the experimentalist an expert puppeteer, able to keep untangled the strands to half-a-dozen independent variables. The correlational psychologist is a mere observer of a play where Nature pulls a thousand strings; but his multivariate methods make him equally an expert, an expert in figuring out where to look for the hidden strings.

His sophistication in data analysis has not been matched by sophistication in theory. The correlational psychologist was led into temptation by his own success, losing himself first in practical prediction, then in a narcissistic program of studying his tests as an end in themselves. A naive operationism enthroned theory of test performance in the place of theory of mental processes. And premature enthusiasm[2] exalted a few measurements chosen almost by accident from the tester's stock as the ruling forces of the mental universe.

In former days, it was the experimentalist who wrote essay after anxious essay defining his discipline and differentiating it from competing ways of studying mind. No doubts plagued correlationists like Hall, Galton, and Cattell. They came in on the wave of evolutionary thought and were buoyed up by every successive crest of social progress or crisis. The demand for universal education, the development of a technical society, the appeals from the distraught twentieth-century parent, and finally the clinical movement assured the correlational psychologist of his great destiny. Contemporary experimentalists, however, voice with ever-increasing assurance their program and social function; and the fact that tonight you have a correlational psychologist discussing disciplinary identities implies that anxiety is now perched on *his* windowledge.

---

2. This judgement is not mine alone; it is the clear consensus of the factor analysts themselves [see 28, pp. 321–325].

Indeed, I do speak out of concern for correlational psychology. Aptitude tests deserve their fine reputation; but, if practical, validated procedures are to be our point of pride, we must be dissatisfied with our progress since 1920. As the Executive Committee of Division 5 itself declared this year, none of our latter-day refinements or innovations has improved practical predictions by a noticeable amount. Correlational psychologists who found their self-esteem upon contributions to theory can point to monumental investigations such as the *Studies of Character* and *The Authoritarian Personality*. Such work does throw strong light upon the human scene and brings important facts clearly into view. But theories to organize these facts are rarely offered and even more rarely solidified [30; 31, p. 55].

**Potential contributions of
the disciplines to one another**

Perhaps it is inevitable that a powerful new method will become totally absorbing and crowd other thoughts from the minds of its followers. It took a generation of concentrated effort to move from Spearman's tetrad equation and Army Alpha to our present view of the ability domain. It took the full energies of other psychologists to move from S-R bonds to modern behavior theory. No doubt the tendency of correlationists to ignore experimental developments is explained by their absorption in the wonders and complexities of the phenomena their own work was revealing. And if experimentalists were to be accused of narrow-minded concentration on one particular style and topic of research, the same comment would apply.

The spell these particular theories and methods cast upon us appears to have passed. We are free at last to look up from our own bedazzling treasure, to cast properly covetous glances upon the scientific wealth of our neighbor discipline. Trading has already been resumed, with benefit to both parties.

The introduction of construct validation into test theory [12] is a prime example. The history of this development, you may recall, was that the APA's Committee on Psychological Tests discovered that available test theory recognized no way of determining whether a proposed psychological interpretation of a test was sound. The only existing theory dealt with criterion validation and could not evaluate claims that a test measured certain psychological traits or states. Meehl, capitalizing on the methodological and philosophical progress of the experimenters, met the testers' need by suggesting the idea of construct validity. A proposed test interpretation, he showed, is a claim that a test measures a construct, i.e., a claim that the test score can be linked to a theoretical network. This network, together with the claim, generates predictions about observations. The test interpretation is justified only if the observations come out as predicted. To decide how well a purported test of anxiety measures anxiety, construct validation is necessary; i.e., we must find out whether scores on the test behave in accordance with the theory that defines anxiety. This theory predicts differences in anxiety between certain groups, and traditional correlational methods can test those predictions. But the theory also predicts variation in anxiety, hence in the test score, as a function of experience or situations, and only an experimental approach can test those predictions.

This new theory of validity has several very broad consequences. It gives the tester a start toward the philosophical sophistication the experimenter has found so illuminating. It establishes the experimental method as a proper and necessary means of validating tests. And it re-establishes research on tests as a valuable and even indispensable way of extending psychological theory.

We may expect the test literature of the future to be far less saturated with correlations of tests with psychologically enigmatic criteria, and far richer in studies which define test variables by their responsiveness to practice at different ages, to drugs, to altered instructions, and to other experimentally manipulated variables. A pioneering venture in this direction is Fleishman's revealing work [21, 22] on changes in the factorial content of motor skills as a function of practice. These studies go far beyond a mere exploration of certain tests; as Ferguson has shown [19, 20], they force upon us a theory which treats abilities as a product of learning, and a theory of learning in which previously acquired abilities play a major role.

Perhaps the most valuable trading goods the correlator can offer in return is his multivariate conception of the world.

No experimenter would deny that situations and responses are multifaceted, but rarely are his procedures designed for a systematic multivariate analysis. The typical experimental design and the typical experimental law employ a single dependent variable. Even when more than one outcome is measured, the outcomes are analyzed and interpreted separately. No response measure, however, is an adequate measure of a psychological construct. Every score mixes general construct-relevant variance with variance specific to the particular measuring operation. It is all right for the agriculturist to consider size of crop as the fundamental variable being observed: that is the payoff for him. Our task, however, is to study changes in fundamental aspects of behavior, and these are evidenced only indirectly in any one measure of outcome.

The correlational psychologist discovered long ago that no observed criterion is truly valid and that simultaneous consideration of many criteria is needed for a satisfactory evaluation of performance. This same principle applies in experimentation. As Neal Miller says in a recent paper on experiments with drugs:

Where there are relatively few facts it seems easy to account for them by a few simple generalizations . . . . As we begin to study the effects of a variety of drugs on a number of different behavioral measures, exceptions and complexities emerge. We are forced to reexamine and perhaps abandon common-sense categories of generalization according to convenient words existing in the English language. As new and more comprehensive patterns of results become available, however, new and more precise generalizations may emerge. We may be able to "carve nature better to the joint" and achieve the simplicity of a much more exact and powerful science [32, pp. 326–327].

Theoretical progress is obstructed when one restricts himself to a single measure of response [34]. Where there is only one dependent variable, it is pointless to introduce intervening variables or constructs. When there are many response variables, however, it is mandatory to subsume them under constructs, since otherwise we must have a separate set of laws for every measure of outcome. Dealing with multiple response variables is, as Miller says [33], precisely the problem with which the factor analysts have been concerned. Factor analysis, by substituting formal for intuitive methods, has been of great help in locating constructs with which to summarize observations about abilities. It is reasonable to expect that multivariate treatment of response measures would have comparable value in experimental psychology.

Experimenters very probably have even more to gain from treating *in*dependent variables as a continuous multivariate system. The manifold treatment categories in a Fisherian design are established a priori. In agriculture, the treatment dimensions the farmer can manipulate are obvious: fertilizer, water, species of seed, and so on. In a more basic science, we require genotypic constructs to describe situations, constructs like the physical scientist's temperature and pressure. The conditions the psychologist most easily manipulates— stimulus form, injunction to the subject, strength of electric shock —are not chosen because we intend to apply these specific conditions when we get around to "controlling behavior." They are used because these conditions, we hope, embody scientifically useful constructs.

The experimenter has no systematic way to classify and integrate results from different tasks or different reinforcers. As Ferguson remarks [20, p. 130; see also 19, p. 100]: "No satisfactory methodology has emerged for describing particular learning tasks, or indicating how one task differs from another, other than by a process of simple inspection." We depend wholly on the creative flair of the theorist to collate the experiments and to invent constructs which might describe particular situations, reinforcements, or injunctions in terms of more fundamental variables. The multivariate techniques of psychometrics are suited for precisely this task of grouping complex events into homogeneous classes or organizing them along major dimensions. These methods are frankly heuristic, but they are systematically heuristic. They select variables with minimal redundancy, and they permit us to obtain maximum information from a minimum of experimental investment.

In suggesting that examining treatment conditions as a statistical universe is a possible way to advance experimental thinking, I am of course echoing the recommendations of Egon Brunswik [6, esp. pp. 39–58]. Brunswik criticized the Fisherian experimenter for his *ad hoc* selection of treatments and recommended that he apply the sampling principles of differential psychology in choosing stimuli and conditions. A sampling procedure such as Brunswik suggests will often be a forward step, but the important matter is not to establish laws which apply loosely to a random, unorganized collection of situations. The important matter is to discover the organization among the situations, so that we can describe situational differences as systematically as we do individual differences.

Research on stress presents a typical problem of organization. Multivariate psychophysiological data indicate that different taxing situations have different effects. At present, stressors can be described and classified only superficially, by inspection. A correlational or distance analysis of the data groups treatments which have similar effects and ultimately permits us to locate each treatment within a continuous multidimensional structure having constructs as reference axes. Data from a recent study by Wenger, Clemens, and Engel [50] may be used as an illustration. Figure 2 shows the means of standardized physiological scores under four different stress conditions: mental arithmetic, a letter association test, hyperventilation, and a cold pressor. The "profiles" for the four conditions are very significantly different. I have made a distance analysis to examine the similarity between conditions, with the results diagrammed in Figure 3. There is a general factor among all the treatments, which distinguishes them from the resting state, and a notable group factor among three of them. According to these data, a mental test seems to induce the same physiological state as plunging one's foot into ice water!

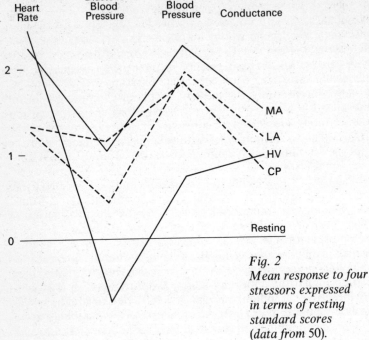

Fig. 2
Mean response to four
stressors expressed
in terms of resting
standard scores
(data from 50).

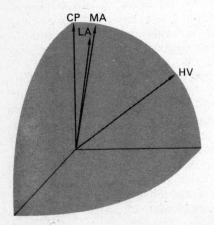

Fig. 3
Multivariate diagram
showing similarity between
four stressors.

Much larger bodies of data are of course needed to map the treatment space properly. But the aptness of an attempt in this direction will be apparent to all who heard Selye's address to the APA last year. His argument [40] that all stressful situations lead to a similar syndrome of physiological changes is strongly reminiscent of Spearman's argument regarding a general factor linking intellectual responses. The disagreement between Selye and other students of stress clearly reduces to a quantitative question of the relative size of specific and nonspecific or general factors in the effects of typical stressors.

Applied psychology divided against itself

Let us leave for the moment questions of academic psychology and consider the schism as it appears in applied psychology. In applied psychology, the two disciplines are in active conflict; and unless they bring their efforts into harmony, they can hold each other to a standstill. The conflict is especially obvious at this moment in the challenge the young engineering psychology offers to traditional personnel psychology.

The program of applied experimental psychology is to modify treatments so as to obtain the highest average performance when all persons are treated alike—a search, that is, for "the one best way." The program of applied correlational psychology is to raise average performance by treating persons differently—different job assignments, different therapies, different disciplinary methods. The correlationist is utterly antagonistic to a doctrine of "the one best way," whether it be the heartless robot-making of Frederick Taylor or a doctrinaire permissiveness which tries to give identical encouragement to every individual. The ideal of the engineering psychologist, I am told, is to simplify jobs so that every individual in the working population will be able to perform them satisfactorily, i.e., so that differentiation of treatment will be unnecessary. This goal guides activities ranging from the sober to the bizarre: from E. L. Thorndike and Skinner, hunting the one best sequence of problems for teaching arithmetic, to Rudolf Flesch and his admirers, reducing *Paradise Lost* to a comic book. If the engineering psychologist succeeds: information rates will be so reduced that the most laggard of us can keep up, visual displays will be so enlarged that the most myopic can see them, automatic feedback will prevent the most accident-prone from spoiling the work or his fingers.

Obviously, with every inch of success the engineer has, the tester must retreat a mile. A slight reduction in information rate, accomplished once, reduces forever the validity and utility of a test of ability to process data. If, once the job is modified, the myopic worker can perform as well as the man with 20/20 vision, Snellen charts and orthoraters are out of business. Nor is the threat confined to the industrial scene. If tranquilizers make everybody happy, why bother to diagnose patients to determine which treatments they should have? And if televised lessons can simplify things so that every freshman will enjoy and understand quantum mechanics, we will need neither college aptitude tests nor final examinations.

It is not my intention to warn testers about looming unemployment. If test technology is not greatly improved, long before the applied experimentalists near their goals, testing deserves to disappear. My message is my belief that the conflicting principles of the tester and the experimenter can be fused into a new and integrated applied psychology.

To understand the present conflict in purposes, we must look again at historical antecedents. Pastore [36] argues with much justice that the testers and classifiers have been political conservatives, while those who try to find the best common treatment for all—particularly in education—have been the liberals. This essential conservatism of personnel psychology traces back to the days of Darwin and Spencer.

The theory of evolution inspired two antagonistic movements in social thought [10, 42]. Darwin and Herbert Spencer were real determinists. The survival of the fittest, as a law of Nature, guaranteed man's superiority and the ultimate triumph of the natural aristocrats among men. As Dewey put it Spencer saw "a rapid transit system of evolution . . . carrying us automatically to the goal of perfect man in perfect society" [17, p. 66]. Men vary in their power of adaptation, and institutions, by demanding adaptation, serve as instruments of natural selection among men. The essence of freedom is seen as the freedom to compete for survival. To Spencer, to Galton, and to their successors down to the present day, the successful are those who have the greatest adjustive capacity. The psychologist's job, in this tradition, is to facilitate or anticipate natural selection. He seeks only to reduce its cruelty and wastage by predicting who will survive in schools and other institutions as they are. He takes the system for granted and tries to identify who will fit into it. His devices have a conservative influence because they identify persons who will succeed in the existing institution. By reducing failures, they remove a challenge which might otherwise force the institution to change [49].

The experimental scientist inherits an interpretation of evolution associated with the names of Ward, James, and Dewey. For them, man's progress rests on his intelligence; the great struggle for survival is a struggle against environment, not against competitors. Intelligent man must reshape his environment, not merely conform to it. This spirit, the very antithesis of Spencerian laissez-faire, bred today's experimental social science which accepts no institution and no tradition as sacred. The individual is seen as inherently self-directing and creative. One can not hope to predict how he will meet his problems, and applied differential psychology is therefore pointless [39, p. 37].

Thus we come to have one psychology which accepts the institution, its treatment, and its criterion and finds men to fit the institution's needs. The other psychology takes man—generalized man—as given and challenges any institution which does not conform to the measure of this standard man.

A clearer view of evolution removes the paradox:

The entire significance of the evolutionary method in biology and social history is that every distinct organ, structure, or formation, every grouping of cells or elements, has to be treated as an instrument of adjustment or adaptation to a particular environing situation. Its meaning, its character, its value, is known when, and only when, it is considered as an arrangement for meeting the conditions involved in some specific situation [16, p. 15].

We are not on the right track when we conceive of adjustment or adjustive capacity in the abstract. It is always a capacity to respond to a particular treatment. The organism which adapts well under one condition would not survive under another. If for each environment there is a best organism, for every organism there is a best environment. The job of applied psychology is to improve decisions about people. The greatest social benefit will come from applied psychology if we can find for each individual the treatment to which he can most easily adapt. This calls for the joint application of experimental and correlational methods.

Interaction of treatment and individual in practical decisions

Goldine Gleser and the writer have recently published a theoretical analysis [11] which shows that neither the traditional predictive model of the correlator nor the traditional experimental comparison of mean differences is an adequate formulation of the decisions confronting the applied psychologist. Let me attempt to give a telescoped version of the central argument.

The decision maker has to determine what treatment shall be used for each individual or each group of individuals. Psychological data help a college, for example, select students to be trained as scientists. The aim of any decision maker is to maximize expected payoff. There is a payoff function relating outcome (e.g., achievement in science) to aptitude dimensions for any particular treatment. Figure 4 shows such a function for a single aptitude. Average payoff—if everyone receives the treatment—is indicated by the arrow. The experimentalist assumes a fixed population and hunts for the treatment with the highest average and the least variability. The correlationist assumes a fixed treatment and hunts for aptitudes which maximize the slope of the payoff function. In academic selection, he advises admission of students with high scores on a relevant aptitude and thus raises payoff for the institution (Figure 5).

Pure selection, however, almost never occurs. The college aptitude test may seem to be intended for a selection decision; and, insofar as the individual college is concerned only with those it accepts, the conventional validity coefficient does indicate the best test. But from a societal point of view, the rejects will also go on into other social institutions, and their profit from this treatment must be weighed in the balance along with the profit or social contribution from the ones who enter college. Every decision is really a choice between treatments. Predicting outcome has no social value unless the psychologist or the subject himself can use the information to make better choices of treatment. The prediction must help to determine a treatment for every individual.

Even when there are just two treatments, the payoff functions have many possible relationships. In Figure 6 we have a mean difference between treatments, and a valid predictor. The predictor—though valid—is useless. We should give everyone Treatment A. In Figure 7, on the other hand, we should divide the group and give different treatments. This gives greater payoff than either treatment used uniformly will give.

Assigning everyone to the treatment with the highest average, as the experimentalist tends to recommend, is rarely the best decision. In Figure 8, Treatment C has the best average, and we might assign everyone to it. The outcome is greater, however, if we assign some persons to each treatment. The psychologist making an experimental comparison arrives at the wrong conclusion if he ignores the aptitude variable and recommends C as a standard treatment.

Applied psychologists should deal with treatments and persons simultaneously. Treatments are characterized by many dimensions; so are persons. The two sets of dimensions together determine a payoff

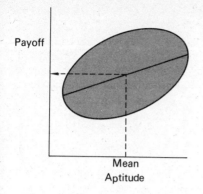

Fig. 4
Scatter diagram and payoff
function showing outcome as a
function of individual differences.

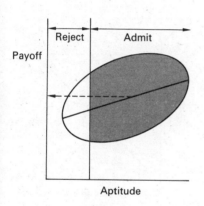

Fig. 5
Increase in payoff as a result of
selection.

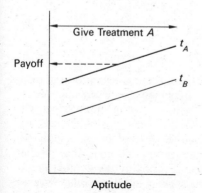

Fig. 6
Payoff functions for two
treatments.

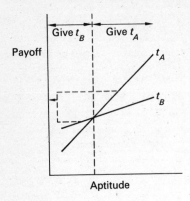

Fig. 7
Payoff functions for two treatments.

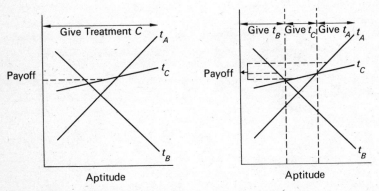

Fig. 8
Payoff functions for three treatments.

surface. For any practical problem, there is some best group of treatments to use and some best allocation of persons to treatments. We can expect some attributes of persons to have strong interactions with treatment variables. These attributes have far greater practical importance than the attributes which have little or no interaction. In dividing pupils between college preparatory and noncollege studies, for example, a general intelligence test is probably the wrong thing to use. This test, being general, predicts success in all subjects, therefore tends to have little interaction with treatment, and if so is not the best guide to differential treatment. We require a measure of aptitude which predicts who will learn better from one curriculum than from the other; but this aptitude remains to be discovered. Ultimately we should *design* treatments, not to fit the average person, but to fit groups of students with particular aptitude patterns. Conversely, we should seek out the aptitudes which correspond to (interact with) modifiable aspects of the treatment.

My argument rests on the assumption that such aptitude-treatment interactions exist. There is, scattered in the literature, a remarkable amount of evidence of significant, predictable differences in the way people learn. We have only limited success in predicting which of two *tasks* a person can perform better, when we allow enough training to compensate for differences in past attainment. But we do find that a person learns more easily from one *method* than another, that this best method differs from person to person, and that such between-treatments differences are correlated with tests of ability and personality. The studies showing interaction between personality and conditions of learning have burgeoned in the past few years, and the literature is much too voluminous to review in passing. Just one recent finding will serve in the way of specific illustration, a study done by Wolfgang Böhm at Vienna [38, pp. 58–59]. He showed his experimental groups a sound film about the adventures of a small boy and his toy elephant at the zoo. At each age level, a matched control group read a verbatim text of the sound track. The differences in average comprehension between the audiovisual and the text presentations were trivial. There was, however, a marked interaction. For some reason yet unexplained, a general mental test correlated only .30 with text learning, but it predicted film learning with an average correlation of .77.[3] The difference was consistent at all ages.

Such finding as this, when replicated and explained, will carry us into an educational psychology which measures readiness for different types of teaching and which invents teaching methods to fit different types of readiness. In general, unless one treatment is clearly best for everyone, treatments should be differentiated in such a way as to maximize their interaction with aptitude variables. Conversely, persons should be allocated on the basis of those aptitudes which have the greatest interaction with treatment variables. I believe we will find these aptitudes to be quite unlike our present aptitude measures chosen to predict differences *within* highly correlated treatments.

---

3.   Personal communication.

**The shape of a
united discipline**

It is not enough for each discipline to borrow from the other. Correlational psychology studies only variance among organisms; experimental psychology studies only variance among treatments. A united discipline will study both of these, but it will also be concerned with the otherwise neglected interactions between organismic and treatment variables [41]. Our job is to invent constructs and to form a network of laws which permits prediction. From observations we must infer a psychological description of the situation and of the present state of the organism. Our laws should permit us to predict, from this description, the behavior of organism-in-situation.

There was a time when experimental psychologists concerned themselves wholly with general, nonindividual constructs, and correlational psychologists sought laws wholly within developmental variables. More and more, nowadays, their investigations are coming to bear on the same targets. One psychologist measures ego involvement by a personality test and compares the behavior of high- and low-scoring subjects. Another psychologist heightens ego involvement experimentally in one of two equated groups and studies the consequent differences in behavior. Both investigators can test the same theoretical propositions, and to the extent that their results agree they may regard both procedures as embodiments of the same construct.

Constructs originating in differential psychology are now being tied to experimental variables. As a result, the whole theoretical picture in such an area as human abilities is changing. Piaget [37] correlates reasoning processes with age and discovers a developmental sequence of schemata whose emergence permits operational thought; Harlow [24] begins actually to create similar schemata in monkeys by means of suitable training. It now becomes possible to pursue in the controllable monkey environment the questions raised by Piaget's unique combination of behavioral testing and interviewing, and ultimately to unite the psychology of intelligence with the psychology of learning.

Methodologies for a joint discipline have already been proposed. R. B. Cattell [8] has offered the most thorough discussion of how a correlationist might organize data about treatment and organism simultaneously. His factor analytic procedures are only one of many choices, however, which modern statistics offers. The experimenters, some of them, have likewise seen the necessity for a united discipline. In the very issue of *Psychological Review* where the much-too-famous

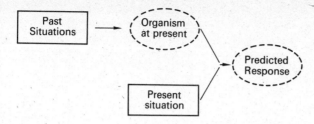

Fig. 9
Theoretical model for prediction from historic data.

distinction between *S-R* and *R-R* laws was introduced, Bergmann and Spence [3] declared that (at the present stage of psychological knowledge) the equation $R = f(S)$ must be expanded into

$$R = f(S, T, D, I)$$

The added variables are innate differences, motivation, and past experience—differential variables all. Hull [26, 27] sought general laws just as did Wundt, but he added that organismic factors can and must be accounted for. He proposed to do this by changing the constants of his equations with each individual. This is a bold plan, but one which has not yet been implemented in even a limited way. It is of interest that both Hull [27, p. 116] and Tolman [47, p. 26] have stated specifically that for their purposes factor analytic methods seem to have little promise. Tucker, though, has at least drawn blueprints of a method for deriving Hull's own individual parameters by factor analysis [48]. Clearly, we have much to learn about the most suitable way to develop a united theory, but we have no lack of exciting possibilities.

The experimenter tends to keep his eye on *ultimate* theory. Woodworth once described psychological laws in terms of the *S-O-R* formula which specifically recognizes the individual. The revised version of his *Experimental Psychology* [53, p. 3], however, advocates an *S-A-R* formula, where *A* stands for "antecedent conditions." This formulation, which is generally congenial to experimenters, reduces the present state of the organism to an intervening variable (Figure 9). A theory of this type is in principle entirely adequate to explain, predict, and control the behavior of organisms; but, oddly enough, it is a theory which can account only for the behavior of organisms of the next generation, who have not yet been conceived.

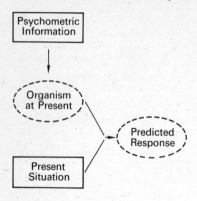

Fig. 10
Theoretical model for prediction from ahistoric data.

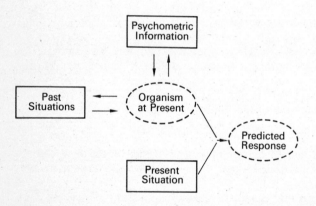

Fig. 11
Theoretical network to be developed by a united discipline.

The psychologist turns to a different type of law (Figure 10) whenever he deals with a subject whose life history he has not controlled or observed in every detail. A theory which involves only laws of this type, while suitable for prediction, has very limited explanatory value. The theory psychology really requires is a redundant network like Figure 11. This network permits us to predict from the past experience or present characteristics of the organism, or a combination of the two, depending on what is known. Filling in such a network is clearly a task for the joint efforts of experimental and correlational psychology.

In both applied work and general scientific work, psychology requires combined, not parallel, labors from our two historic disciplines. In this common labor, they will almost certainly become one, with a common theory, a common method, and common recommendations for social betterment. In the search for interactions we will invent new treatment dimensions and discover new dimensions of the organism. We will come to realize that organism and treatment are an inseparable pair and that no psychologist can dismiss one or the other as error variance.

Despite our specializations, every scientific psychologist must take the same scene into his field of vision. Clark Hull, three sentences before the end of his *Essentials of Behavior* [27, p. 116], voiced just this need. Because of delay in developing methodology, he said, individual differences have played little part in behavior theory, and "a sizeable segment of behavioral science remains practically untouched." This untouched segment contains the question we really want to put to Nature, and she will never answer until our two disciplines ask it in a single voice.

References

1. Bartlett, F. C. Fifty years of psychology. *Occup. Psychol.*, 1955, **29**, 203–216.

2. Beach, F. A. The snark was a boojum. *Amer. Psychologist*, 1950, **5**, 115–124.

3. Bergmann, G. and Spence, K. W. The logic of psychophysical measurement. *Psychol. Rev.*, 1944, **51**, 1–24.

4. Bindra, D. and Scheier, I. H. The relation between psychometric and experimental research in psychology. *Amer. Psychologist*, 1954, **9**, 69–71.

5. Boring, E. G. *History of experimental psychology*. (2nd ed.) New York: Appleton-Century-Crofts, 1950.

6. Brunswik, E. *Perception and the representative design of psychological experiments.* Berkeley: Univer. California Press, 1956.

7. Cattell, J. McK. The biological problems of today: Psychology. *Science*, 1898, **7**, 152–154.

8. Cattell, R. B. *Factor analysis.* New York: Harper, 1952.

9. Clark, K. E. *America's psychologists.* Washington, D.C.: APA, 1957.

10. Corwin, E. S. The impact of the idea of evolution on the American political and constitutional tradition. In S. Persons (Ed.), *Evolutionary thought in America*. New Haven: Yale Univer. Press, 1950. Pp. 182–201.

11. Cronbach, L. J. and Gleser, Goldine C. *Psychological tests and personnel decisions*. Urbana: Univer. Illinois Press, 1957.

12. Cronbach, L. J. and Meehl, P. E. Construct validity in psychological tests. *Psychol. Bull.*, 1955, **52,** 281–302.

13. Cronbach, L. J. and Neff, W. D. Selection and training. In Com. on Undersea Warfare Panel on Psychology and Physiology, *Human Factors in Undersea Warfare*. Washington, D.C.: Nat. Res. Coun., 1949. Pp. 491–516.

14. Daniel, R. S. and Louttit, C. M. *Professional problems in psychology*. New York: Prentice-Hall, 1953.

15. Dashiell, J. F. Some rapprochements in contemporary psychology. *Psychol. Bull.*, 1939, **36,** 1–24.

16. Dewey, J. *Studies in logical theory*. Chicago: Univer. Chicago Press, 1903.

17. Dewey, J. *The influence of Darwin on philosophy and other essays*. New York: Holt, 1910.

18. Eysenck, H. J. Reminiscence, drive, and personality theory. *J. abnorm. soc. Psychol.*, 1956, **53,** 328–333.

19. Ferguson, G. A. On learning and human ability. *Canad. J. Psychol.*, 1954, **8,** 95–112.

20. Ferguson, G. A. On transfer and human ability. *Canad. J. Psychol.*, 1956, **10,** 121–131.

21. Fleishman, E. A. Predicting advanced levels of proficiency in psychomotor skills. In *Proc. Sympos. on Human Engng*. Washington, D.C.: Nat. Acad. Sci., 1956, Pp. 142–151.

22. Fleishman, E. A. and Hempel, W. E., Jr. Changes in factor structure of a complex psychomotor test as a function of practice. *Psychometrika*, 1954, **19,** 239–252.

23. Ford, C. S. and Beach, F. A. *Patterns of sexual behavior*. New York: Harper, 1952.

24. Harlow, H. F. The formation of learning sets. *Psychol. Rev.*, 1949, **56,** 51–65.

25. Harlow, H. F. Mice, men, monkeys, and motives. *Psychol. Rev.*, 1953, **60,** 23–32.

26. Hull, C. L. The place of innate individual and species differences in a natural-science theory of behavior. *Psychol. Rev.*, 1945, **52,** 55–60.

27. Hull, C. L. *Essentials of behavior*. New Haven: Yale Univ. Press, 1951.

28. Laugier, H. (Ed.) L'analyse factorielle et ses applications. Paris: Centre National de la Recherche Scientifique, 1955.

29. Lazarus, R. S. and Baker, R. W. Personality and psychological stress—a theoretical and methodological framework. *Psychol. Newsletter*, 1956, **8**, 21–32.

30. McCandless, B. R. and Spiker, C. C. Experimental research in child psychology. *Child Develpm.*, 1956, **27**, 75–80.

31. McClelland, D. C. Personality. In P. R. Farnsworth (Ed.) *Annu. Rev. Psychol.*, 1956. Stanford: Annual Reviews, 1956. Pp. 39–62.

32. Miller, N. E. Effects of drugs on motivation: The value of using a variety of measures. *Ann. N.Y. Acad. Sci.*, 1956, **65**, 318–333.

33. Miller, N. E. Liberalization of basic S-R concepts: Extensions to conflict behavior and social learning. In S. Koch (Ed.), *Psychology: A study of a science*. Vol. II. *General systematic formulations, learning, and special processes*. New York: McGraw-Hill, in press.

34. Miller, N. E. Objective techniques for studying motivational effects of drugs on animals. In E. Trabucchi (Ed.), *Proc. Int. Sympos. on Psychotropic Drugs*. Amsterdam, Netherlands: Elsevier Publishing Co., in press.

35. Murphy, G. *An historical introduction to modern psychology.* (3rd ed.) New York: Harcourt, Brace, 1932.

36. Pastore, N. *The nature-nurture controversy.* New York: Kings Crown Press, 1949.

37. Piaget, J. *Psychology of intelligence.* M. Piercy and D. E. Berlyne (Trans.). London: Routledge and Kegan Paul, 1950.

38. Rohracher, H. Aus der wissenschaftlichen Arbeit des Psychologischen Institutes der Universität Wien. *Wiener Z. Phil., Psychol., Pädag.*, 1956, **6**, 1–66.

39. Scoon, R. The rise and impact of evolutionary ideas. In S. Persons (Ed.), *Evolutionary thought in America*. New Haven, Yale Univer. Press, 1950. Pp. 4–43.

40. Selye, H. Stress and disease. *Science*, 1955, **122**, 625–631.

41. Shen, E. The place of individual differences in experimentation. In Q. McNemar and M. A. Merrill (Eds.), *Studies in personality*. New York: McGraw-Hill, 1942. Pp. 259–283.

42. Spengler, J. J. Evolutionism in American economics. In S. Persons (Ed.), *Evolutionary thought in America*. New Haven: Yale Univer. Press, 1950. Pp. 202–266.

43. Terman, L. M. The mental test as a psychological method. *Psychol. Rev.*, 1924, **31**, 93–117.

44. Thorndike, R. L. The psychological value systems of psychologists. *Amer. Psychologist*, 1954, **9**, 787–790.

45. Thurstone, L. L. The stimulus-response fallacy in psychology. *Psychol. Rev.*, 1923, **30**, 354–369.

46. Titchener, E. B. The past decade in experimental psychology. *Amer. J. Psychol.*, 1910, **21**, 404–421.

47. Tolman, E. C. The determinants of behavior at a choice point. *Psychol. Rev.*, 1938, **45**, 1–41.

48. Tucker, L. R. Determination of parameters of a functional relation by factor analysis. *ETS Res. Bull.*, 1955, **55**, No. 10.

49. Tyler, R. W. Can intelligence tests be used to predict educability? In K. Eells *et al.*, *Intelligence and cultural differences.* Chicago: Univer. Chicago Press, 1951. Pp. 39–47.

50. Wenger, M. A., Clemens, T. L., and Engel, B. T. Autonomic response patterns to four stimuli. Unpublished manuscript, 1957.

51. Woodworth, R. S. *Dynamic psychology.* New York: Holt, 1918.

52. Woodworth, R. S. *Experimental psychology.* New York: Holt, 1938.

53. Woodworth, R. S. and Schlosberg, H. *Experimental psychology.* (2nd ed.) New York: Holt, 1954.

54. Wundt, W. *Principles of physiological psychology.* Vol. 1. (5th ed.) E. B. Titchener (Trans.) New York: Macmillan, 1904.

55. Yerkes, R. M. Comparative psychology: A question of definitions. *J. Phil. Psychol., and sci. Methods*, 1913, **10**, 580–582.

56. Yerkes, R. M. The study of human behavior. *Science*, 1914, **29**, 625–633.

8

the use of extreme groups to test for the presence of a relationship

Leonard S. Feldt

In the exploratory stages of the investigation of a psychological construct, a two-stage experimental design is frequently employed. In the first stage, a random sample of subjects from a hypothetical or real population is evaluated via a crude measure of the construct, and from the distribution of scores which results, an arbitrary definition is derived for "High" and "Low" subgroups. In the second stage, the high and low groups are exposed to one or several treatment conditions. It is hypothesized that if the initial classification was even moderately valid, the treatment should produce a different distribution of treatment criterion scores for the high and low subpopulations. Usually such a difference is assessed through a comparison of the means of the groups.

Examples of this design are quite common in the psychological literature. It was frequently used, for example, in the early studies of McClelland's Achievement Need [7]. It was also extensively employed in the preliminary validation of Taylor's Manifest Anxiety Scale [11]. In the latter studies the second stage often involved fairly complex

From *Psychometrika*, Vol. 26 (No. 3), pp. 307–316, September, 1961. Reprinted by permission of the author and Psychometric Corporation.

and time consuming treatment conditions, such as eyelid conditioning. Thus, as is often the case, the use of extreme groups was prompted in part by the necessity to limit the total number of subjects.

An important consideration in such a design is the choice of upper and lower percentiles which define the extreme groups. Current experimental practice evidences considerable variation in this aspect of the design. Some investigators have employed extreme tenths or fifths, others have utilized upper and lower halves. In all cases the decision appears to have been quite arbitrary, or dictated by necessity. The primary purpose of this paper is to derive a definition of optimal extreme groups for investigations of this kind. A second purpose is to compare the efficiency of this design to the correlation approach which provides an obvious alternative procedure.

Definitions and assumptions

In the following development, the initial classification variable, the validity of which is under test, will be designated as X. The criterion measure taken in the second stage of the experiment—strength of eyelid conditioning in the Taylor Scale example—will be designated Y. Measures X and Y will be assumed to give rise to a normal bivariate surface with correlation ρ_{xy} in the population of potential experimental subjects. The experiment itself consists of obtaining measure X on a random sample from the subject population, defining equal extreme subgroups on X, imposing treatments conditions and obtaining the Y criterion score on each subject, and finally testing the significance of the difference between Y means for the two groups via a t test.

In the definition of optimal extreme groups, the criterion employed will be the power of the final t test. For a given level of significance the power of this test is dependent upon three quantities: (i) the variability of the Y measures within each extreme group, (ii) the magnitude of the true difference between the Y means; and (iii) the size of the extreme groups. Each of these factors is functionally related to the percentiles chosen to define the groups. It is the nature of linear regression that the more extreme the subpopulations, the larger the difference between the Y means. A large difference is clearly advantageous, for it will result in a more powerful test than will a small difference. But it is also true that the more select the subpopulations, the smaller the number of subjects available. This, in turn, tends to increase the standard error of the difference. Thus, if only the upper and lower ten percent of subjects is employed, both the difference and the standard error of the difference will be larger than if upper and lower halves are used. The value of the variance of Y scores within the subpopulations will also vary with the "extremeness" of the subpopulations. The problem thus becomes one of deriving symmetrical upper and lower percentiles which will result in a combination of true difference, group size, and within-group variance that will yield the most powerful test.

Optimal definition of extreme groups

For the t test of the difference between means of extreme samples let N represent the total number of subjects initially classified, p the proportion of subjects in each extreme group, $n = pN$ the number of subjects in each group, S^2 the sample variance, and the subscripts U and L the upper and lower groups respectively. It should be noted that in this situation N is fixed; the problem involves the determination of the optimal value of p. The t test for equal groups may be written as follows:

$$t = \frac{|\bar{Y}_U - \bar{Y}_L|}{\sqrt{(S_U^2 + S_L^2)/(n - 1)}}.$$

The power of this test is governed by the parameter ϕ, defined as follows [10]:

$$\phi = \mu_w/\sqrt{2}\,\sigma_w. \tag{1}$$

In this formula μ_w is the expected value or mean of a normally distributed variable, say w, and σ_w is its population standard deviation. In the present context $(\bar{Y}_U - \bar{Y}_L)$ is the normally distributed variable, $(\mu_U - \mu_L)$ is its expected value, and $\sigma_{\bar{Y}_U - \bar{Y}_L}$ is its population standard deviation. Thus

$$\phi = \frac{|\mu_U - \mu_L|}{\sqrt{2}\,\sigma_{\bar{Y}_U - \bar{Y}_L}} = \frac{|\mu_U - \mu_L|}{\sqrt{2(\sigma_{Y_U}^2 + \sigma_{Y_L}^2)/pN}}. \tag{2}$$

The value of σ_{Y_U} or σ_{Y_L} is given in [2] as $\sigma_Y^2(1 - c\rho^2)$. In this relationship, σ_Y^2 is the variance of the total population on the treatment criterion, ρ is the population value of the linear correlation between the classification variable and the treatment criterion, and c is a constant dictated by the degree of "extremeness" of the upper and lower groups. The defining relationship for c is

$$c = 1 - \frac{\sigma_{x\,\text{extreme}}^2}{\sigma_{x\,\text{total}}^2}. \tag{3}$$

The second term on the right-hand side is the ratio of the variance within either subpopulation (they are equally variable) to the variance for the total population on the classification variable.

For the normal surface here assumed, the value of the ratio may be computed, by integration by parts, for any selected segment of the distribution [4]. Substitution of this result in (3) yields

$$c = \frac{z^2}{p^2} - \frac{xz}{p},$$ (4)

where x is the positive or negative standard normal deviate defining the extreme groups, and z is the ordinate of the standard normal curve at x. It may also be noted that μ_{Y_U} and μ_{Y_L} are defined by the regression line of Y on X as follows:

$$\mu_{Y_U} = \mu_Y + \rho \frac{\sigma_Y}{\sigma_X} (\mu_{X_U} - \mu_X);$$

$$\mu_{Y_L} = \mu_Y + \rho \frac{\sigma_Y}{\sigma_X} (\mu_{X_L} - \mu_X).$$

The difference thus equals

$$\mu_{Y_U} - \mu_{Y_L} = \rho \frac{\sigma_Y}{\sigma_X} (\mu_{X_U} - \mu_{X_L}).$$ (5)

By appropriate integration, the values of μ_{X_U} and μ_{X_L} may be derived for any segment of a normal curve [4]. In the notation previously introduced, the means for equal extreme segments are $\mu_X \pm (z/p)\sigma_X$. Upon substitution of these expressions into the previous equation, the difference becomes

$$\mu_{Y_U} - \mu_{Y_L} = \frac{2\rho\sigma_Y z}{p}.$$ (6)

Substitution of results (4) and (6) into (2) and the division of numerator and denominator by $2\sigma_Y$ yields the following expression for ϕ:

$$\phi = \frac{\rho \dfrac{z}{p}}{\sqrt{\dfrac{1 - \rho^2(z^2/p^2 - xz/p)}{pN}}}.$$ (7)

To secure maximum power in the test of the difference between $\bar{Y}_U$ and $\bar{Y}_L$, ϕ must be maximized. This is accomplished by appropriate choice of x, and of z and p, which are both functionally related to x. Since the quantity N is fixed in the context of this problem, its value

Table 1
Extreme groups which result in mean difference tests of maximum power

ρ	Percent in Each Extreme Group
.10	27.0
.20	26.9
.30	26.6
.40	26.3
.50	25.8
.60	25.1
.70	24.2
.80	23.3

may be ignored. The condition for a maximum is obtained by setting the first derivative of ϕ with respect to x equal to zero. The process of taking this derivative and of solving the resultant equation involves some rather tedious algebra, and hence it will not be presented here. The end result, however, may be stated quite simply. The maximum value of ϕ occurs when

$$\rho^2\left(1 + x^2 - \frac{z^2}{p^2}\right) + \frac{2px}{z} = 1.00. \tag{8}$$

The nature of this relationship makes it difficult to solve analytically for x and p, given a specific value of ρ. However, the comprehensive normal curve tables of Kelley [5] permit a sufficiently exact approximation for p for select values of ρ. A number of such pairs of values are tabulated in Table 1.

These values indicate that the definition of the optimal extreme groups remains remarkably constant over a rather wide range of values for ρ. For $\rho = .10$, the function reaches a maximum at $p = .27$; for $\rho = .80$, the maximum occurs at $p = .23$. This finding has important implications for researchers employing the difference approach for testing relationships. It suggests that extreme groups of from 25 to 27 percent provide the most powerful test of the existence of a moderate linear relationship. This size group is especially appropriate when the relationship is weak, as it usually is in the experimental context here considered.

From a practical point of view, it is extremely fortunate that this maximum power is reached when groups smaller than the upper and lower halves are employed. Frequently the nature of the experimental treatment or the need to share the pool of experimental subjects forces the investigator to use only a fraction of those originally tested. These results prove that such a restriction can result in greater, rather than less, power in the crucial statistical tests.

Comparison of difference and correlation approaches

If a limited subgroup of subjects may be used to investigate the presence of a linear relationship between X and Y, should the experimenter draw all of his subjects from the extreme portions of the X distribution and test the difference between Y means, or should he draw subjects at random from the entire range on X, estimate the linear correlation, and test it for significance? The answer to this question is clearly pertinent to the development of an adequate research strategy. As in the previous discussion, design efficiency will be evaluated by the power of the statistical tests that are involved.

The test of significance of a product-moment correlation or, more precisely, the test of the linear regression coefficient is

$$t = \frac{r\sqrt{N_0 - 2}}{\sqrt{1 - r^2}}. \tag{9}$$

The power parameter for this test may be obtained by substitution of the appropriate values into formula (1). In this case, the regression coefficient is the normally distributed variable; the population standard deviation is the standard error of the regression coefficient,

$$\sigma_Y \sqrt{1 - \rho^2}/\sqrt{N_0}\,\sigma_X.$$

After algebraic simplification, ϕ is found to equal

$$\phi_r = \frac{\beta}{\sqrt{2}\,\sigma_b} = \frac{\rho\sigma_Y/\sigma_X}{\sqrt{2}\,\sigma_Y\sqrt{1 - \rho^2}/(\sqrt{N_0}\,\sigma_X)} \tag{10}$$

$$= \frac{\rho\sqrt{N_0}}{\sqrt{2}\sqrt{1 - \rho^2}}.$$

With $2pN$ subjects this reduces to

$$\phi_r = \frac{\rho\sqrt{pN}}{\sqrt{1 - \rho^2}}. \tag{11}$$

For the difference test based on pN subjects per group, the value of ϕ reduces to

$$\phi_d = \frac{z\rho}{\sqrt{p(1 - c\rho^2)/N}}. \tag{12}$$

The comparative power of the difference test and the correlation test may be most easily inferred from the ratio of ϕ_d to ϕ_r. Where the ratio exceeds 1.0, the difference test is more powerful; where the ratio is less than 1.0, the correlation test is more powerful.

In general terms, the ratio equals

$$\frac{\phi_d}{\phi_r} = \frac{z/\sqrt{p(1 - c\rho^2)}}{\sqrt{p}/\sqrt{1 - \rho^2}}. \tag{13}$$

It may be noted that the value of the ratio depends upon both p and ρ. The magnitude of ρ is, of course, unknown. The value of p, on the other hand, is partially within the control of the experimenter and partially dictated by the nature of the experiment. In some situations the experimenter might be limited by practical considerations to the use of no more than a small proportion of the subjects in the pool. In other instances, it might be quite feasible to obtain X and Y measures on all N subjects.

To reveal the conditions under which each approach is the more powerful, the ratio was evaluated for various conditions of subject availability. These conditions, which indicate the proportion of subjects available for the second stage of the experiment, range from 20 to 100 percent. (Since the difference technique achieves close to maximum power when upper and lower quarters are used, the value of ϕ_d was based on $p = .25$ for all availability percentages above 50.) For each experimental condition the value of ρ was determined which would make the ratio greater than 1.0. These results are reported in Table 2.

The data in this table reveal that as the availability percentage increases, the choice of design strategy gradually shifts in favor of the correlation approach. However, the advantage of the extreme group design holds until the availability percentage is quite large or the population correlation is quite high. The two-stage design here considered would generally be applied in instances where only a moderate degree of relationship holds. Values of .50 or higher are probably relatively rare in this preliminary stage of construct definition. In view of this fact, a fairly clear-cut recommendation may be made. If less than 75 percent of the subject pool can be used in the experiment, the difference approach will almost surely be the more powerful.

Table 2
Comparative power of difference and correlation
approaches for testing the presence of relationship

Percent of Subjects Available for Treatments	More Powerful Approach
20	Difference when $\rho < .962$ Correlation when $\rho > .962$
30	Difference when $\rho < .938$ Correlation when $\rho > .938$
40	Difference when $\rho < .902$ Correlation when $\rho > .902$
50	Difference when $\rho < .847$ Correlation when $\rho > .847$
60	Difference when $\rho < .768$ Correlation when $\rho > .768$
70	Difference when $\rho < .624$ Correlation when $\rho > .624$
75	Difference when $\rho < .492$ Correlation when $\rho > .492$
80	Difference when $\rho < .198$ Correlation when $\rho > .198$
More Than 80	Correlation for all values of ρ

If more than 80 percent of the subjects can be employed in the second portion of the experiment, the correlation approach will almost certainly be the more powerful.

The above comparison does not take into account the added degrees of freedom of the test of r when the availability percentage is greater than 50. Therefore, the values of ρ noted in Table 2 must be regarded as approximate. However, the power function charts of Pearson and Hartley indicate that for a given value of ϕ the power of a t test is only slightly affected by increases in the degrees of freedom beyond 60. Thus, the recommendation above seems sufficiently precise for all practical purposes.

The difference in power of the two approaches may be illustrated by an example. Assume $\rho = .30$ and that a total of 100 subjects was initially tested on the classification variable. If the experimenter used upper and lower quarters, he would have a t test with 48 degrees of freedom. With a 5 percent level of significance, the power of this test would be approximately .78. If, on the other hand, 50 subjects were selected from the entire range of the classification variable and the product-moment coefficient were tested for significance at the same level, the power would equal .57. If 75 subjects were selected from the full range on X, the power of the correlation test would equal .75. If all 100 subjects could be used, the power would equal .87.

At first glance, it may appear paradoxical that throwing away data from the middle half of the distribution improves the difference approach and renders it superior to correlation analysis based on a greater number of subjects. However, these results are consistent with the findings of other investigators [1, 3]. Those familiar with common item analysis procedures will no doubt recognize the analogous results which hold in that field. Indeed, Kelley's proof [6] that item discrimination is most efficiently assessed through the use of the upper and lower twenty-seven percents follows a very similar line. The discard of the middle portion of the distribution does not merely reduce the *quantity* of the information—a practice which rarely, if ever, works to benefit of a statistical procedure—but also changes the *nature* of data. When the full import of the modifications of both quantity and quality are appreciated, the result no longer seems quite so anomalous.

It should be emphasized that these results apply only to data which conform to the bivariate normal distribution. Of particular importance is the assumption of linear correlation. Where the hypothesis of a curvilinear relationship can be seriously entertained, it would clearly be unwise to sample in a fashion which did not permit close study of the nature of the relationship. Thus preference should be given to the difference approach only when the assumption of linearity is strongly tenable.

Estimating the correlation from extreme group statistics

The foregoing development has been concerned only with the evaluation of the presence of a linear relationship, not with estimation of the strength of that relationship. As McNemar [8] has succinctly pointed out, such a methodology is almost certain to be abused, for it can easily lead the experimenter to exaggerate the importance of trivial results. If the distributions of X and Y are normal, or approximately so, and if the relationship is linear, a useful approximation of the product-moment coefficient may be obtained from statistics derived from the extreme groups.

From (6) the difference between means is seen to equal

$$\mu_{Y_U} - \mu_{Y_L} = 2\rho z \sigma_Y/p,$$

and the variance within either extreme group, as derived in [2], equals

$$\sigma_{Y_U}^2 = \sigma_Y^2 \left(1 - \rho^2 \left[\frac{z^2}{p^2} - \frac{xz}{p} \right] \right).$$

Thus

$$\sigma_Y = \frac{\sigma_{Y_U}}{\sqrt{1 - \rho^2[z^2/p^2 - xz/p]}},$$

and

$$\mu_{Y_U} - \mu_{Y_L} = \frac{2\rho z \sigma_{Y_U}}{p\sqrt{1 - \rho^2[z^2/p^2 - xz/p]}}.$$

Solving this equation for ρ yields

$$\rho = \frac{\mu_{Y_U} - \mu_{Y_L}}{\sqrt{4z^2\sigma_{Y_U}^2/p^2 + (z^2/p^2 - xz/p)(\mu_{Y_U} - \mu_{Y_L})^2}}. \tag{14}$$

If the upper and lower quarters are used to test for the presence of a relationship, (14) becomes

$$\rho = \frac{\mu_{Y_U} - \mu_{Y_L}}{\sqrt{6.4630\sigma_{Y_U}^2 + (.7584)(\mu_{Y_U} - \mu_{Y_L})^2}}.$$

Using sample means to estimate population means and the mean square within groups to estimate the variance within extreme populations, the estimate of ρ becomes

$$\tilde{\rho} = \frac{\bar{Y}_U - \bar{Y}_L}{\sqrt{6.4630 \, \text{MS}_{\text{within}} + .7584(\bar{Y}_U - \bar{Y}_L)^2}}. \tag{15}$$

This estimate represents a solution to a special case of the problem of estimating ρ from data obtained on extreme groups. A solution for the more general problem, in which no restriction is imposed on the comparative size of the extreme groups, has been presented by Peters and Van Voorhis [9]. Such estimates should be used, of course, only when the assumptions of normality and linearity are tenable.

References

1. Bartlett, M. S. Fitting a straight line when both variables are subject to error. *Biometrics*, 1949, **5**, 207–212.

2. Feldt, L. S. A comparison of the precision of three experimental designs employing a concomitant variable. *Psychometrika*, 1958, **23**, 335–353.

3. Gibson, W. M. and Jowett, G. H. "Three-group" regression analysis. I. Simple regression analysis. *Appl. Statist.*, 1957, **6**, 114–122.

4. Kelley, T. L. *Fundamentals of statistics*. Cambridge, Mass.: Harvard Univ. Press, 1947.

5. Kelley, T. L. *The Kelley statistical tables*. Cambridge, Mass.: Harvard Univ. Press, 1948.

6. Kelley, T. L. The selection of upper and lower groups for the validation of test items. *J. educ. Psychol.*, 1939, **30**, 17–24.

7. McClelland, D. C. *et al. The achievement motive*. New York: Appleton-Century-Crofts, 1953.

8. McNemar, Q. At random: Sense and nonsense. *Amer. Psychologist*, 1960, **15**, 295–300.

9. Peters, C. C. and Van Voorhis, W. R. *Statistical procedures and their mathematical bases*. New York: McGraw-Hill, 1940.

10. Pearson, E. S. and Hartley, H. O. *Biometrika tables for statisticians, Vol. I*. Cambridge, England: University Press, 1956.

11. Taylor, J. A. Drive theory and manifest anxiety. *Psychol. Bull.*, 1956, **53**, 303–320.

9

dependence of empirical laws upon the source of experimental variation[1]

G. Robert Grice

—

It is the intent of this paper to discuss two matters of experimental design which have arisen in the course of the author's research. While in some ways unrelated, both are illustrations of a common principle: the nature of an observed relationship between variables is dependent upon the nature of the particular experimental design used to observe the relationship. More specifically, the relation depends upon the particular source of experimental variation which the design explores. This point is not profound, but is merely part of the general principle that the laws relating a set of variables require a rather complete specification of the context in which they apply. The point is not trivial, however, because there appears to be sometimes a rather uncritical assumption that quite different research designs are equivalent if they include the same experimental variables. Choice of the source of experimental variations is not a matter for arbitrary decision, but should be based upon the nature of the scientific problem.

From *Psychological Bulletin*, Vol. 66, (No. 6), 1966, pp. 488–498. Copyright 1966 by the American Psychological Association. Reproduced by permission.

1. Preparation of this paper was supported by Grant MH 08033 from the National Institute of Mental Health.

Between-subjects and
within-subjects designs

It is quite common to hear an experimenter say, with obvious pride, that in this experiment, each subject served as his own control. The reasons for the pride are obvious. After all, what more comparable control group can there be than the same group? Furthermore, the method is efficient and economical, and one has done something elegant. However, such an experiment may or may not be a *proper* source of pride, and one very simple point should be raised: a subject who has served as his own control may not be the same subject that he would have been if he had not. If the experience in the control condition in any way influences performance in the experimental condition, then a different result may be obtained than if a separate control group had been employed. Such an experiment may be good or bad, but if the experimenter thinks that he has merely done, more efficiently, the same investigation as the independent group experiment, he is mistaken. This problem has not gone unnoticed. Solomon (1949) and Campbell and Stanley (1963) have proposed designs concerned with evaluating the effects of pretesting in experiments dealing with such problems as transfer of training, attitude change, and teaching methods. The excellent discussion of Campbell and Stanley, in particular, should be read by investigators contemplating this type of design. The design in which the control group consists of the same subjects as the experimental group is a simple instance of the more general class of "within-subject" designs which have become widely prevalent in psychological research. These designs, of course, involve the administration of a number of experimental treatments or a number of values of some experimental variable to the same subject. When certain treatments are administered to separate groups of subjects while others are administered to the same subjects, these are called "mixed" designs because they contain both within-subjects and between-subjects effects. Most modern statistical textbooks dealing with psychological research have full treatments of such designs. There are two common reasons for obtaining a number of measures from the same subject. In the first place, certain variables are inherently within-subjects effects. For example, in studying learning as a function of practice, it would be absurd to run a separate group of subjects for each number of trials if a continuous performance measure were available. In such experiments, we are specifically interested in the effect which earlier treatments have on later performance. However, the other, and perhaps more common, reason for such procedures is purely statistical and has nothing to do with the scientific logic or purpose of the investigation. The elimination of individual difference variance from differences between treatment means and from the associated error terms may result in a more efficient and less costly experiment. It is quite natural that such designs should have great appeal to experimenters.

In spite of the obvious advantages of within-subjects experiments, their use frequently may lead to incorrect interpretation of their results.[2] The danger is that the experimenter may believe that the design is simply more efficient, but otherwise equivalent to an experiment in which the same treatments were administered to separate groups of subjects. The fact is that the reasoning applied above to the simple control-group experiment applies equally to all within-subjects designs. In spite of the fact that the experimental conditions or values of the experimental variables may be the same, the two kinds of experiments are not the same, and actually investigate different problems. While it is true that textbook authors may state that one must assume that the administration of one treatment has no effect upon the others, this assumption is often made rather easily and based upon no evidence. Frequently, the matter is merely ignored, and the assumption of the equivalence of the designs is implicit rather than explicit.

Recognition that these two types of designs are not equivalent, and are likely to yield different relationships among experimental variables, suggests the possibility of an additional and potentially important kind of experiment. This is one in which the two procedures are directly compared. Such an experiment would, of course, answer the question of the equivalence of the two methods for any particular set of experimental variables. However, it should not be concluded that the experiment would be a mere methodological exercise. If the two procedures result in the discovery of different laws relating experimental variables, this may be a fact of considerable scientific interest. It may lead to an improved understanding of the phenomena and suggest further hypotheses concerning their nature. In spite of the reasonability and potential importance of such experiments, they are strangely rare in the psychological literature—almost to the point of nonexistence. The basic form of the experiment is suggested in Table 1. The columns indicate a number of experimental treatments, which could be simply different procedures or ordered values of some independent variable. In the latter instance, the investigator would study the form of some quantitative function. The upper row would comprise a between-

---

2. Objections which have been raised on purely statistical grounds to common uses of such designs are not considered here (see, e.g., Lana and Lubin, 1963).

Table 1

Design for comparison of between-subjects and
within-subjects experiments

Condition of Administration	Treatment					
	T_1	.	.	T_j	. .	.	T_k
Between	n_{b1}	.	.	n_{bj}	. .	.	n_{bk}
Within	n_{w1}	.	.	n_{wj}	.	.	n_{wk}

subjects experiment, and would contain k independent groups of
subjects, each receiving just one of the treatments. The lower row
would be made up of subjects who received all of the k treatments.
As in any two-dimensional design, the between-cells variance of the
table could be analyzed into three components; however, only two of
these would be of interest in the present instance. The row effect would
indicate whether one of the two conditions resulted in overall superior
performance. Generally, however, the chief interest would be in the
interaction. If significant, it would indicate that the differences
among the treatments depended upon the type of experiment. In the
case of an ordered independent variable, it would indicate that the
functions were of different form. In addition to simple significance
testing, it might be desirable to apply curve-fitting or trend-analysis
procedures. The column effect would ordinarily not be of interest in
this design.

The analysis of such an experimental design does pose certain
problems. If the lower Within row is filled with the same subjects in
all cells, ordinary analysis-of-variance procedures do not apply since
the cells in this row are correlated and those based on independent
groups in the Between condition are not. One solution to this problem,
which we have used, is to run k groups of Within subjects. The data
from only one treatment from each of these groups is then used. The
Within row is then filled with data from independent groups, but is
still, in effect, a "within" condition because all of the subjects have
experienced all of the treatments. Statistically, however, the experiment
may be analyzed in a straightforward manner as an independent
groups design. This procedure does appear to be wasteful of data,
because only $1/k$ of the data for each Within subject is used in the table.
This is true, however, only for the significance testing, and all data
may be used for plotting stable within-subjects functions. In the case
of a quantified independent variable, there is one possibility which

might be employed, using all of the data. A function might be fitted to the data for one condition and then tested for goodness of fit to the other as if it were a rational equation. This procedure is less adequate statistically, but if the data points were stable, it could produce a rather convincing comparison. This is similar to procedures used by Grice and Reynolds (1952) and Newman and Grice (1965) in other contexts, and by Kalish and Haber (1963) in the present context.

The author's own interest in this problem first occurred in connection with the effect of variations in stimulus intensity upon response evocation. The interest arose originally, not from methodological considerations, but from experimental data obtained at the University of Illinois laboratory. In a study of CS intensity in eyelid conditioning, Beck (1963) studied the intensity variable as a within-subjects effect. Surprisingly, she obtained an effect which was much larger than had ever before been obtained. Since all of the previous data came from between-subjects experiments, it was concluded that the effect must have been produced by the fact that each subject experienced the different stimulus intensities. As a result of this reasoning, an experiment similar to that described above was conducted by Grice and Hunter (1964). Two intensities of an auditory CS were used—a 1000-cycle tone at 50 or 100 decibels sound-pressure level. Two groups in the Between condition received only one CS each, either the loud or the soft tone. The Within subjects received both. In an experiment of this kind, the question of order of presentation will always arise for the Within condition. In this instance, the subjects were merely presented with the two stimuli in an irregular order throughout the 100 conditioning trials. In some experiments, each treatment would have to be administered all at once, and the order could be randomized or counterbalanced unless some considerations dictated otherwise. Presumably, the solution would ordinarily be the same as if only the Within experiment were conducted. The result of the Grice and Hunter experiment was quite dramatic. The difference due to the intensity effect obtained under the two procedures was five times as great for the Within condition as it was for the Between condition. When analyzed by the independent groups method suggested above, the interaction term was statistically significant.

A second experiment by Grice and Hunter (1964) dealt with signal intensity in simple reaction time. Reaction time has frequently been found to be related to stimulus intensity and has been discussed in relation to theoretical interpretations of intensity effects. The experiment was conducted in essentially the same manner as the previous one. Again, although less dramatically, the intensity effect was greater for the Within condition. The interaction effect was significant. This time, however, there was a general slowing of response in the two-stimulus situation so that the Condition of Administration effect was also significant. It appears probable that the uncertainty as to which stimulus would occur produced slower reactions, but a greater difference between the loud and soft tones appeared, nevertheless.

Recently, Behar and Adams (1966) obtained a similar result with foreperiod signal intensity in reaction time. Using three intensities of the ready signal, they found reaction time to be a significantly decreasing function of intensity for a within-subjects condition, but not for a between-subjects condition. However, their design did not provide for a test of the significance of the interaction.

These findings concerning stimulus intensity effects have made necessary some readjustments in our theorizing concerning the operation of this variable. For example, Hull's (1949) theory of the stimulus intensity dynamism, which simply assumed that dynamogenic effects were a function of the amount of stimulus energy, was shown to be inadequate. Grice and Hunter suggested that concepts such as adaptation level or contrast were necessary to describe the phenomena more fully. Additional experiments of the within-subjects type have been undertaken to further investigate these ideas. Another result of this second experiment was that it cast considerable doubt on the adequacy of the generalization theory of intensity effects proposed by Perkins (1953) and Logan (1954). This, too, has led to further investigation (Grice, Masters, and Kohfeld, 1966). The general outcome of the Grice and Hunter experiments was that the stimulus intensity variable is of considerably more interest as a within-subjects than as a between-subjects effect. This, in turn, is leading to more within-subjects experiments—not because of statistical considerations, but because of the greater interest in these relationships. It is suggested that this may frequently turn out to be the case for other variables.

The area of stimulus generalization is one in which investigators have for some time been aware of the potential difference between these two classes of experimental designs, although the problem has not been phrased in just this way. The problem arises because it is necessary to test at several stimulus values in order to determine a generalization gradient. Some years ago, Grice (1951) said:

Strictly speaking, only one valid measurement of generalization may be made for a particular subject. This is because of possible effects of one test trial on subsequent ones. If test trials are reinforced, such reinforcement would have the effect of extending the generalization gradient. On the other hand, if the test trials are not reinforced, the picture is complicated by the effects of differential reinforcement [p. 151].

Differential reinforcement is known to have the effect of steepening the gradient (see, e.g., Raben, 1949). Both kinds of studies have actually been conducted. Typical of the within-subjects approach is the well-known study of Hovland (1937) in which the subjects were tested at all tones with order counterbalanced. Counterbalancing of order, however, does not alter the fact that the subjects were exposed to all stimuli during testing. Typical of the between-subjects approach is the study by Grice and Saltz (1950) in which separate groups were tested to each stimulus. In spite of excellent reasons for thinking that the two kinds of experiments should yield different functions, the relation between the two procedures has never been thoroughly investigated. Wickens, Schroder, and Snide (1954) did do a partial replication of the Hovland (1937) pitch generalization experiment using independent groups rather than the counterbalancing method. They obtained a convex generalization gradient as opposed to Hovland's concave functions. It seems likely that this difference is dependent on the difference in experimental design, but one cannot be certain without direct comparison under identical laboratory conditions.

The introduction by Guttman and Kalish (1956) of their operant conditioning techniques for studying generalization suggested, on logical grounds, that this within-subjects procedure might yield results nearly equivalent to a comparable between-subjects procedure. They explained as follows:

The obtaining of generalization gradients for individual S's in this experiment is an outcome of the fact that aperiodic reinforcement greatly increases resistance to extinction, such that the introduction of a test stimulus during extinction reduces the response strength by a small fraction of its total extent . . . [p. 80].

One direct comparison has actually been made between this procedure and an experiment in which separate groups were tested with each stimulus. Hiss and Thomas (1963), studying wave-length generalization in the pigeon, used three separate groups which were trained to one stimulus and then individually tested at the CS and two generalized stimuli. The function obtained in this way was compared with those from a single group tested on all three stimuli as done by Guttman and Kalish. Gradients of four different response measures were compared. The method of comparison requires comment: Aware of the problems involved, they devised a method which they hoped would be an appropriate solution. For the Between condition, triplets were selected at random with one value for each of the three stimuli. For each triplet, an index of steepness of slope was obtained by computing the percentage of total responses made to the CS. In the case of latency measures, the percentages were based on time rather than number of responses. Percentage values were also obtained for the Within condition, apparently based on individual animals although this is not entirely clear. The authors regarded this test as "conservative" on the grounds that the triplets are more variable than a single animal. This ignores, however, the fact that the gradient points for the Between condition include individual difference variance, and any appropriate test must take this into account. The concept of "conservatism" is often of dubious validity when applied to a statistical test. Presumably, Hiss and Thomas meant conservative with respect to the commission of a Type I error. In this instance, however, a Type II error would be at least as serious, since the chief interest appeared to be in establishing the equivalence of the two procedures. In any case, the percentages were compared by means of the Mann-Whitney U test. There is at least one question concerning the applicability of this test to these data. Each random trial was based on data for three subjects, and data from each of these subjects was represented in two other trials. This means that a complex set of correlations would exist between the percentages, thus violating the assumption of independence underlying the U test. The degree to which this violation was important is difficult to evaluate.

If the conclusions to be drawn from the Hiss and Thomas study are correct, they are of considerable interest. For latency of the first response, and for number of responses in the first 30-second test, the slopes were significantly steeper for the Between condition than for the Within condition. The difference was also in this direction for rate of responding on the first five test trials, but did not reach significance. The reason for interest is that the outcome is the direct opposite of what would ordinarily be expected, if extinction test trials were to steepen the gradient. This unexpected finding is not readily predictable from existing theory, and would not have been discovered without such an experiment. It clearly deserves further investigation. That this finding will turn out to be typical, however, is to be doubted. Kalish and Haber (1963) have reported a wave-length generalization study in which each subject was tested at only one value. The between-subjects gradient was flatter than the within-subjects function obtained in the original Guttman and Kalish (1956) experiment.

The present discussion began with the point that within-subjects experimental designs in which two or more experimental treatments are applied to the same subjects are not equivalent to designs in which each subject receives only one of the treatments. This is true even though the experimental conditions may be otherwise identical. It was then suggested that it may frequently be desirable or even necessary to conduct experiments in which the two procedures are directly compared. It turns out that such experiments may be of considerable substantive scientific interest, and may lead to new discoveries and to advancement in the understanding of the phenomena. While the examples given were limited to the areas of stimulus intensity and stimulus generalization, it is suggested that this is a matter of general importance and has wide implications for behavioral research.

Between-conditions and within-conditions correlation

The point to be made in this section has one principle in common with that made in the first section. The nature of an observed empirical relationship will depend upon the source of variance used by the investigator to look for it. Here, however, we begin with a particular use of the correlation coefficient. In psychological theory, the question arises as to whether two response measures may be regarded as indicants of a single theoretical variable. One obvious approach to this problem is to examine the correlation between the two measures. A high correlation would tend to support the view that they are determined by the same underlying variable, while a low correlation would indicate that both may not be measures of the same process. For example, this question has arisen in connection with the Hullian concept of reaction potential, which Hull (1949) conceived as determining several measures of response strength. From time to time the validity of this construct has been questioned on the grounds that correlations obtained between the response measures have not been satisfactorily high. The suggestion is made here that the particular kind of correlation usually used for this purpose does not provide a satisfactory basis for such an evaluation.

When a correlation is to be computed for a sample consisting of a number of subgroups, the total correlation may be partitioned into two components—between-groups and within-groups. This is strictly analogous to the partition of variance in an ordinary analysis of variance. The subgroups may be selected on the basis of some criterion, or may be randomly selected groups receiving different experimental treatments. The within-groups correlation is an "average" correlation within the groups; the between-groups correlation is the correlation of group means for the two response measures. These two correlations are independent.[3] To put this

---

3.   A readily available reference to the logic and computations involved in the partitioning of covariance is to be found in Lindquist (1953, Chapter 14).

another way, the within-groups correlation is a measure of covariation dependent on individual differences, while the between-groups correlation is a measure of the covariation produced by the experimental treatment. With the matter clarified in this way, one should now raise the question as to what kind of a relation it is proper to consider for any particular purpose. It seems clear that a major determining factor should be the nature of the theoretical concepts under study. If the concepts are conceived as relatively stable traits of individuals, then it would appear that the within-groups correlation would be most appropriate since it maximally reflects individual difference variance under constant experimental conditions. If, on the other hand, the concepts are designed to predict the effects of experimental variables upon behavior, the between-groups correlation should be more appropriate, because it indicates the variation resulting from manipulation of these variables. The correlations between various response measures in learning which have typically been reported (Kimble, 1961) have been based on a single experimental condition following a given amount of training. This is, they have been within-condition correlations and no covariation attributable to manipulation of experimental variables has been included.

The first demonstration of the potential significance of this type of reasoning came from an analysis made by Grice (1956) of stimulus generalization data collected by Grice and Saltz (1950). The experiment was a study of size generalization in the rat and was composed of nine experimental groups. The group means yielded orderly gradients indicating varying amounts of generalization decrement. The measure reported by Grice and Saltz was the number of responses in extinction to the test stimuli. Speed of the first test trial, not included in the original report, was reported in the analysis by Grice. The total correlation between these two measures was then analyzed into two components. While the within-groups correlation was only .10, the between-groups correlation was .89. A second analysis of this kind has been reported by Newman and Grice (1965). This was also a size generalization experiment including the additional variable of drive level. The experiment was designed to test theoretical predictions concerning the effect of drive on generalization gradients. There were four generalization test stimuli which were tested under 12 and 48 hours of food deprivation. Thus there were eight independent groups with the same two response measures used by Grice and Saltz. In this instance, the within-conditions correlation was .22, but the between-conditions correlation was .99. In spite of the fact that this correlation clearly indicates the high degree of linearity, it is still instructive to examine the scatter plot of the eight pairs of group means presented in

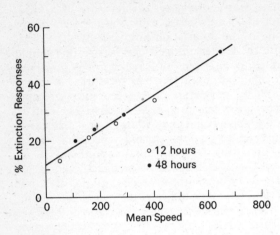

Fig. 1
Between-conditions
relation of extinction
and speed. (Data
from Newman and
Grice, 1965.)

Figure 1.[4] The filled circles indicate the groups tested under 48 hours of deprivation while the hollow circles are for the 12-hour groups. The difference in level of these two conditions indicates the effect of the drive variable. The difference among the points for each drive indicates varying degrees of stimulus generalization. There might be a number of possible explanations for this relationship. However, an obvious and parsimonious interpretation would be that the two response measures are similarly related to a single theoretical state, which, in turn, is influenced by the independent, experimental variables. Of course, this is the way the reaction potential construct is supposed to behave. There are several things which may be said about the difference in the size of the relationship obtained from these two sources. In the first place, training and testing a group of subjects under identical conditions should tend to make the group homogeneous or reduce systematic individual differences in reaction potential. It also seems

---

4.   In this type of relationship, one would ordinarily not be interested in the regression in one direction more than the other, but in a function which simply describes the relationship. For this reason, the line fitted to these data and those in subsequent examples are mutual regression lines. This is the line which minimizes the sum of the sums of the squared residuals for the two variables when both variables are scaled in standard deviation units. The equation for such a line is:

$$y = \frac{\sigma_y}{\sigma_x} x + M_y - \frac{\sigma_y}{\sigma_x} M_x.$$

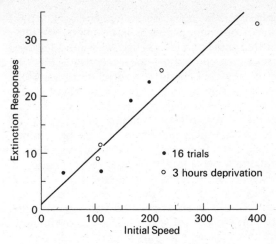

Fig. 2
*Between-conditions
relation of extinction
and initial speed.
(Data from Perrin,
1942.)*

likely that there may be large individual differences in the response measures themselves which are unrelated to reaction potential. For example, some subjects probably are inherently faster responders than others. Moment to moment oscillation in reaction potential will also serve to reduce the within-subjects relationship. In the treatment means, on the other hand, the contribution of individual differences variance is reduced by a factor of $1/n$. The main point about the between-treatments relationship, however, is that the experimental treatments introduce systematic variation in reaction potential. In analysis-of-variance terms, this is a fixed effect rather than a random effect. Since the concern of the theory is with the effect of the experimental variable on reaction potential, it seems clear that the between-treatments effect is the one to examine if one wishes to ascertain whether both response measures are indicants of the theoretical state. Basically, the question reduces to whether or not the measures yield similar S-R laws when experimental variables are manipulated.

A similar example of the relationship between resistance to extinction and response speed is a set of data reported by Perin (1942). The experiment was an attempt to determine reaction potential as a joint function of amount of training and degree of hunger. Five levels of initial training and four levels of food deprivation were employed in a discrete trial bar-pressing situation. The measure usually cited for this study is resistance to extinction, but initial latency measures were also reported. The latency measures have been converted to speed, and the between-conditions relation between speed and number of extinction trials is presented in Figure 2. Variation attributable to the deprivation variable is indicated by the hollow circles, and that attributable to the number of training trials is indicated by the filled circles. It may be seen that these points are fairly well-indicated by a linear function. The between-conditions linear correlation is .94. Data for computation of a within-conditions correlations were not presented, but it is probably safe to assume that it was low. These data, plus those of the previous studies, suggest that there exists a domain in which resistance to extinction and response speed do measure the same thing, and that this underlying state may be manipulated by amount of training, level of deprivation, and stimulus similarity.

In the above examples in which a total correlation was partitioned into within- and between-conditions correlations, the two response measures were obtained from the same subjects. It should be pointed out, however, that a *between-conditions* correlation is still meaningful even though the two response measures were obtained from different subjects. There are various reasons why this might be desirable or necessary. In the first place, the nature of the measures might be such that it is impossible or inconvenient to obtain both. Another possibility is that obtaining one measure might invalidate a second to be taken later. A third situation is one in which there is another experimental variable in addition to the one over which the correlation is to be obtained. It may be that the same response measure is not available in all states of this additional variable. An example of this is to be found in an experiment by Grice (1949). This experiment was a comparison of visual discrimination learning in the rat with simultaneous and successive presentation of stimuli. In the situation in which the two stimuli are presented simultaneously, learning is measured by the percentages of choices of the positive stimulus. In the situation in which only one stimulus is presented on a trial, learning is measured by the increasing difference in latency of response to the positive and negative stimuli. Theoretical considerations provide the rationale by means of which these two measures may be related. The percentage-correct measure may be regarded as a function of the difference in reaction potential between the positive and negative stimuli, or as a measure of overlap between the two reaction potential distributions. This measure was presented for successive blocks of 10 trials. A similar measure of overlap in reaction potential can be obtained from the latency measures from the successive condition. For each block of 10 trials, the number of times that latency to the positive stimulus was faster than a response to the negative stimulus was obtained. This turns out to be the familiar U statistic. A percentage value may be obtained by determining the percent this value is of the total number of opportunities for response to the positive stimulus to be faster

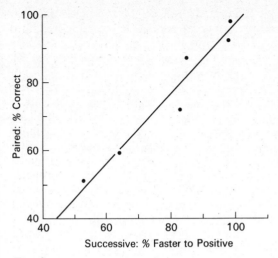

Fig. 3
Between-conditions relation between percent correct choices for paired
presentation and percent faster responses to positive stimulus for single
presentation. (Points are for blocks of 10 trials during learning. Data
from Grice, 1949.)

$(U/U_{max} \times 100)$.[5] The choice measure is plotted as a function of the
measure derived from latency in Figure 3. The correlation over the
10-trial blocks was .97. Under the assumption, on theoretical grounds,
that the two measures are approximately comparable, the linear
function with a slope of about 45 degrees indicates that the level of
learning in these two situations was about the same at all levels of
practice. A slope other than 45 degrees or departure from linearity
would indicate differences in rate of learning or differences in form of
learning functions.

Miller (1959) has suggested a type of analysis which uses what is
essentially the present type of reasoning. He was concerned with the
legitimacy of the introduction of intervening variables and suggested
that the only efficient use of such theoretical entities is when multiple
experimental variables and multiple response measures are employed.
Subsequently, Miller (1961) presented a set of data illustrating the
reasoning. Three experimental variables which might be presumed to

---

5.   This is not the same measure reported in the original paper, but it is closely
     related to it and is believed to be somewhat superior.

influence thirst in the rat and three response measures which might be presumed to measure it were employed. The first independent variable consisted of four amounts of predrinking, varying from 0 to 15 milliliters. The second variable consisted of 15 milliliters of water injected directly into the stomach by means of a fistula. The third was the filling of a balloon in the stomach with 15 milliliters of water. The three response measures were the subsequent amount of water intake, the concentration of quinine in the water required to stop drinking, and bar pressing on a VI schedule rewarded by water. Miller presented the data in a series of bar graphs, but they lend themselves especially well to the kind of analysis used here. A plot of the between-conditions relation between water intake and the quinine measure is presented in Figure 4A. The between-conditions correlation is .97, and the strong linear relation suggests that the two measures reflect a single underlying state —presumably thirst. One would also conclude that the balloon had little, if any, effect on thirst; and that the fistula load did reduce thirst, but less than an equal amount of water taken by mouth. In Figures 4B and C, bar pressing is plotted as a function of water intake and the quinine score. Here the picture is quite different. It appears that bar pressing is a good measure of thirst only when it is manipulated by predrinking. The between-conditions correlation for this variable alone is .98 with water intake, and .99 for quinine. However, the inclusion of the other two conditions reduces both correlations to .52. It is clear that the stomach balloon and, to a lesser extent, the fistula load, reduce bar pressing to a level below what would be predicted on the basis of level of thirst. Miller rightly pointed out that had bar pressing alone been used, there could have been the erroneous conclusion that the balloon reduced thirst. He suggested that an additional variable, such as pain, is operating with the bar pressing measure. One additional point that this analysis makes clear is that Miller's exercise would have been more elegant had he included additional values of the fistula and balloon variable. If these could be added to the two graphs of Figures 4B and C, they would provide additional functions leading to a fuller understanding of the relationships.

More recently, Stricker and Miller (1965) added an additional measure of thirst consisting of licking an empty drinking tube only rarely containing water. This measure has the advantage of not satiating the animal. Over six values of the predrinking variable, the between-conditions correlation with the intake measure was .998. The within-conditions correlation was .31. It was possible to compute both of these coefficients from data presented in the paper.

In the examples presented here, the product-moment correlation has been used as an index of the degree of the between-conditions

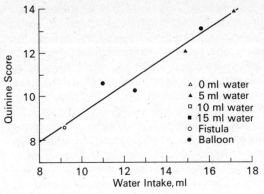

*Fig. 4
Between-conditions
relations between
presumed measures of
thirst.* (*Data from
Miller*, 1961.)

(A) *Quinine score and
water intake.*

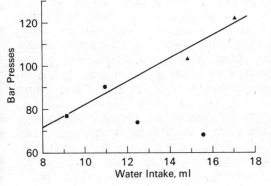

(B) *Bar pressing and
water intake.*

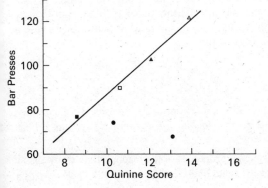

(C) *Bar pressing and
quinine score.*

relationship. These correlations frequently turn out to be substantially higher than those usually encountered in individual difference work. This should not come as a great surprise, however, since the covariation in these examples contains an effect due to systematic, and presumably strategic, manipulation of experimental variables, rather than being entirely dependent on sampling. An additional implication of this is that the significance of these correlations may not be appropriately tested by the usual method. However, analysis-of-variance methods may be adapted to obtain tests of the significance of linear regression and of departure from linearity. In the case of small, but systematic, departures from linearity, it appears that one might frequently be more interested in the "eyeball" test of goodness of fit than in statistical significance. In the case of monotonic but curvilinear relations, one might be interested in the use of transforming functions which could become statements within a theory. Ideally, it would be most satisfactory if such functions could be rationally derived from theoretical considerations. Another point which should be made about these correlations is that their value is specific to a particular experiment, since their size will depend upon the range of the experimental variable manipulated. Further, it should be noted that between-conditions correlations are not independent of sample size for the treatments, because of the dependence of the variability of the mean on sample size.

In summary, it is emphasized that the main point is not the use of correlation measures. The point is that it is important to determine the extent to which two or more response measures yield similar laws when experimental variables are manipulated. Such information can never be obtained from studies of individual differences under constant experimental conditions. In more general terms, the problem may be stated as *comparing* the nature of the laws into which different response measures enter. For, in the long run, the conditions under which measures are not related in a simple fashion are of as much significance as those in which they are. Analysis of this kind appears to provide a useful approach to theory development.

References

Beck, S. B. Eyelid conditioning as a function of CS intensity, UCS intensity, and Manifest Anxiety Scale score. *Journal of Experimental Psychology*, 1963, **66,** 429–438.

Behar, I. and Adams, C. K. Some properties of the reaction time ready signal. *American Journal of Psychology*, 1966, **79,** 419–426.

Campbell, D. T. and Stanley, J. C. Experimental and quasi-experimental designs for research on teaching. In N. L. Gage (Ed.), *Handbook of research on teaching.* Chicago: Rand McNally, 1963. Pp. 171–246.

Grice, G. R. Visual discrimination learning with simultaneous and successive presentation of stimuli. *Journal of Comparative and Physiological Psychology,* 1949, **42,** 365–373.

Grice, G. R. Comments on Razran's discussion of stimulus generalization. *Psychological Bulletin,* 1951, **48,** 150–152.

Grice, G. R. Response speed and size generalization. *Psychological Reports,* 1956, **2,** 246.

Grice, G. R. and Hunter, J. J. Stimulus intensity effects depend upon the type of experimental design. *Psychological Review,* 1964, **71,** 247–256.

Grice, G. R., Masters, L., and Kohfeld, D. L. Classical conditioning without discrimination training. *Journal of Experimental Psychology,* 1966, **72,** 510–513.

Grice, G. R. and Reynolds, B. Effect of varying amounts of rest on conventional and bilateral transfer "reminiscence." *Journal of Experimental Psychology,* 1952, **44,** 247–252.

Grice, G. R. and Saltz, E. The generalization of an instrumental response to stimuli varying in the size dimension. *Journal of Experimental Psychology,* 1950, **40,** 702–708.

Guttman, N. and Kalish, H. I. Discriminability and stimulus generalization. *Journal of Experimental Psychology,* 1956, **51,** 79–88.

Hiss, R. H. and Thomas, D. R. Stimulus generalization as a function of testing procedure and response measure. *Journal of Experimental Psychology,* 1963, **65,** 587–592.

Hovland, C. I. The generalization of conditioned response: I. The sensory generalization of conditioned responses with varying frequencies of tone. *Journal of General Psychology,* 1937, **17,** 279–291.

Hull, C. L. Stimulus intensity dynamism (*V*) and stimulus generalization. *Psychological Review,* 1949, **56,** 67–76.

Kalish, H. I. and Haber, A. Generalization: I. Generalization gradients from single and multiple stimulus points. II. Generalization of inhibition. *Journal of Experimental Psychology,* 1963, **65,** 176–181.

Kimble, G. A. (Ed.) *Hilgard and Marquis' conditioning and learning.* New York: Appleton-Century-Crofts, 1961.

Lana, R. E. and Lubin, A. The effect of correlation on the repeated measures design. *Educational and Psychological Measurement,* 1963, **23,** 729–739

Lindquist, E. J. *Design and analysis of experiments in psychology and education.* Boston: Houghton Mifflin 1953.

Logan, F. A. A note on stimulus intensity dynamism (*V*). *Psychological Review*, 1954, **61**, 77–80.

Miller, N. E. Liberalization of basic S-R concepts: Extensions to conflict behavior, motivation, and social learning. In S. Koch (Ed.), *Psychology: A study of a science*. Vol. 2 *General systematic formulations, learning, and special processes*. New York: McGraw-Hill, 1959. Pp. 196–292.

Miller, N. E. Analytical studies of drive and reward. *American Psychologist*, 1961, **16**, 739–754.

Newman, J. R. and Grice, G. R. Stimulus generalization as a function of drive level, and the relation between two measures of response strength. *Journal of Experimental Psychology*, 1965, **69**, 357–362.

Perin C. T. Behavior potentiality as a joint function of the amount of training and the degree of hunger at the time of extinction. *Journal of Experimental Psychology*, 1942, **30**, 93–113.

Perkins, C. C., Jr. The relation between conditioned stimulus intensity and response strength. *Journal of Experimental Psychology*, 1953, **46**, 225–231.

Raben, M. W. The white rat's discrimination of differences in intensity of illumination measured by running response. *Journal of Comparative and Physiological Psychology*, 1949, **42**, 254–272.

Solomon, R. L. An extension of control group design. *Psychological Bulletin*, 1949, **46**, 137–150.

Stricker, E. M. and Miller, N. E. Thirst measured by licking reinforced on interval schedules: Effects of prewatering and of a bacterial endotoxin. *Journal of Comparative and Physiological Psychology*, 1965, **59**, 112–115.

Wickens, D. D., Schroder, H. M., and Snide, J. D. Primary stimulus generalization of the GSR under two conditions. *Journal of Experimental Psychology*, 1954, **47**, 52–56.

10

a note on functional relations obtained from group data

Murray Sidman

The empirical determination of functional relations between behavior and its controlling variables forms a large part of modern behavioral research. One important aspect of this type of experimentation is the method of distributing subjects among the various points which determine an empirical curve.

The most direct method is to use a single organism, and the same organism, to obtain every point on the curve. This procedure is not always practicable, however, for one or both of two reasons.

1. Intra-organism variability may be so great as to obscure any lawful relation. It is sometimes possible to avoid this problem by taking several determinations at each point and using a statistical measure, a common technique in obtaining threshold measurements [2].

2. Even this procedure will not be effective if, as is often the case, the experimental operations involved in determining one point on the curve have an effect upon the values of other points. For example, one cannot use the same organism to determine all the points on a function

From *Psychological Bulletin*, Vol. 49, 1952, pp. 263–269. Copyright 1952 by the American Psychological Association. Reproduced by permission.

relating extinction responding to number of reinforcements. One reason for this is that the extinction operation is itself a variable entering into extinction results subsequently to reconditioning [4]. It is seldom, if ever, possible to get around this difficulty by using a different individual for each point on the curve. Here inter-organism variability comes into the picture to obscure lawfulness.

Faced with these problems, most experimenters turn to group data. One technique is to employ the same group of organisms to obtain all the points. This procedure, however, is also ruled out if the second situation mentioned above is in effect (unless, of course, this is the problem under investigation). The only recourse remaining is to use a different group to determine each point. The rest of this paper will be devoted to a discussion of certain considerations involved in this latter method of obtaining an empirical function.

Individual vs. averaged functions

The first point to be made is that the mean curve obtained by such a procedure is not necessarily of the same shape as the inferred individual curves. (The term "inferred" is used here since this method is generally employed when the individual curves cannot be obtained directly.) The following development brings this out clearly. For the purpose of demonstration we take as our example the negatively accelerated positive growth function which has achieved a certain prominence in behavior theory. This function can be expressed as

$$y = M - Me^{-kx}, \tag{1}$$

where M is the asymptote approached by y, and k determines the rate of approach to M. If the curves for individual organisms are of this shape, inter-organism variability might occur in the asymptotes approached by the curves, in the rates of approach to the asymptotes, or both. Figure 1 represents a set of individual curves which vary with respect to both constants. (Although, for the sake of simplicity in Figure 1, M and k are assumed to be positively correlated, this assumption is not necessary.) When, for the reasons mentioned above, it is not possible to obtain these individual curves empirically, the procedure generally followed is to expose a different sample of the population of subjects to each value of the independent variable, x, and to take the mean of the dependent variable as the corresponding value of y. On the assumption that each of the samples is equally representative of the population, this procedure is represented in Figure 1 by the broken

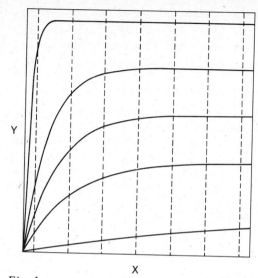

Fig. 1

Sample set of individual curves of the form, $y = M - Me^{-kx}$. Each curve differs with respect to both M and k.

lines drawn from selected values of x. These lines simply indicate that, in a given experiment, the distribution of functions is cut through at selected values of the independent variable.

Corresponding to the curves of Figure 1, we can write the following equations:

$$y_1 = M_1 - M_1 e^{-k_1 x}$$

$$y_2 = M_2 - M_2 e^{-k_2 x}$$

$$\vdots \tag{2}$$

$$y_n = M_n - M_n e^{-k_n x}.$$

To determine the mean value of y for a given value of x we sum equations (2) and divide by n, which results in the expression,

$$n^{-1} \sum_{i=1}^{n} y_i = \bar{y} = n^{-1} \left(\sum_{i=1}^{n} M_i - \sum_{i=1}^{n} M_i e^{-k_i x} \right), \tag{3}$$

which can be written

$$\bar{y} = n^{-1}\left[\sum_{i=1}^{n} M_i - (M_1 e^{-k_1 x} + M_2 e^{-k_2 x} + \cdots + M_n e^{-k_n x})\right]. \quad (4)$$

Each of the exponentials in

$$S = M_1 e^{-k_1 x} + M_2 e^{-k_2 x} + \cdots + M_n e^{-k_n x} \quad (5)$$

can be expanded to give

$$\begin{aligned}
S = &[M_1 + M_1(-k_1)x + M_1(-k_1)^2 x^2/2! \\
&+ M_1(-k_1)^3 x^3/3! + \cdots] \\
&+ [M_2 + M_2(-k_2)x + M_2(-k_2)^2 x^2/2! \\
&+ M_2(-k_2)^3 x^3/3! + \cdots] + \cdots \\
&+ [M_n + M_n(-k_n)x + M_n(-k_n)^2 x^2/2! \\
&+ M_n(-k_n)^3 x^3/3! + \cdots].
\end{aligned} \quad (6)$$

Upon rearranging coefficients we have

$$\begin{aligned}
S = &\sum_{i=1}^{n} M_i + [M_1(-k_1) + M_2(-k_2) + \cdots + M_n(-k_n)]x \\
&+ [M_1(-k_1)^2 + M_2(-k_2)^2 + \cdots + M_n(-k_n)^2]x^2/2! + \cdots \\
&+ [M_1(-k_1)^m + M_2(-k_2)^m + \cdots + M_n(-k_n)^m]x^m/m! + \cdots.
\end{aligned} \quad (7)$$

This can be expressed

$$S = \sum_{i=1}^{n} M_i + A_1 x + A_2 x^2/2! + \cdots + A_m x^m/m! + \cdots, \quad (8)$$

where

$$A_m = M_1(-k_1)^m + M_2(-k_2)^m + \cdots + M_n(-k_n)^m. \quad (9)$$

Substituting equation (8) into equation (4) we arrive at

$$\bar{y} = [1 - (1 + A_1 x + A_2 x^2/2! + \cdots + A_m x^m/m! + \cdots)]n^{-1}. \quad (10)$$

Equation (10) will reduce to the form (1) if and only if

$$A_i = A_j \quad (11)$$

for all i, j, or if

$$A_i = A_1^i. \quad (12)$$

Condition (11) is impossible, since the A's are alternately negative and positive. Condition (12) is easily demonstrated to be impossible unless the A's all equal unity, in which event (12) becomes a special case of (11).

It has been shown, then, that for individual curves of the form (1), if inter-organism variability occurs both in the asymptotes and in the rates of approach to these asymptotes, the average curve *cannot* be described by an equation of the form (1).[1] It can be seen from equations (7) to (10) that this will also be the case if the asymptotes are equal and variability occurs only in the rates of approach. Only when the rates of approach are equal will the mean curve be of the form (1). Thus, under the assumption that

$$k_i = k_j \tag{13}$$

for all i, j, equation (4) can be rewritten

$$\bar{y} = n^{-1}\left(\sum_{i=1}^{n} M_i - \sum_{i=1}^{n} M_i e^{-kx} \right). \tag{14}$$

As far as this writer is aware, the assumption that the rates of approach to the asymptotes are equal for all the organisms in a given experiment has never been explicitly acknowledged by any experimenter or theorist who has fitted this growth function to data obtained by the method under discussion.[2]

At this point it may be argued that although the mean curve is not the same as the individual curves, it is similar enough that, within the limits of experimental error, it can be fitted satisfactorily by the same function. Although this argument possesses dubious merit on grounds of theoretical consistency, it can also be attacked by demonstrating that many other types of individual curve will, if averaged, give as good an approximation to (1) as will equation (10).

For example, if the individual curves are straight lines of the form

$$y = mx \tag{15}$$

up to a given value of x, at which point there occurs a discontinuity (see Figure 2) after which

$$y = c, \tag{16}$$

---

1. The author is indebted to Mr. L. A. Gardner, Jr. for the essential elements of this demonstration.

2. Hull appears actually to have made the opposite assumption. He states, "The 'constant' numerical values appearing in equations representing primary molar behavioral laws vary ... from individual to individual ..." [3, Postulate 18].

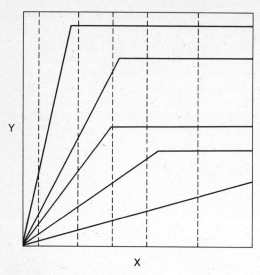

Y

X

Fig. 2
Sample set of individual curves of the form $y = mx$ up to a point of discontinuity, after which $y = c$.

it can be shown that the mean curve can be described by

$$\bar{y} = f(x)(1 - ax) + aBx, \tag{17}$$

where B is the sum of the maximum values of y and a is a proportionality constant between the slope, m, and the maximum value, y_c, of y. (This assumption of proportionality is not necessary, but is made merely to simplify the discussion.) $f(x)$ is a function describing the relationship between x and the sum of the y_c which have been reached at any value of x. (It can be seen from Figure 2 that, as x increases, more of the individual curves will reach their maximum values of y.) $f(x)$ will be determined by the frequency distribution of y_c and the relation, if any, between y_c and x. The form of $f(x)$ will determine how closely equation (16) approximates equation (1). We see, then, that if the individual curves are of the form indicated in Figure 2, the mean curve may approximate equation (1) or any one of a large number of other forms.

Although this discussion has treated only two specific cases in any detail, the same type of analysis can be carried out for any functional relation. In some cases it will be found that the mean curve will be of the same form as the individual curves, e.g., the straight line. However, many functions will show the property discussed above, namely, that the mean curve cannot be of the same form as the individual curves except under special conditions. Furthermore, given a particular mean curve, the form of the individual curves is not uniquely specified. It appears, then, that when different groups of subjects are used to obtain the points determining a functional relation, the mean curve does not provide the information necessary to make statements concerning the function for the individual.

Alternative procedures

Given a situation like that outlined above, there are several alternatives open to experimenters and theorists. First the suggestion might be made that all data obtained by the averaging procedure outlined above be ignored and that the questions which such data attempt to answer not be asked. This radical solution is probably not necessary. Such mean curves may give some valuable information, depending upon the validity of the assumptions one is willing to make concerning the general lawfulness of individual behavior. If it is assumed that all individuals of a certain class will display the same type of functional relation in a given situation, then the mean curve will tell something about that function. If, under this assumption, we obtain the mean curve described by equation (10), it will be known that the individual curves are increasing functions of x and that they either reach a maximum or approach an asymptote.

However, we are not forced to make such an assumption. The mean curve of equation (10), for instance, can be obtained even if the individual curves are so irregular that they cannot be described by any useful equation. A more profitable approach might be to obtain and present all data in the form of distributions, to specify the distributions by their form and by their parameters, and to relate these distributions to the independent variables. (Such procedures would, of course, apply also to experiments in which the same group of subjects is used to determine all points on a function, but where it is observed that the individual data are not amenable to a functional description.)

A third alternative is to develop techniques which will produce lawful individual functions and to present the data without averaging. Although many methods have already been developed for work with individuals [e.g., 1, 5, 6, 7], many more would have to be worked out either by devising new measuring techniques or by attaining more rigorous control over extraneous variables. Statistical procedures would enter into these methods in at least two ways. Replicative statistics would be necessary to determine the reliability of the individual curves, and information would probably be needed concerning the population distribution of the curve constants. Even if these methods were highly developed, however, there are still some data (such as speed of acquisition of behavior under different motivating conditions) which will probably never be amenable to individual treatment. It will, in such cases, be necessary to forego such data or to use statistical analysis. If the latter is done there remains the problem of theoretical integration of data obtained by two different procedures. A decision among the alternate choices will be made only on the basis of further empirical investigation.

References

1. Frick, F. C. and Miller, G. A. A statistical description of operant conditioning. *Amer. J. Psychol.*, 1951, **64,** 20–36.

2. Graham, C. H. and Veniar, F. A. The influence of size of test field surround on visual intensity discrimination. *Proc. nat. Acad. Sci.*, 1950, **36,** 17–25.

3. Hull, C. L. Behavior postulates and corollaries—1949. *Psychol. Rev.*, 1950, **57,** 173–180.

4. Perkins, C. C., Jr. and Cacioppo, A. J. The effect of intermittent reinforcement on the change in extinction rate following successive reconditionings. *J. exp. Psychol.*, 1950, **40,** 794–801.

5. Skinner, B. F. *The behavior of organisms: an experimental analysis.* New York: Appleton-Century, 1938.

6. Skinner, B. F. Are theories of learning necessary? *Psychol. Rev.*, 1950, **57,** 193–216.

7. Skinner, B. F. and Campbell, S. L. An automatic shocking-grid apparatus for continuous use. *J. comp. physiol. Psychol.*, 1947, **40,** 305–307.

11

the problem of inference
from curves based
on group data

W. K. Estes

Papers by Sidman [8], Hayes [4], and Merrill [6] have raised serious questions about the validity of inferences from curves of functional relationship based on averaged data. By means of mathematical arguments and numerical illustrations, these writers have shown convincingly that " ... given a mean curve, the form of the individual curves is not uniquely specified" [8, p. 268]. This demonstration strikes close to home for the learning theorist. In the study of learning, we are interested in describing behavioral changes in individuals, but owing to limited control over behavioral variability must frequently depend upon averages for groups of organisms to determine functional relationships. In many areas we could scarcely remain in business if it were actually true that " ... the mean curve does not provide the information necessary to make statements concerning the function for the individual" [8, p. 268]. Unfortunately it is true. More accurately, it is true *if* we regard the mean curve solely as a source of inductive generalizations. This qualification suggests that possibly the fault lies, not in the averaged curves, but in our customary interpretations of them.

It is noteworthy that learning theory, even quantitative learning theory, has made rather steady progress in spite of the widespread acceptance of a false methodological assumption. Apparently inferences from averaged curves, although not necessarily correct, must in fact often be so. This being the case, researchers in learning are unlikely to give up readily the habit of computing mean curves of functional relationship. My purpose in this note is to show that we need not feel obliged to try. The group curve will remain one of our most useful devices both for summarizing information and for theoretical analysis provided only that it is handled with a modicum of tact and understanding.

The principal point to be made is that the valid treatment of averaged curves depends upon the same principles of statistical inference that have become familiar to all of us in such cases as the analysis of variance and the chi-square test. Just as any mean score for a group of organisms could have arisen from sampling any of an infinite variety of populations of scores, so also could any given mean curve have arisen from any of an infinite variety of populations of individual curves. Therefore no "inductive" inference from mean curve to individual curve is possible and the uncritical use of mean curves even for such purposes as determining the effect of an experimental treatment upon rate of learning or rate of extinction is attended by considerable risk. These considerations set rather severe limitations upon the use of mean curves in the study of learning. Nonetheless we can anticipate that, as so regularly turns out to be the case in scientific research, our virtue in accepting these limitations will not go unrewarded. The same type of theoretical inquiry that has led to recognition of the need for caution in handling averaged data may be turned in a constructive direction and lead to more effective exploitation of the one defensible and important theoretical application that remains for the averaged curve—the testing of exact hypotheses about individual functions.

The first step in this direction is to recognize that the effects of averaging are not in any way capricious or unpredictable and need not be regarded as artifacts or distortions. Distortion arises only if unwarranted inferences are drawn from the mean curves. But given any specified assumption about the form of individual functions, we can proceed to deduce the characteristics to be expected of an averaged curve and then to test these predictions against obtained data. As in any problem of statistical inference, it will always be true that other assumptions might yield the same predictions. The task undertaken will be, however, to test, not the infinity of possible hypotheses, but only the one hypothesis under consideration.

In testing quantitative theories against averaged data we may be concerned either (a) with the form of a functional relationship or (b) with parameter values for the population of organisms sampled. Case a is illustrated by the formerly popular pastime of trying to determine "the form of the learning curve" or by the attempts to verify Hull's hypothesis that habit strength is an exponential function of number of reinforcements [5]. Case b is illustrated by attempts to determine whether the slope parameter of the habit growth curve depends upon amount of reinforcement [11] or whether the rate and asymptote of maze learning are functions of stimulus variability [9].

In studies involving Case a, it has been customary to operate on the tacit assumption that the form of a mean curve will reflect faithfully the form of the individual curves. Since this assumption is now recognized to be unwarranted, we can no longer expect averaged data to yield any direct answer to the question, "What is the form of the individual function?" We can, however, replace this question with one which can be answered, namely, "Is the form of the mean empirical curve in accord with the assumption that the individual functions are of a given form, say $y = f(x, a, b, \dots)$?" (In the remainder of the discussion we shall represent by f the function relating a dependent variable y to an independent variable x and parameters a, b, etc.) It becomes a specific mathematical or statistical research problem to determine for any given function f what testable predictions can be made concerning the mean curve for a group of organisms. Some preliminary considerations that may be helpful in dealing with this type of problem will be discussed below.

In studies involving Case b the assumption has frequently been made that if the function obtained for the individual organism is $y = f(x, a, b, \dots)$, then the function describing the mean curve for a group of organisms should be $y = f(x, \bar{a}, \bar{b}, \dots)$, i.e., a curve of the same form with parameters equal to the means of the corresponding individual parameters. Since the assumption is not generally true, the treatment of this case will require, first, recognizing the instances in which the assumption holds, and, second, investigating instances in which it does not hold in order to determine what information about parameter values is obtainable from the mean curve.

Classification of functions

Relative to these problems, the mathematical functions that we will have occasion to deal with can be classified into three types, each calling for somewhat different treatment. Let us consider briefly the problems that will arise in dealing with each of these types and illustrate some of the procedures that will prove useful in dealing with them.

Class A.   Functions
unmodified by averaging

In these cases the mean curve for the group has the form of the individual function and the parameters of the mean curve are simply the means of the corresponding individual parameters. The chief problem here is that of defining the class of functions so that we will recognize instances of it. The essential characteristics of the class will be apparent from consideration of a few examples:

1. $y = a + bx$
2. $y = a + bx + cx^2$
3. $y = a \log x$
4. $y = a \sin x + b \cos x$
5. $y = a/x$.

A numerical illustration involving one of these examples will show in a concrete way how the averaging process works out for this type of function. Suppose that we have two organisms whose behavior in a learning situation is described by the function $y = a \log x$, where a is a constant which varies in value from one organism to another, but remains fixed in value throughout learning for any one organism. Let y_1 and y_2 be response measures for the two organisms, and let the value of a be 1 for the first organism and 2 for the second. Then the course of learning for the two organisms will be described by the equations

$$y_1 = \log x$$

and

$$y_2 = 2 \log x, \text{ respectively.}$$

Now we compute the "empirical" response measures for each organism for the first four values of the independent variable x as indicated in Table 1. Then by averaging the two response measures at each value of x, we obtain the mean "empirical" curve represented by the values in the column headed $\bar{y}$. It is clear, however, that the column of mean values also represents the values of the function $\bar{y} = 1.5 \log x$. Therefore the function describing the mean curve is of the same form as the individual functions, and the parameter of the function describing the mean curve is the mean of the individual parameters.

All functions belonging to this class work out similarly.[1] Stated in

---

1.   See Mathematical Note 1.

Table 1
Effect of averaging a simple logarithmic function

x	log x	y_1	y_2	$\bar{y}$	1.5 log x
1	.00	.00	.00	.00	.00
2	.30	.30	.60	.45	.45
3	.48	.48	.96	.72	.72
4	.60	.60	1.20	.90	.90

the simplest terms, what they all have in common is that each parameter in the function appears either alone or as a coefficient multiplying a quantity which depends only on the independent variable x. In averaging, any quantity of the latter sort factors out at each value of x and appears in the mean curve, multiplying the mean value of the parameter.

Class B.   Functions for which averaging complicates the interpretation of parameters but leaves form unchanged

Examples of functions falling in this class[2] are

1. $y = \log bx$

2. $y = \dfrac{1}{a} + \dfrac{b}{ax}$.

In the first example, we can rewrite the function in the form

$$y = \log b + \log x;$$

then it is apparent that the mean curve for a group of organisms which differ with respect to parameter b will be logarithmic in form, for the same reasons discussed in the preceding section, but will have the mean value of log b rather than log $\bar{b}$ as the intercept constant. Thus from a mean empirical curve, we can obtain an estimate of the geometric mean of the parameter b for the organisms sampled, but no estimate of the arithmetic mean of b.

In the second example, the mean curve of y vs. $1/x$ will be linear,

---

2.   See Mathematical Note 2.

but the parameters of the mean curve will be the mean values of $1/a$ and b/a for the organisms sampled, so no estimate of $\bar{a}$ or $\bar{b}$ can be obtained from the averaged data.

The testing of hypotheses involving functions in this class raises no difficulties if we are interested only in the form of the function; if we wish to estimate parameter values or to test hypotheses involving changes in parameter values as a function of experimental treatments, then care must be taken to allow for the effects of averaging.

*Class C. Functions
modified in form by
averaging*

A function will fall in this class[3] if it contains any terms involving the independent variable x which will not factor out when we sum values of y over a group of organisms for a constant value of x. The most familiar example of a function belonging to this class is the "growth" curve

$$y = a + be^{-cx}$$

encountered in some guise or other in many learning theories, and given detailed discussion in Sidman's paper [8].

In some cases, a function belonging to this class can be moved into Class B or even Class A by means of an appropriate transformation. Take, for example, the exponential function given above. If the value of the parameter a is known for all individuals, it can be subtracted from the response measure y, leaving us with the simpler equation

$$y' = y - a = be^{-cx}.$$

The latter can be made more tractable by the logarithmic transformation

$$\log y' = \log b - cx$$

which when averaged yields

$$E(\log y') = E(\log b) - \bar{c}x,$$

where $E(\ )$ represents the mean, or expected, value of the term in

---

3.   See Mathematical Note 3.

parentheses. If, then, we take logarithms (base e) of the dependent variable y' and plot the transformed variable as a function of x, both the curve for any individual and the averaged curve for a group will be linear; from the mean curve we can obtain estimates of the mean value of the parameter c and of the geometric mean of the parameter b. By means of this stratagem the problem of testing the hypothesis that an exponential function holds for individual organisms has been reduced to the very simple problem of determining whether the mean curve plotted from the transformed data departs significantly from linearity. Similarly, other hypotheses that might be tested against the group data are greatly simplified. Suppose, for example, that a theoretical curve of extinction took the form of this exponential function, with y being a response measure, x number of trials, and the asymptote a equal to zero, and that we were interested in the question whether some difference in the experimental treatments given two groups of organisms influenced rate of extinction; by means of the suggested transformation, this problem would reduce to that of testing for a difference in slope between two regression lines. A variety of transformations which may be useful in situations of this sort have been discussed by Mueller [7].

Even when functions in Class C cannot be moved into one of the more docile classes by any available transformation, or when for some reason transformation of the data is undesirable (as might be the case if a contemplated transformation produced heterogeneity of variances along the curve), we are not necessarily helpless. The extent to which functional form is modified by averaging will generally depend upon the dispersion of parameter values in the group of organisms sampled; thus in some cases it may be possible by studying individual curves to estimate the dispersion of parameter values in the group and determine whether the form of the mean curve can be expected to conform closely to the form of the individual functions; see, e.g., [3]. Further, even in the case of the most refractory functions, it will usually be possible by appropriate mathematical analysis to derive the main characteristics that should be predicted for an averaged curve; an analysis of this sort for a "growth" function has been described in a recent paper [2].

The role of
experimental error

The analysis given here might be objected to on the grounds that we have considered only the effects of averaging upon data obtained from idealized organisms which behave strictly in accordance with theoretical functions. Response measures obtained from real organisms may, on the other hand, be influenced by various sources of experimental error as well as by the variables taken account of in a given theory. The objection is pertinent, but not fatal. The answer is that in testing a theoretical prediction one must make some explicit assumption about the role of experimental error in the test situation. And as in any statistical test, the validity of the conclusions will be conditional upon the degree to which such assumptions are satisfied. In some instances, it may be reasonable to assume that the contribution of experimental error is negligible; then the analyses given above will apply without modification. Frequently it will be more reasonable to operate under the assumption, routinely made in working with analysis-of-variance models, that error combines additively with treatment effects to determine the observed response measures. In this case, if we wish to test the hypothesis that a function $y = f(x, a, b, \ldots)$ holds for individuals, we will assume that the observed response measure Y for any individual is equal to the sum of y and a random variable e which represents the contribution of experimental error, i.e.,

$$Y = y + e = f(x, a, b, \ldots) + e.$$

Now if the error variable e is independent of x, and if the function f falls in our Class A, averaging of individual curves will yield a mean curve described by the function

$$\bar{Y} = \bar{y} + \bar{e} = f(x, \bar{a}, \bar{b}, \ldots) + \bar{e}.$$

If the mean value of e is zero, which will, for example, be the case whenever the distribution of errors is normal, then the form of the mean curve will be unaffected by the error term; if the mean is not zero, then the mean function will be modified only by the addition of a constant and the plotted mean curve will be changed only by a vertical displacement. In some cases the error variable may interact with experimental variables. If the nature of the interaction can be stated explicitly, then its effects upon the averaging process can be determined by appropriate analysis. In situations where error variables and experimental variables interact in complex or unknown ways, exact tests of quantitative hypotheses will generally be impossible.

Summary

These comments are not meant to provide an exhaustive treatment of the problem of averaging. The one point I have tried to bring out clearly is that the valid interpretation of group curves[4] depends on the principles common to all problems of statistical inference. Although the form of a group mean curve does not determine the forms of the individual curves, it does provide a means of testing exact hypotheses about them. In each particular case, the procedure must be to state explicitly the hypothesis under test, and then to derive the properties that should hold for the averaged curve if the hypothesis is correct. If the predictions thus derived are in accord with data, the hypothesis remains tenable; if they are not, then the hypothesis can be rejected at some specified level of confidence. Utilized within this framework, the averaged curve can be expected to remain one of the most valuable techniques for the analysis of behavioral data, and in fact to increase progressively in value as mathematical and statistical research continues to enlarge our repertory of special devices for the handling of particular problems.

Mathematical notes

1. A more formal criterion for class inclusion is desirable for some purposes, and may be formulated as follows.[5] Let us consider a function $y = f(x, a, b, \ldots)$. At any given value of x, we may regard y as a

---

4. Throughout this discussion we have spoken in terms of mean curves obtained from groups of organisms. Similar problems arise, and similar considerations apply, however, in the case of a curve whose points represent means of repeated measures on the same organism. Parameter values associated with an individual organism may vary either systematically or randomly during the course of an experiment. In either case, we may think of each possible combination of parameter values as determining a hypothetical curve, this population of curves being sampled at each value of the independent variable. Whether the obtained mean curve should be expected to have the same form as the hypothetical individual curves will depend on the nature of the mathematical function describing the latter and on the role of experimental error, just as in the case of a group curve.

5. A criterion proposed by Bakan [1], which involves expanding the function in a Maclaurin series around the point $x = 0$, is not entirely satisfactory. For one thing it is frequently inapplicable. Take, for example, the functions $y = a \log x$ or $y = x^a$; in neither case are the derivatives all continuous at $x = 0$, so in neither case will the series generally represent the function. The criterion suggested in the present paper will hold for all functions which can be expanded by Taylor's theorem, a class which includes all the elementary functions and, in fact, all explicit functions that the psychologist is apt to have dealings with.

function of the parameters a, b, etc., and expand the function in a Taylor's series around the mean values of the parameters [6, 10], obtaining the relation

$$y = f(x, \bar{a}, \bar{b}, \dots) + (\Delta a)f_a + (\Delta b)f_b + \cdots + \frac{(\Delta a)^2}{2} f_a^2 + \cdots$$

where $\bar{a} + \Delta a$ is the value of the a parameter for a given organism; f_a^i represents the ith derivative of y with respect to a, evaluated at $a = \bar{a}$; and so on. When the function is averaged over a group of individuals, we obtain

$$\bar{y} = f(x, \bar{a}, \bar{b}, \dots) + \tfrac{1}{2}\sigma_a^2 f_a^2 + \tfrac{1}{2}\sigma_b^2 f_b^2 + \cdots.$$

Our criterion for inclusion of a function in Class A may now be stated: if in the Taylor's series development, all second and higher order partial derivatives of the function with respect to parameters are zero, then the function is unmodified by averaging. Applying the criterion to $y = a \log x$, we have $f_a = \log x$; $f_a^2 = 0$; and therefore $\bar{y} = \bar{a} \log x$, in agreement with the conclusion reached above by a more informal route.

2.   A sufficient criterion for inclusion of a function $y = f(x, a, b, \dots)$ in Class B is that it does not satisfy the criterion of Class A when expanded around $\bar{a}$, $\bar{b}$, etc., but does satisfy that criterion when rewritten $y = f(x, u, v, \dots)$ and expanded around $\bar{u}$, $\bar{v}$, etc. (u, v, etc. being functions of the parameters a, b, $\dots$). In the first example under Class B above, this criterion is satisfied if we let $\log b = u$; in the second example, it is satisfied if we let $1/a = u$ and $b/a = v$.

3.   If a function falls in Class C, then in the Taylor's series developments described above, some of the second or higher order derivatives will depend on x regardless of how u, v, etc. are chosen, and thus the criteria for Class A or Class B cannot be satisfied.

It will be noted that these formal criteria provide more rigorous definitions of the various classes than can be given in nonmathematical terms. However, it should be emphasized that the conclusions about inference from averaged curves that we have reached in this paper do not depend on abstruse mathematical analyses. In many practical situations, questions concerning the effects of averaging can be handled by simple numerical methods of the type illustrated in an earlier section.

References

1.   Bakan, D. A generalization of Sidman's results on group and individual functions and a criterion. *Psychol. Bull.*, 1954, **51**, 63–64.

2. Estes, W. K. and Burke, C. J. A theory of stimulus variability in learning. *Psychol. Rev.*, 1953, **60,** 276–286.

3. Estes, W. K. and Straughan, J. H. Analysis of a verbal conditioning situation in terms of statistical learning theory. *J. exp. Psychol.*, 1954, **47,** 225–234.

4. Hayes, K. J. The backward curve: a method for the study of learning. *Psychol. Rev.*, 1953, **60,** 269–275.

5. Hull, C. L. *Principles of behavior.* New York: Appleton-Century-Crofts, 1943.

6. Merrill, Margaret. The relationship of individual growth to average growth. *Hum. Biol.*, 1931, **3,** 37–70.

7. Mueller, C. G. Numerical transformations in the analysis of experimental data. *Psychol. Bull.*, 1949, **46,** 198–223.

8. Sidman, M. A note on functional relations obtained from group data. *Psychol. Bull.*, 1952, **49,** 263–269.

9. Wolfle, D. L. The relative efficiency of constant and varied stimulation. III. The objective extent of stimulus variation. *J. comp. Psychol.*, 1936, **22,** 375–381.

10. Woods, F. S. *Advanced calculus.* New York: Ginn, 1934.

11. Zeaman, D. Response latency as a function of the amount of reinforcement. *J. exp. Psychol.*, 1949, **39,** 466–483.

12

N = 1

William F. Dukes

In the search for principles which govern behavior, psychologists generally confine their empirical observations to a relatively small sample of a defined population, using probability theory to help assess the generality of the findings obtained. Because this inductive process commonly entails some knowledge of individual differences in the behavior involved, studies employing only one subject ($N = 1$) seem somewhat anomalous. With no information about intersubject variability in performance, the general applicability of findings is indeterminate.

Although generalizations about behavior rest equally upon adequate sampling of both subjects and situations, questions about sampling most often refer to subjects. Accordingly, the term "$N = 1$" is used throughout the present discussion to designate the *reductio ad absurdum* in the sampling of subjects. It might, however, equally well (perhaps better, in terms of frequency of occurrence) refer to the limiting case in the sampling of situations—for example, the use of one maze in an investigation of learning, or a simple tapping task in a study

From *Psychological Bulletin*, Vol. 64 (No. 1), 1965, pp. 74–79. Copyright 1965 by the American Psychological Association. Reproduced by permission.

of motivation. With respect to the two samplings, Brunswik (1956), foremost champion of the representative design of experiments, speculated:

In fact, proper sampling of situations and problems may in the end be more important than proper sampling of subjects, considering the fact that individuals are probably on the whole much more alike than are situations among one another [p. 39].

As a corollary, the term $N = 1$ might also be appropriately applied to the sampling of experimenters. Long recognized as a potential source of variance in interview data (e.g., Cantril, 1944; Katz, 1942), the investigator has recently been viewed as a variable which may also influence laboratory results (e.g., McGuigan, 1963; Rosenthal, 1963).

Except to note these other possible usages of the term $N = 1$, the present paper is not concerned with one-experimenter or one-situation treatments, but is devoted, as indicated previously, to single-subject studies.

Despite the limitation stated in the first paragraph, $N = 1$ studies cannot be dismissed as inconsequential. A brief scanning of general and historical accounts of psychology will dispel any doubts about their importance, revealing, as it does, many instances of pivotal research in which the observations were confined to the behavior of only one person or animal.

Selective historical review

Foremost among $N = 1$ studies is Ebbinghaus' (1885) investigation of memory. Called by some authorities "a landmark in the history of psychology ... a model which will repay careful study [McGeoch and Irion, 1952, p. 1]," considered by others "a remedy ... at least as bad as the disease [Bartlett, 1932, p. 3]," Ebbinghaus' work established the pattern for much of the research on verbal learning during the past 80 years. His principal findings, gleaned from many self-administered learning situations consisting of some 2,000 lists of nonsense syllables and 42 stanzas of poetry, are still valid source material for the student of memory. In another well-known pioneering study of learning, Bryan and Harter's (1899) report on plateaus, certain crucial data were obtained from only one subject. Their letter-word-phrase analysis of learning to receive code was based on the record of only one student. Their motion of habit hierarchies derived in part from this analysis is, nevertheless, still useful in explaining why plateaus may occur.

Familiar even to beginning students of perception is Stratton's (1897) account of the confusion from and the adjustment to wearing inverted lenses. In this experiment according to Boring (1942), Stratton, with only himself as subject;

> settled both Kepler's problem of erect vision with an inverted image, and Lotze's problem of the role of experience in space perception, by showing that the "absolute" localization of retinal positions—up-down and right-left—are learned and consist of bodily orientation as context to the place of visual excitation [p. 237].

The role of experience was also under scrutiny in the Kelloggs' (1933) project of raising one young chimpanzee, Gua, in their home. (Although observations of their son's behavior were also included in their report, the study is essentially of the $N = 1$ type, since the "experimental group" consisted of one.) This attempt to determine whether early experience may modify behavior traditionally regarded as instinctive was for years a standard reference in discussions of the learning-maturation question.

Focal in the area of motivation is the balloon-swallowing experiment of physiologists Cannon and Washburn (1912) in which kymographic recordings of Washburn's stomach contractions were shown to coincide with his introspective reports of hunger pangs. Their findings were widely incorporated into psychology textbooks as providing an explanation of hunger. Even though in recent years greater importance has been attached to central factors in hunger, Cannon and Washburn's work continues to occupy a prominent place in textbook accounts of food-seeking behavior.

In the literature on emotion, Watson and Rayner's study (1920) of Albert's being conditioned to fear a white rat has been hailed as "one of the most influential papers in the history of American psychology" [Miller, 1960, p. 690]. Their experiment, Murphy (1949) observes,

> immediately had a profound effect on American psychology; for it appeared to support the whole conception that not only simple motor habits, but important, enduring traits of personality, such as emotional tendencies, may in fact be 'built into' the child by conditioning [p. 261].

Actually the Albert experiment was unfinished because he moved away from the laboratory area before the question of fear removal could be explored. But Jones (1924) provided the natural sequel in Peter, a child who, through a process of active reconditioning, overcame a nonlaboratory-produced fear of white furry objects.

In abnormal psychology few cases have attracted as much attention as Prince's (1905) Miss Beauchamp, for years the model case in accounts of multiple personality. An excerpt from the Beauchamp case was recently included, along with selections from Wundt, James, Pavlov, Watson, and others, in a volume of 36 classics in psychology (Shipley, 1961). Perhaps less familiar to the general student but more significant in the history of psychology is Breuer's case (Breuer and Freud, 1895) of Anna O., the analysis of which is credited with containing "the kernel of a new system of treatment, and indeed a new system of psychology [Murphy, 1949, p. 307]." In the process of examining Anna's hysterical symptoms, the occasions for their appearance, and their origin, Breuer claimed that with the aid of hypnosis these symptoms were "talked away." Breuer's young colleague was Sigmund Freud (1910), who later publicly declared the importance of this case in the genesis of psychoanalysis.

There are other instances, maybe not so spectacular as the preceding, of influential $N = 1$ studies—for example, Yerkes' (1927) exploration of the gorilla Congo's mental activities; Jacobson's (1931) study of neuromuscular activity and thinking in an amputee; Culler and Mettler's (1934) demonstration of simple conditioning in a decorticate dog; and Burtt's (1932) striking illustration of his son's residual memory of early childhood.

Further documentation of the significant role of $N = 1$ research in psychological history seems unnecessary. A few studies, each in impact like the single pebble which starts an avalanche, have been the impetus for major developments in research and theory. Others, more like missing pieces from nearly finished jigsaw puzzles, have provided timely data on various controversies.

This historical recounting of "successful" cases is, of course, not an exhortation for restricted subject samplings, nor does it imply that their greatness is independent of subsequent related work.

Frequency and range of topics

In spite of the dated character of the citations—the latest being 1934—$N = 1$ studies cannot be declared the product of an era unsophisticated in sampling statistics, too infrequent in recent psychology to merit attention. During the past 25 years (1939–1963) a total of 246 $N = 1$ studies, 35 of them in the last 5-year period, have appeared in the following psychological periodicals: the *American Journal of Psychology, Journal of Genetic Psychology, Journal of Abnormal and Social Psychology, Journal of Educational Psychology, Journal of Comparative and Physiological Psychology, Journal of Experimental Psychology, Journal of Applied Psychology, Journal of General Psychology, Journal of Social Psychology, Journal of Personality, and*

Journal of Psychology. These are the journals, used by Bruner and Allport (1940) in their survey of 50 years of change in American psychology, selected as significant for and devoted to the advancement of psychology as science. (Also used in their survey were the *Psychological Review*, *Psychological Bulletin*, and *Psychometrika*, excluded here because they do not ordinarily publish original empirical work.) Although these 246 studies constitute only a small percent of the 1939–1963 journal articles, the absolute number is noteworthy and is sizable enough to discount any notion that $N = 1$ studies are a phenomenon of the past.

When, furthermore, these are distributed, as in Table 1, according to subject matter, they are seen to coextend fairly well with the range of topics in general psychology. As might be expected, a large proportion of them fall into the clinical and personality areas. One cannot, however, explain away $N = 1$ studies as case histories contributed by clinicians and personologists occupied less with establishing generalizations than with exploring the uniqueness of an individual and understanding his total personality. Only about 30% (74) are primarily oriented toward the individual, a figure which includes not only works in the "understanding" tradition, but also those treating the individual as a universe of responses and applying traditionally nomothetic techniques to describe and predict individual behavior (e.g., Cattell and Cross, 1952; Yates, 1958).

In actual practice, of course, the two orientations—toward uniqueness or generality—are more a matter of degree than of mutual exclusion, with the result that in the literature surveyed purely idiographic research is extremely rare. Representative of that approach are Evans' (1950) novel-like account of Miller who "spontaneously" recovered his sight after more than 2 years of blindness, Rosen's (1949) "George X: A self-analysis by an avowed fascist," and McCurdy's (1944) profile of Keats.

Rationale for $N = 1$

The appropriateness of restricting an idiographic study to one individual is obvious from the mean of the term. If uniqueness is involved, a sample of one exhausts the population. At the other extreme, an N of 1 is also appropriate if complete population generality exists (or can reasonably be assumed to exist). That is, when between-individual variability for the function under scrutiny is known to be negligible or the data from the single subject have a point-for-point congruence with those obtained from dependable collateral sources, results from a second subject may be considered redundant. Some $N = 1$ studies may be regarded as approximations of this ideal case,

Table 1
Total distribution of N = 1 *studies (1939–1963)*

Category	f	Examples
Maturation development	29	Sequential development of prehension in a macaque (Jensen, 1961); smiling in a human infant (Salzen, 1963)
Motivation	7	Differential reinforcement effects of true, esophageal, and sham feeding in a dog (Hull, Livingston, Rouse, and Barker, 1951)
Emotion	12	Anxiety levels associated with bombing (Glavis, 1946)
Perception, sensory processes	25	Congenital insensitivity to pain in a 19-year-old girl (Cohen, Kipnis, Kunkle, and Kubzansky, 1955); figural aftereffects with a stabilized retinal image (Krauskopf, 1960)
Learning	27	Delayed recall after 50 years (Smith, 1963); imitation in a chimpanzee (Hayes and Hayes, 1952)
Thinking, language	15	"Idealess" behavior in a chimpanzee (Razran, 1961); opposite speech in a schizophrenic patient (Laffal and Ameen, 1959)
Intelligence	14	Well-adjusted congenital hydrocephalic with IQ of 113 (Teska, 1947); intelligence after lobectomy in an epileptic (Hebb, 1939)
Personality	51	Keats' personality from his poetry (McCurdy, 1944); comparison in an adult of P and R techniques (Cattell and Cross, 1952)
Mental health, psychotherapy	66	Multiple personality (Thigpen and Cleckley, 1954); massed practice as therapy for patient with tics (Yates, 1958)
Total	246	

as for example, Heinemann's (1961) photographic measurement of retinal images and Bartley and Seibel's (1954) study of entoptic stray light, using the flicker method.

A variant on this typicality theme occurs when the researcher, in order to preserve some kind of functional unity and perhaps to dramatize a point, reports in depth one case which exemplifies many.

Thus Eisen's (1962) description of the effects of early sensory deprivation is an account of one quondam hard-of-hearing child, and Bettelheim's (1949) paper on rehabilitation a chronicle of one seriously delinquent child.

In other studies an N of 1 is adequate because of the dissonant character of the findings. In contrast to its limited usefulness in *establishing* generalizations from "positive" evidence, an N of 1 when the evidence is "negative," is as useful as an N of 1,000 in *rejecting* an asserted or assumed universal relationship. Thus Krauskopf's (1960) demonstration with one stopped-image subject eliminates motion of the retinal image as necessary for figural aftereffects; and Lenneberg's (1962) case of an 8-year-old boy who lacked the motor skills necessary for speaking but who could understand language makes it "clear that hearing oneself babble is not a necessary factor in the acquisition of understanding ... [p. 422]." Similarly Teska's (1947) case of a congenital hydrocephalic, $6\frac{1}{2}$ years old, with an IQ of 113, is sufficient evidence to discount the notion that prolonged congenital hydrocephaly results in some degree of feeblemindedness.

While scientists are in the long run more likely to be interested in knowing *what is* than *what is not* and more concerned with how many exist or in what proportion they exist than with the fact that at least one exists, one negative case can make it necessary to revise a traditionally accepted hypothesis.

Still other $N = 1$ investigations simply reflect a limited opportunity to observe. When the search for lawfulness is extended to infrequent "nonlaboratory" behavior, individuals in the population under study may be so sparsely distributed spatially or temporally that the psychologist can observe only one case, a report of which may be useful as a part of a cumulative record. Examples of this include cases of multiple personality (Thigpen and Cleckly, 1954), unilateral color blindness (Graham, Sperling, Hsia, and Coulson, 1961), congenital insensitivity to pain (Cohen *et al.*, 1955), and mental deterioration following carbon monoxide poisoning (Jensen, 1950). Situational complexity as well as subject sparsity may limit the opportunity to observe. When the situation is greatly extended in time, requires expensive or specialized training for the subject, or entails intricate and difficult to administer controls, the investigator may, aware of their exploratory character, restrict his observations to one subject. Projects involving home-raising a chimpanzee (Hayes and Hayes, 1952) or testing after 16 years for retention of material presented during infancy (Burtt, 1941), would seem to illustrate this use of an N of 1.

Not all $N = 1$ studies can be conveniently fitted into this rubric; nor is this necessary. Instead of being oriented either toward the person (uniqueness) or toward a global theory (universality), researchers may sometimes simply focus on a problem. Problem-centered research on only one subject may, by clarifying questions, defining variables, and indicating approaches, make substantial contributions to the study of behavior. Besides answering a specific question, it may (Ebbinghaus' work, 1885, being a classic example) provide important groundwork for the theorists.

Regardless of rationale and despite obvious limitations, the usefulness of $N = 1$ studies in psychological research seems, from the preceding historical and methodological considerations, to be fairly well established. (See Shapiro, 1961, for an affirmation of the value of single-case investigations in fundamental clinical psychological research.) Finally, their status in research is further secured by the statistician's assertion (McNemar, 1940) that:

The statistician who fails to see that important generalizations from research on a single case can ever be acceptable is on a par with the experimentalist who fails to appreciate the fact that some problems can never be solved without resort to numbers [p. 361].

References

Bartlett, F. C. *Remembering.* Cambridge, England: University Press, 1932.

Bartley, S. H. and Seibel, Jean L. A. A further study of entoptic stray light. *Journal of Psychology*, 1954, **38**, 313–319.

Bettelheim, B. H. A study in rehabilitation. *Journal of Abnormal and Social Psychology*, 1949, **44**, 231–265.

Boring, E. G. *Sensation and perception in the history of experimental psychology.* New York: Appleton-Century, 1942.

Breuer, J. and Freud, S. Case histories. (Orig. publ. 1895; trans. by J. Strachey) In J. Strachey (Ed.), *The standard edition of the complete psychological works of Sigmund Freud.* Vol. 2. London: Hogarth Press, 1955, Pp. 19–181.

Bruner, J. S. and Allport, G. W. Fifty years of change in American psychology. *Psychological Bulletin*, 1940, **37**, 757–776.

Brunswik, E. *Perception and the representative design of psychological experiments.* Berkeley: Univer. California Press, 1956.

Bryan, W. L. and Harter, N. Studies on the telegraphic language. The acquisition of a hierarchy of habits. *Psychological Review*, 1899, **6**, 345–375.

Burtt, H. E. An experimental study of early childhood memory. *Journal of Genetic Psychology*, 1932, **40**, 287–295.

Burtt, H. E. An experimental study of early childhood memory: Final report. *Journal of Genetic Psychology*, 1941, **58**, 435–439.

Cannon, W. B. and Washburn, A. L. An explanation of hunger. *American Journal of Physiology*, 1912, **29**, 441–454.

Cantril, H. *Gauging public opinion.* Princeton: Princeton Univer. Press, 1944.

Cattell, R. B. and Cross, K. P. Comparison of the ergic and self-sentiment structures found in dynamic traits by R- and P-techniques. *Journal of Personality*, 1952, **21**, 250–271.

Cohen, L. D., Kipnis, D., Kunkle, E. C., and Kubzansky, P. E. Observations of a person with congenital insensitivity to pain. *Journal of Abnormal and Social Psychology*, 1955, **51**, 333–338.

Culler, E. and Mettler, F. A. Conditioned behavior in a decorticate dog. *Journal of Comparative Psychology*, 1934, **18**, 291–303.

Ebbinghaus, H. *Über das Gedächtnis.* Leipzig: Duncker and Humblot, 1885.

Eisen, N. H. Some effects of early sensory deprivation on later behavior: The quondam hard-of-hearing child. *Journal of Abnormal and Social Psychology*, 1962, **65**, 338–342.

Evans, Jean Miller. *Journal of Abnormal and Social Psychology*, 1950, **45**, 359–379.

Freud, S. The origin and development of psycho-analysis. *American Journal of Psychology*, 1910, **21**, 181–218.

Glavis, L. R., Jr. Bombing mission number fifteen. *Journal of Abnormal and Social Psychology*, 1946, **41**, 189–198.

Graham, C. H., Sperling, H. G., Hsia, Y., and Coulson, A. H. The determination of some visual functions of a unilaterally color-blind subject: *Journal of Psychology*, 1961, **51**, 3–32.

Hayes, K. J. and Hayes, Catherine. Imitation in a home-raised chimpanzee. *Journal of Comparative and Physiological Psychology*, 1952, **45**, 450–459.

Hebb, D. O. Intelligence in man after large removals of cerebral tissue: Defects following right temporal lobectomy. *Journal of General Psychology*, 1939, **21**, 437–446.

Heinemann, E. G. Photographic measurement of the retinal image. *American Journal of Psychology*, 1961, **74**, 440–445.

Hull, C. L., Livingston, J. R. Rouse, R. O., and Barker, A. N. True, sham, and esophageal feeding as reinforcements. *Journal of Comparative and Physiological Psychology*, 1951, **44**, 236–245.

Jacobson, E. Electrical measurements of neuromuscular states during mental activities: VI. A note on mental activities concerning an amputated limb. *American Journal of Physiology*, 1931, **96**, 122–125.

Jensen, G. D. The development of prehension in a macaque. *Journal of Comparative and Physiological Psychology*, 1961, **54**, 11–12.

Jensen, M. B. Mental deterioration following carbon monoxide poisoning. *Journal of Abnormal and Social Psychology*, 1950, **45**, 146–153.

Jones, Mary C. A laboratory study of fear: The case of Peter. *Journal of Genetic Psychology*, 1924, **31**, 308–315.

Katz, D. Do interviewers bias poll results? *Public Opinion Quarterly*, 1942, **6**, 248–268.

Kellogg, W. N. and Kellogg, Luella. *The ape and the child*. New York: McGraw-Hill, 1933.

Krauskopf, J. Figural after-effects with a stabilized retinal image. *American Journal of Psychology*, 1960, **73**, 294–297.

Laffal, J. and Ameen, L. Hypotheses of opposite speech. *Journal of Abnormal and Social Psychology*, 1959, **58**, 267–269.

Lenneberg, E. H. Understanding language without ability to speak: A case report. *Journal of Abnormal and Social Psychology*, 1962, **65**, 419–425.

McCurdy, H. G. *La belle dame sans merci*. *Character and Personality*, 1944, **13**, 166–177.

McGeoch, J. A. and Irion, A. L. *The psychology of human learning*. New York: Longmans, Green, 1952.

McGuigan, F. J. The experimenter: A neglected stimulus object. *Psychological Bulletin*, 1963, **60**, 421–428.

McNemar, Q. Sampling in psychological research. *Psychological Bulletin*, 1940, **37**, 331–365.

Miller, D. R. Motivation and affect. In Paul H. Mussen (Ed.), *Handbook of research methods in child development*. New York: Wiley, 1960. Pp. 688–769.

Murphy, G. *Historical introduction to modern psychology*. New York: Harcourt, Brace, 1949.

Prince, M. *The dissociation of a personality*. New York: Longmans, Green, 1905.

Razran, G. Raphael's "idealess" behavior. *Journal of Comparative and Physiological Psychology*, 1961, **54**, 366–367.

Rosen, E. George X: The self-analysis of an avowed fascist. *Journal of Abnormal and Social Psychology*, 1949, **44**, 528–540.

Rosenthal, R. Experimenter attributes as determinants of subjects' responses. *Journal of Projective Techniques*, 1963, **27**, 324–331.

Salzen, E. A. Visual stimuli eliciting the smiling response in the human infant. *Journal of Genetic Psychology*, 1963, **102**, 51–54.

Shapiro, M. B. The single case in fundamental clinical psychological research. *British Journal of Medical Psychology*, 1961, **34,** 255–262.

Shipley, T. (Ed.) *Classics in psychology.* New York: Philosophical Library, 1961.

Smith, M. E. Delayed recall of previously memorized material after fifty years. *Journal of Genetic Psychology*, 1963, **102,** 3–4.

Stratton, G. M. Vision without inversion of the retinal image. *Psychological Review*, 1897, **4,** 341–360, 463–481.

Teska, P. T. The mentality of hydrocephalics and a description of an interesting case. *Journal of Psychology*, 1947, **23,** 197–203.

Thigpen, C. H. and Cleckley, H. A case of multiple personality. *Journal of Abnormal and Social Psychology*, 1954, **49,** 135–151.

Watson, J. B. and Rayner, Rosalie. Conditioned emotional reactions. *Journal of Experimental Psychology*, 1920, **3,** 1–14.

Yates, A. J. The application of learning theory to the treatment of tics. *Journal of Abnormal and Social Psychology*, 1958, **56,** 175–182.

Yerkes, R. M. The mind of a gorilla. *Genetic Psychology Monographs*, 1927, **2,** 1–193.

block 3

13. Nunnally, J. The place of statistics in psychology, *Educational and Psychological Measurement*, 1960, **20**, 641–650.

14. Tukey, J. W. Conclusions vs. decisions, *Technometrics*, 1960, **2**, 1–11.

15. Rozeboom, W. W. The fallacy of the null-hypothesis significance test. *Psychological Bulletin*, 1960, **57**, 416–428.

16. Bakan, D. The test of significance in psychological research. *Psychological Bulletin*, 1966, **66**, 423–437.

17. Lykken, D. T. Statistical significance in psychological research. *Psychological Bulletin*, 1968, **70**, 151–159.

18. Meehl, P. E. Theory testing in psychology and physics: a methodological paradox. *Philosophy of Science*, 1967, **34**, 103–115.

19. Grant, D. A. Testing the null hypothesis and the strategy and tactics of investigating theoretical models. *Psychological Review*, 1962, **69**, 54–61.

20. Binder, A. Further considerations on testing the null hypothesis and the strategy and tactics of investigating theoretical models. *Psychological Review*, 1963, **70**, 107–115.

21. Wilson, W. R. and Miller, H. A note on the inconclusiveness of accepting the null hypothesis. *Psychological Review*, 1964, **71**, 238–242.

22. Edwards, W. Tactical note on the relation between scientific and statistical hypotheses. *Psychological Bulletin*, 1965, **63**, 400–402.

23. Wilson, W. R., Miller, H. L., and Lower, J. S. Much ado about the null hypothesis. *Psychological Bulletin*, 1967, **67**, 188–197.

The final block of readings deals with the role of statistics in research, with null hypothesis testing, and with tests of significance. In the article by Nunnally there is a description of what the author believes to be misconceptions about the use of statistical methods. Nunnally discusses what he terms some psychologists' "preoccupation with statistics" and the hypothesis testing model for finding "significant differences." The author reminds us that the task of psychologists is to discover lawful relations in behavior, not significant differences. In the next article, by Tukey, a distinction is made between conclusions and decisions. Also included in the article is a discussion of tests of significance, tests of hypotheses, and point estimates.

Since null hypothesis testing has been of central concern to many psychologists, a number of articles are included in this block which critically evaluate the strengths and weaknesses of this procedure. Rozeboom's article contains serious objections to the "traditional null-hypothesis significance-test method." Among other things, he is critical of what he calls "decisions to accept or to reject hypotheses," and he would prefer to use "degrees of believing or disbelieving." At the conclusion of his article a number of suggestions are found for strengthening our data evaluation procedures.

The article by Bakan contains a further discussion of the test of significance. Bakan takes the null hypothesis to task and points out that it is generally false under any circumstances. In addition, the article contains a review of both the Fisher and the Bayesian approach as a basis for inference, and concludes with the suggestion that the Bayesian approach may be the more appropriate of the two. A critique of the emphasis placed on statistical significance is also found in the article by Lykken. Lykken's conclusion is that statistical significance may be the least important characteristic of good research. The point is made that other things determine the value of research, such as the degree of experimental control, the measuring techniques used, and the scientific or practical importance of the phenomenon. Lykken also emphasizes the importance of replication and distinguishes among several kinds.

The differences in theory testing between psychology and physics are discussed in Meehl's article. Meehl points out that the role of statistical significance in psychology is the reverse of that in physics. In addition to discussing the logic and methodology of science, Meehl presents a brief review of the process of statistical inference.

Several of the articles deal specifically with the problems associated with testing the null hypothesis and provide a series of arguments and counterarguments. Grant argues that accepting the null hypothesis is an inappropriate way of seeking support for a theory. Binder makes rebuttal to this argument, and the argument is carried even further by Wilson and Miller. The latter two authors tend to agree with Grant in that they also argue that rejection is better than acceptance of the null hypothesis. Disagreement with the rejection-support position is found in the article by Edwards. Edwards notes that classical statistics—in contrast to Bayesian statistics—is strongly biased against the null hypothesis. He feels that a conservative investigator should identify his theory with the null hypothesis. Several of the points made in the article by Edwards are challenged in the paper by Wilson, Miller, and Lower.

13

the place of statistics
in psychology

Jum Nunnally

Most psychologists probably will agree that the emphasis on statistical methods in psychology is a healthy sign. Although we sometimes substitute statistical elegance for good ideas, and over-embellish small studies with elaborate analyses, we are probably on a firmer basis than we were in the prestatistical days. However, it will be argued that there are some serious misemphases in our use of statistical methods, which are retarding the growth of psychology.

The purpose of this article is to criticize the use of statistical "hypothesis-testing" models and some related concepts. It will be argued that the hypothesis-testing models have little to do with the actual testing of hypotheses and that the use of the models has encouraged some unhealthy attitudes toward research. Some alternative approaches will be suggested.

Few, if any, of the criticisms which will be made were originated by the author, and, taken separately, each is probably a well-smitten "straw man." However, it is hoped that when the criticisms are brought

From *Educational and Psychological Measurement*, Vol. 20 (No. 4), 1960, pp. 641–650. Reprinted by permission of J. Nunnally and *Educational and Psychological Measurement*.

together they will argue persuasively for a change in viewpoint about statistical logic in psychology.

What is wrong?

Most will agree that science is mainly concerned with finding functional relations. A particular functional relationship may be studied either because it is interesting in its own right or because it helps clarify a theory. The functional relations most often sought in psychology are correlations between psychological variables, and differences in central tendency in differently treated groups of subjects. Saying it in a simpler manner, psychological results are usually reported as correlation coefficients (or some extension thereof, such as factor analysis) and differences between means (or some elaboration, such as a complex analysis of variance treatment).

Hypothesis testing

After an experiment is completed, and the correlations or differences between means have been obtained, the results must be interpreted. The experimenter is aware of sampling error and realizes that if the experiment is run on different groups of subjects the obtained relations will probably not be the same. How then should he take into account the chance element in the obtained relationship? In order to interpret the results, the experimenter would, as most of us have, rely on the statistical models for hypothesis testing. It will be argued that the hypothesis-testing models are inappropriate for nearly all psychological studies.

Statistical hypothesis testing is a decision theory: you have one or more alternative courses of action, and the theory leads to the choice of one or several of these over the others. Although the theory is very useful in some practical circumstances (such as in "quality control"), it is misnamed. It has very little to do with hypothesis testing in the way that hypotheses are tested in the work-a-day world of scientific activity.

The most misused and misconceived hypothesis-testing model employed in psychology is referred to as the "null-hypothesis" model. Stating it crudely, one null hypothesis would be that two treatments do not produce different mean effects in the long run. Using the obtained means and sample estimates of "population" variances, probability statements can be made about the acceptance or rejection of the null hypothesis. Similar null hypotheses are applied to correlations, complex experimental designs, factor-analytic results, and most all experimental results.

Although from a mathematical point of view the null-hypothesis models are internally neat, they share a crippling flaw: in the real world the null hypothesis is almost never true, and it is usually nonsensical to perform an experiment with the *sole* aim of rejecting the null hypothesis. This is a personal point of view, and it cannot be proved directly. However, it is supported both by common sense and by practical experience. The common-sense argument is that different psychological treatments will almost always (in the long run) produce differences in mean effects, even though the differences may be very small. Also, just as nature abhors a vacuum, it probably abhors zero correlations between variables.

Experience shows that when large numbers of subjects are used in studies, nearly all comparisons of means are "significantly" different and all correlations are "significantly" different from zero. The author once had occasion to use 700 subjects in a study of public opinion. After a factor analysis of the results, the factors were correlated with individual-difference variables such as amount of education, age, income, sex, and others. In looking at the results I was happy to find so many "significant" correlations (under the null-hypothesis model)—indeed, nearly all correlations were significant, including ones that made little sense. Of course, with an N of 700 correlations as large as .08 are "beyond the .05 level." Many of the "significant" correlations were of no theoretical or practical importance.

The point of view taken here is that if the null hypothesis is not rejected, it usually is because the N is too small. If enough data is gathered, the hypothesis will generally be rejected. If rejection of the null hypothesis were the real intention in psychological experiments, there usually would be no need to gather data.

The arguments above apply most straightforwardly to "two-tail tests," which are used in most experiments. A somewhat better argument can be made for using the null hypothesis in the one-tail test. However, even in that case, if rejection of the null hypothesis is not obtained for the specified direction, the hypothesis can be reversed and rejection will usually occur.

Perhaps my intuitions are wrong—perhaps there are many cases in which different treatments produce the same effects and many cases in which correlations are exactly zero. Even so, the emphasis on the null-hypothesis models is unfortunate. As is well recognized, the mere rejection of a null hypothesis provides only meager information. For example, to say that a correlation is "significantly" different from zero provides almost no information about the relationship. Some would argue that finding "significance" is only the first step, but how many psychologists ever go beyond this first step?

Psychologists are usually not interested in finding tiny relationships. However, once this is admitted, it forces either a modification or an abandonment of the null-hypothesis model.

An alternative to the null hypothesis is the "fixed-increment" hypothesis. In this model, the experimenter must state in advance how much of a difference is an important difference. The model could be used, for example, to test the differential effect of two methods of teaching psychology, in which an achievement test is used to measure the amount of learning. Suppose that the regular method of instruction obtains a mean achievement test score of 45. In the alternative method of instruction, laboratory sessions are used in addition to lectures. The experimenter states that he will consider the alternative method of instruction better if, in the long run, it produces a mean achievement test score which is at least ten points greater than the regular method of instruction. Suppose that the alternative method actually produces a mean achievement test score of 65. The probability can then be determined as to whether the range of scores from 55 upwards covers the "true" value (the parameter).

The difficulty with the "fixed-increment" hypothesis-testing model is that there are very few experiments in which the increment can be stated in advance. In the example above, if the desired statistical confidence could not be found for a ten point increment, the experimenter would probably try a nine point increment, then an eight point increment, and so on. Then the experimenter is no longer operating with a hypothesis-testing model. He has switched to a *confidence-interval* model, which will be discussed later in the article.

The small N fallacy

Closely related to the null hypothesis is the notion that only enough subjects need be used in psychological experiments to obtain "significant" results. This often encourages experimenters to be content with very imprecise estimates of effects. In those situations where the dispersions of responses are small, only a small number of subjects is required. However, such situations are seldom encountered in psychology. The question, "When is the N large enough?" will be discussed later in the article.

Even if the object in experimental studies were to test the null hypothesis, the statistical test is often compromised by the small N. The tests depend on assumptions like homogeneity of variance, and the small N study is not sufficient to say how well the assumptions hold. The small N experiment, coupled with the null hypothesis, is usually an illogical effort to leap beyond the confines of limited data to document lawful relations in human behavior.

The sampling fallacy

In psychological experiments we speak of the group of subjects as a "sample" and use statistical sampling theory to assess the results. Of course, we are seldom interested only in the particular group of subjects, and it is reasonable to question the generality of the results in wider collections of people. However, we should not take the sampling notion too seriously, because in many studies no sampling is done. In many studies we are content to use any humans available. College freshmen are preferred, but in a pinch we will use our wives, secretaries, janitors, and anyone else who will participate. We should then be a bit cautious in applying a statistical sampling theory, which holds only when individuals are randomly or systematically drawn from a defined population.

The crucial experiment

Related to the misconceptions above are some misconceptions about crucial experiments. Before the points are argued, a distinction should be made between crucial designs and crucial sets of data. A crucial design is an agreed-on experimental procedure for testing a theoretical statement. Even if the design is accepted as crucial, a particular set of data obtained with the design may not be accepted as crucial.

Although crucial designs have played important parts in some areas of science, few of them are, as yet, available in psychology. In psychology it is more often the case that experimenters propose different designs for testing the same theoretical statement. Experimental designs that apparently differ in small ways often produce different relationships. However, this is not a serious bother. Antithetical results should lead to more comprehensive theory.

A more serious concern is whether particular sets of experimental data can be regarded as crucial. Even when different psychologists employ the same design they often obtain different relationships. Such inconsistencies are often explained by "sampling error," but this is not a complete explanation. Even when the N's are large, it is sometimes reported that Jones finds a positive correlation, Smith a negative correlation, and Brown a nil correlation. The results of psychological studies are sometimes particular to the experimenter and the time and place of the experiment. This is why most psychologists would place more faith in the results of two studies, each with 50 subjects, performed by different investigators in different places, than in the results obtained by one investigator for 100 subjects. Then we must be concerned not only with the sampling of people but with the sampling of experimental environments as well. The need to "sample" experimental environments is much greater in some types of studies than in others. For example, the need probably would be greater in group dynamic studies than in studies of depth perception.

What should be done?

Estimation

Hypotheses are really tested by a process of *estimation* rather than with statistical hypothesis-testing models. That is, the experimenter wants to determine what the mean differences are, how large the correlation is, what form the curve takes, and what kinds of factors occur in test scores. If, in the long run, substantial differences are found between effects or if substantial correlations are found, the experimenter can then speak of the theoretical and practical implications.

To illustrate our dependence on estimation, analysis of variance should be considered primarily an estimation device. The variances and ratios of variances obtained from the analysis are unbiased estimates of different effects and their interactions. The proper questions to ask are, "How large are the separate variances?" and "How much of the total variance is explained by particular classifications?" Only as a minor question should we ask whether or not the separate sources of variance are such as to reject the null hypothesis. Of course, if the results fail to reject the null hypothesis, they should not be interpreted further; but if the hypothesis is rejected, this should be considered only the beginning of the analysis.

Once it is realized that the basis for testing psychological hypotheses is that of estimation, other issues are clarified. For example, the Gordian-knot can be cut on the controversial issue of "proving" the null hypothesis. If, in the long run, it is found that the means of two differently treated groups differ inconsequentially, there is nothing wrong with believing the results as they stand.

Confidence intervals

It is not always necessary to use a large *N*, and there are ways of telling when enough data has been gathered to have faith in statistical estimates. Most of the statistics which are used (means, variances, correlations, and others) have known distributions, and, from these, confidence intervals can be derived for particular estimates. For example, if the estimate of a correlation is .50, a confidence interval can be set for the inclusion of the "true" value. It might be found in this way that the probability is .99 that the "true" value[1] is at least as high as .30. This would supply a great deal more information than to reject the null hypothesis only.

The statistical hypothesis-testing models differ in a subtle, but important, way from the confidence methods. The former make decisions for the experimenter on an all-or-none basis. The latter tell the experimenter how much faith he can place in his estimates, and they indicate how much the N needs to be increased to raise the precision of estimates by particular amounts.

The null-hypothesis model occurs as a special case of the confidence models. If, for example, in a correlational study the confidence interval covers zero, then, in effect, the null hypothesis is not rejected. When this occurs it usually means that not enough data has been gathered to answer the questions at issue.

Discriminatory power

In conjunction with making estimates and using confidence methods with those estimates, methods are needed for demonstrating the strength of relationships. In correlational studies, this need is served by the correlations themselves. In measuring differences in central tendency for differently treated groups, no strength-of-relationship measure is generally used.

One measure that is sometimes used is obtained by converting mean differences for two groups into a point-biserial correlation. This is easily done by giving the members of one group a "group score" of 1 and the members of the other group a "group score" of 2 (any other two numbers would serve the purpose). The dichotomous "group scores" are then correlated with the dependent variable. When the N is large, it is an eye-opener to learn what small correlations correspond to "highly significant" differences.

There is a general strength-of-relationship measure that can be applied to all comparisons of mean differences. The statistic is Epsilon, which was derived by Kelley (1935) and extended by Peters and Van Voorhis (1940). The latter showed how Epsilon applies to analysis of variance methods and recommended its use in general. Their advice was not followed, and the suggestion here is that we reconsider Epsilon.

Epsilon is an unbiased estimate of the correlation ratio, Eta. It is unbiased because "degrees of freedom" are employed in the variance

---

1. Technically, it would be more correct to say that the probability is .99 that the range from .30 to 1.00 covers the parameter.

estimates. To show how Epsilon is applied, consider the one-classification analysis of variance results shown in Table 1.

Epsilon is obtained by dividing the error variance (in the example in Table 1, the within columns variance) by the total variance, subtracting that from one, and taking the square-root of the result. The one classification in Table 1 explains 49 percent of the total variance, which shows that the classification has high discriminatory power. Of course, in this case, the null hypothesis would have been rejected, but that is not nearly as important as it is to show that the classification produces strong differences.

Table 1
Hypothetical results illustrating the use of epsilon

Source	Sums of squares	df	Variance Est.
Experimental treatments (between column means)	510	4	127.50
Within columns	490	119	4.12
Total	1000	123	8.13

$$(Epsilon)^2 = 1 - \frac{Within\ var.}{Total\ var.}$$

$$= 1 - \frac{4.12}{8.13}$$

$$= .49$$

$$Epsilon = .70$$

Whereas Epsilon was applied in Table 1 to the simplest analysis of variance design, it applies equally well to complex designs. Each classification produces an Epsilon, which shows directly the discriminatory power of each (see Peters and Van Voorhis, 1940).

Epsilon is simply a general measure of correlation. If levels within a classification are ordered on a quantitative scale and regressions are linear, Epsilon reduces to the familiar r.

A point of view

Statisticians are not to blame for the misconceptions in psychology about the use of statistical methods. They have warned us about the use of the hypothesis-testing models and the related concepts. In particular they have criticized the null-hypothesis model and have recommended alternative procedures similar to those recommended here. (See Savage, 1957; Tukey, 1954; and Yates, 1951.)

People are complicated, and it is hard to find principles of human behavior. Consequently, psychological research is often difficult and frustrating, and the frustration can lead to a "flight into statistics." With some, this takes the form of a preoccupation with statistics to the point of divorcement from the headaches of empirical study. With others, the hypothesis-testing models provide a quick and easy way of finding "significant differences" and an attendant sense of satisfaction.

The emphasis that has been placed on the null hypothesis and its companion concepts is probably due in part to the professional milieu of psychologists. The "reprint race" in our universities induces us to publish hastily-done, small studies and to be content with inexact estimates of relationships.

There is a definite place for small N studies in psychology. A chain of small studies, each elaborating and modifying the hypotheses and procedures, can eventually lead to a good understanding of a domain of behavior. However, if such small studies are taken out of context and considered (or published) separately, they usually are of little value, even if null hypotheses are successfully rejected.

Psychology had a proud beginning, and it would be a pity to see it settle for the meager efforts which are encouraged by the use of the hypothesis-testing models. The original purpose was to find lawful relations in human behavior. We should not feel proud when we see the psychologist smile and say "the correlation is significant beyond the .01 level." Perhaps that is the most that he can say, but he has no reason to smile.

References

Kelley, T. L. "An unbiased correlation ratio measure." *Proceedings of the National Academy of Science*, Washington, XXI (1935), 554–559.

Peters, C. C. and Van Voorhis, W. R. *Statistical Procedures and Their Mathematical Bases*. New York: McGraw-Hill, 1940.

Savage, R. J. "Nonparametric statistics." *Journal of the American Statistical Association*, LII (1957), 332–333.

Tukey, J. W. "Unsolved problems of experimental statistics." *Journal of the American Statistical Association*, XLIX (1954), 710.

Yates, F. "The influence of *Statistical Methods for Research Workers* on the development of the science of statistics." *Journal of the American Statistical Association*, XLVI (1951), 32–33.

14

*conclusions vs. decisions**

John W. Tukey

With the exception of appendices 2 and 3, the following is based on the after dinner talk given by Professor John W. Tukey at the first meeting of the Section of the Physical and Engineering Sciences of the American Statistical Association held in New York City on May 26, 1955. This talk was repeated at a later date before a dinner meeting of the Metropolitan Section of the American Society for Quality Control. On both occasions considerable discussion ensued. The talk is published here both for the record, and in the hope that some readers may be stimulated to prepare written rejoinders.

Introduction

My subject tonight should be both interesting and professionally relevant and yet should not involve formulas or a blackboard. Of the topics most professionally relevant to statisticians, I must choose between human relations, as between statistician and client, and statistical philosophy, both subjects where our practices often outshine our formal philosophy, both subjects where more discussion and better understanding are needed if our practices are to improve as fast as they should.

It is especially important that our discussion and understanding of statistical philosophy be firm and well-balanced. For one-sided development, no matter how important the single aspect may be, will ultimately deflect some, if not all, of our practices into unwise bypaths.

From *Technometrics*, Vol. 26 (No. 4), November, 1960. Reprinted by permission of the author and the American Statistical Association.

* Prepared in part in connection with research sponsored by the Office of Naval Research.

I have been concerned for a number of years with the tendency of decision theory to attempt the conquest of all statistics. This concern has been founded, in large part, upon my belief that science does not live by decisions alone—that its main support is a different sort of inference.

Effective discussion of this problem, and a real start toward the development of a consensus of opinion, has been retarded by the absence of a word for this other sort of inference, a word which could be contrasted with "decisions." For me, there is now a word. (Some dislike it, but no one has suggested a better choice.) The word is "conclusions." Conclusion theory is intended, not to replace decision theory, but to stand firm beside it.

Because I believe that conclusions are even more important to science than decisions, it is particularly appropriate that I am able to speak to the first meeting of the ASA's new Section on Physical and Engineering Sciences about the relations, and the differences, between decisions and conclusions. I know of no better way to wish the Section well than to encourage its membership to thought and discussion on a topic which I believe will remain important to the carrying out of the functions of all of its members.

Decisions, what are they?

Some of us have read about decision theory, most of us have heard of it, and all of us make decisions. But do we have a clear idea of what a decision-theorist's decision is? Have the books made the essential situation clear? Or have they discussed only the externals of a single formulation? In fact, there has been so little discussion of essentials that I have had to formulate my own idea of what a "decision", in the sense of modern decision theory, really is.

The decisions of practice are far more nearly of the form "let us decide to act for the present as if" than of the form long conventional in treatments of decision theory—"we accept." The distinction is important and too often neglected. The restrictions "act . . . as if" and "for the present" convey two separate and important ideas, ideas which serve to distinguish conclusions from decisions, ideas which epitomize much of what I wish to say.

When an engineer must choose at once between two ways of building a bridge, or a doctor must choose which of two treatments to apply to a patient who is critically ill, or when a businessman must choose between two policies for the season that is now upon him, each must *weigh* alternative A against alternative B in this *immediate* situation, and strive to select the alternative that will yield the bigger reward, whether this reward be a cheaper safe bridge, a better chance of recovery for the patient, or a more profitable season. The possible actions are defined, their consequences in various "states of nature" are understood, and some evidence about these states of nature is at hand. In each instance the individual must judge whether to act as if the reward from alternative A will indeed prove to be greater than that from alternative B (which we may abbreviate "$A > B$"), or whether the opposite is true ("$A < B$").

The three alternative decisions:

1. to act in the present situation as if $A > B$,
2. to act in the present situation as if $A = B$,
3. to act in the present situation as if $A < B$

seem to me reasonably stated, while the conventional statements of the alternatives:

1'. to accept $A > B$,
2'. to accept $A = B$,
3'. to accept $A < B$

seem to have been (unconsciously) well calculated to mislead the reader or student.

When we say "act as if $A > B$," we have made *no* judgment as to the "truth" or "certainty beyond a reasonable doubt" of the statement "$A > B$." When we say "for the present," we are referring only to the particular situation under consideration at present. Thus what we have done is to weight both the *evidence* concerning the relative merits of A and B and also *the probable consequences in the present situation* of various actions (actions, not decisions!). Finally, we have decided that the particular course of action which would be appropriate if A were truly $>B$ is the most reasonable one to adopt *in the specific situation* that faces us.

When we say "act as if $A > B$" and "in the present situation," we assert *no* judgment as to the "truth" or "certainty beyond a reasonable doubt" of the statement "$A > B$," and we make no judgment about the wisdom of choosing among actions in all, or even many, of the situations in which a knowledge that A was truly $>B$ would determine a wise man's choice. The consequences in *other* situations of acting as if $A > B$ have not been considered. It is important that we have not done these things; it is perhaps even more important that we know that we have not done them.

What has been done is simple and specific. The *evidence* concerning the relative rewards from the alternatives has been weighed: The *consequences in the present situation* of various actions (not decisions!) have been assessed. We have decided that, in this single specific situation, the particular action that would be appropriate if A were truly $> B$ is the most reasonable action to take.

Two sorts of special cases may help to tie down these remarks: It is often necessary to make a decision on the basis of no formal data at all. (Consider the hen crossing the road!) It may be reasonable to make two opposite decisions at the same time with regard to different actions. (How many of us both save for *our own* future and carry life insurance, perhaps even in a single policy? One is a decision to act as if we will live, the other a decision to act as if we will die!)

Decisions to "act for the present as if" are attempts to do as well as possible in specific situations, to choose wisely among the available gambles.

Conclusions, what may they be?

Like any other human endeavor, science involves many decisions, but it progresses by the building up of a fairly well established body of knowledge. (One whose relevance is supposed to be broad.) This body grows by the reaching of conclusions—by acts whose essential characteristics differ widely from the making of decisions. Conclusions are established with careful regard to evidence, but without regard to consequences of specific actions in specific circumstances. (They are, of course, based on specific experiments or observations.) Conclusions are withheld until adequate evidence has accumulated.

A conclusion is a statement which is to be accepted as applicable to the conditions of an experiment or observation unless and until unusually strong evidence to the contrary arises. This definition has three crucial parts; two explicit, and the third implicit. It emphasizes "acceptance", in the original, strong sense of that word; it speaks of "unusually strong evidence"; and it implies the possibility of later rejection.

First, the conclusion is to be *accepted*. It is taken into the body of knowledge, not just into the guidebook of advice for immediate action, as would be the case with a decision. It is something of lasting value extracted from the data.

Indeed, the conclusion is to remain accepted, unless and until *unusually strong* evidence to the contrary arises. This implies that only a small percentage of all conclusions will, in due course, be upset.

Third, a conclusion is accepted subject to future *rejection*, when and if the evidence against it becomes strong enough. (Only a small proportion of conclusions will be rejected.) It is taken to be of lasting value, but not necessarily of everlasting value.

These characteristics are very different from those of a decision-theorist's decision. The differences are extremely important.

It has been wisely said that "science is the use of alternative working hypotheses." Wise scientists use great care and skill in selecting the bundle of alternative working hypotheses they use. Conclusions typically reduce the spread of the bundle of those working hypotheses which are regarded as still consistent with the observations. Hence conclusions must be reached cautiously, firmly, not too soon and not too late. And they must be judged by their long run effects, by their "truth," not by specific consequences of specific actions.

Statistical vs. experimenter's conclusions

As statisticians we must insist upon more than one kind of conclusion, upon the difference between "statistical conclusions" and "experimenter's conclusions." A "statistical conclusion" applies to the *actual* conditions of the experiment. If a consistent blunder were made, if the instruments or measurements yield substantial systematic errors (they will always have some systematic errors, though we may hope that these are small), if the measurements were reduced according to a theory which is incomplete in some important way (it will always be incomplete to a certain extent), if the conditions or measurements were incorrectly recorded, if the importance of important variables were not recognized (so that their values were not recorded or reported), the stated conclusions are likely to be wrong. Errors for such reasons are not to be charged against *statistical* conclusions.

But experimenter's conclusions, be they physical conclusions, chemical conclusions, biological conclusions or engineering conclusions, must take account of all these possibilities. In most areas of experiment or observation it will be either desirable or necessary for the experimenter to make specific allowance, beyond the statistically recognizable uncertainty, for such deviations of the actual situation from the supposed situation. For this reason, his conclusions will be weaker than the statistical ones.

This difference, which arises from what may loosely be called the problem of systematic error, is an important challenge to the statistician. Both the statistician's morale and his integrity are tested when, for example, he has to face the possibility of a really substantial systematic error just after he has used all his skill to reduce, in the same experiment, the effects of fluctuating errors to 95% of their former value. It challenges his relationship to his clients in two opposite ways. When his client is quantitatively sophisticated, as many physical and engineering scientists are, he must face the systematic errors or lose his client's respect. When his client is not quantitatively sophisticated, as is often the case in other fields, he must educate the client at the proper rate, not too rapidly and not too slowly—first, perhaps, about fluctuating errors, but eventually about systematic errors, too!

Asymmetry can be essential

We have emphasized the most important differences between decisions and conclusions. There is another difference which is not quite among the most important, but which yet deserves a place of its own. This is the treatment of doing nothing.

In most accounts of decision theory, the decision to do nothing is either ignored (which is probably the worst thing to do in practice) or treated on a par with all the other decisions. In conclusion theory, on the other hand, not coming to a conclusion plays a very special role. Three instances may help us to reflect on this distinction:

1. All of us who were originally brought up in physical or biological science feel quite clearly, I am sure, that "to be not yet certain" is very different from other attitudes about a question.

2. We may be surprised to find a related attitude among administrators—Chester I. Barnard, on page 194 of *The Functions of the Executive* [1] says (his italics) "*The fine art of executive decision consists in not deciding questions that are now not pertinent, in not deciding prematurely, in not making decisions that cannot be made effective, and in not making decisions that others should make.*"

3. An active worker in decision theory told me recently that the decision to do nothing was "the only decision without a loss function."

Each of these emphasizes, in a different way, the distinctive character of "doing nothing." Each deserves further examination. [Appendix 2 will treat (1).]

Barnard's statement implies that the "decisions" of the executive are much more nearly what we have called *conclusions* than what we have called *decisions*. They are not to be entered upon lightly, and there is a clear implication that, once reached, they are to be referred to for some time as part of a growing body of doctrine.

The decision-theorist's statement in (3) reveals him, it seems to me, as one who is really in search of conclusions. Why else is "doing nothing" so different? It is an action, one that can, in particular, lose money.

Decision theory ought to be *symmetrical* with regard to the action "do nothing." Conclusion theory must be *unsymmetrical* with regard to the action "conclude nothing."

Tests of significance

The prototype of modern experimental statistics was the test of significant difference. It came first as a tool of analysis and inference, not as a tool of mere description. When we examine its purport in the framework we are describing, we find that it is a *qualitative conclusion* procedure. Its purpose is to answer the question "Dare we conclude that this difference is not zero?"

We may, on the basis of a test of significance, *conclude* that $A \neq B$, or even more specifically that $A < B$ or $A > B$. But failure to attain significance is not, of itself, intended to produce a conclusion, is not intended to be accepted, in that strong sense of the word "accept" which is relevant to conclusions.

Where do we stand when the difference between A and B has not reached "significance?" Some would like to wield Occam's razor and say that "We have shown that $A = B$." Surely we have not *concluded* that $A = B$. For no quantitative evidence can establish that A is not just a very little different from B. Perhaps we have *decided* that $A = B$, but if so, for what specific situation, on what evidence, and with what assessment of consequences?

To interpret appropriately a failure to attain significance, it is necessary to know something about the precision of the comparison, to know how close there is reason to believe A is to B. Only by advancing into the use of confidence techniques (about which more anon) can a negative statement about significance be converted into a positive conclusion of established smallness of difference.

Tests of hypothesis

Symmetry, and mathematical simplicity, seemed to lead along a straight path from tests of significance to tests of hypothesis. As the procession traversed this path, few if any stopped to see where they had gone—to notice that they had left a qualitative conclusion procedure and had come to what was suspiciously like a qualitative decision procedure.

The choice between two simple hypotheses can be viewed in two quite different ways:

1.   as an attempt to choose the best risk, without regard to certainty—which is surely a decision procedure, or

2.   as an attempt to control, often by a sequential procedure, both kinds of error (both the error of accepting the hypothesis when it is false, and the error of rejecting it when it is true) at suitably low levels—which is, on the face of it, a conclusion procedure.

The aim of (2) can be expressed as follows: "We will take enough observations to allow us to dare to conclude either that the first hypothesis is false, or that the second hypothesis is false, but we shall not try to conclude that both are false, even if the observations prove adequate to do this." The form of this statement is clearly that of a conclusion procedure, though it is natural to wonder at the presence of its last proviso.

If, on the other hand, the aim is really (1), to choose the best risk, then there is no real place in the procedure for the artificial limitations of 5%, of 1%, or of any of the conventional significance or confidence levels. If nothing is to be concluded, only something decided, there is no need to control the probability of error. (Only the mathematical expectation of gain needs to be positive to make a small gamble profitable. There is no need for high confidence in winning individual bets. A coin which comes heads 60% of the time will win more money safely than one that comes heads 95% or 99% of the time.)

Until we go through the accounts of the testing of hypotheses, separating decision elements from conclusion elements, the intimate mixture of disparate elements will be a continual source of confusion. The writer looks forward to the day when the history and status of tests of hypotheses will have been disentangled. (See also Appendix 3.)

Estimation

Older by far than any other statistical techniques are point estimates, each a simple indication of the value the data seem to point out or suggest. They are quantitative, where the other classical procedures we have so far discussed are qualitative. They are attempts to do the best that we can, not to do only what we can be certain about. Hence they are decision procedures, more specifically, quantitative decision procedures. So far as our classification goes, they offer no problems.

Probably the greatest ultimate importance, among all types of statistical procedures we now know, belongs to *confidence procedures* which, by making interval estimates, attempt to reach as strong conclusions as are reasonable by pointing out, not single likely values, but rather whole classes (intervals, regions, etc.) of *possible* values, so chosen that there can be high confidence that the "true" value is *somewhere among them.* Such procedures are clearly quantitative conclusion procedures. They make clear the essential "smudginess" of experimental knowledge.

The twin dichotomies

Keeping the varied sorts of statistical inference procedures separate, and yet properly related to one another, is important to every statistician. Hopefully, the distinction between decisions and conclusions, as well as the distinction between qualitative and quantitative, are now clear.

The writer has found, and continues to find, these twin dichotomies (qualitative-quantitative and conclusion-decision) most helpful in organizing the procedures of statistics into a pattern which is useful both for application and reflection.

Surely the quantitative is preferable to the qualitative whenever both are equally available and equally relevant. Thus most qualitative statistical procedures are interim measures, introduced to serve until equally relevant quantitative procedures become available.

If we use the phrases "to do one's best" and "to state only that which is certain" as typifying decisions on the one hand, and conclusions on the other, we can see that there is a real place for both. And in particular situations we can usually tell what these places are.

To sum things up: the case of qualitative vs. quantitative should have a mixed verdict, granting "qualitative" squatters rights, but only until "quantitative" is ready to move in; while the case of conclusion vs. decisions should be settled out of court, with an understanding that cooperation is vital to both parties. There is a place for both "doing one's best" and "saying only what is certain," but it is important to know, in each instance, both which one is being done, and which one ought to be done.

APPENDIX 1

Some confusing relations

So long as we lacked clearly contrasted words, confusion between decisions and conclusions was very easy, especially since they are so thoroughly combined, both so frequently, and in almost every possible way.

Both decisions and conclusions are required in almost every field of human endeavor, yet the proportions, mutual relations and relative dominance which are appropriate vary greatly from one field to another. The aim and purpose of pure science lies in the *conclusions* which build up knowledge. Yet these conclusions are reached because individual scientists *decide* to attack certain problems in certain ways. (They rarely, if ever, know enough to *conclude* which problems they should attack, or how.) In most fields of engineering much must depend on the wisdom of experience, on engineering judgment, on engineering decisions. Yet these *decisions* are built upon the *conclusions* of pure and applied science. Engineering uses decisions fortified with conclusions, just as science uses decisions to reach conclusions.

In statistics, too, conclusions and decisions are interrelated and intertwined. It is not infrequent that we come to *conclusions* about *decision procedures*. What may prove to be one of the greatest monuments to Abraham Wald's memory is the notion of admissibility. And one of its more important elements is the fact that we may *conclude* (in this instance purely from theory and presuppositions) that one *decision procedure* is always worse than another.

We have seen that point estimates may reasonably be regarded as decisions. If we have a situation in which alternative point estimates are investigated by experimental sampling, and if the sampling is continued until the effects of sampling fluctuations fall below a prechosen standard of smallness, we are really experimenting until we can reach a *conclusion* about competing *decision procedures*. A third instance, closer in feeling to the first, is provided by R. A. Fisher's classical paper of 1920, "A Mathematical Examination of the Methods of Determining the Accuracy of an Observation by the Mean Error, and by the Mean Square Error" [2], one of many objective comparisons of estimators.

On the other hand, all of us make *decisions* about *conclusion procedures*. Some of us do it every day. "How is it best to analyze this data?" is a question which cannot be left to the experimenter alone, which the statistician is bound by his profession to try to answer. If the answer should clearly be a procedure to provide a conclusion, then he must do something about a *conclusion procedure*. Does he *decide* about it, or *conclude* about it? As an inherent conservative (professionally, anyway!), he would like to conclude. But will he have enough firm evidence? Often he will not!

When a transformation is chosen, whether for an analysis of variance, for a quantal response assay, or for some other statistical procedure, how often does the chooser know what is *the* best transformation? In a theoretical sense, the answer is "never," for he will have only a finite amount of information—since his estimate of "best" will have a finite standard deviation—and transformations can be varied in arbitrarily small steps. In practice, it must be recognized that *exactly the best* transformation is not required, so that such an argument is not compelling. Yet, even in a practical sense, the answer is "not nearly often enough," for adequate information is often, or even usually, lacking. Who knows of an instance, to take a concrete example, where the choice between probits and logits for a quantal response assay was a conclusion and not a decision?

In handling complex data by analysis of variance, how shall we set up the analysis? How detailed shall be our computations? On what orthogonal functions shall we calculate regressions? Can any of you recall situations where the answer to any of these was a conclusion?

APPENDIX 2

Conclusion theory
as an action system

Insofar as man's organized activities can be regarded as striving toward at least dimly recognized goals, it is easy to argue that the individual actions which make up these activities should be guided by some appropriate form of decision theory. Actions are to be taken in specific instances, and the gains or losses resulting from specific combinations of actions and states of nature can, in principle, be at least roughly assessed. Why then should there be a place for conclusion theory, which seems from such a broad viewpoint to be a poor substitute for what is really needed? At least four classes of important reasons loom up over the horizon: problems of communication, problems of assessment of gain and loss, problems of assessment of the *a priori*, problems of adequate mathematical treatment.

Most human affairs are not conducted by a single individual, nor even by a single executive hierarchy. Science, in the broadest sense, is both one of the most successful of human affairs, and one of the most decentralized. In principle, each of us puts his evidence (his observations, experimental or not, and their discussion) before all the others, and in due course an adequate consensus of opinion develops. In the early decades of the Royal Society of London, this was indeed very nearly how things were. But the number of working scientists has doubled, and redoubled very many times since then. As a consequence, problems of communication have probably come to dominate the problems of scientific method. And the practices of science have developed to meet the challenge. Outstanding among these practices is the use of conclusions. A scientist is helped little to know that another, given different evidence and facing a different specific situation, decided (even decided wisely) to act as if so-and-so were the true state of nature. The communication (for information, not as directives) of decisions is often inappropriate, and usually inefficient. A scientist is helped much to know that another reached a certain conclusion, that he felt that the correctness of so-and-so was established with high confidence. In order to replace conclusions as the basic means of communication, it would be necessary to rearrange and replan the entire fabric of science. No statistician should dare to attempt such a task on the basis of his limited area of specialized knowledge.

But suppose a new fabric of science were to be developed. How could the old be compared with the new? Let us admit for simplicity that rapidity of progress is what is desired. (To do this for argument's sake alone does not mean that the intellectual and artistic aspects of science are being neglected in comparison with its pragmatic aspects.) Can one judge now how far science will progress (using the old fabric) in twenty years? And if not, how could we judge whether twenty years' use of a new fabric had done better or worse? If twenty years of trial would not be adequate for evaluation, how can an advance assessment give any useful idea of the gains and losses to be expected from a change to a new fabric?

If there were to be a change to a new fabric of science, one based more explicitly on decision-theoretic principles, how would the choice among many such fabrics be made? There would be a need to choose something like an *a priori* state of the whole world, more precisely to choose an *a priori* distribution of probability over all the possible states of the whole world, since just as the admissible decision procedures are the Bayesian solutions (those solutions which are optimum for suitable assumptions about the *a priori* probabilities of all "states of nature" considered) so too the admissible decision fabrics are to be expected to be Bayesian fabrics. And it is a little too much to ask of those who have learned to study certain limited aspects of the world, and who are striving to learn a little more of these aspects, that they envisage all possible worlds and distribute probability among them.

Finally, there are problems of adequate mathematical treatment. Statistics can solve a few vastly over-simplified problems in great generality or great detail, but it has barely begun to chew out a few little entrances into many problems of moderate difficulty. Problems of the order of difficulty of finding a Bayesian fabric, given the gains and losses, are wholly outside its present grasp. Today it has not provided even a beginning of an answer for such vastly simpler problems as: given samples of moderate size from each of two populations, given that the populations are so nearly normal (i.e., Gaussian) that samples of 1000 have no more than an even chance of detecting (at 5 % significance) that the populations are not normal, and (even) given that the populations are symmetrical, what is the safest way to compare the centers of the two populations on the basis of the samples, where safety combines (1) reasonable reliability of significance or confidence percentages and (2) avoidance of procedures which are relatively very wasteful for particular population shapes. (Notes: (a) Even these many words, of course, have not completely specified a problem. (b) Adding a probability distribution over shapes to the hypotheses seems unlikely to make the problem easier.)

There are four types of difficulty, then, ranging from communication through assessment to mathematical treatment, each of which by itself will be sufficient, for a long time, to prevent the replacement, in science, of the system of conclusions by a system based more closely on today's decision theory. Once these four have been examined, the natural question becomes: "How did the conclusion system escape the parallel sets of difficulties?" The answer is simple and clear. It grew. This means that it evolved; that many minor alternatives were tried, often unconsciously, that most were found wanting, and were discarded; that this process of trial and selection went through cycle after cycle. The strength of the *process of science* today comes from *ex*perience rather than *in*sight, and this state of affairs may be expected to continue for a long time. Indeed, it will not be easy to gain the limited insight required to understand how the present processes of science do as well as they do.

APPENDIX 3

What of tests of hypothesis?

In view of Neyman's continued insistence on "inductive behavior," words which relate more naturally to decisions than to conclusions, it is reasonable to suppose that the Neyman-Pearson theory of testing hypotheses was, at the very least, a long step in the direction of decision theory, and that the appearance of 5%, 1% and the like in its development and discussion was a carryover from the then dominant qualitative conclusion theory, the theory of tests of significance. If this view is correct, Wald's decision theory now does much more nearly what tests of hypothesis were intended to do. Indeed, there are three ways in which it does better. First, it has given up a fixed probability for errors of the first kind, and has focussed on gains, losses or regrets (be they average or minimax). Secondly, it has made it somewhat easier to consider a much wider variety of specifications, to make much less stringent assumptions. And finally it has shown that one should expect mathematics to provide, not a single best procedure, but rather an assortment of good procedures (e.g., a complete class of admissible procedures) from which judgment and insight into a particular instance (perhaps expressed in the form of an a priori distribution) must be used to select the "best" procedure.

If one aspect of the theory of testing hypotheses has been embodied in modern decision theory, what of its other aspects? The notion of the power function of a test, which is of course strictly analogous to the notion of the operating characteristic of a sampling plan, is just as applicable to tests of significance (conclusions) as to tests of hypotheses (decisions). And, indeed, its natural generalization to confidence procedures (conclusions) seems more natural and reasonable than such conventional criteria as the average length of confidence intervals.

Conclusion theory can take over these nondecisional aspects of the theory of testing hypotheses. Its main concern in so doing must be caution about over-narrow specifications. To know that a certain confidence procedure is optimum, so long as the underlying observations follow a normal (i.e., Gaussian) distribution precisely, is not enough, if the procedure is poor for distributions whose shapes are very difficult to distinguish (in practice) from normality. (And such situations exist, at least in large samples, cf. [3].)

In the long run, then, the theory of testing hypotheses can be absorbed into the contrasted bodies of decision theory and conclusion theory. (And the Neyman-Pearson lemma can serve, in its proper place, in both.)

Acknowledgment

Like most of the writer's papers, the present one owes much to conversations with, and careful readings of drafts by many friends and colleagues. Outstanding in this instance are Dr. Edgar Anderson and Dr. Jayarajan Chanmugan. My thanks go to all who have helped.

References

1. Barnard, Chester I.   *The Functions of the Executive*, Cambridge, Massachusetts, Harvard University Press, 1938, 334 pp.

2. Fisher, R. A. "A mathematical examination of methods of determining the accuracy of an observation by the mean error, and by the mean square error," *Monthly Notices of the Royal Astronomical Society*, Vol. 80, No. 8, pp. 758–770, June, 1920. Reprinted as paper 2 in his *Contributions to Mathematical Statistics*, John Wiley & Sons, Inc., New York, 1950.

3. Tukey, John W. "A survey of sampling from contaminated distributions," pp. 448–485 in *Contributions to Probability and Statistics: Essays in Honor of Harold Hotelling*, Ed. Olkin and others, Stanford University Press, Stanford, California, 1960.

15

the fallacy of the
null-hypothesis
significance test

William W. Rozeboom

The theory of probability and statistical inference is various things to various people. To the mathematician, it is an intricate formal calculus, to be explored and developed with little professional concern for any empirical significance that might attach to the terms and propositions involved. To the philosopher, it is an embarrassing mystery whose justification and conceptual clarification have remained stubbornly refractory to philosophical insight. (A famous philosophical epigram has it that induction [a special case of statistical inference] is the glory of science and the scandal of philosophy.) To the experimental scientist, however, statistical inference is a research instrument, a processing device by which unwieldy masses of raw data may be refined into a product more suitable for assimilation into the corpus of science, and in this lies both strength and weakness. It is strength in that, as an ultimate *consumer* of statistical methods, the experimentalist is in position to demand that the techniques made available to him conform to his actual needs. But it is also weakness in that, in his need for the tools constructed by a highly technical formal discipline, the

From *Psychological Bulletin*, Vol. 57 (No. 5), 1960, pp. 416–428. Copyright 1960 by the American Psychological Association. Reproduced by permission.

experimentalist, who has specialized along other lines, seldom feels competent to extend criticisms or even comments; he is much more likely to make unquestioning application of procedures learned more or less by rote from persons assumed to be more knowledgeable of statistics than he. There is, of course, nothing surprising or reprehensible about this—one need not understand the principles of a complicated tool in order to make effective use of it, and the research scientist can no more be expected to have sophistication in the theory of statistical inference than he can be held responsible for the principles of the computers, signal generators, timers, and other complex modern instruments to which he may have recourse during an experiment. Nonetheless, this leaves him particularly vulnerable to misinterpretation of his aims by those who build his instruments, not to mention the ever present dangers of selecting an inappropriate or outmoded tool for the job at hand, misusing the proper tool, or improvising a tool of unknown adequacy to meet a problem not conforming to the simple theoretical situations in terms of which existent instruments have been analyzed. Further, since behaviors once exercised tend to crystallize into habits and eventually traditions, it should come as no surprise to find that the tribal rituals for data-processing passed along in graduate courses in experimental method should contain elements justified more by custom than by reason.

In this paper, I wish to examine a dogma of inferential procedure which, for psychologists at least, has attained the status of a religious conviction. The dogma to be scrutinized is the "null-hypothesis significance test" orthodoxy that passing statistical judgment on a scientific hypothesis by means of experimental observation is a decision procedure wherein one rejects or accepts a null hypothesis according to whether or not the value of a sample statistic yielded by an experiment falls within a certain predetermined "rejection region" of its possible values. The thesis to be advanced is that despite the awesome pre-eminence this method has attained in our experimental journals and textbooks of applied statistics, it is based upon a fundamental misunderstanding of the nature of rational inference, and is seldom if ever appropriate to the aims of scientific research. This is not a particularly original view—traditional null-hypothesis procedure has already been superseded in modern statistical theory by a variety of more satisfactory inferential techniques. But the perceptual defenses of psychologists are particularly efficient when dealing with matters of methodology, and so the statistical folkways of a more primitive past continue to dominate the local scene.

To examine the method in question in greater detail, and expose some of the discomfitures to which it gives rise, let us begin with a hypothetical case study.

**A case study in null-
hypothesis procedure; or,
a quorum of embarrassments**

Suppose that according to the theory of behavior, T_0, held by most right-minded, respectable behaviorists, the extent to which a certain behavioral manipulation M facilitates learning in a certain complex learning situation C should be null. That is, if "ϕ" designates the degree to which manipulation M facilitates the acquisition of habit H under circumstances C, it follows from the orthodox theory T_0 that $\phi = 0$. Also suppose, however, that a few radicals have persistently advocated an alternative theory T_1 which entails, among other things, that the facilitation of H by M in circumstances C should be appreciably greater than zero, the precise extent being dependent upon the values of certain parameters in C. Finally, suppose that Igor Hopewell, graduate student in psychology, has staked his dissertation hopes on an experimental test of T_0 against T_1 on the basis of their differential predictions about the value of ϕ.

Now, if Hopewell is to carry out his assessment of the comparative merits of T_0 and T_1 in this way, there is nothing for him to do but submit a number of S's to manipulation M under circumstances C and compare their efficiency at acquiring habit H with that of comparable S's who, under circumstances C, have *not* been exposed to manipulation M. The difference, d, between experimental and control S's in average learning efficiency may then be taken as an operational measure of the degree, ϕ, to which M influences acquisition of H in circumstances C. Unfortunately, however, as any experienced researcher knows to his sorrow, the interpretation of such an observed statistic is not quite so simple as that. For the observed dependent variable d, which is actually a performance measure, is a function not only of the extent to which M influences acquisition of H, but of many additional major and minor factors as well. Some of these, such as deprivations, species, age, laboratory conditions, etc., can be removed from consideration by holding them essentially constant. Others, however, are not so easily controlled, especially those customarily subsumed under the headings of "individual differences" and "errors of measurement." To curtail a long mathematical story, it turns out that with suitable (possibly justified) assumptions about the distributions of values for these uncontrolled variables, the manner in which they influence the dependent variable, and the way in which experimental and control S's were selected and manipulated, the observed sample statistic d may be regarded as the value of a normally distributed random variate whose average value is ϕ and whose variance, which is independent of ϕ, is unbiasedly estimated by the square of another sample statistic, s, computed from the data of the experiment.[1]

The import of these statistical considerations for Hopewell's dissertation, of course, is that he will not be permitted to reason in any simple way from the observed d to a conclusion about the comparative merits of T_0 and T_1. To conclude that T_0, rather than T_1, is correct, he must argue that $\phi = 0$, rather than $\phi > 0$. But the observed d, whatever its value, is logically compatible both with the hypothesis that $\phi = 0$ and the hypothesis that $\phi > 0$. How then, can Hopewell use his data to make a comparison of T_0 and T_1? As a well-trained student, what he *does*, of course, is to divide d by s to obtain what, under H_0, is a t statistic, consult a table of the t distributions under the appropriate degrees-of-freedom, and announce his experiment as disconfirming or supporting T_0, respectively, according to whether or not the discrepancy between d and the zero value expected under T_0 is "statistically significant"—i.e., whether or not the observed value of d/s falls outside of the interval between two extreme percentiles (usually the 2.5th and 97.5th) of the t distribution with that df. If asked by his dissertation committee to justify this behavior, Hopewell would rationalize something like the following (the more honest reply, that this is what he has been taught to do, not being considered appropriate to such occasions):

In deciding whether or not T_0 *is correct, I can make two types of mistakes: I can reject* T_0 *when it is in fact correct [Type I error], or I can accept* T_0 *when in fact it is false [Type II error]. As a scientist, I have a professional obligation to be cautious, but a 5% chance of error is not unduly risky. Now if all my statistical background assumptions are correct, then, if it is really true that* $\phi = 0$ *as* T_0 *says, there is only one chance in 20 that my observed statistic* d/s *will be smaller than* $t_{.025}$ *or larger than* $t_{.975}$, *where by the latter I mean, respectively, the 2.5th and 97.5th percentiles of the* t *distribution with the same degrees-of-freedom as in my experiment. Therefore, if I reject* T_0 *when* d/s *is smaller than* $t_{.025}$ *or larger than* $t_{.975}$, *and accept* T_0 *otherwise, there is only a 5% chance that I will reject* T_0 *incorrectly.*

If asked about his Type II error, and why he did not choose some other rejection region, say between $t_{.475}$ and $t_{.525}$, which would yield the same probability of Type I error, Hopewell should reply that although he has no way to compute his probability of Type II error under the assumptions traditionally authorized by null-hypothesis procedure, it

---

1. s is here the estimate of the standard error of the difference in means, not the estimate of the individual SD.

is presumably minimized by taking the rejection region at the extremes of the t distribution.

Let us suppose that for Hopewell's data, $d = 8.50$, $s = 5.00$, and $df = 20$. Then $t_{.975} = 2.09$ and the acceptance region for the null hypothesis $\phi = 0$ is $-2.09 < d/s < 2.09$, or $-10.45 < d < 10.45$. Since d does fall within this region, standard null-hypothesis decision procedure, which I shall henceforth abbreviate "NHD," dictates that the experiment is to be reported as supporting theory T_0. (Although many persons would like to conceive NHD testing to authorize only rejection of the hypothesis, not, in addition, its acceptance when the test statistic fails to fall in the rejection region, if failure to reject were not taken as grounds for acceptance, then NHD procedure would involve no Type II error, and no justification would be given for taking the rejection region at the extremes of the distribution, rather than in its middle.) But even as Hopewell reaffirms T_0 in his dissertation, he begins to feel uneasy. In fact, several disquieting thoughts occur to him:

1. Although his test statistic falls within the orthodox acceptance region, a value this divergent from the expected zero should nonetheless be encountered less than once in 10. To argue in favor of a hypothesis on the basis of data ascribed a p value no greater than .10 (i.e., 10%) by that hypothesis certainly does not seem to be one of the more impressive displays of scientific caution.

2. After some belated reflection on the details of theory T_1, Hopewell observes that T_1 not only predicts that $\phi > 0$, but with a few simplifying assumptions no more questionable than is par for this sort of course, the value that ϕ should have can actually be computed. Suppose the value derived from T_1 in this way is $\phi = 10.0$. Then, rather than taking $\phi = 0$ as the null hypothesis, one might just as well take $\phi = 10.0$; for under the latter, $(d - 10.0)/s$ is a 20 df t statistic, giving a two-tailed, 95% significance, acceptance region for $(d - 10.0)/s$ between $-.209$ and 2.09. That is, if one lets T_1 provide the null hypothesis, it is accepted or rejected according to whether or not $-.45 < d < 20.45$, and by this latter test, therefore, Hopewell's data must be taken to support T_1—in fact, the likelihood under T_1 of obtaining a test statistic this divergent from the expected 10.0 is a most satisfactory three chances in four. Thus it occurs to Hopewell that had he chosen to cast his professional lot with the T_1-ists by selecting $\phi = 10.0$ as his null hypothesis, he could have made a strong argument in favor of T_1 by precisely the same line of statistical reasoning he has used to support T_0 under $\phi = 0$ as the null hypothesis. That is, he could have

made an argument that persons partial to T_1 would regard as strong. For behaviorists who are already convinced that T_0 is correct would howl that since T_0 is the dominant theory, only $\phi = 0$ is a legitimate null hypothesis. (And is it not strange that what constitutes a valid statistical argument should be dependent upon the majority opinion about behavior theory?)

3.   According to the NHD test of a hypothesis, only two possible final outcomes of the experiment are recognized—either the hypothesis is rejected or it is accepted. In Hopewell's experiment, all possible values of d/s between -2.09 and 2.09 have the same interpretive significance, namely, indicating that $\phi = 0$, while conversely, all possible values of d/s greater than 2.09 are equally taken to signify that $\phi \neq 0$. But Hopewell finds this disturbing, for of the various possible values that d/s might have had, the significance of $d/s = 1.70$ for the comparative merits of T_0 and T_1 should surely be more similar to that of, say, $d/s = 2.10$ than to that of, say, $d/s = -1.70$.

4.   In somewhat similar vein, it also occurs to Hopewell that had he opted for a somewhat riskier confidence level, say a Type I error of 10% rather than 5%, d/s would have fallen outside the region of acceptance and T_0 would have been rejected. Now surely the degree to which a datum corroborates or impugns a proposition should be independent of the datum-assessor's personal temerity. Yet according to orthodox significance-test procedure, whether or not a given experimental outcome supports or disconfirms the hypothesis in a question depends crucially upon the assessor's tolerance for Type I risk.

Despite his inexperience, Igor Hopewell is a sound experimentalist at heart, and the more he reflects on these statistics, the more dissatisfied with his conclusions he becomes. So while the exigencies of graduate circumstances and publication requirements urge that his dissertation be written as a confirmation of T_0, he nonetheless resolves to keep an open mind on the issue, even carrying out further research if opportunity permits. And reading his experimental report, so of course would we— has any responsible scientist ever made up his mind about such a matter on the basis of a single experiment? Yet in this obvious way we reveal how little our actual inferential behavior corresponds to the statistical procedure to which we pay lip-service. For if we did, in fact, accept or reject the null hypothesis according to whether the sample statistic falls in the acceptance or in the rejection region, then there would be no replications of experimental designs, no multiplicity of experimental approaches to an important hypothesis—a single experiment would, by definition of the method, make up our mind about the hypothesis in question. And the fact that in actual practice, a single finding seldom even tempts us to such closure of judgment reveals how little the conventional model of hypothesis testing fits our actual evaluative behavior.

Decisions vs. degrees of belief

By now, it should be obvious that something is radically amiss with the traditional NHD assessment of an experiment's theoretical import. Actually, one does not have to look far in order to find the trouble—it is simply a basic misconception about the purpose of a scientific experiment. The null-hypothesis significance test treats acceptance or rejection of a hypothesis as though these were *decisions* one makes on the basis of the experimental data—i.e., that we elect to adopt one belief, rather than another, as a result of an experimental outcome. *But the primary aim of a scientific experiment is not to precipitate decisions, but to make an appropriate adjustment in the degree to which one accepts, or believes, the hypothesis or hypotheses being tested.* And even if the purpose of the experiment *were* to reach a decision, it could not be a decision to accept or reject the hypothesis, for decisions are voluntary commitments to action—i.e., are *motor* sets—whereas acceptance or rejection of a hypothesis is a *cognitive* state which may provide the basis for rational decisions, but is not itself arrived at by such a decision (except perhaps indirectly in that a decision may initiate further experiences which influence the belief).

The situation, in other words, is as follows: As scientists, it is our professional obligation to reason from available data to explanations and generalities—i.e., beliefs—which are supported by these data. But belief in (i.e., acceptance of) a proposition is not an all-or-none affair; rather, it is a matter of degree, and the extent to which a person believes or accepts a proposition translates pragmatically into the extent to which he is willing to commit himself to the behavioral adjustments prescribed for him by the meaning of that proposition. For example, if that inveterate gambler, Unfortunate Q. Smith, has complete confidence that War Biscuit will win the fifth race at Belmont, he will be willing to accept any odds to place a bet on War Biscuit to win; for if he is absolutely *certain* that War Biscuit will win, then odds are irrelevant—it is simply a matter of arranging to collect some winnings after the race. On the other hand, the more that Smith has doubts about War Biscuit's prospects, the higher the odds he will demand before betting. That is, the *extent* to which Smith accepts or rejects the hypothesis that War Biscuit will win the fifth at Belmont is an important determinant of his betting decisions for that race.

Now, although a scientist's data supply *evidence* for the conclusions he draws from them, only in the unlikely case where the conclusions are logically deducible from or logically incompatible with the data do the data warrant that the conclusions be entirely accepted or rejected. Thus, e.g., the fact that War Biscuit has won all 16 of his previous starts is strong evidence in favor of his winning the fifth at Belmont, but by no means warrants the unreserved acceptance of this hypothesis. More generally, the data available confer upon the conclusions a certain *appropriate degree of belief*, and it is the inferential task of the scientist to pass from the data of his experiment to whatever *extent* of belief these and other available information justify in the hypothesis under investigation. In particular, the proper inferential procedure is *not* (except in the deductive case) a matter of deciding to accept (without qualification) or reject (without qualification) the hypothesis: even if adoption of a belief were a matter of voluntary action—which it is not—neither such extremes of belief or disbelief are appropriate to the data at hand. As an example of the disastrous consequences of an inferential procedure which yields only two judgment values, acceptance and rejection, consider how sad the plight of Smith would be if, whenever weighing the prospects for a given race, he always worked himself into either supreme confidence or utter disbelief that a certain horse will win. Smith would rapidly impoverish himself by accepting excessively low odds on horses he is certain will win, and failing to accept highly favorable odds on horses he is sure will lose. In fact, Smith's two judgment values need not be *extreme* acceptance and rejection in order for his inferential procedure to be maladaptive. All that is required is that the degree of belief arrived at be in general inappropriate to the likelihood conferred on the hypothesis by the data.

Now, the notion of "degree of belief appropriate to the data at hand" has an unpleasantly vague, subjective feel about it which makes it unpalatable for inclusion in a formalized theory of inference. Fortunately, a little reflection about this phrase reveals it to be intimately connected with another concept relating conclusion to evidence which, though likewise in serious need of conceptual clarification, has the virtues both of intellectual respectability and statistical familiarity. I refer, of course, to the *likelihood*, or *probability*, conferred upon a hypothesis by available evidence. Why should not Smith *feel* certain, in view of the data available, that War Biscuit will win the fifth at Belmont? Because it *is* not certain that War Biscuit will win. More generally, what determines how strongly we should accept or reject a proposition is the probability given to this hypothesis by the information at hand. For while our voluntary actions (i.e., decisions) are determined by our intensities of belief in the relevant propositions, not by their actual probabilities, expected utility is maximized when the cognitive weights given to potential but not yet known-for-certain pay-off events are represented in the decision procedure by the probabilities of these events. We may thus relinquish the concept of "appropriate degree of belief" in favor of "probability of the hypothesis," and our earlier contention about the nature of data-processing may be rephrased to say that the proper inferential task of the experimental scientist is not a simple acceptance or rejection of the tested hypothesis, but determination of the probability conferred upon it by the experimental outcome. This likelihood of the hypothesis relative to whatever data are available at the moment will be an important determinant for decisions which must currently be made, but is not itself such a decision and is entirely subject to revision in the light of additional information.

In brief, what is being argued is that the scientist, whose task is not to prescribe actions but to establish rational beliefs upon which to base them, is fundamentally and inescapably committed to an explicit concern with the problem of inverse probability. What he wants to know is how plausible are his hypotheses, and he is interested in the probability ascribed by a hypothesis to an observed experimental outcome only to the extent he is able to reason backwards to the likelihood of the hypothesis, given this outcome. Put crudely, no matter how improbable an observation may be under the hypothesis (and when there are an infinite number of possible outcomes, the probability of any particular one of these is, usually, infinitely small—the familiar p value for an observed statistic under a hypothesis H is not actually the probability of that outcome under H, but a partial integral of the probability-density function of possible outcomes under H), it is still confirmatory (or at least nondisconfirmatory, if one argues from the data to rejection of the background assumptions) so long as the likelihood of the observation is even smaller under the alternative hypotheses. To be sure, the theory of hypothesis-likelihood and inverse probability is as yet far from the level of development at which it can furnish the research scientist with inferential tools he can apply mechanically to obtain a definite likelihood estimate. But to the extent a statistical method does not at least move in the *direction* of computing the probability of the hypothesis, given the observation, that method is not truly a method of *inference*, and is unsuited for the scientist's cognitive ends.

**The methodological status
of the null-hypothesis
significance test**

The preceding arguments have, in one form or another, raised several doubts about the appropriateness of conventional significance-test decision procedure for the aims it is supposed to achieve. It is now time to bring these charges together in an explicit bill of indictment.

1. The null-hypothesis significance test treats "acceptance" or "rejection" of a hypothesis as though these were decisions one makes. But a hypothesis is not something, like a piece of pie offered for dessert, which can be accepted or rejected by a voluntary physical action. Acceptance or rejection of a hypothesis is a cognitive process, a *degree* of believing or disbelieving which, if rational, is not a matter of choice but determined solely by how likely it is, given the evidence, that the hypothesis is true.

2.   It might be argued that the NHD test may nonetheless be regarded as a legitimate decision procedure if we translate "acceptance (rejection) of the hypothesis" as meaning "acting as though the hypothesis were true (false)." And to be sure, there are many occasions on which one must base a course of action on the credibility of a scientific hypothesis. (Should these data be published? Should I devote my research resources to and become identified professionally with this theory? Can we test this new Z bomb without exterminating all life on earth?) But such a move to salvage the traditional procedure only raises two further objections. (a) While the scientist—i.e., the person—must indeed make decisions, his *science* is a systematized body of (probable) *knowledge*, not an accumulation of decisions. The end product of a scientific investigation is a degree of confidence in some set of propositions, which then constitutes a *basis* for decisions. (b) Decision theory shows the NHD test to be woefully inadequate as a decision procedure. In order to decide most effectively when or when not to act as though a hypothesis is correct, one must know both the probability of the hypothesis under the data available and the utilities of the various decision outcomes (i.e., the values of accepting the hypothesis when it is true, of accepting it when it is false, of rejecting it when it is true, and of rejecting it when it is false). But traditional NHD procedure pays no attention to utilities at all, and considers the probability of the hypothesis, given the data—i.e., the inverse probability—only in the most rudimentary way (by taking the rejection region at the extremes of the distribution rather than in its middle).

Failure of the traditional significance test to deal with inverse probabilities invalidates it not only as a method of rational inference, but *also* as a useful decision procedure.

3. The traditional NHD test unrealistically limits the significance of an experimental outcome to a mere two alternatives, confirmation or disconfirmation of the null hypothesis. Moreover, the transition from confirmation to disconfirmation as a function of the data is discontinuous—an arbitrarily small difference in the value of the test statistic can change its significance from confirmatory to disconfirmatory. Finally, the point at which this transition occurs is entirely gratuitous. There is absolutely no reason (at least provided by the method) why the point of statistical "significance" should be set at the 95% level, rather than, say the 94% or 96% level. Nor does the fact that we sometimes select a 99% level of significance, rather than the usual 95% level, mitigate this objection—one is as arbitrary as the other.

4. The null-hypothesis significance test introduces a strong bias in favor of one out of what may be a large number of reasonable alternatives. When sampling a distribution of unknown mean μ, different assumptions about the value of μ furnish an infinite number of alternate null hypotheses by which we might assess the sample mean, and whichever hypothesis is selected is thereby given an enormous, in some cases almost insurmountable, advantage over its competitors. That is, NHD procedure involves an inferential double standard—the favored hypothesis is held innocent unless proved guilty, while any alternative is held guilty until no choice remains but to judge it innocent. What is objectionable here is not that some hypotheses are held more resistant to experimental extinction than others, but that the differential weighing is an all-or-none side effect of a personal choice, and especially, that the method *necessitates* one hypothesis being favored over all the others. In the classical theory of inverse probability, on the other hand, all hypotheses are treated on a par, each receiving a weight (i.e., its "a priori" probability) which reflects the credibility of that hypothesis on grounds other than the data being assessed.

5. Finally, if anything can reveal the practical irrelevance of the conventional significance test, it should be its failure to see genuine application to the inferential behavior of the research scientist. Who has ever given up a hypothesis just because one experiment yielded a test statistic in the rejection region? And what scientist in his right mind would ever feel there to be an appreciable difference between the interpretive significance of data, say, for which one-tailed $p = .04$

and that of data for which $p = .06$, even though the point of "significance" has been set at $p = .05$? In fact, the reader may well feel undisturbed by the charges raised here against traditional NHD procedure precisely because, without perhaps realizing it, he has never taken the method seriously anyway. Paradoxically, it is often the most firmly institutionalized tenet of faith that is most susceptible to untroubled disregard—in our culture, one must early learn to live with sacrosanct verbal formulas whose import for practical behavior is seldom heeded. I suspect that the primary reasons why null-hypothesis significance testing has attained its current ritualistic status are (a) the surcease of methodological insecurity afforded by having an inferential algorithm on the books, and (b) the fact that a by-product of the algorithm is so useful, and its end product so obviously inappropriate, that the latter can be ignored without even noticing that this has, in fact, been done. What has given the traditional method its spurious feel of usefulness is that the *first*, and by far most laborious, step in the procedure, namely, estimating the probability of the experimental outcome under the assumption that a certain hypothesis is correct, is also a crucial first step toward what one is genuinely concerned with, namely, an idea of the likelihood of that hypothesis, given this experimental outcome. Having obtained this most valuable statistical information under pretext of carrying through a conventional significance test, it is then tempting, though of course quite inappropriate, to heap honor and gratitude upon the method while overlooking that its actual *result*, namely, a decision to accept or reject, is not used at all.

**Toward a more realistic
appraisal of
experimental data**

So far, my arguments have tended to be aggressively critical—one can hardly avoid polemics when butchering sacred cows. But my purpose is not just to be contentious, but to help clear the way for more realistic techniques of data assessment, and the time has now arrived for some constructive suggestions. Little of what follows pretends to any originality; I merely urge that ongoing developments along these lines should receive maximal encouragement.

For the statistical theoretician, the following problems would seem to be eminently worthy of research:

1. Of supreme importance for the theory of probability is analysis of what we mean by a proposition's "probability," relative to the evidence

provided. Most serious students of the philosophical foundations of probability and statistics agree (cf. Braithwaite, pp. 119f.) that the probability of a proposition (e.g., the probability that the General Theory of Relativity is correct) does not, prima facie, seem to be the same sort of thing as the probability of an event-class (e.g., the probability of getting a head when this coin is tossed). Do the statistical concepts and formulas which have been developed for probabilities of the latter kind also apply to hypothesis likelihoods? In particular, are the probabilities of hypotheses quantifiable at all, and for the theory of inverse probability, do Bayes' theorem and its probability-density refinements apply to hypothesis probabilities? These and similar questions are urgently in need of clarification.

2. If we are willing to assume that Bayes' theorem, or something like it, holds for hypothesis probabilities, there is much that can be done to develop the classical theory of inverse probability. While computation of inverse probabilities turns essentially upon the parametric a priori probability function, which states the probability of each alternative hypothesis in the set under consideration prior to the outcome of the experiment, it should be possible to develop theorems which are invariant over important sub-classes of a priori probability functions. In particular, the difference between the a priori probability function and the "a posteriori" probability function (i.e., the probabilities of the alternative hypotheses after the experiment), perhaps analyzed as a difference in "information," should be a potentially fruitful source of concepts with which to explore such matters as the "power" or "efficiency" of various statistics, the acquisition of inductive knowledge through repeated experimentation, etc. Another problem which seems to me to have considerable import, though not one about which I am sanguine, is whether inverse-probability theory can significantly be extended to hypothesis-probabilities, given knowledge which is only probabilistic. That is, can a theory of sentences of form "The probability of hypothesis H, given that E is the case, is p," be generalized to a theory of sentences of form "The probability of hypothesis H, given that the probability of E is q, is p?" Such a theory would seem to be necessary, e.g., if we are to cope adequately with the uncertainty attached to the background assumptions which always accompany a statistical analysis.

My suggestions for applied statistical analysis turn on the fact that while what is desired is the a posteriori probabilities of the various alternative hypotheses under consideration, computation of these by classical theory necessitates the corresponding a priori probability distribution, and in the more immediate future, at least, information about this will exist only as a subjective feel, differing from one person to the next, about the credibilities of the various hypotheses.

3. Whenever possible, the basic statistical report should be in the form of a *confidence interval*. Briefly, a confidence interval is a subset of the alternative hypotheses computed from the experimental data in such a way that for a selected confidence level α, the probability that the true hypothesis is included in a set so obtained is α. Typically, an α-level confidence interval consists of those hypotheses under which the *p* value for the experimental outcome is larger than $1 - \alpha$ (a feature of confidence intervals which is sometimes confused with their definition), in which case the confidence-interval report is similar to a simultaneous null-hypothesis significance test of each hypothesis in the total set of alternatives. Confidence intervals are the closest we can at present come to quantitative assessment of hypothesis-probabilities (see *technical note*, below), and are currently our most effective way to eliminate hypotheses from practical consideration—if we choose to act as though none of the hypotheses not included in a 95% confidence interval are correct, we stand only a 5% chance of error. (Note, moreover, that this probability of error pertains to the incorrect simultaneous "rejection" of a major part of the total set of alternative hypotheses, not just to the incorrect rejection of one as in the NHD method, and is a *total* likelihood of error, not just of Type I error.) The confidence interval is also a simple and effective way to convey that all-important statistical datum, the conditional probability (or probability density) function—i.e., the probability (probability density) of the observed outcome under each alternative hypothesis—since for a given kind of observed statistic and method of confidence-interval determination, there will be a fixed relation between the parameters of the confidence interval and those of the conditional probability (probability density) function, with the end-points of the confidence interval typically marking the points at which the conditional probability (probability density) function sinks below a certain small value related to the parameter α. The confidence-interval report is not biased toward some favored hypothesis, as is the null-hypothesis significance test, but makes an impartial simultaneous evaluation of all the alternatives under consideration. Nor does the confidence interval involve an arbitrary decision as does the NHD test. Although one person may prefer to report, say, 95% confidence intervals while another favors 99% confidence intervals, there is no conflict here, for these are simply two ways to convey the same information. An experimental report can, with complete consistency and some benefit, simultaneously present several confidence intervals

for the parameter being estimated. On the other hand, different choices of significance level in the NHD method is a clash of incompatible decisions, as attested by the fact that an NHD analysis which simultaneously presented two different significance levels would yield a logically inconsistent conclusion when the observed statistic has a value in the acceptance region of one significance level and in the rejection region of the other.

Technical Note: One of the more important problems now confronting theoretical statistics is exploration and clarification of the relationships among inverse probabilities derived from confidence-interval theory, fiducial-probability theory (a special case of the former in which the estimator is a sufficient statistic), and classical (i.e., Bayes') inverse-probability theory. While the interpretation of confidence intervals is tricky, it would be a mistake to conclude, as the cautionary remarks usually accompanying discussions of confidence intervals sometimes seem to imply, that the confidence-level α of a given confidence interval I should not really be construed as a probability that the true hypothesis, H, belongs to the set I. Nonetheless, if I is an α-level confidence interval, the probability that H belongs to I as computed by Bayes' theorem given an a priori probability distribution will, in general, *not* be equal to α, nor is the difference necessarily a small one—it is easy to construct examples where the a posteriori probability that H belongs to I is either 0 or 1. Obviously, when different techniques for computing the probability that H belongs to I yield such different answers, a reconciliation is demanded. In this instance, however, the apparent disagreement is largely if not entirely spurious, resulting from differences in the evidence relative to which the probability that H belongs to I is computed. And if this is, in fact, the correct explanation, then fiducial probability furnishes a partial solution to an outstanding difficulty in the Bayes' approach. A major weakness of the latter has always been the problem of what to assume for the a priori distribution when no pre-experimental information is available other than that supporting the background assumptions which delimit the set of hypotheses under consideration. The traditional assumption (made hesitantly by Bayes, less hesitantly by his successors) has been the "principle of insufficient reason," namely, that given no knowledge at all, all alternatives are equally likely. But not only is it difficult to give a convincing argument for this assumption, it does not even yield a unique a priori probability distribution over a continuum of alternative hypotheses, since there are many ways to express such a continuous set, and what is an equi-likelihood a priori distribution under one of these does not necessarily transform into the same under another. Now, a fiducial probability distribution determined over a set of alternative hypotheses by an experimental observation is a measure of the likelihoods of these hypotheses relative to all the information contained in the experimental data, but based on no pre-experimental information beyond the background assumptions restricting the possibilities to this particular set of hypotheses. Therefore, it seems reasonable to postulate that the no-knowledge a priori distribution in classical inverse probability theory should be that distribution which, when experimental data capable of yielding a fiducial argument are now given, results in an a posteriori distribution identical with the corresponding fiducial distribution.

4. While a confidence-interval analysis treats all the alternative hypotheses with glacial impartiality, it nonetheless frequently occurs that our interest is focused on a certain selection from the set of possibilities. In such case, the statistical analysis should also report, when computable, the precise p value of the experimental outcome, or better, though less familiarly, the probability density at that outcome, under each of the major hypotheses; for these figures will permit an immediate judgment as to which of the hypotheses is most favored by the data. In fact, an even more interesting assessment of the post-experimental credibilities of the hypotheses is then possible through use of "likelihood ratios" if one is willing to put his pre-experimental feelings about their relative likelihoods into a quantitative estimate. For let $Pr(H, d)$, $Pr(d, H)$, and $Pr(H)$ be, respectively, the probability of a hypothesis H in light of the experimental data d (added to the information already available), the probability of data d under hypothesis H, and the pre-experimental (i.e., a priori) probability of H. Then for two alternative hypotheses H_0 and H_1, it follows by classical theory that

$$\frac{Pr(H_0, d)}{Pr(H_1, d)} = \frac{Pr(H_0)}{Pr(H_1)} \times \frac{Pr(d, H_0)}{Pr(d, H_1)} \qquad (1)^2$$

Therefore, if the experimental report includes the probability (or probability density) of the data under H_0 and H_1, respectively, and

2. When the numbers of alternative hypotheses and possible experimental outcomes are transfinite, $Pr(d, H) = Pr(H, d) = Pr(H) = 0$ in most cases. If so, the probability ratios in Formula 1 are replaced with the corresponding probability-density ratios. It should be mentioned that this formula rather idealistically presupposes there to be no doubt about the correctness of the background statistical assumptions.

its reader can quantify his feelings about the relative pre-experimental merits of H_0 and H_1 (i.e., $Pr(H_0)/Pr(H_1)$), he can then determine the judgment he should make about the relative merits of H_0 and H_1 in light of these new data.

5.   Finally, experimental journals should allow the researcher much more latitude in publishing his statistics in whichever form seems most insightful, especially those forms developed by the modern theory of estimates. In particular, the stranglehold that conventional null-hypothesis significance testing has clamped on publication standards must be broken. Currently justifiable inferential algorithm carries us only through computation of conditional probabilities; from there, it is for everyman's clinical judgment and methodological conscience to see him through to a final appraisal. Insistence that published data must have the biases of the NHD method built into the report, thus seducing the unwary reader into a perhaps highly inappropriate interpretation of the data, is a professional disservice of the first magnitude.

Summary

The traditional null-hypothesis significance-test method, more appropriately called "null-hypothesis decision [NHD] procedure," of statistical analysis is here vigorously excoriated for its inappropriateness as a method of *inference*. While a number of serious objections to the method are raised, its most basic error lies in mistaking the aim of a scientific investigation to be a *decision*, rather than a *cognitive* evaluation of propositions. It is further argued that the proper application of statistics to scientific inference is irrevocably committed to extensive consideration of inverse probabilities, and to further this end, certain suggestions are offered, both for the development of statistical theory and for more illuminating application of statistical analysis to empirical data.

Reference

Braithwaite, R. B. *Scientific Explanation.* Cambridge, England: Cambridge University Press, 1953.

the test of significance in psychological research

David Bakan

That which we might identify as the "crisis of psychology" is closely related to what Hogben (1958) has called the "crisis in statistical theory." The vast majority of investigations which pass for research in the field of psychology today entail the use of statistical tests of significance. Most characteristically, when a psychologist finds a problem he wishes to investigate he converts his intuitions and hypotheses into procedures which will yield a test of significance; and will characteristically allow the result of the test of significance to bear the essential responsibility for the conclusions which he will draw.

The major point of this paper is that the test of significance does not provide the information concerning psychological phenomena characteristically attributed to it; and that, furthermore, a great deal of mischief has been associated with its use. What will be said in this paper is hardly original. It is, in a certain sense, what "everybody

From *Psychological Bulletin*, Vol. 66 (No. 6), December, 1966, pp. 423–437. Copyright 1966 by the American Psychological Association. Reproduced by permission. Reprinted in Bakan, D. *On Method: Toward a Reconstruction of Psychological Investigation.* San Francisco: Jossey-Bass, Inc., 1967.

knows." To say it "out loud" is, as it were, to assume the role of the child who pointed out that the emperor was really outfitted only in his underwear. Little of that which is contained in this paper is not already available in the literature, and the literature will be cited.

Lest what is being said in this paper be misunderstood, some clarification needs to be made at the outset. It is not a blanket criticism of statistics, mathematics, or, for that matter, even the test of significance when it can be appropriately used. The argument is rather that the test of significance has been carrying too much of the burden of scientific inference. Wise and ingenious investigators can find their way to reasonable conclusions from data because and in spite of their procedures. Too often, however, even wise and ingenious investigators, for varieties of reasons not the least of which are the editorial policies of our major psychological journals, which we will discuss below, tend to credit the test of significance with properties it does not have.

Logic of the test of significance

The test of significance has as its aim obtaining information concerning a characteristic of a *population* which is itself not directly observable, whether for practical or more intrinsic reasons. What is observable is the *sample*. The work assigned to the test of significance is that of aiding in making inferences from the observed sample to the un-observed population.

The critical assumption involved in testing significance is that, if the experiment is conducted properly, *the characteristics of the population have a designably determinative influence on samples drawn from it*, that, for example, the mean of a population has a determinative influence on the mean of a sample drawn from it. Thus if P, the population characteristic, has a determinative influence on S, the sample characteristic, then there is some license for making inferences from S to P.

If the determinative influence of P on S could be put in the form of simple logical *implication*, that P implies S, the problem would be quite simple. For, then we would have the simple situation: if P implies S, and if S is false, P is false. There are some limited instances in which this logic applies directly in sampling. For example, if the range of values in the population is between 3 and 9 (P), then the range of values in any sample must be between 3 and 9 (S). Should we find a value in a sample of, say, 10, it would mean that S is false; and we could assert that P is false.

It is clear from this, however, that, *strictly speaking*, one can only go from the denial of S to the denial of P; and not from the assertion of S to the assertion of P. It is within this context of simple logical implication that the Fisher school of statisticians have made important contributions—and it is extremely important to recognize this as the context.

In contrast, approaches based on the theorem of Bayes (Bakan, 1953, 1956; Edwards, Lindman, and Savage, 1963; Keynes, 1948; Savage, 1954; Schlaifer, 1959) would allow inferences to P from S even when S is not denied, as S adding something to the credibility of P when S is found to be the case. One of the most viable alternatives to the use of the test of significance involves the theorem of Bayes; and the paper by Edwards *et al.* (1963) is particularly directed to the attention of psychologists for use in psychological research.

The notion of the null hypothesis[1] promoted by Fisher constituted an advance *within this context* of simple logical implication. It allowed experimenters to set up a null hypothesis complementary to the hypothesis that the investigator was interested in, and provided him with a way of positively confirming his hypothesis. Thus, for example, the investigator might have the hypothesis that, say, normals differ from schizophrenics. He would then set up the *null hypothesis* that the means in the population of all normals and all schizophrenics were *equal.* Thus, the rejection of the null hypothesis constituted a way of *asserting* that the means of the populations of normals and schizophrenics *were different*, a completely reasonable device whereby to affirm a logical antecedent.

The model of simple logical implication for making inferences from S to P has another difficulty which the Fisher approach sought to overcome. This is that it is rarely meaningful to set up any simple "P implies S" model for parameters that we are interested in. In the case of the mean, for example, it is rather that P has a determinative influence on the *frequency* of any specific S. But one experiment does not provide many values of S to allow the study of their frequencies. It gives us *only one* value of S. The *sampling distribution* is conceived

---

1. There is some confusion in the literature concerning the meaning of the term null hypothesis. Fisher used the term to designate any exact hypothesis that we might be interested in disproving, and "null" was used in the sense of that which is to be nullified (cf., e.g., Berkson, 1942). It has, however, also been used to indicate a parameter of zero (cf., e.g., Lindquist, 1940, p. 15), that the difference between the population means is zero, or the correlation coefficient in the population is zero, the difference in proportions in the population is zero, etc. Since both meanings are usually intended in psychological research, it causes little difficulty.

which specifies the relative frequencies of all possible values of *S*. Then, with the help of an adopted *level of significance*, we could, *in effect*, say that *S* was false; that is, any *S* which fell in a region whose relative theoretical frequency under the null hypothesis was, say, 5 % would be *considered* false. If such an *S* actually occurred, we would be in a position to declare *P* to be false, still within the model of simple logical implication.

It is important to recognize that one of the essential features of the Fisher approach is what may be called the *once-ness* of the experiment; the inference model takes as critical that the experiment has been conducted *once*. If an *S* which has a low probability under the null hypothesis actually occurs, it is taken that the null hypothesis is false. As Fisher (1947, p. 14) put it, why should the theoretically rare event under the null hypothesis actually occur to "us"? If it does occur, we take it that the null hypothesis is false. Basic is the idea that "the theoretically unusual does not happen to me." [2] It should be noted that the referent for all probability considerations is neither in the population itself nor the subjective confidence of the investigator. It is rather in a hypothetical population of experiments all conducted in the same manner, but *only one of which is actually conducted*. Thus, of course, the probability of falsely rejecting the null hypothesis if it were true is exactly that value which has been taken as the level of significance. Replication of the experiment vitiates the validity of the inference model, unless the replication itself is taken into account in the model and the probabilities of the model modified accordingly (as is done in various designs which entail replication, where, however, the total experiment, including the replications, is again considered as *one* experiment). According to Fisher (1947), "it is an essential characteristic of experimentation that it is carried out with limited resources [p. 18]." In the Fisher approach, the "limited resources" is not only a making of the best out of a limited situation, but is rather an integral feature of the

---

2. I playfully once conducted the following "experiment": Suppose, I said, that every coin has associated with it a "spirit"; and suppose, furthermore, that if the spirit is implored properly, the coin will veer head or tail as one requests of the spirit. I thus invoked the spirit to make the coin fall head. I threw it once, it came up head. I did it again, it came up head again. I did this six times, and got six heads. Under the null hypothesis the probability of occurrence of six heads is $(\frac{1}{2})^6 = .016$, significant at the 2% level of significance. I have never repeated the experiment. But, then, the logic of the inference model does not really demand that I do! It may be objected that the coin, or my tossing, or even my observation was biased. But I submit that such things were in all likelihood not as involved in the result as corresponding things in most psychological research.

inference model itself. Lest he be done a complete injustice, it should be pointed out that he did say, "In relation to the test of significance, we may say that a phenomenon is experimentally demonstrable when we know how to conduct an experiment which will rarely fail to give us statistically significant results [1947, p. 14]." However, although Fisher "himself" believes this, it is *not* built into the inference model.[3]

Difficulties of the null hypothesis

As already indicated, research workers in the field of psychology place a heavy burden on the test of significance. Let us consider some of the difficulties associated with the null hypothesis.

1. The a priori reasons for believing that the null hypothesis is generally false anyway

One of the common experiences of research workers is the very high frequency with which significant results are obtained with large samples. Some years ago, the author had occasion to run a number of tests of significance on a battery of tests collected on about 60,000 subjects from all over the United States. Every test came out significant. Dividing the cards by such arbitrary criteria as east vs. west of the Mississippi River, Maine vs. the rest of the country, North vs. South, etc., all produced significant differences in means. In some instances, the differences in the sample means were quite small, but nonetheless, the *p* values were all very low. Nunnally (1960) has reported a similar experience involving correlation coefficients on 700 subjects. Joseph Berkson (1938) made the observation almost 30 years ago in connection with chi-square:

I believe that an observant statistician who has had any considerable experience with applying the chi-square test repeatedly will agree with my statement that, as a matter of observation, when the numbers in the data are quite large, the P's tend to come out small. Having observed this,

---

3. Possibly not even this criterion is sound. It may be that a number of statistically significant results which are *borderline* "speak for the null hypothesis rather than against it [Edwards *et al.*, 1963, p. 235]." If the null hypothesis were really false, then with an increase in the number of instances in which it can be rejected, there should be some substantial proportion of more dramatic rejections rather than borderline rejections.

and on reflection, I make the following dogmatic statement, referring for illustration to the normal curve: "If the normal curve is fitted to a body of data representing any real observations whatever of quantities in the physical world, then if the number of observations is extremely large—for instance, on an order of 200,000—the chi-square P will be small beyond any usual limit of significance."

This dogmatic statement is made on the basis of an extrapolation of the observation referred to and can also be defended as a prediction from a priori *considerations. For we may assume that it is practically certain that any series of real observations does not actually follow a normal curve with absolute exactitude in all respects, and no matter how small the discrepancy between the normal curve and the true curve of observations, the chi-square P will be small if the sample has a sufficiently large number of observations in it.*

If this be so, then we have something here that is apt to trouble the conscience of a reflective statistician using the chi-square test. For I suppose it would be agreed by statisticians that a large sample is always better than a small sample. If, then, we know in advance the P that will result from an application of a chi-square test to a large sample, there would seem to be no use in doing it on a smaller one. But since the result of the former test is known, it is no test at all [pp. 526–527].

As one group of authors has put it, "in typical applications . . . the null hypothesis . . . is known by all concerned to be false from the outset [Edwards *et al.*, 1963, p. 214]." The fact of the matter is that *there is really no good reason to expect the null hypothesis to be true in any population.* Why should the mean, say, of all scores east of the Mississippi be *identical* to all scores west of the Mississippi? Why should any correlation coefficient be *exactly* .00 in the population? Why should we expect the ratio of males to females be *exactly* 50:50 in any population? Or why should different drugs have *exactly* the same effect on any population parameter (Smith, 1960)? *A glance at any set of statistics on total populations will quickly confirm the rarity of the null hypothesis in nature.*

The reason why the null hypothesis is characteristically rejected with large samples was made patent by the theoretical work of Neyman and Pearson (1933). The probability of rejecting the null hypothesis is a function of five factors: whether the test is one- or two-tailed, the level of significance, the standard deviation, the amount of deviation from the null hypothesis, *and the number of observations.* The choice of a one- or two-tailed test is the investigator's; the level of significance is also based on the choice of the investigator; the standard deviation is a given of the situation, and is characteristically reasonably well estimated; the deviation from the null hypothesis is what is unknown; and the choice of the number of cases in psychological work is characteristically arbitrary or expeditious. Should there be any deviation from the null hypothesis in the population, *no matter how small*—and we have little doubt that such a deviation usually exists—a sufficiently large number of observations will lead to the rejection of the null hypothesis. As Nunnally (1960) put it,

if the null hypothesis is not rejected, it is usually because the N is too small. If enough data are gathered, the hypothesis will generally be rejected. If rejection of the null hypothesis were the real intention in psychological experiments, there usually would be no need to gather data [*p.* 643].

2. Type I error and publication practices

The Type I error is the error of rejecting the null hypothesis when it is indeed true, and its probability is the level of significance. Later in this paper we will discuss the distinction between *sharp* and *loose* null hypotheses. The sharp null hypothesis, which we have been discussing, is an exact value for the null hypothesis as, for example, the difference between population means being precisely zero. A loose null hypothesis is one in which it is conceived of as being *around* null. Sharp null hypotheses, as we have indicated, rarely exist in nature. Assuming that loose null hypotheses are not rare, and that their testing may make sense under some circumstances, let us consider the role of the publication practices of our journals in their connection.

It is the practice of editors of our psychological journals, receiving many more papers than they can possibly publish, to use the magnitude of the *p* values reported as one criterion for acceptance or rejection of a study. For example, consider the following statement made by Arthur W. Melton (1962) on completing 12 years as editor of the *Journal of Experimental Psychology*, certainly one of the most prestigious and scientifically meticulous psychological journals. In enumerating the criteria by which articles were evaluated, he said:

The next step in the assessment of an article involved a judgment with respect to the confidence to be placed in the findings—confidence that the results of the experiment would be repeatable under the conditions described. In editing the Journal *there has been a strong reluctance to accept and publish results related to the principal concern of the research when those results were significant at the .05 level, whether by one- or two-tailed test. This has not implied a slavish worship of the .01 level, as some critics may have implied. Rather, it reflects a belief that it is the responsibility of the investigator in a science to reveal his effect in such a way that no reasonable man would be in a position to discredit the results by saying that they were the product of the way the ball bounces [pp. 553–554].*

His clearly expressed opinion that nonsignificant results should not take up the space of the journals is shared by most editors of psychological journals. It is important to point out that I am not advocating a change in policy in this connection. In the total research enterprise where so much of the load for making inferences concerning the nature of phenomena is carried by the test of significance, the editors can do little else. The point is rather that the situation in regard to publication makes manifest the difficulties in connection with the overemphasis on the test of significance as a principal basis for making inferences.

McNemar (1960) has rightly pointed out that not only do journal editors reject papers in which the results are not significant, but that papers in which significance has not been obtained are not submitted, that investigators select out their significant findings for inclusion in their reports, and that theory-oriented research workers tend to discard data which do not work to confirm their theories. The result of all of this is that "published results are more likely to involve false rejection of null hypotheses than indicated by the stated levels of significance [p. 300]," that is, published results which are significant may well have Type I errors in them far in excess of, say, the 5% which we may allow ourselves.

The suspicion that the Type I error may well be plaguing our literature is given confirmation in an analysis of articles published in the *Journal of Abnormal and Social Psychology* for one complete year (Cohen, 1962). Analyzing 70 studies in which significant results were obtained with respect to the power of the statistical tests used, Cohen found that power, the probability of rejecting the null hypothesis when the null hypothesis was false, was characteristically meager. Theoretically, with such tests, one should not often expect significant results even when the null hypothesis was false. Yet, there they were! Even if deviations from null existed in the relevant populations, the investigations were characteristically not powerful enough to have detected them. This strongly suggests that there is something additional associated with these rejections of the null hypotheses in question. It strongly points to the possibility that the manner in which studies get published is associated with the findings; that *the very publication practices themselves are part and parcel of the probabilistic processes on which we base our conclusions concerning the nature of psychological phenomena.* Our total research enterprise is, at least in part, a kind of scientific roulette, in which the "lucky," or constant player, "wins," that is, gets his paper or papers published. And certainly, going from 5% to 1% does not eliminate the possibility that it is "the way the ball bounces," to use Melton's phrase. It changes the odds in this roulette, but it does not make it less a game of roulette.

The damage to the scientific enterprise is compounded by the fact that the publication of "significant" results tends to stop further investigation. If the publication of papers containing Type I errors tended to foster further investigation so that the psychological phenomena with which we are concerned would be further probed by others, it would not be too bad. But it does not. Quite the contrary. As Lindquist (1940, p. 17) has correctly pointed out, the danger to science of the Type I error is much more serious than the Type II error—for when a Type I error is committed, it has the effect of stopping investigation. A highly significant result appears definitive, as Melton's comments indicate. In the 12 years that he edited the *Journal of Experimental Psychology*, he sought to select papers which were worthy of being placed in the "archives," as he put it. Even the strict repetition of an experiment and not getting significance in the same way does not speak against the result already reported in the literature. For failing to get significance, speaking strictly within the inference model, only means that that experiment is inconclusive; whereas the study already reported in the literature, with a low *p* value, is regarded as conclusive. Thus we tend to place in the archives studies with a relatively high number of Type I errors, or, at any rate, studies which reflect small deviations from null in the respective populations; and we act in such a fashion as to reduce the likelihood of their correction.

**Psychologist's "adjustment"
by misinterpretation**

The psychological literature is filled with misinterpretations of the nature of the test of significance. One may be tempted to attribute this to such things as lack of proper education, the simple fact that humans may err, and the prevailing tendency to take a cookbook approach in which the mathematical and philosophical framework out of which the tests of significance emerge are ignored; that, in other words, these misinterpretations are somehow the result of simple intellectual inadequacy on the part of psychologists. However, such an explanation is hardly tenable. Graduate schools are adamant with respect to statistical education. Any number of psychologists have taken out substantial amounts of time to equip themselves mathematically and philosophically. Psychologists as a group do a great deal of mutual criticism. Editorial reviews prior to publication are carried out with eminent conscientiousness. There is even a substantial literature devoted to various kinds of "misuse" of statistical procedures, to which not a little attention has been paid.

It is rather that the test of significance is profoundly interwoven with other strands of the psychological research enterprise in such a way that it constitutes a critical part of the total cultural-scientific tapestry. To pull out the strand of the test of significance would seem to make the whole tapestry fall apart. In the face of the intrinsic difficulties that the test of significance provides, we rather attempt to make an "adjustment" by attributing to the test of significance characteristics which it does not have, and overlook characteristics that it does have. The difficulty is that the test of significance can, especially when not considered too carefully, do *some* work; for, after all, the results of the test of significance *are* related to the phenomena in which we are interested. One may well ask whether we do not have here, perhaps, an instance of the phenomenon that learning under partial reinforcement is very highly resistant to extinction. Some of these misinterpretations are as follows:

1. Taking the p value as a "measure" of significance

A common misinterpretation of the test of significance is to regard it as a "measure" of significance. It is interpreted as the answer to the question "How significant is it?" A p value of .05 is thought of as less significant than a p value of .01, and so on. The characteristic practice on the part of psychologists is to compute, say, a t, and then "look up" the significance in the table, taking the p value as a *function of* t, and thereby a "measure" of significance. Indeed, since the p value is inversely related to the magnitude of, say, the difference between means *in the sample*, it can function as a kind of "standard score" measure for a variety of different experiments. Mathematically, the t is actually very similar to a "standard score," entailing a deviation in the numerator, and a function of the variation in the denominator; and the p value is a "function" of t. If this use were explicit, it would perhaps not be too bad. But it must be remembered that this is using the p value as a *statistic descriptive of the sample alone*, and does not automatically give an inference to the population. There is even the practice of using tests of significance in studies of total populations, in which the observations cannot by any stretch of the imagination be thought of as having been randomly selected from any designable population.[4] Using the *p* value in this way, in which the statistical inference model is even hinted at, is completely indefensible; for the single function of the statistical inference model is making inferences to populations from samples.

The practice of "looking up" the *p* value for the *t*, which has even been advocated in some of our statistical handbooks (e.g., Lacey, 1953, p. 117; Underwood, Duncan, Taylor, and Cotton, 1954, p. 129), rather than looking up the *t* for a given *p* value, violates the inference model. The inference model is based on the presumption that one *initially* adopts a level of significance as the specification of that probability which is too slow to occur to "us," as Fisher has put it, in this one instance, and under the null hypothesis. A purist might speak of the "delicate problem . . . of fudging with a posteriori alpha values [levels of significance. Kaiser, 1960, p. 165]," as though the levels of significance were initially decided upon, but rarely do psychological research workers or editors take the level of significance as other than a "measure."

But taken as a "measure," it is only a measure of the sample. Psychologists often erroneously believe that the *p* value is "the probability that the results are due to chance," as Wilson (1961, p. 230) has pointed out; that a *p* value of .05 means that the chances are .95 that the scientific hypothesis is correct, as Bolles (1962) has pointed out; that it is a measure of the power to "predict" the behavior of a population (Underwood *et al.*, 1954, p. 107); and that it is a measure of the "confidence that the results of the experiment would be repeatable under the conditions described," as Melton put it. Unfortunately, none of these interpretations are within the inference model of the test of significance. Some of our statistical handbooks have "allowed" misinterpretation. For example, in discussing the erroneous rhetoric associated with talking of the "probability" of a population parameter (in the inference model there is no probability associated with something which is either true or false), Lindquist (1940) said, "For most practical purposes, the end result is the same as if the 'level of confidence' type of interpretation is employed [p. 14]." Ferguson (1959) wrote, "The .05 and .01 probability levels are descriptive of our degree of confidence [p. 133]." There is little question but that sizable differences, correlations, etc., in *samples*, especially samples of reasonable size, speak more

---

4. It was decided not to cite any specific studies to exemplify points such as this one. The reader will undoubtedly be able to supply them for himself.

strongly of sizable differences, correlations, etc., in the population; and there is little question but that if there is real and strong effect in the population, it will continue to manifest itself in further sampling. However, these are inferences which *we* may make. They are outside the inference model associated with the test of significance. The *p* value within the inference model is only the value which we take to be as how improbable an event could be under the null hypothesis, which we judge will not take place to "us," in this one experiment. *It is not a "measure" of the goodness of the other inferences which we might make.* It is an a priori condition that we set up whereby we decide whether or not we will reject the null hypothesis, not a measure of significance.

There is a study in the literature (Rosenthal and Gaito, 1963) which points up sharply the lack of understanding on the part of psychologists of the meaning of the test of significance. The subjects were 9 members of the psychology department faculty, all holding doctoral degrees, and 10 graduate students, at the University of North Dakota; and there is little reason to believe that this group of psychologists was more or less sophisticated than any other. They were asked to rate their degree of belief or confidence in results of hypothetical studies for a variety of *p* values, and for *n*'s of 10 and 100. That there should be a relationship between the average rated confidence or belief and *p* value, as they found, is to be expected. What is shocking is that these psychologists indicated substantially greater confidence or belief in results associated with the larger sample size for the same *p* values! According to the theory, especially as this has been amplified by Neyman and Pearson (1933), the probability of rejecting the null hypothesis for any given deviation from null and *p* value *increases* as a function of the number of observations. The rejection of the null hypothesis when the number of cases is small speaks for a more dramatic effect in the population; and if the *p* value is the same, the probability of committing a Type I error remains the same. Thus one can be more confident with a small *n* than a large *n*. The question is, how could a group of psychologists be so wrong? I believe that this wrongness is based on the commonly held belief that the *p* value is a "measure" of degree of confidence. Thus, the reasoning behind such a wrong set of answers by these psychologists may well have been something like this: the *p* value is a measure of confidence; but a larger number of cases also increases confidence; therefore, for any given *p* value, the degree of confidence should be higher for the larger *n*. The wrong conclusion arises from the erroneous character of the first premise, and from the failure to recognize that the *p* value is a function of sample size for any given deviation from null in the population. The author knows of instances in which editors of very reputable psychological journals have rejected papers in which the p values and n's were small on the grounds that there were not enough observations, clearly demonstrating that the same mode of thought is operating in them. Indeed, rejecting the null hypothesis with a small n is indicative of a strong deviation from null in the population, the mathematics of the test of significance having already taken into account the smallness of the sample. Increasing the n increases the probability of rejecting the null hypothesis; and in these studies rejected for small sample size, that task has already been accomplished. These editors are, of course, in some sense the ultimate "teachers" of the profession; and they have been teaching something which is patently wrong!

2. Automaticity of inference

What may be considered to be a dream, fantasy, or ideal in the culture of psychology is that of achieving complete automaticity of inference. The making of inductive generalizations is always somewhat risky. In Fisher's *The Design of Experiments* (1947, p. 4), he made the claim that the methods of induction could be made rigorous, exemplified by the procedures which he was setting forth. This is indeed quite correct in the sense indicated earlier. In a later paper, he made explicit what was strongly hinted at in his earlier writing, that the methods which he proposed constituted a relatively *complete* specification of the process of induction:

That such a process induction existed and was possible to normal minds, has been understood for centuries; it is only with the recent development of statistical science that an analytic account can now be given, about as satisfying and complete, at least, as that given traditionally of the deductive processes [Fisher, 1955, p. 74].

Psychologists certainly took the procedures associated with the t test, F test, and so on, in this manner. *Instead* of having to engage in inference themselves, they had but to "run the tests" for the purpose of making inferences, since, as it appeared, the statistical tests were analytic analogues of inductive inference. The "operationist" orientation among psychologists, which recognized the contingency of knowledge on the knowledge-getting operations and advocated their specification, could, it would seem, "operationalize" the inferential processes simply by reporting the details of the statistical analysis! It thus removed the burden of responsibility, the chance of being wrong, the necessity for making inductive inferences, from the shoulders of the investigator and placed them on the tests of significance. The contingency of the conclusion upon the experimenter's decision of the level of significance was managed in two ways. The first, by resting on a kind of social agreement that 5 % was good, and 1 % better. The second in the manner which has already been discussed, by not making a decision of the level of significance, but only reporting the *p* value as a "result" and a presumably objective "measure" of degree of confidence. But that the probability of getting significance is also contingent upon the number of observations has been handled largely by ignoring it.

A crisis was experienced among psychologists when the matter of the one- versus the two-tailed test came into prominence; for here the contingency of the result of a test of significance on a decision of the investigator was simply too conspicuous to be ignored. An investigator, say, was interested in the difference between two groups on some measure. He collected his data, found that Mean A was greater than Mean B in the sample, and ran the ordinary two-tailed *t* test; and, let us say, it was not significant. Then he bethought himself. The two-tailed test tested against *two* alternatives, that the population Mean A was greater than population Mean B and vice versa. But then, he really wanted to know whether Mean A was greater than Mean B. Thus, he could run a one-tailed test. He did this and found, since the one-tailed test is more powerful, that his difference was now significant.

Now here there was a difficulty. The test of significance is not nearly so automatic an inference process as had been thought. It is manifestly contingent on the decision of the investigator as to whether to run a one- or a two-tailed test. And somehow, making the decision *after* the data were collected and the means computed, seemed like "cheating." How should this be handled? Should there be some central registry in which one registers one's decision to run a one- or two-tailed test before collecting the data? Should one, as one eminent psychologist once suggested to me, send oneself a letter so that the postmark would prove that one had pre-decided to run a one-tailed test? The literature on ways of handling this difficulty has grown quite a bit in the strain to somehow overcome this particular clear contingency of the results of a test of significance on the decision of the investigator. The author will not attempt here to review this literature, except to cite one very competent paper which points up the intrinsic difficulty associated with this problem, the *reductio ad absurdum* to which one comes. Kaiser (1960), early in his paper, distinguished between the *logic* associated with the test of significance and other forms of inference, a distinction which, incidentally, Fisher would hardly have allowed: "The arguments developed in this paper are based on logical considerations in statistical inference. (We do not, of course, suggest that statistical inference is the only basis for scientific inference) [p. 160]." But then, having taken the position that he is going to follow the logic of statistical inference relentlessly, he said (Kaiser's italics): "*we cannot logically make a directional statistical decision or statement when the null hypothesis is rejected on the basis of the direction of the difference in the observed sample means* [p. 161]." One really needs to strike oneself in the head! If Sample Mean A is greater than Sample Mean B, and there is reason to reject the null hypothesis, in what other direction can it reasonably be? What kind of logic is it that leads one to believe that it could be otherwise than that Population Mean A is greater than Population Mean B? We do not know whether Kaiser intended his paper as a *reductio ad absurdum*, but it certainly turned out that way.

The issue of the one- versus the two-tailed test genuinely challenges the presumptive "objectivity" characteristically attributed to the test of significance. On the one hand, it makes patent what was the case under any circumstances (at the least in the choice of level of significance, and the choice of the number of cases in the sample), that the conclusion is contingent upon the decision of the investigator. An astute investigator, who foresaw the results, and who therefore pre-decided to use a one-tailed test, will get one *p* value. The less astute but honorable investigator, who did not foresee the results, would feel obliged to use a two-tailed test, and would get another *p* value. On the other hand, if one decides to be relentlessly logical within the logic of statistical inference, one winds up with the kind of absurdity which we have cited above.

3. The confusion of induction to the aggregate with induction to the general

Consider a not atypical investigation of the following sort: A group of, say, 20 normals and a group of, say, 20 schizophrenics are given a test. The tests are scored, and a *t* test is run, and it is found that the means differ significantly at some level of significance, say 1 %. What inference can be drawn? As we have already indicated, the investigator could have insured this result by choosing a sufficiently large number of cases. Suppose we overlook this objection, which we can to some extent, by saying that the difference between the means in the population must have been *large enough* to have manifested itself with only 40 cases. But still, what do we know from this? The *only* inference which this allows is that the mean of all normals is different from the mean of all schizophrenics in the populations from which the samples have presumably been drawn at random. (Rarely is the criterion of randomness satisfied. But let us overlook this objection too.)

The common rhetoric in which such results are discussed is in the form "Schizophrenics differ from normals in such and such ways." The sense that both the reader and the writer have of this rhetoric is that it has been justified by the finding of significance. Yet clearly it does not mean *all* schizophrenics and *all* normals. All that the test of significance justifies is that *measures of central tendency of the aggregates* differ in the populations. The test of significance has *not* addressed itself to anything about the schizophrenia or normality which characterizes *each* member of the respective populations. Now it is certainly possible for an investigator to develop a hypothesis about the nature of schizophrenia *from which he may infer* that there should be differences between the means in the populations; and his finding of a significant difference in the means of his sample would add to the credibility of the former. However, that 1% which he obtained in his study bears only on the means of the populations, and is not a "measure" of the confidence that he may have in his hypothesis concerning the nature of schizophrenia. There are *two* inferences that he must make. One is that of the sample to the population, for which the test of significance is of some use. The other is from his inference concerning the population to his hypothesis concerning the nature of schizophrenia. The *p* value does not bear on this second inference. The psychological literature is filled with assertions which confound these two inferential processes.

Or consider another hardly atypical style of research. Say an experimenter divides 40 subjects at random into two groups of 20 subjects each. One group is assigned to one condition and the other to another condition, perhaps, say, massing and distribution of trials. The subjects are given a learning task, one group under massed conditions, the other under distributed conditions. The experimenter runs a *t* test on the learning measure and again, say, finds that the difference is significant at the 1% level of significance. He may then say in his report, being more careful than the psychologist who was studying the difference between normals and schizophrenics (being more "scientific" than his clinically-interested colleague), that "the mean in the population of learning under massed conditions is lower than the mean in the population of learning under distributed conditions," feeling that he can say this with a good deal of certainty because of his test of significance. But here too (like his clinical colleague) he has made *two* inferences, and not one, and the 1% bears on the one but not the other. The statistical inference model certainly allows him to make his statement for the population, but only for *that* learning task, and the *p* value is appropriate only to that. But the generalization to "massed conditions" and "distributed conditions" beyond that particular learning task is a second inference with respect to which the *p* value is not relevant. The psychological literature is plagued with any number of instances in which the rhetoric indicates that the *p* value does bear on this second inference.

Part of the blame for this confusion can be ascribed to Fisher who, in *The Design of Experiments* (1947, p. 9), suggested that the mathematical methods which he proposed were exhaustive of scientific induction, and that the principles he was advancing were "common to all experimentation." What he failed to see and to say was that after an inference was made concerning a population parameter, *one still needed to engage in induction* to obtain meaningful scientific propositions.

To regard the methods of statistical inference as exhaustive of the inductive inferences called for in experimentation is completely confounding. When the test of significance has been run, the necessity for induction has hardly been completely satisfied. However, the research worker knows this, in some sense, and proceeds, as he should, to make further inductive inferences. He is, however, still ensnarled in his test of significance and the presumption that *it* is the whole of his inductive activity, and thus mistakenly takes a low *p* value for the measure of the validity of his *other* inductions.

The seriousness of this confusion may be seen by again referring back to the Rosenthal and Gaito (1963) study and the remark by Berkson which indicate that research workers believe that a large sample is better than a small sample. We need to refine the rhetoric somewhat. Induction consists in making inferences from the particular to the general. It is certainly the case that as confirming particulars are added, the credibility of the general is increased. However, *the addition of observations to a sample is*, in the context of statistical inference, *not the addition of particulars* but the modification of what is *one particular* in the inference model, the sample aggregate. In the context of statistical inference, it is not necessarily true that "a large sample is better than a small sample." For, as has been already indicated, obtaining a significant result with a small sample suggests a larger deviation from null in the population, and may be considerably more meaningful. Thus more particulars are better than fewer particulars on the making of an inductive inference; but not necessarily a larger sample.

In the marriage of psychological research and statistical inference, psychology brought its own reasons for accepting this confusion, reasons which inhere in the history of psychology. Measurement psychology arises out of two radically different traditions, as has been pointed out by Guilford (1936, pp. 5 ff.) and Cronbach (1957), and the matter of putting them together raised certain difficulties. The one tradition seeks to find propositions concerning the nature of man in *general*—propositions of a general nature, with each *individual a particular* in which the general is manifest. This is the kind of psychology associated with the traditional experimental psychology of Fechner, Ebbinghaus, Wundt, and Titchener. It seeks to find the laws which characterize the "generalized, normal, human, adult mind [Boring, 1950, p. 413]." The research strategy associated with this kind of psychology is straightforwardly inductive. It seeks inductive generalizations which will apply to *every* member of a designated class. A single particular in which a generalization fails forces a rejection of the generalization, calling for either a redefinition of the class to which it applies or a modification of the generalization. The other tradition is the psychology of individual differences, which has its roots more in England and the United States than on the continent. We may recall that when the young American, James McKeen Cattell, who invented the term *mental test*, came to Wundt with his own problem of individual differences, it was regarded by Wundt as *ganz Amerikanisch* (Boring, 1950, p. 324).

The basic datum for an individual-differences approach is not anything that characterizes *each* of two subjects, but the *difference between them*. For this latter tradition, it is the *aggregate* which is of interest, and not the general. One of the most unfortunate characteristics of many studies in psychology, especially in experimental psychology, is that the data are treated as aggregates while the experimenter is trying to infer general propositions. There is hardly an issue of most of the major psychological journals reporting experimentation in which this confusion does not appear several times; and in which the test of significance, which has some value in connection with the study of aggregates, is not interpreted as a measure of the credibility of the general proposition in which the investigator is interested.

The distinction between the aggregate and the general may be illuminated by a small mathematical exercise. The methods of analysis of variance developed by Fisher and his school have become techniques of choice among psychologists. However, at root, the methods of analysis of variance do not deal with that which any two or more subjects may have in common, but consider only *differences between* scores. This is all that is analyzed by analysis of variance. The following identity illustrates this clearly, showing that the original total sum squares, of which everything else in any analysis of variance is simply the partitioning of, is based on the literal difference between each pair of scores (cf. Bakan, 1955). Except for n, it is the only information used from the data:

$$\sum_{i=1}^{n} (X_i - \bar{X})^2 = \frac{1}{2}\left[\frac{(X_1 - X_2)}{1}\right]^2$$

$$+ \frac{2}{3}\left[\frac{(X_1 - X_3) + (X_2 - X_3)}{2}\right]^2 + \cdots$$

$$+ \frac{n-1}{n}\left[\frac{(X_1 - X_n) + \cdots + (X_{n-1} - X_n)}{n-1}\right]^2.$$

Thus, what took place historically in psychology is that instead of attempting to *synthesize* the two traditional approaches to psychological phenomena, which is both possible and desirable, a syncretic combination took place of the methods appropriate to the study of aggregates with the aims of a psychology which sought for general propositions. One of the most overworked terms, which added not a little to the essential confusion, was the term "error," which was a kind of umbrella term for (at the least) variation among scores from different individuals, variation among measurements for the same individual, and variation among samples.

Let us add another historical note. In 1936, Guilford published his well-known *Psychometric Methods*. In this book, which became a kind of "bible" for many psychologists, he made a noble effort at a "Rapprochement of Psychophysical and Test Methods" (p. 9). He observed, quite properly, that mathematical developments in each of the two fields might be of value in the other, that "Both psychophysics and mental testing have rested upon the same fundamental statistical devices [p. 9]." There is no question of the truth of this. However, what he failed to emphasize sufficiently was that mathematics is so abstract that the same mathematics is applicable to rather different fields of investigation without there being any necessary further identity between them. (One would not, for example, argue that business and genetics are essentially the same because the same arithmetic is applicable to market research and in the investigation of the facts of heredity.) A critical point of contract between the two traditions was in connection with scaling in which Cattell's principle that "equally often noticed differences are equal unless always or never noticed [Guilford, 1936, p. 217]" was adopted as a fundamental assumption. The "equally often noticed differences" is, of course, based on aggregates. By means of this assumption, one could collapse the distinction between the two areas of investigation. Indeed, this is not really too bad if one is alert to the fact that *it is* an assumption, one which even has considerable pragmatic value. As a set of techniques whereby data could be analyzed, that is, as a set of techniques whereby one could *describe* one's findings, and then make inductions about the nature of the psychological phenomena, that which Guilford put together in his book was eminently valuable. However, around this time the work of Fisher and his school was coming to the attention of psychologists. It was attractive for several reasons. It offered advice for handling "small samples." It offered a number of eminently ingenious new ways of organizing and extracting information from data. It offered ways by which several variables could be analyzed simultaneously, away from the old notion that one had to keep everything constant and vary only one variable at a time. It showed how the effect of the "interaction" of variables could be assessed. But it also claimed to have mathematized induction! The Fisher approach was thus "bought," and psychologists got a theory of induction in the bargain, a theory which seemed to exhaust the inductive processes. Whereas the question of the "reliability" of statistics had been a matter of concern for some time before (although frequently very garbled), it had not carried the burden of induction to the degree that it did with the Fisher approach. With the "buying" of the Fisher approach the psychological research worker also brought, and then overused, the test of significance, employing it as the measure of the significance, in the largest sense of the word, of his research efforts.

Sharp and loose
null hypotheses

Earlier, a distinction was made between sharp and loose null hypotheses. One of the major difficulties associated with the Fisher approach is the problem presented by sharp null hypotheses; for, as we have already seen, there is reason to believe that the existence of sharp null hypotheses is characteristically unlikely. There have been some efforts to correct for this difficulty by proposing the use of loose null hypotheses; in place of a single point, a region being considered null. Hodges and Lehmann (1954) have proposed a distinction between "statistical significance," which entails the sharp hypothesis, and "material significance," in which one tests the hypothesis of a deviation of a stated amount from the null point instead of the null point itself. Edwards (1950, pp. 30–31) has suggested the notion of "practical significance" in which one takes into account the meaning, in some practical sense, of the magnitude of the deviation from null together with the number of observations which have been involved in getting statistical significance. Binder (1963) has equally argued that a subset of parameters be equated with the null hypothesis. Essentially what has been suggested is that the investigator make some kind of a decision concerning "How much, say, of a difference makes a difference?" The difficulty with this solution, which is certainly a sound one technically, is that in psychological research we do not often have very good grounds for answering this question. This is partly due to the inadequacies of psychological measurement, but mostly due to the fact that the answer to the question of "How much of a difference makes a difference?" is not forthcoming outside of some particular practical context. The question calls forth another question, "How much of a difference makes a difference *for what?*"

Decisions vs. assertions

This brings us to one of the major issues within the field of statistics itself. The problems of the research psychologist do not generally lie within practical contexts. He is rather interested in making assertions concerning psychological functions which have a reasonable amount of credibility associated with them. He is more concerned with "What is the case?" than with "What is wise to do?" (cf. Rozeboom, 1960).

It is here that the decision-theory approach of Neyman, Pearson, and Wald (Neyman, 1937, 1957; Neyman and Pearson, 1933; Wald, 1939, 1950, 1955) becomes relevant. The decision-theory school, still basing itself on some basic notions of the Fisher approach, deviated from it in several respects:

1. In Fisher's inference model, the two alternatives between which one chose on the basis of an experiment were *reject* and *inconclusive*. As he said in *The Design of Experiments* (1947), "the null hypothesis is never proved or established, but is possibly disproved, in the course of experimentation [p. 16]." In the decision-theory approach, the two alternatives are rather *reject* and *accept*.

2. Whereas in the Fisher approach the interpretation of the test of significance critically depends on having one sample from a *hypothetical* population of experiments, the decision-theory approach conceives of, is applicable to, and is sensible with respect to numerous repetitions of the experiment.

3. The decision-theory approach added the notions of the Type II

error (which can be made only if the null hypothesis is accepted) and power as significant features of their model.

4.   The decision-theory model gave a significant place to the matter of what is concretely lost if an error is made in the practical context, on the presumption that accept entailed one concrete action, and reject another. It is in these actions and their consequences that there is a basis for deciding on a level of confidence. The Fisher approach has little to say about the consequences.

As it has turned out, the field of application par excellence for the decision-theory approach has been the sampling inspection of mass-produced items. In sampling inspection, the acceptable deviation from null can be specified; both accept and reject are appropriate categories; the alternative courses of action can be clearly specified; there is a definite measure of loss for each possible action; and the choice can be regarded as one of a series of such choices, so that one can minimize the overall loss (cf. Barnard, 1954). Where the aim is only the acquisition of knowledge without regard to a specific practical context, these conditions do not often prevail. Many psychologists who learned about analysis of variance from books such as those by Snedecor (1946) found the examples involving log weights, etc., somewhat annoying. The decision-theory school makes it clear that such practical contexts are not only "examples" given for pedagogical purposes, but actually are essential features of the methods themselves.

The contributions of the decision-theory school essentially revealed the intrinsic nature of the test of significance beyond that seen by Fisher and his colleagues. They demonstrated that the methods associated with the test of significance constitute not an assertion, or an induction, or a conclusion calculus, but a decision- or risk-evaluation calculus. Fisher (1955) has reacted to the decision-theory approach in polemic style, suggesting that its advocates were like "Russians [who] are made familiar with the ideal that research in pure science can and should be geared to technological performance, in the comprehensive organized effort of a five-year plan for the nation." He also suggested an American "ideological" orientation: "In the U.S. also the great importance of organized technology has I think made it easy to confuse the process appropriate for drawing correct conclusions, with those aimed rather at, let us say, speeding production, or saving money [p. 70]." [5] But perhaps a more reasonable way of looking at this is to regard the decision-theory school to have explicated what was already implicit in the work of the Fisher school.

---

5.   For a reply to Fisher, see Pearson (1955).

Conclusion

What then is our alternative, if the test of significance is really of such limited appropriateness as has been indicated? At the very least it would appear that we would be much better off if we were to attempt to *estimate* the magnitude of the parameters in the populations; and recognize that we then need to make other inferences concerning the psychological phenomena which may be manifesting themselves in these magnitudes. In terms of a statistical approach which is an alternative, the various methods associated with the theorem of Bayes which was referred to earlier may be appropriate; and the paper by Edwards *et al.* (1963) and the book by Schlaifer (1959) are good starting points. However, that which is expressed in the theorem of Bayes alludes to the more general process of inducing propositions concerning the nonmanifest (which is what the population is a special instance of) and ascertaining the way in which that which is manifest (which the sample is a special instance of) bears on it. This is what the scientific method has been about for centuries. However, if the reader who might be sympathetic to the considerations set forth in this paper quickly goes out and reads some of the material on the Bayesian approach with the hope that thereby he will find a *new basis for automatic inference*, this paper will have misfired, and he will be disappointed.

That which we have indicated in this paper in connection with the test of significance in psychological research may be taken as an instance of a kind of essential mindlessness in the conduct of research which may be, as the author has suggested elsewhere (Bakan, 1965), related to the presumption of the nonexistence of mind in the subjects of psychological research. Karl Pearson once indicated that higher statistics were only common sense reduced to numerical appreciation. However, that base in common sense must be maintained with vigilance. When we reach a point where our statistical procedures are substitutes instead of aids to thought, and we are led to absurdities, then we must return to the common sense basis. Tukey (1962) has very properly pointed out that statistical procedures may take our attention away from the data, which constitute the ultimate base for any inferences which we might make. Robert Schlaifer (1959, p. 654) has dubbed the error of the misapplication of statistical procedures the "error of the third kind," the most serious error which can be made. Berkson has suggested the use of "the interocular traumatic test, you know what the data mean when the conclusion hits you between the eyes [Edwards *et al.*, 1963, p. 217]." We must overcome the myth that if our treatment of our subject matter is mathematical it is therefore precise and valid. Mathematics can serve to obscure as well as reveal.

Most importantly, we need to get on with the business of generating *psychological* hypotheses and proceed to do investigations and make inferences which bear on them; instead of, as so much of our literature would attest, testing the statistical null hypothesis in any number of contexts in which we have every reason to suppose that it is false in the first place.

References

Bakan, D. Learning and the principle of inverse probability. *Psychological Review*, 1953, **60,** 360–370.

Bakan, D. The general and the aggregate: A methodological distinction. *Perceptual and Motor Skills*, 1955, **5,** 211–212.

Bakan, D. Clinical psychology and logic. *American Psychologist*, 1956, **11,** 655–662.

Bakan, D. The mystery-mastery complex in contemporary psychology. *American Psychologist*, 1965, **20,** 186–191.

Barnard, G. A. Sampling inspection and statistical decisions. *Journal of the Royal Statistical Society* (B), 1954, **16,** 151–165.

Berkson, J. Some difficulties of interpretation encountered in the application of the chi-square test. *Journal of the American Statistical Association*, 1938, **33,** 526–542

Berkson, J. Tests of significance considered as evidence. *Journal of the American Statistical Association*, 1942, **37,** 325–335.

Binder, A. Further considerations on testing the null hypothesis and the strategy and tactics of investigating theoretical models. *Psychological Review*, 1963, **70,** 101–109.

Bolles, R. C. The difference between statistical hypotheses and scientific hypotheses. *Psychological Reports*, 1962, **11,** 639–645.

Boring, E. G. *A history of experimental psychology.* (2nd ed.) New York: Appleton-Century-Crofts, 1950.

Cohen, J. The statistical power of abnormal-social psychological research: A review. *Journal of Abnormal and Social Psychology*, 1962, **65,** 145–153.

Cronbach, L. J. The two disciplines of scientific psychology. *American Psychologist*, 1957, **12,** 671–684.

Edwards, A. L. *Experimental design in psychological research.* New York: Rinehart, 1950.

Edwards, W., Lindman, H., and Savage, L. J. Bayesian statistical inference for psychological research. *Psychological Review*, 1963, **70,** 193–242.

Ferguson, L. *Statistical analysis in psychology and education.* New York: McGraw-Hill, 1959.

Fisher, R. A. *The design of experiments.* (4th ed.) Edinburgh: Oliver and Boyd, 1947.

Fisher, R. A. Statistical methods and scientific induction. *Journal of the Royal Statistical Society* (B), 1955, **17,** 69–78.

Guilford, J. P. *Psychometric methods.* New York: McGraw-Hill, 1936.

Hodges, J. L. and Lehman, E. L. Testing the approximate validity of statistical hypotheses. *Journal of the Royal Statistical Society* (B), 1954, **16,** 261–268.

Hogben, L. *The relationship of probability, credibility and error: An examination of the contemporary crisis in statistical theory from a behaviourist viewpoint.* New York: Norton, 1958.

Kaiser, H. F. Directional statistical decision. *Psychological Review,* 1960, **67,** 160–167.

Keynes, J. M. *A treatise on probability.* London: Macmillan, 1948.

Lacey, O. L. *Statistical methods in experimentation.* New York: Macmillan, 1953.

Lindquist, E. F. *Statistical analysis in educational research.* Boston: Houghton Mifflin, 1940.

McNemar, Q. At random: Sense and nonsense. *American Psychologist,* 1960, **15,** 295–300.

Melton, A. W. Editorial. *Journal of Experimental Psychology,* 1962, **64,** 553–557.

Neyman, J. Outline of a theory of statistical estimation based on the classical theory of probability. *Philosophical Transactions of the Royal Society* (A), 1937, **236,** 333–380.

Neyman, J. "Inductive behavior" as a basic concept of philosophy of science. *Review of the Mathematical Statistics Institute,* 1957, **25,** 7–22.

Neyman, J. and Pearson, E. S. On the problem of the most efficient tests of statistical hypotheses. *Philosophical Transactions of the Royal Society* (A), 1933, **231,** 289–337.

Nunnally, J. The place of statistics in psychology. *Education and Psychological Measurement,* 1960, **20,** 641–650.

Pearson, E. S. Statistical concepts in their relation to reality. *Journal of the Royal Statistical Society* (B), 1955, **17,** 204–207.

Rosenthal, R. and Gaito, J. The interpretation of levels of significance by psychological researchers. *Journal of Psychology,* 1963, **55,** 33–38.

Rozeboom, W. W. The fallacy of the null-hypothesis significance test. *Psychological Bulletin,* 1960, **57,** 416–428.

Savage, L. J. *The foundations of statistics.* New York: Wiley, 1954.

Schlaifer, R. *Probability and statistics for business decisions.* New York: McGraw-Hill, 1959.

Smith, C. A. B. Review of N. T. J. Bailey, *Statistical methods in biology. Applied Statistics,* 1960, **9,** 64–66.

Snedecor, G. W. *Statistical methods.* (4th ed.; orig. publ. 1937) Ames, Iowa: Iowa State College Press, 1946.

Tukey, J. W. The future of data analysis. *Annals of Mathematical Statistics,* 1962, **33,** 1–67.

Underwood, B. J., Duncan, C. P., Taylor, J. A., and Cotton, J. W. *Elementary statistics.* New York: Appleton-Century-Crofts, 1954.

Wald, A. Contributions to the theory of statistical estimation and testing hypotheses. *Annals of Mathematical Statistics,* 1939, **10,** 299–326.

Wald, A. *Statistical decision functions.* New York: Wiley, 1950.

Wald, A. *Selected papers in statistics and probability.* New York: McGraw-Hill, 1955.

Wilson, K. V. Subjectivist statistics for the current crisis. *Contemporary Psychology,* 1961, **6,** 229–231.

statistical significance in psychological research

David T. Lykken

In a recent journal article Sapolsky (1964) developed the following substantive theory: Some psychiatric patients entertain an unconscious belief in the "cloacal theory of birth" which involves the notions of oral impregnation and anal parturition. Such patients should be inclined to manifest eating disorders: compulsive eating in the case of those who wish to get pregnant and anorexia in those who do not. Such patients should also be inclined to see cloacal animals, such as frogs, on the Rorschach. This reasoning led Sapolsky to predict that Rorschach frog responders show a higher incidence of eating disorders than patients not giving frog responses. A test of this hypothesis in a psychiatric hospital showed that 19 of 31 frog responders had eating disorders indicated in their charts, compared to only 5 of the 31 control patients. A highly significant chi-square was obtained.

It will be an expository convenience to analyze Sapolsky's article in considerable detail for purposes of illustrating the methodological issues which are the real subject of this paper. My intent is not to criticize a particular author but rather to examine a kind of epistemic confusion which seems to be endemic in psychology, especially, but by

From *Psychological Bulletin*, Vol. 70 (No. 3), 1968, pp. 151–159. Copyright 1968 by the American Psychological Association. Reproduced by permission.

no means exclusively, in its "softer" precincts. One would like to demonstrate this generality with multiple examples. Having just combed the latest issues of four well-known journals in the clinical and personality areas, I could undertake to identify several papers in each issue wherein, because they were able to reject a directional null hypothesis at some high level of significance, the authors claimed to have usefully corroborated some rather general theory or to have demonstrated some important empirical relationship. To substantiate that these claims are overstated and that much of this research has not yet earned the right to the reader's overburdened attentions would require a lengthy analysis of each paper. Such profligacy of space would ill become an essay one aim of which is to restrain the swelling volume of the psychological literature. Therefore, with apologies to Sapolsky for subjecting this one paper to such heavy handed scrutiny, let us proceed with the analysis.

Since I regarded the prior probability of Sapolsky's theory (that frog responders unconsciously believe in impregnation per os) to be nugatory and its likelihood unenhanced by the experimental findings, I undertook to check my own reaction against that of 20 colleagues, most of them clinicians, by means of a formal questionnaire. The 20 estimates of the prior probability of Sapolsky's theory, which these psychologists made before being informed of his experimental results, ranged from 10^{-6} to .13 with a median value of .01, which can be interpreted to mean, roughly, "I don't believe it." Since the prior probability of many important scientific theories is considered to be vanishingly small when they are first propounded, this result provides no basis for alarm. However, after being given a fair summary of Sapolsky's experimental findings, which "corroborate" the theory by confirming the operational hypothesis derived from it with high statistical significance, these same psychologists attached posterior probabilities to the theory which ranged from 10^{-5} to .14, with the median unchanged at .01. I interpret this consensus to mean, roughly, "I still don't believe it." This finding, I submit, *is* alarming because it signifies a sharp difference of opinion between, for example, the consulting editors of the journal and a substantial segment of its readership, a difference on the very fundamental question of what constitutes good (i.e., publishable) clinical research.

The thesis of the present paper is that Sapolsky and the editors were in fact following, with reasonable consistency, our traditional rules for evaluating psychological research, but that, as the Sapolsky paper exemplifies, at least two of these rules should be reconsidered. One of the rules examined here asserts roughly the following: "When a prediction or hypothesis derived from a theory is confirmed by experiment, a nontrivial increment in one's confidence in that theory should result, especially when one's prior confidence is low." Clearly, my 20 colleagues were violating this rule here since their confidence in the frog responder-cloacal birth theory was not, on the average, increased by the contemplation of Sapolsky's highly significant chi-square. From their comments it seems that they found it too hard to accept that a belief in oral impregnation could lead to frog responding merely because the frog has a cloacus. (One must, after all, admit that few patients know what a cloacus is or that a frog has one and that those few who do know probably will also know that the frog's eggs are both fertilized and hatched externally so neither oral impregnation nor anal birth are in any way involved. Hence, *neither* the average patient *nor* the biologically sophisticated patient should logically be expected to employ the frog as a symbol for an unconscious belief in oral con-ception.) My colleagues, on the contrary, found it relatively easy to believe that the observed association between frog responding and eating problems might be due to some other cause entirely (e.g., both symptoms are immature or regressive in character; the frog, with its disproportionately large mouth and voice may well constitute a common orality totem and hence be associated with problems in the oral sphere; "squeamish" people might tend both to see frogs and to have eating problems; and so on.)

Assuming that this first rule *is* wrong in this instance, perhaps it could be amended to allow one to make exceptions in cases resembling this illustration. For example, one could add the codicil: "This rule may be ignored whenever one considers the theory in question to be overly improbable or whenever one can think of alternative explana-tions for the experimental results." But surely such an amendment would not do. ESP, for example, could never become scientifically respectable if the first exception were allowed, and one consequence of the second would be that the importance attached to one's findings would always be inversely related to the ingenuity of one's readers. The burden of the present argument is that this rule is wrong not only in a few exceptional instances *but as it is routinely applied to the majority of experimental reports in the psychological literature.*

Corroborating theories by
experimental confirmation
of theoretical predictions[1]

Most psychological experiments are of three kinds: (a) studies of the effect of some treatment on some output variables, which can be

---

1. Much of the argument in this section is based upon ideas developed in certain unpublished memoranda by P. E. Meehl (personal communication, 1963) and in a recent article (Meehl, 1967).

regarded as a special case of (b) studies of the difference between two or more groups of individuals with respect to some variable, which in turn are a special case of (c) the study of the relationship or correlation between two or more variables within some specified population. Using the bivariate correlation design as paradigmatic, then, one notes first that the strict null hypothesis must always be assumed to be false (this idea is not new and has recently been illuminated by Bakan, 1966). Unless one of the variables is wholly unreliable so that the values obtained are strictly random, it would be foolish to suppose that the correlation between any two variables is identically equal to .0000 . . . (or that the effect of some treatment of the difference between two groups is exactly *zero*). The molar dependent variables employed in psychological research are extremely complicated in the sense that the measured value of such a variable tends to be affected by the interaction of a vast number of factors, both in the present situation and in the history of the subject organism. It is exceedingly unlikely that any two such variables will not share at least some of these factors and equally unlikely that their effects will exactly cancel one another out.

It might be argued that the more complex the variables the smaller their average correlation ought to be since a larger pool of common factors allows more chance for mutual cancellation of effects in obedience to the Law of Large Numbers. However, one knows of a number of unusually potent and pervasive factors which operate to unbalance such convenient symmetries and to produce correlations large enough to rival the effects of whatever casual factors the experimenter may have had in mind. Thus, we know that (a) "good" psychological and physical variables tend to be positively correlated; (b) experimenters, without deliberate intention, can somehow subtly bias their findings in the expected direction (Rosenthal, 1963); (c) the effects of common method are often as strong as or stronger than those produced by the actual variables of interest (e.g., in a large and careful study of the factorial structure of adjustment to stress among officer candidates, Holtzman and Bitterman, 1956, found that their 101 original variables contained five main common factors representing, respectively, their rating scales, their perceptual-motor tests, the McKinney Reporting Test, their GSR variables, and the MMPI); (d) transitory state variables such as the subject's anxiety level, fatigue, or his desire to please, may broadly affect all measures obtained in a single experimental session.

This average shared variance of "unrelated" variables can be thought of as a kind of ambient noise level characteristic of the domain. It would be interesting to obtain empirical estimates of this quantity in our field to serve as a kind of Plimsoll mark against which to compare obtained relationships predicted by some theory under test. If, as I think, it is not unreasonable to suppose that "unrelated" molar psychological variables share on the average about 4% to 5% of common variance, then the expected correlation between any such variables would be about .20 in absolute value and the expected difference between any two groups on some such variable would be nearly .5 standard deviation units. (Note that these estimates assume zero measurement error. One can better explain the near-zero correlations often observed in psychological research in terms of unreliability of measures than in terms of the assumption that the true scores are in fact unrelated.)

Suppose now that an investigator predicts that two variables are positively correlated. Since we expect the null hypothesis to be false, we expect his prediction to be confirmed by experiment with a probability of very nearly .5; by using a large enough sample, moreover, he can achieve any desired level of statistical significance for this result. If the ambient noise level for his domain is represented by correlations averaging, say, .20 in absolute value, then his chances of finding a statistically significant confirmation of his prediction with a reasonable sample size will be quite high (e.g., about 1 in 4 for $N = 100$) even if there is no truth whatever to the theory on which the prediction was based. Since most theoretical predictions in psychology, especially in the areas of clinical and personality research, specify no more than the direction of a correlation, difference or treatment effect, we must accept the harsh conclusion that a single experimental finding of this usual kind (confirming a directional prediction), no matter how great its statistical significance, will seldom represent a large enough increment of corroboration for the theory from which it was derived to merit very serious scientific attention. (In the natural sciences, this problem is far less severe for two reasons: (a) theories are powerful enough to generate point predictions or at least predictions of some narrow range within which the dependent variable is expected to lie; and (b) in these sciences, the degree of experimental control and the relative simplicity of the variables studied are such that the ambient noise level represented by unexplained and unexpected correlations, differences, and treatment effects is often vanishingly small.)

**The significance
of large correlations**

It might be argued that, even where only a weak directional prediction is made, the obtaining of a result which is not only statistically significant but large in absolute value should constitute a stronger corroboration of the theory. For example, although Sapolsky predicted only that frog responding and eating disorders would be positively related, the fourfold point correlation (phi coefficient) between these variables in his sample was about .46, surely much larger than the average relationship expected between random pairs of molar variables on the premise that "everything is related to everything else." Does not such a large effect therefore provide stronger corroboration for the theory in question?

One difficulty with this reasonable sounding doctrine is that, in the complex sort of research considered here, *really large* effects, differences, or relationships are not usually to be expected and, when found, may even argue *against* the theory being tested. To illustrate this, let us take Sapolsky's theory seriously and, by making reasonable guesses concerning the unknown base rates involved, attempt to estimate the actual size of the relationship between frog responding and eating disorders which the theory should lead us to expect. Sapolsky found that 16% of his control sample showed eating disorders; let us take this value as the base rate for this symptom among patients who do not hold the cloacal theory of birth. Perhaps we can assume that all patients who do hold this theory will give frog responses but surely not all of these will show eating disorders (any more than will all patients who believe in vaginal conception be inclined to show coital or urinary disturbances); it seems a reasonable assumption that no more than 50% of the believers in oral conception will therefore manifest eating problems. Similarly, we can hardly suppose that the frog response *always* implies an unconscious belief in the cloacal theory; surely this response can come to be emitted now and then for other reasons. Even with the greatest sympathy for Sapolsky's point of view, we could hardly expect more than, say, 50% of frog responders to believe in oral impregnation. Therefore, we might reasonably predict that 16 of 100 nonresponders would show eating disorders in a test of this theory, 50 of 100 frog responders would hold the cloacal theory and half of these show eating disorders, while 16% or 8 of the remaining 50 frog responders will show eating problems too, giving a total of 33 eating disorders among the 100 frog responders. Such a finding would produce a significant chi-square but the actual degree of relationship as indexed by the phi coefficient would be only about .20. In other words, if one considers the supplementary assumptions which would be required to make a theory compatible with the actual results obtained, it becomes apparent that the finding of a really strong association may actually embarrass the theory rather than support it (e.g., Sapolsky's finding of 61% eating disorders among his frog responders is *significantly larger* ($p < .01$) than the 33% generously estimated by the reasoning above).

Multiple corroboration

In the social, clinical, and personality areas especially, we must expect that the size of the correlations, differences, or effects which might reasonably be predicted from our theories will typically not be very large relative to the ambient noise level of correlations and effects due solely to the "all-of-a-pieceness of things." The conclusion seems inescapable that the only really satisfactory solution to the problem of corroborating such theories is that of *multiple corroboration*, the derivation and testing of a number of separate, quasi-independent predictions. Since the prior probability of such a multiple corroboration may be on the order of $(.5)^n$, where n is the number of independent[2] predictions experimentally confirmed, a theory of any useful degree of predictive richness should in principle allow for sufficient empirical confirmation through multiple corroboration to compel the respect of the most critical reader or editor.

The relation of experimental findings to empirical facts

We turn now to the examination of a second popular rule for the evaluation of psychological research, which states roughly that "When no obvious errors of sampling or experimental method are apparent, one's confidence in the general proposition being tested (e.g., Variables A and B are positively correlated in Population C) should be proportional to the degree of statistical significance obtained." We are following this rule when we say, "Theory aside, Sapolsky has at least demonstrated an empirical fact, namely, that frog responders have more eating disturbances than patients in general." This conclusion means, of course, that in the light of Sapolsky's highly significant findings we should be willing to give very generous odds that any other competent investigator (at another hospital, administering the Rorschach in his own way, and determining the presence of eating problems in whatever manner seems reasonable and convenient for him) will also find a substantial positive relationship between these two variables.

---

2. Tests of predictions from the same theory are seldom strictly independent since they often share some of the same supplementary assumptions, are made at the same time on the same sample, and so on.

Let us be more specific. Given Sapolsky's fourfold table showing 19 of 31 frog responders to have eating disorders (61%), it can be shown by chi-square that we should have 99% confidence that the true population value lies between 13/31 and 25/31 (between 42% and 81%). With 99% confidence that the population value is at least 13 in 31, we should have $.99(99) = 98\%$ confidence that a new sample from that population should produce at least 6 eating disorders among each 31 frog responders, assuming that 5 of each 31 nonresponders show eating problems also as Sapolsky reported. That is, we should be willing to bet $98 against only $2 that a replication of this experiment will show *at least as many* eating disorders among frog responders as among nonresponders. The reader may decide for himself whether his faith in the "empirical fact" demonstrated by this experiment can meet the test of this gambler's challenge.

Three kinds of replication

If, as suggested above, "demonstrating an empirical fact" must involve a claim of confidence in the replicability of one's findings, then to clearly understand the relation of statistical significance to the probability of a "successful" replication it will be helpful to distinguish between three rather different methods of replicating or cross-validating an experiment. *Literal replication*, of course, would involve exact duplication of the first investigator's sampling procedure, experimental conditions, measuring techniques, and methods of analysis; asking the original investigator to simply run more subjects would perhaps be about as close as we could come to attaining literal replication and even this, in psychological research, might often not be close enough. In the case of *operational replication*, on the other hand, one strives to duplicate exactly just the sampling and experimental procedures given in the first author's report of his research. The purpose of operational replication is to test whether the investigator's "experimental recipe"— the conditions and procedures he considered salient enough to be listed in the "Methods" section of his report—will in other hands produce the results that he obtained. For example, replication of the "Clever Hans" experiment revealed that the apparent ability of that remarkable horse to add numbers had been due to an uncontrolled and unsuspected factor (the presence of the horse's trainer within his field of view). This factor, not being specified in the "methods recipe" for the result, was omitted in the replication which for that reason failed. Operational replication would be facilitated if investigators would accept more responsibility for specifying what they believe to be the minimum essential conditions and controls for producing their results. Psychologists tend to be inconsistently prolix in describing their experimental methods; thus, Sapolsky tabulates the age, sex, and diagnosis for each of his 62 subjects. Does he mean to imply that the experiment will not work if these details are changed?—surely not, but then why describe them?

In the quite different process of *constructive replication*, one deliberately avoids imitation of the first author's methods. To obtain an ideal constructive replication, one would provide a competent investigator with *nothing more than* a clear statement of the empirical "fact" which the first author would claim to have established—for example, "psychiatric patients who give frog responses on the Rorschach have a greater tendency toward eating disorders than do patients in general"—and then let the replicator formulate his own methods of sampling, measurements, and data analysis. One must keep in mind that the data, the specific results of a particular experiment, are only seldom of any real interest in themselves. The "empirical facts" which we value so highly consist usually of confirmed conceptual or constructive (not operational) hypotheses of the form "Construct A is positively related to Construct B in Population C." We are interested in the *construct* "tendency toward eating disorders," not in the *datum* "has reference made to overeating in the nurse's notes for May 15th." An operational replication tests whether we can duplicate our findings using the same methods of measurement and sampling; a constructive replication goes further in the sense of testing the validity of these methods.

Thus, if I cannot confirm Sapolsky's results for patients from my hospital, assessing eating disorders by means of informant interviews, say, or actual measurements of food intake, then clearly Sapolsky has *not* demonstrated any "fact" about eating disorders among psychiatric patients in general. I could then revert to an operational replication, assessing eating problems from the psychiatric notes as Sapolsky did and selecting my sample to conform with the age, sex, and diagnostic properties of his, although I might not regard this endeavor to be worth the effort since, under these circumstances, even a successful operational replication could not establish an empirical conclusion of any great generality or interest. Just as a reliable but invalid test can be said to measure something, but not what it claimed to measure, so an experiment which replicates operationally but not constructively could be said to have demonstrated something, but not the relation between meaningful constructs, generalizable to some broad reference population, which the author originally claimed to have established.[3]

Relation of the significance test to the probability of a "successful" replication

The probability values resulting from significance testing can be directly used to measure one's confidence in expecting a "successful" literal replication only. Thus, we can be 98% confident of finding at least 6 of 31 frog responders to have eating problems only if we reproduce all of the conditions of Sapolsky's experiment with absolute fidelity, something that he himself could not undertake to do at this point. Whether we are entitled to anything approaching such high confidence that we could obtain such a result from an operational replication depends entirely upon whether Sapolsky has accurately specified all of the conditions which were in fact determinative of his results. That he did not in this instance is suggested by the fact that, investigating the feasibility of replicating his experiment at the University of Minnesota Hospitals, I found that I should have to review several thousand case records in order to turn up a sample of 31 frog responders like his. Although he does not indicate how many records he examined, one strongly suspects that the base rate of Rorschach frog responding must have been higher at Sapolsky's hospital, either because of some difference in the patient population or, more probably, because an investigator's being interested in some class of responses will tend to subtly elicit such responses at a higher rate unless the testing procedure is very rigorously controlled. If the base rates for frog responding are so different at the two hospitals, it seems doubtful that the response can have the same correlates or meaning in the two populations and therefore one would be reckless indeed to offer high odds on the outcome of even the most careful operational replication. The likelihood of a successful constructive replication is, of course,

---

3.   This distinction between operational and constructive replication seems to have much in common with that made by Sidman (1960) between what he calls "direct" and "systematic" replication. However, in the operant research context to which Sidman directs his attention, "replication" means to run another animal or the same animal again; thus, direct replication involves maintaining the same experimental conditions in detail whereas in systematic replication one allows all supposedly irrelevant factors to vary from one subject to the next in the hope of demonstrating that one has correctly identified the variables which are really in control of the behavior being studied.

still smaller since it depends on the additional assumptions that Sapolsky's samples were truly representative of psychiatric patients in general and that his method of assessing eating problems was truly valid, that is, would correlate highly with a different, equally reasonable appearing method.

Another example

It is not my purpose, of course, to criticize statistical theory or method but rather to suggest ways in which these tools are sometimes misused or misinterpreted by writers or readers of the psychological literature. Nor do I mean to abuse a particular investigator whose research report happened to serve as a convenient illustration of the components of the argument. An abundance of articles can be found in the journals which exemplify these points quite as well as Sapolsky's but space limitations forbid multiple examples. As a compromise, therefore, I offer just one further illustration, showing how the application of these same critical principles might have increased a reader's—and perhaps even an editor's—skepticism concerning some research of my own.

The purpose of the experiment in question (Lykken, 1957) was to test the hypothesis that the "primary" psychopath has reduced ability to condition anxiety or fear. To segregate a subgroup in which such primary psychopaths might be concentrated, I asked prison psychologists to separate inmates already diagnosed as psychopathic personalities into one group that met 14 rather specific clinical criteria specified by Cleckley (1950, pp. 355–392) and to identify another group which clearly did not fit some of these criteria. The normal control subjects were comparable to the psychopathic groups in age, IQ, and sex. Fear conditioning was assessed using the GSR as the dependent variable and a rather painful electric shock as the unconditioned stimulus (UCS). On the index used to measure rate of conditioning, the primary psychopathic group scored significantly lower than did the controls. By the usual reasoning, therefore, one might conclude that this result demonstrates that primary psychopaths are abnormally slow to condition the GSR, at least with an aversive UCS, and this empirical fact in turn provides significant support for the theory that primary psychopaths have defective fear-learning ability (i.e., a low "anxiety IQ").

But to anyone who has actually participated in research of this kind, this seemingly straightforward reasoning must appear appallingly oversimplified. It is quite impossible to obtain anything resembling a truly random sample of psychopaths (or of nonpsychopathic normals either, for that matter) and it is a matter of unquantifiable conjecture how a sample obtained by a different investigator using equally defensible methods might perform on the tests which I employed. Even with the identical sample, no two investigators are likely to measure the GSR in the same way, use the same conditioned stimulus (CS) and UCS or the same pattern of reinforced and CS-only trials. Given even the same set of protocols, there is no standard formula for obtaining an index of degree or rate of conditioning; the index I used was essentially abitrary and whether it was a good one is a matter of opinion. My own evaluation of the methods used, together with a complex set of supplementary assumptions difficult to explicate, leads me to believe that these results increase the likelihood that primary psychopaths have slower GSR conditioning with an aversive UCS; I might now give odds of two to one that this empirical generalization is true and odds of three to two that another investigator would be able to confirm it by means of a constructive replication. But this already biased claim is far more modest than the one which is implicit in the significance testing operation, namely, "such a mean difference would only be expected 5 times in 100 if the [generalization] is not true."

This empirical generalization, about GSR conditioning, is derivable from the hypothesis of interest, that psychopaths have a low anxiety IQ, by a chain of reasoning so complex and elliptical and so burdened with accessory assumptions as to be quite impossible to spell out in the detail required for rigorous logical analysis. Psychologists knowledgeable in the area can evaluate whether it is a reasonable derivation but their opinions will not necessarily agree. Moreover, even if the derivation could pass the scrutiny of some "Certified Public Logician," confirmation of the prediction about GSR conditioning should add only very slightly to our confidence in the hypothesis about fear conditioning. Even if this confirmation were made relatively more firm by, for example, constructive replication of the generalization, "aversive GSR conditioning is retarded in primary psychopaths," the hypothesis that these individuals have a low anxiety IQ could still be said to have passed only the weakest kind of test. This is so because such simple directional predictions about group differences have nearly a 50–50 chance of being true a priori even if our particular hypothesis is false. There are doubtless many possible explanations for low GSR conditioning scores in psychopaths other than the possibility of defective fear conditioning. Indeed, some of my subjects whose conditioning scores were nearly as low as those of the most extreme primary psychopaths seemed to me to be clearly neurotic with considerable anxiety and I attempted to account for their GSR performance with an ad hoc conjecture involving a kind of repression phenomenon, that is, a denial that a low GSR index implied poor fear conditioning in their cases.

A redeeming feature of this study was that two other related but distinguishable predictions from the same hypothesis were tested at the same time, namely, that primary psychopaths should do as well as normals on a learning task involving positive reward but less well on an avoidance learning problem, and that they should be more willing than normals to choose embarrassing or frightening situations in preference to alternatives involving tedium, frustration, physical discomfort, and the like. Tests of these predictions gave affirmative results also, thus providing some of the multiple corroboration necessary for the hypothesis to claim the attention of other experimenters.

Obviously, I do not mean to criticize the editor's decision to publish my (1957) paper. The tendency to evaluate research in terms of mechanical rules based on the results of the significance tests should not be replaced by equally rigid requirements concerning replication or corroboration. This study, like Sapolsky's or most others in this field, can be properly evaluated only by a qualified reader who can substitute his own informed judgment and scientific intuition for the rigorous reasoning and experimental control that is usually not achievable in clinical and personality research. As it happens, subsequent work has provided some encouraging support for my 1957 findings. The two additional predictions mentioned above have received operational replication (i.e., the same test methods used in a different context) by Schachter and Latené (1964). The prediction that psychopaths show slower GSR conditioning with an aversive UCS has been constructively replicated (i.e., independently tested with no attempt to copy my procedures) by Hare (1965a). Finally, two additional predictions from the theory that the primary psychopath has a low anxiety IQ have been tested with affirmative results (Hare, 1965b; 1966). All told, then, this hypothesis can now boast of having led to at least five quasi-independent predictions which have been experimentally confirmed and three of which have been replicated. The hypothesis is therefore entitled to serious consideration although one would be rash still to regard it as proven. At least one alternative hypothesis, that the psychopath has an unusually efficient mechanism for inhibiting emotional arousal, can account equally well for the existing findings so that, as is usually the case, further research is called for.

Conclusions

The moral of this story is that the finding of statistical significance is perhaps the least important attribute of a good experiment; it is *never* a sufficient condition for concluding that a theory has been corroborated, that a useful empirical fact has been established with reasonable confidence—or that an experimental report ought to be published. The value of any research can be determined, not from the statistical results, but only by skilled, subjective evaluation of the coherence and reasonableness of the theory, the degree of experimental control employed, the sophistication of the measuring techniques, the scientific or practical importance of the phenomena studied, and so on. Ideally, all experiments would be replicated before publication but this goal is impractical. "Good" experiments will tend to replicate better than poor ones (and, when they do not, the failures will tend to be informative in themselves, which is not true for poor experiments) and should be published so that they may stimulate replication and extension by others. Editors must be bold enough to take responsibility for deciding which studies are good and which are not, without resorting to letting the *p* value of the significance tests determine this decision. There is little real danger that anything of value will be lost through this approach since the unpublished investigator can always resort to constructive replication to induce editorial acceptance of his empirical conclusions or to multiple corroboration to compel editorial respect for his theory. Since operational replication must really be done by an independent second investigator and since constructive replication has greater generality, its success strongly implying that an operational replication would have succeeded also, one should usually replicate one's own work constructively, using different sampling and measurement procedures within the purview of the same constructive hypothesis. If only unusually well done, provocative, and important research were published without prior authentication, operational replication of such research by others would become correspondingly more valuable and entitled to the respect now accorded capable replication in the other experimental sciences.

References

Bakan, D. The test of significance in psychological research. *Psychological Bulletin*, 1966, **66,** 423–437.

Cleckley, H. *The mask of sanity.* Saint Louis: C. V. Mosby, 1950.

Hare, R. D. Acquisition and generalization of a conditioned fear response in psychopathic and nonpsychopathic criminals. *Journal of Psychology*, 1965, **59,** 367–370. (a)

Hare, R. D. Temporal gradient of fear arousal in psychopaths. *Journal of Abnormal Psychology*, 1965, **70**, 442–445. (b)

Hare, R. D. Psychopathy and choice of immediate versus delayed punishment. *Journal of Abnormal Psychology*, 1966, **71**, 25–29.

Holtzman, W. H. and Bitterman, M. E. A factorial study of adjustment to stress. *Journal of Abnormal and Social Psychology*, 1956, **52**, 179–185.

Lykken, D. T. A study of anxiety in the sociopathic personality. *Journal of Abnormal and Social Psychology*, 1957, **55**, 6–10.

Meehl, P. E. Theory-testing in psychology and physics: A methodological paradox. *Philosophy of Science*, 1967, **34**, 103–115.

Rosenthal, R. On the social psychology of the psychological experiment: The experimenter's hypothesis as unintended determinant of experimental results. *American Scientist*, 1963, **51**, 268–283.

Sapolsky, A. An effort at studying Rorschach content symbolism: The frog response. *Journal of Consulting Psychology*, 1964, **28**, 469–472.

Schachter, S. and Latené, B. Crime, cognition and the autonomic nervous system. *Nebraska Symposium on motivation*, 1964, **12**, 221–273.

Sidman, M. *Tactics of scientific research*. New York: Basic Books, 1960.

18

theory-testing in psychology and physics:

a methodological paradox

Paul E. Meehl[1]

The purpose of the present paper is not so much to propound a doctrine or defend a thesis (especially as I should be surprised if either psychologists or statisticians were to disagree with whatever in the nature of a "thesis" it advances), but to call the attention of logicians and philosophers of science to a puzzling state of affairs in the currently accepted methodology of the behavior sciences which I, a psychologist, have been unable to resolve to my satisfaction. The puzzle, sufficiently striking (when clearly discerned) to be entitled to the designation "paradox," is the following: *In the physical sciences, the usual result of an improvement in experimental design, instrumentation, or numerical mass of data, is to increase the difficulty of the "observational hurdle" which the physical theory of interest must successfully surmount; whereas, in psychology and some of the allied behavior sciences, the usual effect*

From *Philosophy of Science* Vol. 34 (No. 2), June, 1967. Reprinted by permission of Paul E. Meehl and The Philosophy of Science Association.

1. I wish to express my indebtedness to Dr. David T. Lykken, conversations with whom have played a major role in stimulating my thinking along these lines, and whose views and examples have no doubt influenced the form of the argument in this paper. For an application of these and allied considerations to a specific example of poor research in psychology, see [7].

of such improvement in experimental precision is to provide an easier hurdle for the theory to surmount. Hence what we would normally think of as improvements in our experimental method tend (when predictions materialize) to yield *stronger* corroboration of the theory in physics, since to remain unrefuted the theory must have survived a more difficult test; by contrast, such experimental improvement in psychology typically results in a *weaker* corroboration of the theory, since it has now been required to survive a more lenient test [3] [9] [10].

Although the point I wish to make is one in logic and methodology of science and, as I think, does not presuppose adoption of any of the current controversial viewpoints in technical statistics, a brief exposition of the process of statistical inference as we usually find it in the social sciences is necessary. (The philosopher who is unfamiliar with this subject-matter may be referred to any good standard text on statistics, such as the widely used book by Hays [5] which includes a clear and succinct treatment of the main points I shall briefly summarize here.)

On the basis of a substantive psychological theory T in which he is interested, a psychologist derives (often in a rather loose sense of 'derive') the consequence that an observable variable x will differ as between two groups of subjects. Sometimes, as in most problems of clinical or social psychology, the two groups are defined by a property the individuals under study already possess, e.g., social class, sex, diagnosis, or measured I.Q. Sometimes, as is more likely to be the case in such fields as psychopharmacology or psychology of learning, the contrasted groups are defined by the fact that the experimenter has subjected them to different experimental influences, such as a drug, a reward, or a specific kind of social pressure. Whether the contrasted groups are specified by an "experiment of nature" where the investigator takes the organisms as he finds them, or by a true "experiment" in the more usual sense of the word, is not crucial for the present argument; although, as will be seen, the implications of my puzzle for theory-testing are probably more perilous in the former kind of research than in the latter.

According to the substantive theory T, the two groups are expected to differ on variable x, but it is recognized that errors of (a) measurement and (b) random sampling will, in general, produce *some* observed difference between the averages of the groups studied, even if their total population did not differ in the true value of $\bar{x}$ [= mean of x].

Example: We are interested in the question whether girls are brighter than boys (i.e., that $\mu_g - \mu_b \doteq \delta_{gb} > 0$). We do not have perfectly reliable measures of intelligence, and we are furthermore not in a position to measure the intelligence of all boys and girls in the hypothetical population about which we desire to make a general statement.

Instead we must be content with fallible I.Q. scores, and with a sample of school children drawn from the hypothetical population. Each of these sources of error, measurement error and random sampling error, contributes to an untrustworthiness in the computed value we obtain for the average intelligence $\bar{x}_b$ of the boys and also for $\bar{x}_g$, that of the girls. If we observe a difference of, say $d = 5$ I.Q. points in a sample of 100 boys and 100 girls, we must have some method to infer whether this obtained observational difference between the two groups reflects a real difference or one which is merely apparent, i.e., due to the combined effect of errors of measurement and sampling. We do this by means of a "statistical significance test," the mathematics of which is not relevant here, except to say that by combining the principles of probability with a characterization of the procedure by which the samples were constituted, and quantifying the variation in observed intelligence score *within* each of the two groups being contrasted, it is possible to employ a formula which utilizes the observed averages together with the observed variations and sample sizes so as to answer certain relevant kinds of questions. Among such questions is the following: "If there were, in fact, no real difference in average I.Q. between the population of boys and girls, with what relative frequency would an investigator find a difference—in relation to the observed intragroup variation—of the magnitude our observations have actually found"?

The statistical hypothesis, that there is no population difference between boys and girls in I.Q., which is called the "null hypothesis" $[H_0 : \bar{\delta} = 0]$ is used to generate a random sampling distribution of the statistic ("t-test") employed in testing the presence of a significant difference. If the observed data would be very improbable on the hypothesis that H_0 obtained, we abandon H_0 in favor of its alternative. We conclude that since H_0 is false, its alternative, i.e., that there exists a real average difference between the sexes, obtains. In the past, it was customary to deal with what may be called the "print null" hypothesis which says that there is zero difference between the two averages in the populations. In recent years it has been more explicitly recognized that what is of theoretical interest is not the mere presence of *difference* (i.e., that H_0 is false, i.e., that $\mu_b \neq \mu_g$) but rather the presence of a difference *in a certain direction* (in this case, that $\mu_g > \mu_b$). It is therefore increasingly frequent that the behavior scientist employs the so-called "directional null hypothesis," say H_2, instead of the point-null hypothesis H_0. If our substantive theory T involves the prediction that the average I.Q. of girls in the entire population exceeds that of boys, we test the alternative to this statistical hypothesis about the population, i.e., that *either the average I.Q. of boys exceeds that of girls*

(H_2) *or that there is no difference* (H_0). That is, we adopt for statistical test (with the anticipation of refuting it) a disjunction of the old-fashioned point-null hypothesis H_0 with the hypothesis H_2 that H_0 is false and it is false in a direction *opposite* to that implied by our substantive theory. However, this directional null hypothesis ($H_{02} : \mu_g \leq \mu_b$), unlike the old-fashioned point-null hypothesis ($H_0 : \mu_g = \mu_b$), does not generate a theoretically expected distribution, because it is not precise, i.e., it does not specify a point-value for the unknown parameter $\delta = \mu_{girls} - \mu_{boys}$. However, we can employ it as we do the point-null hypothesis, by reasoning that *if* the point-null hypothesis H_0 obtained in the state of nature, *then* an observed difference (in the direction that our substantive theory predicts) of such-and-such magnitude, has a calculable probability; and that calculable probability is an upper bound upon the desired (but unknown) probability based on $H_{02} : \mu_g \leq \mu_b$. That is to say, if the probability of observed girl-over-boy difference ($\bar{d}_{gb} = \bar{x}_g - \bar{x}_b$) arising through random error is p, given the point-null hypothesis $H_0 : \mu_g = \mu_b$, then the probability of the observed difference arising randomly given any of the point-hypotheses constituting $H_2 : \mu_g < \mu_b$ will of course be less than p. Hence p is an upper bound on this probability for the inexact directional null hypothesis ($H_{02} : \mu_g \leq \mu_b$). Proceeding in this way directs our interest to only one tail of the theoretical random sampling distribution instead of both tails, which has given rise to a certain amount of controversy among statisticians, but that controversy is not relevant here. (For an excellent clarifying discussion, see Kaiser [6]). Suffice it to say that having formulated a directional null hypothesis H_{02} which is the alternative to the statistical hypothesis of interest H_1, and which includes the point-null hypothesis H_0 as one (very unlikely) possibility for the state of nature, we then carry out the experiment with the anticipation of *refuting* this directional null hypothesis, thereby confirming the alternative statistical hypothesis of interest (H_1), and, since H_1 in turn was implied by the substantive theory T, of corroborating T.

In such a situation we know in advance that we are in danger of making either of two sorts of "errors," not in the sense of committing scientific mistakes but in the sense of (rationally) inferring what is objectively a false conclusion. If the null hypothesis (point or directional) is in fact true, but due to the combination of measurement and sampling errors we obtain a value which is so improbable upon H_2 or H_0 that we decide in favor of their alternative H_1, we will then have committed what is known as an *error of the first kind* or *Type I Error*. An error of the first kind is a statistical inference that the null hypothesis is false, when in the state of nature it is actually true. This means we will have concluded in favor of a statistical statement H_1 which flowed as a consequence of our substantive theory T, and therefore we will believe ourselves to have obtained empirical support for T, whereas in reality this statistical conclusion is false and, consequently, such support for the substantive theory is objectively lacking. Measurement and sampling error may, of course, also result in a sampling deviation in the opposite direction; or, the true difference $\bar{\delta}$ may be so small that even if our sample values were to coincide exactly with the true ones, the sheer algebra of the significance test would not enable us to reach the prespecified level of statistical significance. If we conclude until further notice that the directional null hypothesis H_{02} is tenable, on the grounds that we have failed to refute it by our investigation, then we have failed to support its statistical alternative H_1, and therefore failed to confirm one of the predictions of the substantive theory T. Retention of the null hypothesis H_{02} when it is in fact false is known as an *error of the second kind* or *Type II Error*.

In the biological and social sciences there has been widespread adoption of the probabilities .01 or .05 as the allowable theoretical frequency of Type I errors. These values are called the 1% and 5% "levels of significance." It is obvious that there is an inverse relationship between the probabilities of the two kinds of errors, so that if we adopt a significance level which increases the frequency of Type I errors, such a policy will lead to a greater number of claims of statistically significant departure from the null hypothesis; and, therefore, in whatever unknown fraction of all experiments performed the null hypothesis is in reality false, we will more often (correctly) conclude its falsity, i.e., we will thereby be reducing the proportion of Type II errors.

Suppose we hold fixed the theoretically calculable incidence of Type I errors. Thus, we determine that *if* the null hypothesis is in fact true in the state of nature, we do not wish to risk erroneously concluding that it is false more than, say, five times in 100. Holding this 5% significance level fixed (which, as a form of scientific strategy, means leaning over backward not to conclude that a relationship exists when there isn't one, or when there is a relationship in the wrong direction), we can decrease the probability of Type II errors by improving our experiment in certain respects. There are three general ways in which the frequency of Type II errors can be decreased (for fixed Type I error-rate), namely, (a) by improving the logical structure of the experiment, (b) by improving experimental techniques such as the control of extraneous variables which contribute to intragroup variation (and hence appear in the denominator of the significance test), and (c) by increasing the size of the sample. Given a specified true difference in the range of H_1, the complement $(1 - p)$ of the probability of a Type II error is known as the *power*, and an improvement in the experiment by any or all of these three methods yields an increase in power (or, to use words employed by R. A. Fisher, the experiments "sensitiveness" or "precision.") For many years relatively little emphasis was put upon the problem of power, but recently this concept has come in for a good deal of attention. Accordingly, up-to-date psychological investigators are normally expected to include some preliminary calculations regarding power in designing their experiments. We select a logical design and choose a sample size such that it can be said in advance that if one is interested in a true difference provided it is at least of a specified magnitude (i.e., if it is smaller than this we are content to miss the opportunity of finding it), the probability is high (say, 80%) that we will successfully refute the null hypothesis. See, for example, Cohen's literature sampling [4] on the problem of power. For an incisive critique of the whole approach, a critique which has been given far less respectful attention than it deserves (conspiracy of silence?), I recommend Rozeboom's excellent contribution [11]. But I should emphasize that my argument in this paper does not hinge upon the reader's agreement with Rozeboom's very strong attack (although I, myself, incline to go along with him).

It is important to keep clear the distinction between the *substantive theory* of interest and the *statistical hypothesis* which is derived from it [2]. In the I.Q. example there was almost no substantive theory or a very impoverished one; i.e., the question being investigated was itself stated as a purely statistical question about the average I.Q. of the two sexes. In the great majority of investigations in psychology the situation is otherwise. Normally, the investigator holds some substantive theory about unconscious mental processes, or physiological or genetic entities, or perceptual structure, or about learning influences in the person's past, or about current social pressures, which contains a great deal more content than the mere statement that the population parameter of an observational variable is greater for one group of individuals than for another. While no competent psychologist is unaware of this obvious distinction between a substantive psychological theory T and a statistical hypothesis H is implied by it, in practice there is a tendency to conflate the substantive theory with the statistical hypothesis, thereby illicitly conferring upon T somewhat the same degree of support given H by a successful refutation of the null hypothesis. Hence the investigator, upon finding an observed difference which has an extremely small probability of occurring on the null hypothesis, gleefully records the tiny probability number "$p < .001$," and there is a tendency to feel that the extreme smallness of this probability of a Type I error is somehow transferrable to a small probability of "making a theoretical mistake." It is as if, when the observed statistical result would be expected to arise only once in a thousand times through a Type I statistical error given H_{02}, therefore one's substantive theory *T*, which entails the alternative H_1, has received some sort of direct quantitative support of magnitude around .999 $[= 1 - .001]$.

To believe this literally would, of course, be an undergraduate mistake of which no competent psychologist would be guilty; I only want to point to the fact that there is subtle tendency to "carry over" a very small probability of a Type I error into a sizeable resulting confidence in the truth of the substantive theory, even among investigators who would never make an explicit identification of the one probability number with the complement of the other.

One reason why the directional null hypothesis ($H_{02} : \mu_g \leq \mu_b$) is the appropriate candidate for experimental refutation is the universal agreement that the old point-null hypothesis $H_0 : \mu_g = \mu_b$) is [quasi-] always false in biological and social science. Any dependent variable of interest, such as I.Q., or academic achievement, or perceptual speed, or emotional reactivity as measured by skin resistance, or whatever, depends mainly upon a finite number of "strong" variables characteristic of the organisms studied (embodying the accumulated results of their genetic makeup and their learning histories) plus the influences manipulated by the experimenter. Upon some complicated, unknown mathematical function of this finite list of "important" determiners is then superimposed an indefinitely large number of essentially "random" factors which contribute to the intragroup variation and therefore boost the error term of the statistical significance test. In order for two groups which differ in some identified properties (such as social class, intelligence, diagnosis, racial or religious background) to differ not at all in the "output" variable of interest, it would be necessary that all determiners of the output variable have precisely the same average values in both groups, or else that their values should differ by a *pattern of amounts of difference* which precisely counterbalance one another to yield a net difference of zero. Now our general background knowledge in the social sciences, or, for that matter, even "common sense" considerations, makes such an exact equality of all determining variables, or a precise "accidental" counterbalancing of them, so extremely unlikely that no psychologist or statistician would assign more than a negligibly small probability to such a state of affairs.

Example. Suppose we are studying a simple perceptual-verbal task like rate of color-naming in school children, and the independent variable is father's religious preference. Superficial consideration might suggest that these two variables would not be related, but a little thought leads one to conclude that they will almost certainly be related by *some* amount, however small. Consider, for instance, that a child's reaction to any sort of school-context task will be to some extent dependent upon his social class, since the desire to please academic personnel and the desire to achieve at a performance (just because it is a *task*, regardless of its intrinsic interest) are both related to the kinds of sub-cultural and personality traits in the parents that lead to upward mobility, economic success, the gaining of further education, and the like. Again, since there is known to be a sex difference in color-naming, it is likely that fathers who have entered occupations more attractive to "feminine" males will (on the average) provide a somewhat more feminine father-figure for identification on the part of their male offspring, and that a more refined color vocabulary, making closer discriminations between similar hues, will be characteristic of the ordinary language of such a household. Further, it is known that there is a correlation between a child's general intelligence and its father's occupation, and of course there will be *some* relation, even though it may be small, between a child's general intelligence and his color vocabulary, arising from the fact that *vocabulary in general* is heavily saturated with the general intelligence factor. Since religious preference is a correlate of social class, all of these social class factors, as well as the intelligence variable, would tend to influence color-naming performance. Or consider a more extreme and faint kind of relationship. It is quite conceivable that a child who belongs to a more liturgical religious denomination would be somewhat more color-oriented than a child for whom bright colors were not associated with the religious life. Everyone familiar with psychological research knows that numerous "puzzling, unexpected" correlations pop up all the time, and that it requires only a moderate amount of motivation-plus-ingenuity to construct very plausible alternative theoretical explanations for them.

These armchair considerations are borne out by the finding that in psychological and sociological investigations involving very large numbers of subjects, it is regularly found that almost all correlations or differences between means are statistically significant. See, for example, the papers by Bakan [1] and Nunnally [8]. Data currently being analyzed by Dr. David Lykken and myself, derived from a huge sample of over 55,000 Minnesota high school seniors, reveal statistically significant relationships in 91% of pairwise associations among a congeries of 45 miscellaneous variables such as sex, birth order, religious preference, number of siblings, vocational choice, club membership, college choice, mother's education, dancing, interest in woodworking, liking for school, and the like. The 9% of non-significant associations are heavily concentrated among a small minority of variables having dubious reliability, or involving arbitrary groupings of non-homogeneous or non-monotonic sub-categories. The majority of variables exhibited significant relationships *with all but three of the others*, often at a very high confidence level ($p < 10^{-6}$).

This line of reasoning is perhaps not quite as convincing in the case of true *experiments*, where the subjects are randomly assigned by the investigator to different experimental manipulations. If the reader is disinclined to follow me here, my overall argument will, for him, be applicable to those kinds of research in social science which study the correlational relationships or group differences between subjects "as they come," but not to the type of investigation which constitutes an experiment in the usual scientific sense. However, I myself believe that even in the strict sense of 'experiment,' the argument is still strong, although the quantitative departures from the point-null H_0 would be expected to run considerably lower on the average. Considering the fact that "everything in the brain is connected with everything else," and that there exist several "general state-variables" (such as arousal, attention, anxiety, and the like) which are known to be at least *slightly* influenceable by practically any kind of stimulus input, it is highly unlikely that *any* psychologically discriminable stimulation which we apply to an experimental subject would exert literally *zero* effect upon any aspect of his performance. The psychological literature abounds with examples of small but detectable influences of this kind. Thus it is known that if a subject memorizes a list of nonsense syllables in the presence of a faint odor of peppermint, his recall will be facilitated by the presence of that odor. Or, again, we know that individuals solving intellectual problems in a "messy" room do not perform quite as well as individuals working in a neat, well-ordered surround. Again, cognitive processes undergo a detectable facilitation when the thinking subject is concurrently performing the irrelevant, noncognitive task of squeezing a hand dynamometer. It would require considerable ingenuity to concoct experimental manipulations, except the most minimal and trivial (such as a very slight modification in the word order of instructions given a subject) where one could have confidence that the manipulation would be utterly without effect upon the subject's motivational level, attention, arousal, fear of failure, achievement drive, desire to please the experimenter, distraction, social fear, etc., etc. So that, for example, while there is no very "interesting" psychological theory that links hunger drive with color-naming ability, I myself would confidently predict a significant difference in color-naming ability between persons tested after a full meal and persons who had not eaten for 10 hours, provided the sample size were sufficiently large and the color-naming measurements sufficiently reliable, since one of the effects of the increased hunger drive is heightened "arousal," and anything which heightens arousal would be expected to affect a perceptual-cognitive performance like color-naming. Suffice it to say that there are very good reasons for expecting at least *some* slight influence of almost any experimental manipulation which would differ sufficiently in its form and content from the manipulation imposed upon a control group to be included in an experiment in the first place. In what follows I shall therefore assume that the point-null hypothesis H_0 is, in psychology, [quasi-] always false.

Let us now conceive of a large "theoretical urn" containing counters designating the indefinitely large class of actual and possible substantive theories concerning a certain domain of psychology (e.g., mammalian instrumental learning). Let us conceive of a second urn, the "experimental-design" urn, containing counters designating the indefinitely large set of possible experimental situations which the ingenuity of man could devise. (If anyone should object to my conceptualizing, for purposes of methodological analysis, such a heterogeneous class of theories or experiments, I need only remind him that such a class is universally presupposed in the logic of statistical significance testing.) Since the point-null hypothesis H_0 is [quasi-] always false, almost every one of these experimental situations involves a non-zero difference on its output variable (parameter). Whichever group we (arbitrarily) designated as the "experimental" group and the "control" group, in half of these experimental settings the true value of the dependent variable difference (experimental minus control) will be positive, and in the other half negative.

It may be objected that this is use of the Principle of Insufficient Reason and presupposes one particular answer to some disputed questions in statistical theory (as between the Bayesians and the Fisherians). But I must emphasize that I have said nothing about the *form* or *range* or other parametric characteristics of the distribution of true differences. I have merely said that the point-null hypothesis H_0 is always false, and I have then *assigned*, in a strictly random fashion, the names "experimental" and "control" to the two groups which a given experimental setup treats in two different ways. That is, it makes no difference here whether a group of subjects learning nonsense syllables while squeezing a hand dynamometer is called the experimental group, or whether we call "experimental" the group that learns the nonsense syllables without such squeezing. Hence my use of the

Principle of Insufficient Reason is one of those legitimate, non-controversial uses following directly when the basic principles of probability are applied to a specification of procedure for random assignment.

We now perform a random pairing of the counters from the "theory" urn with the counters from the "experimental" urn, and arbitrarily stipulate—quite irrationally—that a "successful" outcome of the experiment means that the difference favors the experimental group $[\mu_E - \mu_C > 0]$. This preposterous model, which is of course much worse than anything that can exist even in the most primitive of the social sciences, provides us with a lower bound for the expected frequency of a theory's successfully predicting the direction in which the null hypothesis fails, *in the state of nature* (i.e., we are here not considering sampling problems, and therefore we neglect errors of either the first or the second kind). It is obvious that if the point-null hypothesis H_0 is [quasi-]always false, and there is no logical connection between our theories and the direction of the experimental outcomes, then if we arbitrarily assign one of the two directional hypotheses H_1 or H_2 to each theory, that hypothesis will be correct half of the time, i.e., in half of the arbitrary urn-counter-pairings. Since even my late, uneducated grandmother's common-sense psychological theories had nonzero verisimilitude, we can safely say that the value $p = \frac{1}{2}$ is a lower bound on the success-frequency of experimental "tests," assuming our experimental design had perfect power.

Countervailing the unknown increment over $p = \frac{1}{2}$ which arises from the fact that the experimental and theoretical counters are not thus drawn randomly (since our theories do possess, on the average, at least some tiny amount of verisimilitude), there is the statistical factor that among the counter-pairings which are accidentally "successful" (in the sense that the state of nature falsifies the null hypothesis in the expected direction), we will sometimes fail to refute it because of measurement and sampling errors, since our experiments will always, in practice, have less than perfect power. Even though the point-null hypothesis H_0 is always false, so that the directional null hypothesis H_{02} is false in the (theoretically pseudo-predicted) direction half the time, we will sometimes fail to discover this because of Type II errors. Without making illegitimate prior-probability assumptions concerning the actual distribution of true differences in the whole vast world of psychological experimental contexts, one cannot say anything definite about the extent to which this countervailing influence of Type II errors will wash out (or even overcome) the fact that our theories tend to have non-negligible verisimilitude. But by setting aside this latter fact, i.e., by assuming counterfactually that there is *no connection whatever between our theories and our experimental designs* (the two-urn idealization), thereby fixing the expected frequency of successful refutations of the directional null hypothesis H_{02} at $p = \frac{1}{2}$ for experiments of *perfect power;* it follows that as the power of our experimental designs and significance tests is increased by any of the three methods described above, we approach $p = \frac{1}{2}$ as the limit of our expected frequency of "successful outcomes," i.e., of attaining statistically significant experimental results in the theoretically predicted direction.

I conclude that the effect of increased precision, whether achieved by improved instrumentation and control, greater sensitivity in the logical structure of the experiment, or increasing the number of observations, is to yield a probability approaching $\frac{1}{2}$ of corroborating our substantive theory by a significance test, *even if the theory is totally without merit.* That is to say, the ordinary result of improving our experimental methods and increasing our sample size, proceeding in accordance with the traditionally accepted method of theory-testing by refuting a directional null hypothesis, yields a prior probability $p \simeq \frac{1}{2}$ and very likely somewhat above that value by an unknown amount. It goes without saying that successfully negotiating an experimental hurdle of this sort can constitute only an extremely weak corroboration of any substantive theory, *quite apart from currently disputed issues of the Bayesian type regarding the assignment of prior probabilities to the theory itself.*

So far as I am able to discern, this methodological truth is either unknown or systematically ignored by most behavior scientists. I do not know to what extent this is attributable to confusion between the substantive theory T and the statistical hypothesis H_1, with the resulting mis-assignment of the probability $(1 - p_I)$ complementary to the significance level p_I attained, to the "probability" of the substantive theory; or to what extent it arises from insufficient attention to the truism that the point-null hypothesis H_0 is [quasi-]always false. It seems unlikely that most social science investigators would think in their usual way about a theory in meteorology which "successfully predicted" that it would rain on the 17th of April, given the antecedent information that it rains (on the average) during half the days in the month of April!

But this is not the worst of the story. Inadequate appreciation of the extreme weakness of the test to which a substantive theory T is subjected by merely predicting a directional statistical difference $\bar{d} > 0$ is then compounded by a truly remarkable failure to recognize the logical asymmetry between, on the one hand, (formally invalid) "confirmation" of a theory via affirming the consequent in an argument of form: $[T \supset H_1, H_1, \text{infer } T)$, and on the other hand the deductively tight *refutation* of the theory *modus tollens* by a falsified prediction, the logical form being: $[T \supset H_1, \sim H_1, \text{infer } \sim T]$.

While my own philosophical predilections are somewhat Popperian, I daresay any reader will agree that no full-fledged Popperian philosophy of science is presupposed in what I have just said. The destruction of a theory *modus tollens* is, after all, a matter of deductive logic; whereas that the "confirmation" of a theory by its making successful predictions involves a much weaker kind of inference. This much would be conceded by even the most anti-Popperian "inductivist." The writing of behavior scientists often reads as though they assumed—what it is hard to believe anyone would explicitly assert if challenged—that successful and unsuccessful predictions are practically on all fours in arguing for and against a substantive theory. Many experimental articles in the behavioral sciences, and, even more strangely, review articles which purport to survey the current status of a particular theory in the light of all available evidence, treat the confirming instances and the disconfirming instances with equal methodological respect, as if one could, so to speak, "Count noses," so that if a theory has somewhat more confirming than disconfirming instances, it is in pretty good shape evidentially. Since we know that this is already grossly incorrect on purely formal grounds, it is a mistake *a fortiori* when the socalled "confirming instances" have themselves a prior probability, as argued above, somewhere in the neighborhood of $\frac{1}{2}$, quite apart from any theoretical considerations.

Contrast this bizarre state of affairs with the state of affairs in physics. While there are of course a few exceptions, the usual situation in the experimental testing of a physical theory at least involves the prediction of a *form* of function (with parameters to be fitted); or, more commonly, the prediction of a quantitative magnitude (point-value). Improvements in the accuracy of determining this experimental function-form or point-value, whether by better instrumentation for control and making observations, or by the gathering of a larger number of measurements, has the effect of *narrowing* the band of tolerance about the theoretically predicted value. What does this mean in terms of the significance-testing model? It means: *In physics, that which corresponds, in the logical structure of statistical inference, to the old-fashioned point-null hypothesis H_0 is the value which flows as a consequence of the substantive theory T;* so that an increase in what the statistician would call "power" or "precision" has the methodological effect of stiffening the experimental test, of setting up a more difficult observational hurdle for the theory T to surmount. Hence, in physics the effect of improving precision or power is that of *decreasing* the prior probability of a successful experimental outcome if the theory lacks verisimilitude, that is, precisely the reverse of the situation obtaining in the social sciences.

As techniques of control and measurement improve or the number of observations increases, the methodological effect in physics is that a successful passing of the hurdle will mean a greater increment in corroboration of the substantive theory; whereas in psychology, comparable improvements at the experimental level result in an empirical test which can provide only a progressively weaker corroboration of the substantive theory.

In physics, the substantive theory predicts a point-value, and when physicists employ "significance tests," their mode of employment is to compare the theoretically predicted value x_0 with the observed mean $\bar{x}_0$, asking whether they differ (in either direction!) by more than the "probable error" of determination of the latter. Hence H : $H_0 = \mu_x$ functions as a point-null hypothesis, and the prior (logical, antecedent) probability of its being correct in the absence of theory approximates zero. As the experimental error associated with our determination of $\bar{x}_0$ shrinks, values of $\bar{x}_0$ consistent with x_0 (and hence, compatible with its implicans T) must lie within a narrow range. In the limit (zero probable error, corresponding to "perfect power" in the significant test) any nonzero difference $(\bar{x}_0 - x_0)$ provides a *modus tollens* refutation of T. If the theory has negligible verisimilitude, the logical probability of its surviving such a test is negligible. Whereas in psychology, the result of perfect power (i.e., *certain* detection of any non-zero difference in the predicted direction) is to yield a prior probability $p = \frac{1}{2}$ of getting experimental results compatible with T, because perfect power would mean guaranteed detection of whatever difference exists; and a difference [quasi] always exists, being in the "theoretically expected direction" half the time if our substantive theories were all of negligible verisimilitude (two-urn model).

This methodological paradox would exist for the psychologist even if he played his own statistical game fairly. The reason for its existence is obvious, namely, that most psychological theories, especially in the so-called "soft" fields such as social and personality psychology, are not quantitatively developed to the extent of being able to generate point-predictions. In this respect, then, although this state of affairs is surely unsatisfactory from the methodological point of view, and stands in great need of clarification (and, hopefully, of constructive suggestions for improving it) from logicians and philosophers of science, one might say that it is "nobody's fault," it being difficult to see just how the behavior scientist could extricate himself from this dilemma without making unrealistic attempts at the premature construction of theories which are sufficiently quantified to generate point-predictions for refutation.

However, there are five social forces and intellectual traditions at work in the behavior sciences which make the research consequences of this situation even worse than they may have to be, considering the state of our knowledge. In addition to (a) failure to recognize the marked evidential asymmetry between confirmation and *modus tollens* refutation of theories, and (b) inadequate appreciation of the extreme weakness of the hurdle provided by the mere directional significance test, there exists among psychologists (c) a fairly widespread tendency to report experimental findings with a liberal use of *ad hoc* explanations for those that didn't "pan out." This last methodological sin is especially tempting in the "soft" fields of (personality and social) psychology, where the profession highly rewards a kind of "cuteness" or "cleverness" in experimental design, such as a hitherto untried method for inducing a desired emotional state, or a particularly "subtle" gimmick for detecting its influence upon behavioral output. The methodological price paid for this highly-valued "cuteness" is, of course, (d) an unusual ease of escape from *modus tollens* refutation. For, the logical structure of the "cute" component typically involves use of complex and rather dubious auxiliary assumptions, which are required to mediate the original prediction and are therefore readily available as (genuinely) plausible "outs" when the prediction fails. It is not unusual that (e) this *ad hoc* challenging of auxiliary hypotheses is repeated in the course of a series of related experiments, in which the auxiliary hypothesis involved in Experiment 1 (and challenged *ad hoc* in order to avoid the latter's *modus tollens* impact on the theory) becomes the focus of interest in Experiment 2, which in turn utilizes further plausible but easily challenged auxiliary hypotheses, and so forth. In this fashion a zealous and clever investigator can slowly wend his way through a tenuous nomological network, performing a long series of related experiments which appear to the uncritical reader as a fine example of "an integrated research program," *without ever once refuting or corroborating so much as a single strand of the network.* Some of the more horrible examples of this process would require the combined analytic and reconstructive efforts of Carnap, Hempel, and Popper to unscramble the logical relationships of theories and hypothesis to evidence. Meanwhile our eager-beaver researcher, undismayed by logic-of-science considerations and relying blissfully on the "exactitude" of modern statistical hypothesis-testing, has produced a long publication list and been promoted to a full professorship. In terms of his contribution to the enduring body of psychological knowledge, he has done hardly anything. His true position is that of a potent-but-sterile intellectual rake, who leaves in his merry path a long train of ravished maidens but no viable scientific offspring.[2]

Detailed elaboration of the intellectual vices (a)–(e) and their scientific consequences must be left for another place, as must constructive suggestions for how the behavior scientist can improve his situation. My main aim here has been to call the attention of logicians and philosophers of science to what, as I think, is an important and difficult problem for psychology, or for any science which is largely in a primitive stage of development such that its theories do not give rise to point-predictions.

References

1. Bakan, David, "The test of significance in psychological research," *Psychological Bulletin*, Vol. 66 (1966), pp. 423–437.

2. Bolles, Robert C., "The difference between statistical hypotheses and scientific hypotheses," *Psychological Reports*, Vol. 11 (1962), pp. 639–645.

3. Bunge, Mario (ed.), *The critical approach to science and philosophy: essays in honor of Karl R. Popper*, New York: Free Press of Glencoe, Inc., 1964.

4. Cohen, Jacob, "The statistical power of abnormal-social psychological research: a review," *Journal of abnormal and social Psychology*, Vol. 65 (1962), pp. 145–153.

5. Hays, William L., *Statistics for psychologists*, New York: Holt, Rinehart, and Winston, 1963.

6. Kaiser, Henry F., "Directional statistical decisions," *Psychological Review*, Vol. 67 (1960), pp. 160–167.

---

2. Since the readers of this journal cannot, by and large, be expected to possess familiarity with the field of psychology or the contributions of various psychologists, and since quantitative empirical documentation of these admittedly impressionistic comments is still in preparation for subsequent presentation elsewhere, it is perhaps neither irrelevant nor in bad taste to present a few biographical data. Lest the philosophical reader wonder (quite appropriately) whether these impressions of the psychological literature ought perhaps to be dismissed as mere "sour grapes" from an embittered, low-publication psychologist *manqué*, it may be stated that the author (a past president of the American Psychological Association) has published over 70 technical books or articles in both "hard" and "soft" fields of psychology, is a recipient of the Association's Distinguished Scientific Contributor Award, also of the Distinguished Contributor Award of the Division of Clinical Psychology, has been elected to Fellowship in the American Academy of Arts and Sciences, and is actively engaged in both theoretical and empirical research at the present time. He's not mad at anybody—but he is a bit distressed at the state of psychology.

7. Lykken, David T., "Statistical significance in psychiatric research," *Reports from the Research Laboratories of the Department of Psychiatry, University of Minnesota. Report No. PR*-66-9, Minneapolis: December 30, 1966.

8. Nunnally, Jum C., "The place of statistics in psychology," *Educational and Psychological Measurement*, Vol. 20 (1960), pp. 641–650.

9. Popper, Karl R., *The logic of scientific discovery*, New York: Basic Books, 1959.

10. Popper, Karl R., *Conjectures and refutations*, New York: Basic Books, 1962.

11. Rozeboom, William W., "The fallacy of the null-hypothesis significance test," *Psychological Bulletin*, Vol. 67 (1960), pp. 416–428.

testing the null hypothesis and the strategy and tactics of investigating theoretical models

David A. Grant[1]

Testing the null hypothesis, H_0, against alternatives, H_1, is well established and has a proper place in scientific research. However, this testing procedure, when it is routinely applied to comparing experimental outcomes with outcomes that are quantitatively predicted from a theoretical model, can have unintended results and bizarre implications. This paper first outlines three situations in which testing H_0 has conventionally been done by psychologists. In terms of the probable intentions or strategy of the experimenter testing H_0 turns out to be an appropriate tactic in the first situation, but it is

From *Psychological Review*, Vol. 69 (No. 1), 1962, pp. 54–61. Copyright 1962 by the American Psychological Association. Reproduced by permission.

1.   The author is indebted to Arnold M. Binder of Indiana University whose arguments inspired him to make explicit some of the issues involved in using conventional analysis of variance procedures in testing the adequacy of a theoretical model. As this paper went through various revisions over a period of time the writer is correspondingly indebted to a number of supporting agencies: the Graduate Research Committee and the College of Letters and Science of the University of Wisconsin, the National Science Foundation, and finally to the Department of Psychology of the University of California, Berkeley, his host during final preparation of the manuscript.

inadequate in the second situation, and it is self-defeating with curious implications in the last situation. Alternatives to this conventional procedure are then presented along with the considerations which make the alternatives preferable to testing the usual H_0.

Three applications of H_0 testing

Probably the most common application of the tactic of testing H_0 arises when the independent variable has produced a sample difference or set of differences in the magnitude of the dependent variable. Quantitative predictions of the size of the difference or differences are not available. The experimenter wishes to know whether or not differences of the size obtained could have occurred by virtue of the operation of the innumerable nonexperimental factors conventionally designated as random. He sets up H_0 that the differences are zero; chooses a significance level, α; determines the set of hypotheses alternative to H_0 that he is willing to entertain, H_1; selects an appropriate test statistic, t, F, χ^2, U, T, or the like; and proceeds with the test. Rejection of H_0 permits him to assert, with a precisely defined risk of being wrong, that the obtained differences were not the product of chance variation. Failure of the test to permit rejection of H_0, which, unfortunately, is commonly termed "accepting" H_0, means that the obtained differences or greater ones would occur by chance with a probability greater than α. This situation is straight-forward. The experimenter has limited aims. He has asked a simple question, and he has received a simple answer, subject only to those ambiguities which attend all experimental and inductive inference. His tactics are admirably suited to his strategic objective.

Another common but less satisfactory instance of testing H_0 arises when the results of pre-experimental matching or pretesting are to be evaluated. Here the experimenter has measured the dependent variable or some related variable before operation of the independent variable, and he devoutly hopes that the experimental and control groups are alike except for random differences. He is now relieved or chagrined, depending upon whether H_0 is "accepted" or "rejected" as a consequence of his test. Even if H_0 is accepted his relief is tempered by some uneasiness. He knows that he has not proved, and indeed cannot prove, that H_0 is "true." His tactics in testing H_0 seem to be appropriate to the impossible strategic aim of proving the truth of H_0. Certainly, if he had a more reasonable aim he has adopted inappropriate tactics. Utilizing these tactics, the best he can do is to beat a strategic retreat, and if H_0 is accepted he can perhaps point out that he has used a very powerful test and that if there were real differences they were most likely very small. Although psychologists have never to my knowledge done so, he might be able to go one step further and point out that his testing procedure would reject H_0 a given percentage of the time, say, 90 %, if the "true" difference had been as little as, say, one-tenth of an *SD*. This sort of statement of the power of a test is a commonplace in acceptance inspection (Grant, 1952, Ch. 13).

With the advent of more detailed mathematical models in psychology (e.g., Bush, Abelson and Hyman, 1956; Bush and Estes, 1959; Goldberg, 1958; Kemeny, Snell, and Thompson, 1957) a new statistical testing situation is arising more and more frequently. The specificity of the predictions and perhaps the whole philosophy behind model construction pose a different kind of statistical problem than those faced by most psychological investigators in the past. It seems obvious that as the use of models becomes more widespread a greater number of investigators will face the problem of evaluating the correspondence between empirical data points and precise numerical predictions of these points. Unfortunately most of the procedures used to date in testing the adequacy of such theoretical predictions set rather bad examples. Probably the least adequate of these procedures has been that in which an H_0 of exact correspondence between theoretical and empirical points is tested against H_1 covering any discrepancy between predictions and experimental results.

Most models predict a considerable number of different aspects of the data, and some of these aspects are predicted with greater success than others (Bush and Estes, 1959, Chs. 14, 15, 17, 18). We shall restrict our discussion to the prediction of values along a curve which might be a learning curve. An idealized version of such a typical situation is presented in Figure 1. Here, the dependent variable, Y, is plotted on the vertical axis against the independent variable, X, on the horizontal axis. The theoretical model has led to an expression, $Y' = f(X)$, giving a set of k theoretical predictions, $Y'_1, Y'_2, \ldots, Y'_k$. The experiment has produced k empirical data points, a set of mean values, $\bar{Y}_1, \bar{Y}_2, \ldots, \bar{Y}_k$, corresponding to the values of the independent variable that were investigated, namely, $X_1, X_2, \ldots, X_k$. Individual observations tend to form normal distributions about each of the $\bar{Y}_i$, and these normal distributions tend to have equal σ's for all data points. In further discussion we shall assume that inaccuracies in the manipulation of the independent variable, X, can be ignored. The problem now is to investigate the goodness of fit of the Y'_i to the $\bar{Y}_i$ or the correspondence between the Y'_i and the $\bar{Y}_i$.

The tactics oriented toward accepting H_0 as corroborating the theory involve breaking down the jth individual observation from the

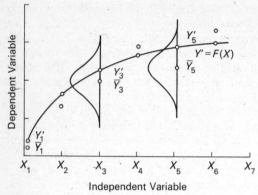

Fig. 1

Idealized situation involving the test of a theoretical function, $Y' = F(X)$. (Theoretical points, Y'_i, are represented by open circles; obtained means, Y_i, are represented by solid circles.)

general mean of all of the observations, as follows:

$$Y_{ij} - \bar{Y} = (Y_{ij} - \bar{Y}_i) + (\bar{Y}_i - Y'_i) + (Y'_i - \bar{Y}) \tag{1}$$

where Y_{ij} is the jth observation in the ith normal distribution, and $\bar{Y}$ is the general mean of all observations. The total sum of squares may then be partitioned as follows:

$$SS_{\text{Tot}} = SS_{\text{Dev Est}} + SS_{\text{Dev Theory}} + SS_{\text{Theory}} \tag{2}$$

where $SS_{\text{Dev Est}}$ is the sum of squares associated with the variation of individual measures from their means, $SS_{\text{Dev Theory}}$ is the sum of squares associated with the systematic departures of empirical data points from the theoretical points, and SS_{Theory} is the sum of squares associated with departures of the theoretical points from the general mean of the whole experiment. If we suppose that the linear model for the analysis of variance holds, then:

$$Y_{ij} = \mu + T_i + D_i + e_{ij} \tag{3}$$

where μ is the population mean for all Y_{ij} over the specific values of the independent variable, X_i; T_i is the departure of the "true" theoretical value of Y'_i from μ; D_i is the discrepancy of the "true" value of $\bar{Y}_i$ from the true value of Y'_i; and e_{ij} is a random element from a normal distribution with a mean of zero and variance, σ^2, for all i. For a fixed set of X_i the T's and D's may be defined so that $\Sigma T_i = \Sigma D_i = 0$. Under H_0 each $D_i = 0$. Under H_i some $D_i \neq 0$, and the variance of the D_i, $\sigma_D^2 \neq 0$. This last variance may be termed the true variance of the discrepancies from the theory over the particular set of X_i that was investigated.

The foregoing is a conventional analysis of variance model, and the F ratio of the $MS_{\text{Dev Theory}}$ divided by the $MS_{\text{Dev Est}}$ provides an excellent and powerful test of H_0 against H_1. The number of degrees of freedom for $SS_{\text{Dev Est}}$ will be $k(n-1)$ where n is the number of observations per data point, and the degrees of freedom for $SS_{\text{Dev Theory}}$ will be $k - n_T$, where n_T is the number of degrees of freedom lost in the process of fitting the model to the data. If this F is significant, we reject H_0, concluding that the discrepancies between the $\bar{Y}_i$ and the Y_i' are too great to be accounted for by the observed random variation in the experiment. In this conclusion we accept the 5 % or 1 % risk implied by our choice of α.

Logical difficulties arise when F fails of significance. H_0 remains tenable but is not proved to be correct. A tenable H_0 provides some support for the theory but only in the negative sense of failing to provide evidence that the theory is faulty. To assert that accepting the H_0 proves that the model provides a satisfactory fit to the data is an inaccurate and misleading statement. We may mean that we are satisfied, but others, especially proponents of other theories, will tend to regard our test as too lenient.

Failure to reject H_0, instead of producing closure, leaves certain annoying ambiguities, but the tactics of testing this particular H_0 imply a strategy that suffers from more serious defects that are readily apparent when the whole conception of testing a theory is carefully considered. To begin with, in view of our present psychological knowledge and the degree of refinement of available theoretical models it seems certain that even the best and most useful theories are not perfect. This means, in terms of the analysis of variance model, there will be some nonzero D_i's. H_0, then, is never really "true." Its "acceptance," rather than "proving" the theory, merely indicates that in this instance the D_i's were too small to be demonstrated by the sensitivity of the experiment in question. The tactics of accepting H_0 as proof and rejecting H_0 as disproof of a theory lead to the anomalous results that a small-scale, insensitive experiment will most often be interpreted as favoring a theory, whereas a large-scale, sensitive experiment will usually yield results opposed to the theory!

Curiously enough, even rejection of H_0 by means of a very stringent experimental test may be quite misleading as far as casting light on the adequacy of the theory is concerned. If the D_i's are very small indeed the theoretical model may be a great improvement over anything else that is available and satisfactory for many purposes even though an extremely sensitive experiment were to reveal the nonzero

D_i's. If our task, as scientists, were to test and accept or reject theories as they came off some assembly line the tactics of testing H_0 could be made in a satisfactory manner simply by requiring that the test be "sufficiently" stringent. In fact, our task and our intentions are usually different from testing products; what we are really up to resembles *quality control* rather than *acceptance inspection*, and statistical procedures suitable for the latter are rarely optimal for the former (Grant, 1952, Chs. 1, 13).

**Hypothesis testing
vs. statistical estimation**

An analogy will make clear the relation between testing tactics and the intention of the tester. Suppose that I wish to test a parachute; how should I go about it? How I should test depends upon my general intentions. If I want to sell the parachute and am testing it only to be able to claim that it has been tested, and I do not care what happens to the purchaser, then I should give the parachute a most lenient, nonanalytic test. If, however, I am testing the parachute to be sure of it for my own use, then I should subject it to a very stringent, nonanalytic test. But if I am in the competitive business of manufacturing and selling parachutes, then I should subject it to a searching, analytic test, designed to tell me as much as possible about the locus and cause of any failure in order that I may improve my product and gain a larger share of the parachute market. My contention is that the last situation is the one that is most analogous to that facing the theoretical scientist. He is not accepting or rejecting a finished theory; he is in the long-term business of constructing better versions of the theory. Progress depends upon improvement or providing superior alternatives, and improvement will ordinarily depend upon knowing just how good the model is and exactly where it seems to need alteration. The large D_i's designate the next point of attack in the continuing project of refining the existing model. Therefore attention should be focused upon the various discrepancies between prediction and outcome instead of on the over-all adequacy of the model.

In view of our long-term strategy of improving our theories, our statistical tactics can be greatly improved by shifting emphasis away from over-all hypothesis testing in the direction of statistical estimation. This always holds true when we are concerned with the actual size of one or more differences rather than simply in the existence of differences. For example, in the second instance of hypothesis testing cited at the beginning of this paper, where the investigator tests a pre-experimental difference, he would do better to obtain 95% or 99%

confidence interval for the pre-experimental difference. If the interval is small and includes zero, he (and any other moderately sophisticated person) knows immediately that he is on fairly safe ground; but if the interval is large, even though it includes zero, it is immediately apparent that the situation is more uncertain. In both instances H_0 would have been accepted.

Testing a revised H_0

Before turning to estimation procedures that are useful in examining the correspondence between experimental outcomes and predictions from a mathematical model, I shall digress briefly to outline a statistical testing method which can legitimately be used in appraising the fit of a model to data as shown in Figure 1. Basically the statistical argument in the proper test is reoriented so that rejection of H_0 constitutes evidence favoring the theory. The new H_0 is that the correlation between the predicted values, $\bar{Y}_i'$, and the obtained values, $\bar{Y}_i$, is zero, after all correlation due to the fitting process has been eliminated. The alternative, H_1, against which H_0 is tested is that there is a correlation greater than zero between theoretical and empirical points. The four simple steps required to obtain the necessary F test are as follows:

1. Calculate $t_i = Y_i' - \bar{Y}$ for all i. $\Sigma t_i = 0$.[2]

2. Calculate $SS_{\text{Correspondence}} = n(\Sigma t_i \bar{Y}_i)^2 / \Sigma t_i^2$, where n is the number of observations upon which each $\bar{Y}_i$ is based. Negative values of $(\Sigma t_i \bar{Y}_i)$ are treated as zero.

3. Obtain $MS_{\text{Correspondence}} = SS_{\text{Correspondence}} / n_T$, where n_T, the number of degrees of freedom involved in fitting the theoretical points to the empirical data, will ordinarily be the number of linearly independent fitting constants in the mathematical expression of the model.

4. Divide $MS_{\text{Correspondence}}$ by $MS_{\text{Dev Est}}$ to give $F_{\text{Correspondence}}$ which has n_T degrees of freedom for its numerator and $k(n - 1)$ degrees of freedom for its denominator, k being the number of $\bar{Y}_i$. The test is one-tailed in the sense that negative values of $\Sigma t_i \bar{Y}$ are treated as zero values, so

---

2. In the unusual event where the general mean of the observations, $\bar{Y}$, is not used as a fitting constant for $Y' = f(X)$, the t_i must be computed as deviations from the mean of all the Y_i', $\bar{Y}'$. The test will then be insensitive to discrepancies between $\bar{Y}'$ and $\bar{Y}$ and the interpretation will be somewhat equivocal. A separate test of H_0 that $\bar{Y}_{\text{population}}$ equals $\bar{Y}'$, is feasible, but here the experimenter is forced into the illicit posture of seeking to embrace H_0.

that the probability values of the F distribution must be halved, an unusual procedure with F tests in analysis of variance.

Following the above procedure, rejection of H_0 now means that there is more than random positive covariation between predicted and obtained values of the dependent variable.

This test is admirable in that it puts the burden of proof on the investigator, because a small-scale, insensitive experiment is unlikely to produce evidence favoring the model. Furthermore, if the model has any merit, the more sensitive the experiment, the more likely it is that a significant F, favoring the theory, will be obtained. Actually, the test is extremely sensitive to virtue in the theory, and therefore in the case of a moderately successful model and a moderately sensitive experiment both this F and the one testing the significance of systematic deviations from the model ($F = MS_{\text{Dev Theory}}/MS_{\text{Dev Est}}$) will tend to be significant. This outcome is no anomaly; it merely indicates that the model predicts some but not all of the systematic variation in the data. In short, progress is being made, but improvement is possible. The fact that simultaneous significance of both F's, indicating general success and specific failures of a model, should be a common-place points up the necessity of turning to methods of statistical estimation for a more adequate examination of the workings of a theoretical model.

Practical estimation methods
for investigation of models

As is true of statistical tests, each method of statistical estimation has its advantages and limitations. In the investigation of the adequacy of theoretical curves in psychology there are reasons to believe that the simpler estimation methods have practical advantages over some of the more elegant procedures. To give a fairly complete view of the situation, methods of point and interval estimation of σ_D^2 and of the individual D_i will be described, and a brief evaluation of each method will be given.

Estimating σ_D^2. The variance of the discrepancies between the Y_i' and the $\bar{Y}_i$ condenses into a single number the adequacy of fit of the theoretical model. As such it is an excellent index for the evaluation of the model. The smaller the variance, σ_D^2, the better the model, and vice versa. As an estimate of the size of the discrepancies one might expect in future similar applications of the model, σ_D^2 is far more informative than any F test. Furthermore σ_D^2 is readily estimated in the case of homogeneity of the error variance, σ_e^2. The expected values of the relevant mean squares are as follows:

$$\exp(MS_{\text{Dev Theory}}) = \sigma_e^2 + n\sigma_D^2 \tag{4}$$

$$\exp(MS_{\text{Dev Est}}) = \sigma_e^2 \tag{5}$$

A maximum likelihood estimate of the variance of the discrepancies, $\hat{\sigma}_D^2$ is then:

$$\hat{\sigma}_D^2 = (MS_{\text{Dev Theory}} - MS_{\text{Dev Est}})/n \tag{6}$$

The accuracy of this estimator depends upon the number of degrees of freedom associated with $SS_{\text{Dev Theory}}$ and $SS_{\text{Dev Est}}$. The latter rarely poses any practical problem, but the former, in view of the predilection of psychologists for minimizing the number of data points, is quite critical. This is readily apparent when interval estimation of σ_D^2 is attempted.

Bross (1950) gives a convenient method for accurate approximation of the fiducial interval for σ_D^2, and in this case the fiducial and confidence intervals are essentially equal. The method will be outlined below for the 5% interval.

1. Obtain $\hat{\sigma}_D^2$ from Equation 6, above. (If the estimate is negative or zero, meaningful limits cannot be obtained.)

2. Find:

$$L = \frac{\dfrac{F}{F_{025(k-n_T,k[n-1])}} - 1}{\dfrac{F \cdot F_{025(k-n_T,\infty)}}{F_{025(k-n_T,k[n-1])}} - 1}$$

where:

$$F = MS_{\text{Dev Theory}}/MS_{\text{Dev Est}}$$

$F_{025(k-n_T,k[n-1])}$ is the entry in the 2.5% F table (Pearson and Hartley, 1954) for $n_1 = k - n_T$ and $n_2 = k[n-1]$; and $F_{025(k-n_T,\infty)}$ is the entry for $n_1 = k - n_T$ and $n_2 = \infty$.

3. Find:

$$L = \frac{F \cdot F_{025(k[n-1],k-n_T)} - 1}{\dfrac{F \cdot F_{025(k[n-1],k-n_T)}}{F_{025(\infty,k-n_T)}} - 1}$$

where $F_{025(k[n-1],k-n_T)}$ is the entry in the 2.5% F table for $n_1 = k[n-1]$, and $n_2 = k - n_T$; $F_{025(\infty,k-n_T)}$ is the entry for $n_1 = \infty$, and $n_2 = k - n_T$.

4. The upper and lower limits are then $\bar{L}\hat{\sigma}_D^2$ and $L\hat{\sigma}_D^2$, respectively. With less than 15–20 data points these limits will be found to be uncomfortably wide, a fact to bear in mind when designing an experimental test of a theoretical model. For example, in Figure 1, with 6 data points and two degrees of freedom for curve fitting, the limits might plausibly be 0–40, whereas with 14 data points the limits might be 0–12.

Aside from the considerable variability in the estimate of σ_D^2 which can be reduced by increasing the number of data points, there are two other important limitations to the use of estimates of the variance of the discrepancies in evaluating a model. First of all, the population value of σ_D^2 is completely dependent upon the particular values of the independent variable, X, which are chosen for the test of the model. Choice of two different sets of X's could well lead to two entirely different values of σ_D^2, and both of these values could be perfectly accurate. Secondly, although σ_D^2 gives an over-all index of the adequacy of the model being tested, it condenses so much information into one measure that it does not permit pin-pointing the especially large D_i's so that they can be given proper attention in considering revision of the model.

Estimating the D_i. The individual D_i may be estimated as points, or intervals may be established for the D_i, collectively or individually. As before, each method has its good points and its limitations.

Point estimation of the individual D_i's consists simply in comparing the individual data points, the $\bar{Y}_i$, with the fitted curve. It is a crude method, but it has served well in the past and represents the beginning of wisdom. For example, in Figure 1, the model builder might well note that the first three data points lie below the curve and ask himself if there is some special reason for this. He would also note that the greatest discrepancy occurs at $\bar{Y}_5$, where the neighboring discrepancies are in the other direction. The weakness of this simple method lies in the absence of a criterion which will assist the investigator in deciding which discrepancies should be singled out for further attention and which may be disregarded because they are within the range of expected random variation. This defect is remedied by the interval estimation techniques.

Probably the ideal method of interval estimation is that in which intervals are established for the whole curve in one operation by finding the 95% confidence band. The method takes the theoretical curve as a point of departure, and the result is a pair of curves above and below the theoretical curve, which will tend in the case of random variation to contain between them 95% of the data points. Points lying outside the band are immediately suspect; they are the most promising candidates for attention in the next version of the model. There are two practical difficulties with this method. First, homogeneity of the error variance, σ_e^2, over all the X_i is required. And secondly, because errors in estimation of each fitting parameter must be taken into account, for all but the simplest curves (Cornell, 1956, pp. 184–186) the bands may be difficult[3] to obtain. Although the method is elegant, in practice it will rarely represent sufficient improvement over the final method, given below, to justify its use.

The last method seems to me to be the most useful and most robust and most flexible method. It can be widely applied, and the relative ease of application, coupled with its ability to discriminate between significant and random discrepancies make it superior to the other estimation methods. It also possesses the homely virtue of being readily understood. In contrast to the preceding method, this one takes as its point of departure the empirical means, and consists, simply, in computing the 95% confidence limits for each of the $\bar{Y}_i$. If there is homogeneity of variance, the error variance of each mean is taken simply as $\hat{\sigma}_e^2/n$; in cases of suspected heterogeneity, each mean must have its own estimate of error variance. This will, of course, be the variance of the distribution of Y_{ij} for each i, divided by n. When these limits have been obtained, attention is directed to instances where the theoretical curve lies outside the limits. In some cases, the investigator might choose to establish the 80% or 90% limits in order to direct his attention to less drastic departures of the experimental results from the model. Choice of an optimum level for the limits is hard to establish on a general a priori basis, but it is likely that limits narrower than the traditional 95% will be found more useful than the broader limits. Simple as this method is, it is hard to improve upon in actual practice. Instead of giving an almost meaningless over-all acceptance or rejection of a model, it directs attention to specific defects, its functioning improves as the precision of the experimental test is improved, and the investigator can set the confidence coefficient so as to increase its sensitivity to defect at a cost of a fairly well-specified percentage of

---

3. A sufficient estimate of the error variance of each parameter must be available and independent of the estimates of all other parameters or else the covariances of all parametric estimates must be found and the theoretical function must have continuous first partial derivatives with respect to the parameters in order that the confidence bands may be found in the asymptotic case (Rao, 1952, pp. 207–208). Where an asymptote is involved in the fitting of the theoretical function, satisfactory independent estimators can rarely be obtained.

false positives or wild goose chases. A final and often crucial advantage is that the confidence intervals, based as they are upon the experimental means, can be obtained in cases where the form of the theoretical function does not permit satisfactory estimation of its parameters, and the analysis of variance and confidence bands methods cannot properly be applied.

Summary and conclusions

In this paper I have attempted to show that the traditional procedure of testing a null hypothesis (H_0) of a zero difference or set of zero differences is quite appropriate to the experimenter's intentions or scientific strategy when he is unable to predict differences of a specified size. When theory or other circumstances permit the prediction of differences of specified size, using these predictions as the values in H_0 is tactically inappropriate, frustrating and self-defeating. This is particularly true when a theoretical curve has been predicted, and H_0 is framed in terms of zero discrepancies from the curve. If rejection of H_0 is interpreted as evidence against the theory, and "acceptance" of H_0 is interpreted as evidence favoring the theory, we find that the larger and more sensitive the experiment is, the more likely it will lead to results opposed to the theory; whereas the smaller and less sensitive the experiment, the more likely the results will favor the theory. Aside from this anomaly, which can be corrected by recasting H_0 in terms of a zero covariance between theoretical prediction and experimental outcome, hypothesis testing as a statistical tactic in this case implies an acceptance-inspection strategy. Acceptance-inspection properly involves examination of finished products with a view to accepting them if they are good enough and rejecting them if they are shoddy enough. The theoretician is not a purchaser but rather he is a producer of goods in a competitive market so that his examination of his theory should be from the standpoint of quality control. His idealized intentions are to detect and correct defects, if possible, so that he can produce a more adequate, more general theoretical model. Because his ideal strategy is not to prove or disprove a theory but rather to seek a better theory, his appropriate statistical tactics should be those involving estimation rather than hypothesis testing.

Examination of alternative techniques available for point or interval estimation of discrepancies between theoretical predictions and experimental outcomes or the over-all variance of these discrepancies suggests strongly that estimation of the confidence intervals for the means found along a theoretical curve is the most practical and most widely applicable general procedure. Other writers have recently emphasized the values of various estimation as opposed to hypothesis testing techniques (e.g., Bolles and Messick, 1958; Gaito, 1958; Savage, 1957) and it is hoped that considerations pointed out by them and points raised in this paper will be helpful to investigators who are in the process of examining theoretical models which lead to specific numerical predictions of experimental outcomes.

References

Bolles, R. and Messick, S. Statistical utility in experimental inference. *Psychol. Rep.*, 1958, **4**, 223–227.

Bross, I. Fiducial intervals for variance components. *Biometrics*, 1950, **6**, 136–144.

Bush, R. R., Abelson, R. P., and Hyman, R. *Mathematics for psychologists: Examples and problems.* New York: Social Science Research Council, 1956.

Bush, R. R. and Estes, W. K. (Eds.) *Studies in mathematical learning theory.* Stanford, Calif.: Stanford Univer. Press, 1959.

Cornell, F. G. *The essentials of educational statistics.* New York: Wiley, 1956.

Gaito, J. The Bolles-Messick coefficient of utility. *Psychol. Rep.*, 1958, **4**, 595–598.

Goldberg, S. *Introduction to difference equations.* New York: Wiley, 1958.

Grant, E. L. *Statistical quality control.* New York: McGraw-Hill, 1952.

Kemeny, J. G., Snell, J. L., and Thompson, G. L. *Introduction to finite mathematics.* Englewood Cliffs, N.J.: Prentice-Hall, 1957.

Pearson, E. S. and Hartley, H. O. (Eds.) *Biometrika tables for statisticians.* Cambridge, England: Cambridge Univer. Press, 1954.

Rao, C. R. *Advanced statistical methods in biometric research.* New York: Wiley, 1952.

Savage, I. R. Nonparametric statistics. *J. Amer. Statist. Ass.*, 1957, **52**, 331–344.

further considerations on testing the null hypothesis and the strategy and tactics of investigating theoretical models

Arnold Binder

The arguments in a recent article by Grant (1962) are directed against experimental designs oriented toward acceptance of the null hypothesis, that is, where support for an empirical hypothesis depends upon acceptance of the null hypothesis. Atkinson and Suppes (1958) provide an excellent example of the type of experimental logic to which Grant objects. These investigators postulated a one-stage Markov model for a zero-sum, two-person game. On the basis of the model they predicted, first, the mean proportion of various responses over asymptotic trials and, second, that the probability of State k given States i and j on the two previous trials is equal to the probability of State k given only State j on the immediately preceding trial (i.e., that a one-stage Markov model accounts for the data). The predictions were then compared with the obtained results by means of a series of t tests, in the former case, and a χ^2 test, in the latter. One of the t tests, for example, involved a comparison of the predicted proportion of .600 against the observed mean proportion of .605, while another a comparison of a predicted value of .667 and an observed value of .670.

From *Psychological Review*, Vol. 70 (No. 1), 1963, pp. 107–115. Copyright 1963 by the American Psychological Association. Reproduced by permission.

Support for the one-stage Markov model was then inferred by the failure of the t tests and the χ^2 to reach the .05 level of significance. That is, support for the empirical model came from acceptance of the null hypotheses. Other examples may be found in Binder and Feldman, 1960; Bower, 1962; Brody, 1958; Bush and Mosteller, 1955; Grant and Norris, 1946; Harrow and Friedman, 1958; Weinstock, 1958; and Witte, 1959.

To facilitate future discussion it is convenient to refer to the procedure where acceptance of the null hypothesis leads to support for an empirical hypothesis as acceptance-support (*a-s*), and to the procedure where empirical support comes from rejection of the null hypothesis as rejection-support (*r-s*).

In addition to the objections to *a-s*, Grant argues that the method of testing statistical hypotheses may not be a very good idea in any case. He thus argues it is wise to shift away from the current emphasis in psychological research on hypothesis testing in the direction of statistical estimation.

Statistical logic

There have been two principal schools of thought in regard to the logical and procedural ramifications of statistical inference. The older of these stems from the writings of Yule, Karl Pearson, and Fisher, while the other comes from the early work of Neyman and Pearson and the more recent developments of Wald. The respective influences of each of these schools on experimental statistics is abundantly evident, but a difficulty in separating these influences is that the actual recommendations for tests and interval estimates in a field like psychology are similar for both.

In the Fisher school one starts the testing process with a hypothesis, called the "null hypothesis," which states that the sample at issue comes from a hypothetical population with a sampling distribution in a certain known class. Using this distribution one rejects the null hypothesis whenever the discrepancy between the statistic and the relevant parameter of the distribution of interest is so large that the probability of obtaining that discrepancy or a larger one is less than the quantity designated α (the significance level). No clear statement is provided for the manner in which the null hypothesis is chosen, but the tests with which Fisher (1949) has been associated are in the form where the null hypothesis is equated with the statement "the phenomenon to be demonstrated is in fact absent" (p. 13).

The concept "rejection of the null hypothesis" is therefore unambiguous in the context of Fisher's viewpoint, but what about "acceptance of the null hypothesis?" Fisher (1949) provides the following statement "the null hypothesis is never proved or established, but is possibly disproved, in the course of experimentation. Every experiment may be said to exist only in order to give the facts a chance of disproving the null hypothesis" (p. 16). This is not very edifying since one does not expect to prove any hypothesis by the methods of probabilistic inference. Hogben (1957) has interpreted these and similar statements of the Yule-Fisher group to mean that a test of significance can lead to one of two decisions: the null hypothesis is rejected at the α level or judgment is reserved in the absence of sufficient basis for rejecting the null hypothesis.

Papers by Neyman and Pearson (1928a, 1928b) pointed out that the choice of a statistical test must involve consideration of alternative hypotheses as well as the hypothesis of central concern. They introduced the distinction between the error of falsely rejecting the null hypothesis and the error of falsely accepting it (rejecting its alternative). Neyman and Pearson's (1933) general theory of hypothesis testing, based on the concepts Type I error, Type II error, power, and critical region, was presented later.

The possible parameters for the distribution of the random variable or variables in a given investigation are conceptually represented by a set of points in what is called a parameter space. This space is considered to be divided into two or more subsets, but we shall restrict our present discussion to the classical case in which there are exactly two subsets of points.

The statistical hypothesis specifies that the parameter point lies in a particular one of these two subsets while the alternative hypothesis specifies the other subset for the point. A statistical test is a procedure for deciding, on the basis of a set of observations, whether to accept or reject the hypothesis. Acceptance of the hypothesis is precisely the same as deciding that the parameter point lies in the set encompassed by the hypothesis, while rejection of the hypothesis is deciding that the point lies in the other subset. A typical test procedure assigns to each possible value of the random variable (statistic) one of the two possible decisions.

Sets of distributions (or their associated parameters), in this mathematical model, may be considered to correspond to the explanations in the empirical world which may account for the possible outcomes of a given experiment. Empirical hypotheses, which specify values or relationships in the scientific world, are translatable on this basis into statistical hypotheses. But the distinction between empirical and statistical hypotheses is quite important: the former refer to scientific results and relationships, the latter to subsets of points in a parameter space; they are related by a set of correspondences between scientific events and parameter sets.

The term "null hypothesis" does not occur in the writings of many of the advocates of the Neyman-Pearson view. Except for one pejorative footnote I was unable to find the term used by Neyman (1942), for example, in any of an extensive array of his publications. In general, these people prefer the term "statistical hypothesis" or simply "hypothesis" in designating the subset of central concern and alternative hypothesis for the other subset. However, null hypothesis has taken on meaning over the years in the context of the Neyman-Pearson tradition among many writers of statistics, particularly those with expository proclivities. In the *Dictionary of Statistical Terms* (Kendall and Buckland, 1957) we find the following definition for null hypothesis: "In general, this term relates to a particular hypothesis under test, as distinct from the alternative hypotheses which are under consideration. It is therefore the hypothesis which determines the Type I Error" (p. 202).

An evaluation[1]

Grant's position in regard to *a-s* is certainly not new or novel since it has been implicit in the writings of Fisher for the past 25 years. Moreover,

---

1.   There is a third viewpoint, represented in the psychological literature by Rozeboom's (1960) recent article, from which Grant's position could be evaluated. This viewpoint emphasizes the importance of the a posteriori probabilities of alternative explanations, in the Bayes sense, rather than the decision aspects of experimentation. However, the philosophical and practical problems of this approach remain enormous as is evident in the debates on this and related topics over the years. See, for example, Jeffreys (1957), Neyman (1952), Hogben (1957), Savage (1954), Chernoff and Moses (1959), von Mises (1942, 1957), and particularly Parzen (1960) who discusses the dangers of using Bayesian inverse probability in applied problems. It is typically not the case in basic research that one can assume that an unknown parameter is a random variable with some specified a priori distribution, and in such cases this approach does not presently provide any adequate answers to the problems of hypothesis evaluation.

   While of a markedly different philosophical persuasion than the present writer, Rozeboom (1960) is equally unsympathetic with the inferential bias represented by Grant. He cuts into an essential component of this bias in the following succinct and effective manner,

   Although many persons would like to conceive NHD [the null hypothesis decision procedure] testing to authorize only rejection of the hypothesis, not, in addition, its acceptance when the test statistic fails to fall in the rejection region, if failure to reject were not taken as grounds for acceptance, then NHD procedure would involve no Type II error, and no justification would be given for taking the rejection region at the extremes of the distribution, rather than in its middle (p. 419).

it has been part of the folklore of statistical advising in psychology at least as far back as my initial exposure to psychological statistics (see Footnote 2). And, in fact, if Grant wishes to argue that his position holds only in the very narrowest interpretation of the Yule-Karl Pearson-Fisher structure, I see no grounds for contesting it. If there are only two possible decisions—reject the null hypothesis or reserve judgment—one would surely not wish to equate the null hypothesis with the empirical hypothesis designating a specific value. Using this logic an investigator could just as well discard as retain a theory when it has led to perfect predictions over a wide range.

In this context I would like to point out that there are many logical difficulties connected with the Fisher formulations which have been brought out dramatically in years of debate (Fisher, 1935, 1950, 1955, 1959, 1960; Neyman, 1942, 1952, 1956, 1961). Moreover there are some people who, while generally sympathetic with the Fisher viewpoint, are quite willing to accept the null hypothesis and conclude that this provides support for an empirical hypothesis (Mather, 1943; Snedecor, 1956).

In the pursuit of evaluating Grant's position from the Neyman-Pearson theory we must remember that the null hypothesis is a statistical hypothesis which designates a particular subset of parameter points. Moreover, the null hypothesis and the alternative hypothesis (the other subset) are mutually exhaustive so that rejection of the one implies acceptance of the other; acceptance of a hypothesis being the belief, at a certain probability level, that the subset specified by the hypothesis includes the parameter point. There can be no question about the legitimacy or acceptability of acceptance of the null hypothesis within this purely mathematical scheme since acceptance and rejection are perfectly complementary.

Consequently any interpretive difficulties which result from accepting the null hypothesis must be in the rules for or manner of relating empirical and statistical (null) hypotheses. The null hypothesis is of course that hypothesis for which the probability of erroneous rejection is fixed at α (or set at a maximum of α); the test (critical region) is chosen so as to maximize power for the given α and the alternative hypothesis. Since therein lies the only feature of the process that differentiates the null hypothesis from the other subset, the relating of empirical and statistical hypotheses must be based upon it.

While there are no firm rules for deciding with which of the two subsets a given empirical hypothesis should be associated, there have been certain practices or conventions used by different writers. Neyman (1942), for example, suggested a most reasonable convention for relating empirical and statistical hypotheses which is to equate with the null hypothesis that empirical hypothesis for which the error of erroneous rejection is more serious than the error of erroneous acceptance so that the more important error is under the direct control of the experimenter. There are a few other conventions based upon the derivational advantages of fixing α for a simple (rather than a composite) hypothesis, but it is quite clear that Grant has not merely restated any of these. In fact, Grant's (1962) strong statement that "using these predictions as the values in H_0 [the null hypothesis] is tactically inappropriate, frustrating, and self-defeating," (p. 61) indicates that his position is much more than a convention of convenience.

The position which I will develop over the remainder of this paper is not that *a-s* is preferable to *r-s*, but that there are no sound foundations for damning *a-s*. In this process let me initially point out that one can be led astray unless he recognizes that when one tests a point prediction he usually knows before the first sample element is drawn that his empirical hypothesis is not precisely true. Consider testing the hypothesis that two groups differ in means by some specified amount. We might test the hypothesis that the difference in means is 0, or perhaps 12, or perhaps even 122.5. But in each case we are certain that the difference is not precisely 0.0000 ... *ad inf.*, or 12.0000 ..., or 122.50000 ... *ad inf.*

Recognition of this state of affairs leads to thinking in terms of differences or deviations that are or are not of importance for a given stage of theory construction or of application. Some express this in terms of differences which do and do not have practical importance, but I prefer the term zone of indifference which is used with important implications in sequential analysis. That is, if, for example, the difference in mean performance between two groups is less than, say, ϵ the two means may be considered equivalent for the given stage of theoretical development. In the case of a prediction of one-third for the proportion of right turns of rats in a maze, one would expect the same courses of action to be followed if the figure were actually .334 or .335. Thus, although we may specify a point null hypothesis for the purpose of our statistical test, we do recognize a more or less broad indifference zone about the null hypothesis consisting of values which are essentially equivalent to the null hypothesis for our present theory or practice.

While the formal procedures for testing statistical hypotheses are based upon the assumption that the sample size (n) is fixed prior to consideration of alternative test procedures, the user of statistical techniques is faced with the problem of choosing n and does so with regard for the magnitude of the discriminations which are or are not important for his particular application or level of theory development.

In the typical case we choose the conditions of experimentation, including sample size, such that we will reject the null hypothesis with a given probability when the parameter difference is a certain magnitude. This is frequently done very formally in fields like agriculture, although rather informally in psychology. For example, in Cochran and Cox (1957) there is an extended discussion of the procedures for choosing the number of replications for an experiment on the basis of the practical importance of true differences. Thus in one of their examples, a difference of 20 % of the mean of two values is considered sufficiently important to warrant a sensitive enough experiment to have an .80 probability of detecting it; that is, if the difference is 20 % a large enough n is desired to insure that the power of the test is .80. Although it may happen that the required sample size is a function of an unknown distribution and not determinable in advance, it can usually be approximated with the tests used most frequently by psychologists.

The choice of sample size is but one feature in the overall planning to obtain an experiment of the desired precision with due consideration for the level of theory development (including alternate theories), the zones of indifference, and the related consequences of decision. However, such other features as the standard error per unit observation and the design efficiency do not have the flexibility of sample size, and, moreover, are usually chosen to maximize precision for reasons of economy. The choice of optimum sample size applies to all experimental strategies, including the nonobjectionable (to Grant) and more usual r-s. It is surely apparent that anyone who wants to obtain a significant difference badly enough can obtain one—if his only consideration is obtaining that significant difference. Accepting that the means, for example, of two groups are never perfectly equal, the difference between them is some value ϵ. It is obviously an easy matter to choose a sample size large enough, for the ϵ, such that we will reject the null hypothesis with a given probability. But the difference may be so slight as to have no practical or theoretical consequences for the given stage of measurement and theory construction. As McNemar (1960) has recently pointed out, in his objections to the use of extreme groups, significant differences may be obtained even when the underlying correlation is as low as .10 which implies a proportion of predicted variance equal to .01.

After arguing against a-s on the basis of the dangers of tests that tend toward leniency, Grant points out that the procedure may be equally objectionable when the test is too stringent. He illustrates the latter by an example of a theory which is useful though far from perfect in its predictions. This particular point is perfectly in accord with my arguments since it demonstrates the parallelism of *a-s* and *r-s*. First, one does not usually want an experiment that is too stringent: in *a-s* because it may not be desirable to reject a useful, though inaccurate theory; in *r-s* because one may accept an extremely poor and practically useless theory. Second, one does not want an experiment that is too lenient or insensitive; in *a-s* because one may accept an extremely poor and practically useless theory; in *r-s* because it may not be desirable to reject a useful, though inaccurate theory (that is, to accept the null hypothesis which implies rejection of its alternative). The identical terms were chosen in the preceding sentences to dramatize the parallel implications for *a-s* and *r-s* of the general desirability of a test that is neither too stringent nor too insensitive. Whether or not the experiment is precise enough is, then, a function of theoretical and practical consequences, and not of whether acceptance or rejection of the null hypothesis leads to support for an empirical theory.

But, one may argue, while there is logical equivalence as stated above, there is not motivational equivalence. That is, while it is agreed that ideally investigators design their experiments (including their choice of sample sizes) in order to be reasonably certain of detecting only differences which are of practical or theoretical importance, in actual practice they are neither so wise nor so pure as to be influenced by these factors to the exclusion of social motivations. And it is indeed much easier to do insensitive rather than precise experimentation. This phenomenon is of course what Grant (1962) referred to in his statement,

The tactics of accepting H_0 *as proof and rejecting* H_0 *as disproof of a theory lead to the anomalous results that a small-scale, insensitive experiment will most often be interpreted as favoring a theory, whereas a large-scale, sensitive experiment will usually yield results opposed to the theory!* (p. 56).

Perhaps that reflects the essential point of Grant's presentation—merely to caution imprudent experimenters that the combination of personal desire to establish one's hypothesis and the ease of performing insensitive experimentation produce a particularly troublesome interaction.

Before proceeding it should be remembered that scientific considerations may be made secondary to personal desires to establish a theory whether the procedure be *a-s* or *r-s* in a perfectly analogous fashion. The only difference involves such practical considerations as the fact that it is usually easier to run 5 or 10 subjects than 100 or 500.

If Grant (1962) merely intended his article to convey this obvious warning, I cannot understand the discussions which involve such statements as the following:

Unfortunately most of the procedures used to date in testing the adequacy of such theoretical predictions [from mathematical models] set rather bad examples. Probably the least adequate of these procedures has been that in which an H_0 of exact correspondence between theoretical and empirical points is tested against H_1 covering any discrepancy between predictions and experimental results (p. 55).

If one is pointing out the dangers of using insensitive *a-s* tests (rather than condemning *a-s* on logical grounds), one would be expected to object to a particular or general use of *a-s* only if the use involved insensitive tests. Thus, it might be argued that experimenter WKE obtained support for his quantitative prediction by the use of *a-s* with a test so insensitive that it could not reasonably detect important discrepancies between predictions and observations. Or, as another fictional example, it might be stated that RRB always used *a-s* and always found support for his linear models, but his *n* was uniformly less than 5. But, unless there were almost uniform use of insensitive tests with *a-s*, this cautionary position could not reasonably lead to a condemnation of *a-s*.

As I see it, moreover, the argument against insensitive *a-s* tests is nothing but a particular form of the more general argument against bad experimentation. It is unquestionably the case that an *a-s* experiment that is too small and insensitive is poor, but the poorness is a property of the insensitivity and not of the *a-s* procedure. An *r-s* experiment that is too small and insensitive is equally poor. Due to the interaction between personal achievement desires and the ease of sloppy experimentation, as referred to previously, it may be necessary to be particularly alert to the usual scientific safeguards when using *a-s*, but that is a trivial matter and hardly worthy of an article.

In summary, it would be perfectly justifiable to argue that *n* is too small (or even too large) for a particular degree of sensitivity required at a given level of scientific development, but that is far from a proscription of designs where acceptance of the null hypothesis is in some way to the experimenter's social or personal advantage.

Grant's position from the viewpoint of scientific development

In the process of concluding this discussion I would like to emphasize and expand on certain factors which seem most critical in the process of evaluating scientific theories, as well as to indicate that my objections to Grant's apparent position are justifiable beyond the confines of the Neyman-Pearson theory.

It is surely clear that at various phases in the development of a scientific field one is faced with the problem of deciding about the suitability of different theories. When a discipline is at an early stage of development, knowledge of empirical relationships is crude so that broad isolation of explanatory constructs may be the most that is obtainable. At this stage one might consider as a significant accomplishment the ruling out of the hypothesis that observed differences are chance phenomena. The empirical hypothesis of central concern would be that there is some relationship of unknown magnitude, while its alternative would be the chance or noise explanation.

With increasing sophistication in the discipline the alternative hypotheses may represent different, but more or less equally well-developed theories. One does not choose between theory and chance, but between theory and theory or between theory and theories. Another aspect of increased sophistication is frequently the greater precision in the prediction of empirical results for the various theories.

The decision as to which of the theories is admissible on the basis of the available data may be accomplished directly within the Neyman-Pearson framework, but that is not necessarily the case. Sometimes the choice among theories depends upon a succession of tests of hypotheses or possibly even upon quite informal considerations; as an example of the latter, one theory may lead to a prediction which is perfectly in accord (within rounding errors) with the observations while the other theory is off by quite a margin—a statistical test would be considered foolish indeed. In disciplines that have markedly smaller observational variability than psychology the most common procedure consists of a subjective comparison between predictions and observations. Moreover, the point that one chooses among alternative hypotheses at various stages of scientific development (whether by statistical methods or otherwise) most certainly does not imply that his efforts stop once he has accepted or rejected a given hypothesis as Grant implies; if the accepted theory, for example, is of any interest he proceeds to make finer analyses and comparisons which may range from orthogonal subcomparisons in the analysis of variance to intuitive rumination. This provides a basis for objecting to Grant's arguments to the effect that hypothesis testing should be replaced (not supplemented) by estimation. The point is that both are usable, but at different phases of investigation.

I will again refer to the Atkinson and Suppes (1958) experiment to illustrate the relative roles of hypothesis testing and subsequent analysis in scientific advancement. Their first strategy was to decide which of two theories—game theory or the Markov model—was most adequate in the given experimental context. This clearly was a problem of testing hypotheses; a choice had to be made and the procedures of estimation could at best provide a substage on the way to the decision. The Markov model was accepted and game theory rejected, as noted above, but this certainly did not lead to a cessation of activity. Instead the investigators initially compared theoretical and observed transition matrices (and found them distinctly different), they then tested the more specific hypothesis of a one-stage Markov model against the alternative of a two-stage model, and finally they investigated the stationarity of the Markov process.

During its early phases, Einstein's general theory of relativity was equivalent to Newtonian theory in the success of explaining various common phenomena and a choice between them could not be made. But the Einstein theory led to certain predictions differing from Newtonian and these in turn led to a series of "crucial" tests. Among these were the exact predictions as to the magnitude of the bending of a light ray from a star by the gravitational field of the sun and the shift of wavelength of light emitted from atoms at the surface of stars. The general theory of relativity, thus, led to predictions which differed from the predictions of the alternative theory (Newton's), and the ultimate correspondence between these predictions and empirical observations (acceptance of no difference between predicted and obtained results) led to support for general relativity. While agreements between theory and observational results have been close they certainly have not been perfect—even physicists have problems of measurement precision and intricacy of mathematical derivation. But to the best judgment of the scientists the closeness of the fit between predictions and observations warrants the conclusion that the data provide support for the theory. Surely, however, despite its tremendous power, physicists do not claim that Einstein's general theory has been proved nor are they convinced that it will not be ultimately replaced by a better theory.

It does not seem reasonable to argue that this method of scientific procedure is not suitable for psychology—just because our measurement precision happens to be lower than in physics and we use statistical tests rather than purely observational comparison.

References

Atkinson, R. C. and Suppes, P. An analysis of two-person game situations in terms of statistical learning theory. *J. exp. Psychol.*, 1958, **55,** 369–378.

Binder, A. and Feldman, S. E. The effects of experimentally controlled experience upon recognition responses. *Psychol. Monogr.*, 1960, **74** (9, Whole No. 496).

Bower, G. H. An association model for response and training variables in paired-associate learning. *Psychol. Rev.*, 1962, **69**, 34–53.

Brody, A. L. Independence in the learning of two consecutive responses per trial. *J. exp. Psychol.*, 1958, **56**, 16–20.

Bush, R. R. and Mosteller, F. *Stochastic models for learning.* New York: Wiley, 1955.

Chernoff, H. and Moses, L. E. *Elementary decision theory.* New York: Wiley, 1959.

Cochran, W. G. and Cox, Gertrude M. *Experimental designs.* (2nd ed.) New York: Wiley, 1957.

Fisher, R. A. The fiducial argument in statistical inference. *Ann. Eugen.*, 1935, **6**, 391–398.

Fisher, R. A. *Statistical methods for research workers.* (10th ed.) Edinburgh: Oliver and Boyd, 1948.

Fisher, R. A. *The design of experiments.* (5th ed.) Edinburgh: Oliver and Boyd, 1949.

Fisher, R. A. The comparison of samples with possibly unequal variances. In, *Contributions to mathematical statistics.* New York: Wiley, 1950.

Fisher, R. A. Statistical methods and scientific induction. *J. Roy. Statist. Soc., Ser. B.*, 1955, **17**, 69–78.

Fisher, R. A. *Statistical methods and scientific inference.* (2nd ed.) Edinburgh: Oliver and Boyd, 1959.

Fisher, R. A. Scientific thought and the refinement of human reasoning. *J. Operat. Res. Soc., Japan*, 1960, **3**, 1–10.

Grant, D. A. Testing the null hypothesis and the strategy and tactics of investigating theoretical models. *Psychol. Rev.*, 1962, **69**, 54–61.

Grant, D. A. and Norris, Eugenia B. Dark adaptation as a factor in the sensitization of the beta response of the eyelid to light. *J. exp. Psychol.*, 1946, **36**, 390–397.

Harrow, M. and Friedman, G. B. Compairing reversal and nonreversal shifts in concept formation with partial reinforcement controlled. *J. exp. Psychol.*, 1958, **55**, 592–598.

Hogben, J. *Statistical theory.* London: Allen and Unwin, 1957.

Jeffreys, H. *Scientific inference.* (2nd ed.) Cambridge: Cambridge Univer. Press, 1957.

Kendall, M. G. and Buckland, W. R. *A dictionary of statistical terms.* Edinburgh: Oliver and Boyd, 1957.

Mather, K. *Statistical analysis in biology.* New York: Interscience, 1943.

McNemar, Q. At random: Sense and nonsense. *Amer. Psychologist,* 1960, **15,** 295–300.

Neyman, J. Basic ideas and theory of testing statistical hypothesis. *J. Roy. Statist. Soc.,* 1942, **105,** 292–327.

Neyman, J. *Lectures and conferences on mathematical statistics and probability.* (2nd ed.) Washington: United States Department of Agriculture, Graduate School, 1952.

Neyman, J. Note on article by Sir Ronald Fisher. *J. Roy. Statist. Soc.,* 1956, **18,** 288–294.

Neyman, J. Silver jubilee of my dispute with Fisher. *J. Operat. Res. Soc., Japan,* 1961, **3,** 145–154.

Neyman, J. and Pearson, E. S. On the use and interpretation of certain test criteria for purposes of statistical inference. Part I. *Biometrika,* 1928, **20A,** 175–240. (a)

Neyman, J. and Pearson, E. S. On the use and interpretation of certain test criteria for purposes of statistical inference. Part II. *Biometrika,* 1928, **20A,** 263–294. (b)

Neyman, J. and Pearson, E. S. On the problem of the most efficient tests of statistical hypotheses. *Phil. Trans. Roy. Soc., Ser. A,* 1933, **231,** 289–337.

Parzen, E. *Modern probability theory and its applications.* New York: Wiley, 1960.

Rozeboom, W. W. The fallacy of the null-hypothesis significance test. *Psychol. Bull.,* 1960, **57,** 416–428.

Savage, L. J. *The foundations of statistics.* New York: Wiley, 1954.

Snedecor, G. W. *Statistical methods.* (5th ed.) Ames: Iowa State Coll. Press, 1956.

von Mises, R. On the correct use of Bayes' formula. *Ann. math. Statist.,* 1942, **13,** 156–165.

von Mises, R. *Probability, statistics and truth.* (2nd ed.) London: Allen and Unwin, 1957.

Weinstock, S. Acquisition and extinction of a partially reinforced running response at a 24-hour intertrial interval. *J. exp. Psychol.,* 1958, **56,** 151–158.

Witte, R. S. A stimulus-trace hypothesis for statistical learning theory. *J. exp. Psychol.,* 1959, **57,** 273–283.

21

a note on the inconclusiveness of accepting the null hypothesis

Warner R. Wilson
Howard Miller

Grant (1962) and Binder (1963) have recently discussed the utility of basing support for a theory on the acceptance of a null hypothesis (H_0) versus basing support on the rejection of a H_0. It is convenient to refer to the procedure where acceptance of a H_0 leads to support for a theory as acceptance-support (*a-s*), and to the procedure where support for a theory comes from rejection of a H_0 as rejection support (*r-s*). Both writers have contributed to the clarification of the issue, but ambiguity and disagreement still remain.

Before discussing the problem it may be desirable to discuss some of the terms to be used. This paper follows the lead of Grant (1962) in viewing the H_0 as a supposition to the effect that no difference or no relationship exists or that no effect is exerted. Seemingly the term null hypothesis is often used in this way, and certainly Grant (1962) used it in this way when he first stated the issue. It is therefore, in this sense, a statistical hypothesis to whose rejection alone a probability estimate may be placed. As Binder points out, those of the Yule-Fisher school view the investigator as having two alternatives: he either rejects the H_0 or reserves judgment. Those following the lead of Neyman and

From *Psychological Review*, Vol. 1 (No. 3), 1964, pp. 238–242. Copyright 1964 by the American Psychological Association. Reproduced by permission.

Pearson either reject the H_0 or accept it.[1] The Yule-Fisher school would seem more compatible with *a-s* since in *a-s* one either rejects the H_0 or withholds judgment. Likewise, the Neyman-Pearson school seems more compatible with *a-s* since it allows acceptance of the H_0, and, in *a-s* it is the acceptance of the H_0 that provides support for a theory which predicted no difference in the first place. However, any reasonable person would concede that if the theory predicts no difference, the failure to find a significant difference gives some comfort to the theory, at least relatively speaking. It would seem, therefore, that it makes little difference which of these views one takes.

This paper suggests that the issue of *a-s* versus *r-s* strategies is broader than Grant and Binder indicate. It is hoped that the additional perspectives presented here will add further clarification and help provide grounds for the resolution of the issue. Grant and Binder discuss primarily a strategy decision which must be made in relation to the analysis of data. This paper points out that a similar decision must be made in relation to the collection of data.

In some cases, experimenters employ theoretical models to predict expected outcomes exactly. Grant and Binder direct most of their attention to situations of this kind. They point out that when evaluating the correspondence between predictions and outcomes, the experimenter has at least two choices: he can test the H_0 of no difference between predicted and actual values, or he can test the H_0 of no significant correspondence between observed and predicted values. In the first case, support for the theory comes from acceptance of a H_0; in the second case, support comes from rejection of a H_0. It may be noted that in this context the experimenter commits himself to an *a-s* or an *r-s* strategy when he decides how to analyze his data. It may be convenient to refer to the two types of analyses as acceptance-support-analysis (*a-s-a*) and rejection-support-analysis (*r-s-a*). A typical *a-s-a* would involve showing, perhaps by means of *t*-tests, that a number of predicted points do not deviate significantly from the points predicted by a theory and concluding that the theory is, therefore, supported. An *r-s-a* of the same data would involve showing a significant correspondence between predicted and observed points by means of correlation or analysis of variance as discussed by Grant.

Grant (1962) makes several objections to *a-s-a*: It is seldom, in psychology at least, that an experimenter can have real faith in the accuracy of his theory. Hence, if an experimenter finds no difference between theoretical and empirical values, that is, if *a-s* is obtained, this

---

1. Binder's (1963) article provides a more detailed and well-documented discussion of these two viewpoints.

result usually merely indicates that the experiment was not sufficiently sensitive to indicate the imperfections in the theory that are almost certainly there. Further, the more insensitive the experiment, the more likely it is to "support" a theory even if the theory is poor. When one seeks *r-s*, however, insensitivity works against acceptance of a theory. Furthermore, it is also difficult to give a satisfactory interpretation to a failure to obtain *a-s* because, if an experiment is very sensitive, it may deny *a-s* to a theory which is really fairly good. When an experimenter seeks *r-s*, however, sensitivity increases his chances of obtaining support.

Binder (1963, cf. p. 111) claims that parallel objections can be made about *r-s-a*. An *r-s-a* may fail to support a good theory if the experiment is very insensitive; and, at the same time, if the experiment is very sensitive, an *r-s-a* may lend support to a worthless theory, that is, one that has negligible predictive utility. Grant's arguments, says Binder, do not add up to an objection against an *a-s* strategy; they add up to an objection against experiments that are either too insensitive or too sensitive. Experiments whose sensitivity is appropriate to the present stage of theory construction and application will enable an experimenter to accept helpful theories and reject useless ones no matter which type of analysis he applies.

While this last point may be sound enough logically, it does not help much practically, since it would seem to be rather difficult to establish any workable formula for deciding what is too precise or imprecise in a given setting. Better to have a strategy that protects against the more serious type of error even if optional sensitivity is not maintained.

Binder (1963) does make a contribution, however, in that he brings to our attention that we can make several different kinds of mistakes. We can (a) accept a false theory; (b) withold judgment about or reject a good theory; or (c) accept a "true but poor" theory (as discussed by Binder, 1963, pp. 111–112). It may be helpful to note the relation among choice of *a-s-a* or *r-s-a*, use of sensitive or insensitive experiments, and the type of error one is subject to:

In an imprecise experiment *a-s-a* leads to Error Type a

In a precise experiment *a-s-a* leads to Error Type b

In an imprecise experiment *r-s-a* leads to Error Type b

In a precise experiment *r-s-a* leads to Error Type c

The choice between *a-s-a* and *r-s-a* would seem to hinge on an evaluation of the seriousness of these different mistakes. Traditionally, Type a is considered much more serious than Type b. Campbell

(1959) has presented a very sophisticated justification of this time-honored assumption. Ordinarily experimenters pay no attention to Type c; most experimenters are content to base r-s on a significant *t* or *F* and to worry not at all if the effect is so small as to be negligible. It is apparently quite rare in psychology for an experimenter to insist that a difference be larger than some minimum before it is accepted as important. And, many psychological theories are able to predict only that differences, of unspecified magnitude, should or should not occur. Some even argue that small effects may be very important from the viewpoint of theory development and maintain, in effect, that when one reports a significant but very small effect he is not making an error at all but being highly virtuous. Nonetheless, it may be unwise to give so little heed to the size of effects, that is, to Error Type c. It could be argued that psychologists may be spending a great deal of their time studying variables better viewed as irrelevant. This would seem to be more a fault of *interpretation* of a detected relationship than its detection itself. Finding a relationship is still a virtue while misusing it may not be.

One could even argue that Error Type a, acceptance of a false theory, is much the same as Error Type c, acceptance of a theory that is true as far as it goes but which is able to predict only a negligible part of the variance in the data. Indeed, Binder presents much of his defense of *a-s* on the fact that while *a-s* may lead to a, *r-s* has a corresponding weakness in that it may lead to *c*. Even if it is granted that Error Types a and c are similar in their consequences—and this is a concession that psychology as a whole apparently does *not* make—one can still note grounds for preferring precise experiments and an *r-s* analysis to imprecise experiments and *a-s* analysis. For one thing, human nature being what it is, more experimenters will probably be tempted to do imprecise experiments than precise experiments. One might argue, however, that this consideration is beside the point. More important is the fact that the precise experiment necessarily provides data to indicate how adequate the theory in question is. To be sure, it is a peculiarity of psychological data reporting that significance of relationship is always indicated while degree of relationship usually is not. Nonetheless, if the degree of relationship is slight, this can readily be inferred if the appropriate computations, or even inspections, are made. The experimenter may accept a theory that predicts very little but he is not likely to be seriously deluded about how much it predicts. One is much more in the dark with the imprecise *a-s-a*, for in this case the data show that the theory may be perfect, but, in the absence of *r-s-a* it may, as far as anyone can tell, also be very poor or even completely worthless.

These various considerations would seem to support Grant's

contention that the usual acceptance-rejection tactics might well be replaced or at least supplemented by a quality control procedure which would indicate not merely if theories predict but how well. The above considerations would not, however, seem to support Binder's contention that *a-s* and *r-s* expose the experimenter to completely parallel and equal serious pitfalls. Indeed, in light of the various stated reasons for viewing Error Type a as more serious than Error Type c (which may not even in itself be an error), it would seem that an evaluation of the various considerations Binder raises would lead to a preference for an *r-s* rather than an *a-s* strategy.

Perhaps some different perspectives can clarify further the basis for this preference. Suppose the same set of data provides both types of support or neither. In such cases it would make little difference which analysis was applied. But suppose the data provide *r-s* but not *a-s*. Such data can be meaningfully interpreted as lending the theory some support as Grant (1962) has pointed out. The critical question is, "What are the implications of accepting *a-s* when *r-s* cannot be claimed?" It is suggested that *a-s* without *r-s* means nothing. This result can seemingly only occur when the experiment *is* too insensitive to justify any conclusion. Although an *a-s* analysis may sometimes be a useful or interesting supplement to the *r-s* analysis, Grant (1962) seems justified in maintaining that *a-s* alone is not enough. To state this conclusion in another way: *a-s-a* is adequate in some situations but in all these cases *r-s-a* will be adequate also, however, in certain other situations, which apparently cannot always be anticipated, *r-s-a* will be adequate but *a-s-a* will lead one astray. Hence, why use *a-s-a*?

Thus far this paper has considered only cases in which the experimenter is comparing the fit between data points and theoretical expectations that take the form of exact quantitative predictions, e.g., the correspondence between an empirical and predicted learning curve. It is hopefully clear that two different approaches can be taken to the analysis of such data, the acceptance-support-analysis or the rejection-support-analysis.

Obviously many, if not most, experiments in psychology do not involve exact predictions. Often it is only the directionality of results that is predicted, e.g., the experimental group is expected to be less than, greater than, or perhaps equal to the control group. Do the issues raised by Grant and Binder in the context of exact quantitative prediction have any relevance to experiments that test theories which predict only whether groups are less than, greater than, or equal to each other? It is suggested that this second context also allows the experimenter to adopt an *a-s* or an *r-s* strategy and that the arguments favoring *r-s* are just as compelling in this situation.

It is true that when prediction is not exact, the kind of analysis applied will almost necessarily be analogous to what has been discussed as *r-s-a*. Suppose one predicts that the experimental group will exceed the control group. The H_0 states no difference. Support for the prediction comes from rejecting this H_0. Application of an *a-s-a*, in this context, would involve conceptualizing the H_0 as follows: "The groups do not differ significantly from the rank order predicted." *A-s* is obtained unless the groups differ significantly in the direction opposite that predicted. One, of course, is not likely to think of an *a-s-a* in this particular context because, in this context, *a-s* is ridiculously easy to obtain. Perhaps, however, this fact only lends support to the assertion made earlier—*a-s* without *r-s* means nothing.

Even when predictions are only directional and an *r-s-a* is used, the experimenter can still adopt an acceptance versus a rejection support strategy by choosing to design his experiment so that his theory predicts no differences versus some differences. It will be convenient to refer to the no-difference experiment as an *a-s*-design (*a-s-d*) and to the some-difference experiment as an *r-s*-design (*r-s-d*). If the experimenter chooses an *a-s-d*, he can claim support for his theory if no differences are found and at the same time present his negative results as evidence against any rival theories that do predict a difference. Rock and others (Rock, 1957; Rock and Heimer, 1959; Rock and Steinfeld, 1963) have used just such a strategy. If the experimenter wishes to use an *r-s* strategy, he adopts an *r-s-d*; and if differences are obtained, he claims support for his position and evidence against any theories that predict no difference. Wilson (1962) has used just such a strategy. The experimenter may, of course, change strategies in midstream. For example, if an experimenter fails to get *r-s*, he may adopt a new theoretical position that predicts no difference and cite his data as giving *a-s* to it. When Thorndike reformulated his law of effect on the basis of negative results, he essentially changed from an *r-s* to an *a-s* strategy. Seemingly, an experimenter could, in theory, start out without a theory and formulate one post hoc, in which case he might claim either *a-s* or *r-s*.

The objections made to *a-s-a* seem to apply with equal or greater force to *a-s-d*. In both cases imprecision increases the danger of accepting an erroneous theory, whereas both *r-s-a* and *r-s-d* protect against erroneous conclusions even in imprecise experiments.

A further important and compelling point would seem to be that in all of these cases we are using statistics because empirical hypotheses do not find absolute acceptance (or rejection). Rather they are accepted with more or less confidence depending on the adequacy of the evidence. Indeed, the main point of inferential statistics would seem to be to attack probability statements to the acceptance of ideas. Unless we are able to predict a necessary *degree* of correspondence or difference (which is rare in psychology), we are only able to attach such a probability statement to the *rejection* of the null hypothesis. For example, in a directional empirical prediction we can say that 1 or 5 % of the time (as we choose) we will be wrong in rejecting the null hypothesis on the basis of such data as these. We cannot, however, conversely say what the probability is of falsely accepting it except for the unlikely event in which we can specify a necessary magnitude. Therefore, only an *r-s* strategy will supply an exact estimate and an *a-s* strategy allows one to "accept" his hypothesis only in the negative sense of having found no evidence against it. This does not seem to be very satisfying grounds especially when error variance is large.

A final consideration has to do with the nontheoretical value of the information obtained from an *a-s-d* vs. an *r-s-d*. It is perhaps not undue to ask of an experimenter what value his information has other than its implications for choosing between theories. It may be noted that *a-s-d* seem to commit one to the cataloging of ineffective variables and procedures. Very likely a cataloging of effective variables and procedures, which is the logical result of *r-s-d*, would be more useful.

Summary

A choice can be made between an acceptance-support and a rejection-support strategy when prediction is merely directional as well as when it is exact. When exact quantitative predictions are derived, one chooses an acceptance-support vs. a rejection-support strategy by choosing an acceptance-support analysis vs. a rejection-support analysis. When only the directionality of the outcome is predicted, a rejection-support analysis is almost sure to be used, but one can still make the choice of an acceptance-support vs. a rejection-support strategy by choosing an acceptance-support design vs. a rejection-support design. In both cases rejection-support seems to be the better strategy, especially in that it enables one to minimize and quantify the danger of accepting an erroneous theory even in imprecise experiments.

References

Binder, A. Further considerations on testing the null hypothesis and the strategy and tactics of investigating theoretical models. *Psychol. Rev.*, 1963, **70**, 107–115.

Campbell, D. T. Methodological suggestions from a comparative psychology of knowledge processes. *Inquiry*, 1959, **2**, 153–182.

Grant, D. A. Testing the null hypothesis and the strategy and tactics of investigating theoretical models. *Psychol. Rev.*, 1962, **69,** 54–61.

Rock, I. The role of repetition in associative learning. *Amer. J. Psychol.*, 1957, **70,** 186–193.

Rock, I. and Heimer, W. Further evidence of one-trial associative learning. *Amer. J. Psychol.*, 1959, **72,** 1–16.

Rock, I. and Steinfeld, G. Methodological questions in the study of one-trial learning. *Science*, 1963, **140,** 822–824.

Wilson, W. R. Learning of paired-associates: Definitely not all-or-none. *Amer. Psychologist*, 1962, **17,** 372. (Abstract)

22

tactical note on the relation between scientific and statistical hypotheses[1]

Ward Edwards

Grant (1962), Binder (1963), and Wilson and Miller (1964) have been debating the question of what should be the appropriate relationship between the scientific hypotheses or theories that a scientist is interested in and the statistical hypotheses, null and alternative, that classical statistics invites him to use in significance tests. Grant rightly notes that using the value predicted by a theory as a null hypothesis puts a premium on sloppy experimentation, since small numbers of observations and large variances favor acceptance of the null hypothesis and "confirmation" of the theory, while sufficiently precise experimentation is likely to reject any null hypothesis and so the theory associated with it, even when that theory is very nearly true. Grant's major recommendation for coping with the problem is to use confidence intervals around observed values; if the theoretical values do not lie within these limits, the theory is suspect. With this technique also,

From *Psychological Bulletin*, Vol. 63 (No. 6), June, 1965, pp. 400–402. Copyright 1965 by the American Psychological Association. Reproduced by permission.

1. This research was supported by the United States Air Force under Contract AF 19 (628)-2823 monitored by the Electronics Systems Division, Air Force Systems Command. I am grateful to L. J. Savage, D. A. Grant, and W. R. Wilson for helpful criticisms of an earlier draft.

sloppy experimentation will favor acceptance of the theory—but at least the width of the intervals will display sloppiness. Grant also suggests testing the hypothesis that the correlation between predicted and observed values is zero (in cases in which a function rather than a point is being predicted), but notes that an experiment of reasonable precision will nearly always reject this hypothesis for theories of even very modest resemblance to the truth. Binder, defending the more classical view, argues that the inference from outcome of a statistical procedure to a scientific conclusion must be a matter of judgment, and should certainly take the precision of the experiment into account, but that there is no reason why the null hypothesis should not, given an experiment of reasonable precision, be identified with the scientific hypothesis of interest. Wilson and Miller point out that the argument concerns not only statistical procedures but also choice of theoretical prediction to be tested, since some predictions are of differences and some of no difference. Their point seems to apply primarily to loosely formulated theories, since precise theories will make specific numerical predictions of the sizes of differences and it would be natural to treat these as null hypothesis values.

Edwards, Lindman, and Savage (1963), in an expository paper on Bayesian statistical inference, have pointed out that from a Bayesian point of view, classical procedures for statistical inference are always violently biased against the null hypothesis, so much so that evidence that is actually in favor of the null hypothesis may lead to its rejection by a properly applied classical test. This fact implies that, other things being equal, a theory is likely to look better in the light of experimental data if its prediction is associated with the alternative hypothesis than if it is associated with the null hypothesis.

For a detailed mathematical exposition of the bias of classical significance tests, see Edwards, Lindman, and Savage (1963) and Lindley (1957). Lindley has proven a theorem frequently illustrated in Edwards, Lindman, and Savage (1963) that amounts to the following. An appropriate measure of the impact of evidence on one hypothesis as against another is a statistical quantity called the likelihood ratio. Name any likelihood ratio in favor of the null hypothesis, no matter how large, and any significance level, no matter how small. Data can always be invented that will simultaneously favor the null hypothesis by at least that likelihood ratio and lead to rejection of that hypothesis at at least that significance level. In other words, data can always be invented that highly favor the null hypothesis, but lead to its rejection by an appropriate classical test at any specified significance level. That theorem establishes the generality and ubiquity of the bias. Edwards, Lindman, and Savage (1963) show that data like those found in psychological experiments leading to .05 or .01 level rejections of null hypotheses are seldom if ever strong evidence against null hypotheses, and often actually favor them.

The following example gives the flavor of the argument, though it is extremely crude and makes no use of such tools as likelihood ratios. The boiling point of statistic acid is known to be exactly 50°C. You, an organic chemist, have attempted to synthesize statistic acid; in front of you is a beaker full of foul-smelling glop, and you would like to know whether or not it is indeed statistic acid. If it is not, it may be any of a large number of related compounds with boiling points diffusely (for the example, that means uniformly) distributed over the region from 130°C to 170°C. By one of those happy accidents so common in statistical examples, your thermometer is known to be unbiased and to produce normally distributed errors with a standard deviation of 1°. So you measure the boiling point of the glop, once.

The example, of course, justifies the use of the classical critical ratio test with a standard deviation of 1°. Suppose that the glop really is statistic acid. What is the probability that the reading will be 151.96° or higher? Since 1.96 is the .05 level on a two-tailed critical ratio test, but we are here considering only the upper tail, that probability is .025. Similarly, the probability that the reading will be 152.58° or greater is .005. So the probability that the reading will fall between 151.96° and 152.58°, if the glop is really statistic acid, is .025–.005 = .02.

What is the probability that the reading will fall in that interval if the glop is not statistic acid? The size of the interval is .62°. If the glop is not statistic acid, the boiling points of the other compounds that it might be instead are uniformly distributed over a 40° region. So the probability of any interval within that region is simply the width of the interval divided by the width of the region, .62/40 = .0155. So if the compound is statistic acid, the probability of a reading between 151.96° and 152.58° is .02, while if it is not statistic acid that probability is only .0155. Clearly the occurrence of a reading in the region, especially a reading near its lower end, would favor the null hypothesis, since a reading in that region is more likely if the null hypothesis is true than if it is false. And yet, any such reading would lead to a rejection of the null hypothesis at the .05 level by the critical ratio test.

Obviously the assumption made about the alternative hypothesis was crucial to the calculation. (Such special features as normality, the literal uniformity of the distribution under the alternative hypothesis, and the particular regions and significance levels chosen are not at all important; they affect only the numerical details, not the basic phenomenon.) The narrower the distribution under the alternative hypothesis, the less striking is the paradox; the wider that distribution, the more striking. That distribution is narrowest if it is a single point, and favors the alternative hypothesis most if that point happens to coincide with the datum. And yet Edwards, Lindman, and Savage (1963) show that even a single-point alternative hypothesis located exactly where the data fall cannot bias the likelihood ratio against the null hypothesis as severely as classical significance tests are biased.

This violent bias of classical procedures is not an unmitigated disaster. Many null hypotheses tested by classical procedures are scientifically preposterous, not worthy of a moment's credence even as approximations. If a hypothesis is preposterous to start with, no amount of bias against it can be too great. On the other hand, if it is preposterous to start with, why test it?

The implication of this bias of classical procedures against null hypotheses seems clear. If classical procedures are to be used, a theory identified with a null hypothesis will have several strikes against it just because of that identification, whether or not the theory is true. And the more thorough the experiment, the larger that bias becomes. The scientific conservative, eager to make sure that error is scotched at any cost, will therefore prefer to test his theories as null hypotheses—to their detriment. The scientific enthusiast, eager to make sure that his good new ideas do not die premature or unnecessary deaths, will if possible test his theories as alternative hypotheses—to their advantage. Often, these men of different temperament will reach different conclusions.

The subjectivity of this conclusion is distressing, though realistic. There should be a better, less subjective approach—and there is. The trouble is that in classical statistics the alternative hypothesis is essentially undefined, and so provides no standard by means of which to judge the congruence between datum and null hypothesis; hence the arbitrariness of the .05, .01, and .001 levels, and their lack of agreement with less arbitrary measures of congruence. A man from Mars, asked whether or not your suit fits you, would have trouble answering. He could notice the discrepancies between its measurements and yours, and might answer no; he could notice that you did not trip over it, and might answer yes. But give him two suits and ask him which fits you better, and his task starts to make sense, though it still has its difficulties. I believe that the argument between Grant and Binder is essentially unresolvable; no procedure can test the goodness of fit of a single model to data in any satisfactory way. But procedures for comparing the goodness of fit of two or more models to the same data are easy to come by, entirely appropriate, and free of the difficulties Binder and Grant have been arguing about. (They do have difficulties.

Most important, either these models must specify to some extent the error characteristics of the data-generating process, or else a special model of the data-generating process, such as the normality assumption concerning the thermometer in the statistic acid example, must also be supplied. But of course this difficulty is common to all of statistics, and is fully as much a difficulty for the approaches I am rejecting as for those I am espousing.) The likelihood-ratio procedures I advocate do not make any use of classical null-hypothesis testing, and so the question of which model to associate with the null hypothesis does not arise. While there is nothing essentially Bayesian about such procedures, I naturally prefer their Bayesian to their non-Bayesian versions, and so refer you to Savage (1962), Raiffa and Schlaifer (1961), Schlaifer (1959, 1961), and Edwards, Lindman, and Savage (1963) as appropriate introductions to them. Unfortunately, I cannot refer you to literature telling you how to invent not just one but several plausible models that might account for your data.

References

Binder, A. Further considerations on testing the null hypothesis and the strategy and tactics of investigating theoretical models. *Psychological Review*, 1963, **70**, 107–115.

Edwards, W., Lindman, H., and Savage, L. J. Bayesian statistical inference for psychological research. *Psychological Review*, 1963, **70**, 193–242.

Grant, D. A. Testing the null hypothesis and the strategy and tactics of investigating theoretical models. *Psychological Review*, 1962, **69**, 54–61.

Lindley, D. V. A statistical paradox. *Biometrika*, 1957, **44**, 187–192.

Raiffa, H. and Schlaifer, R. *Applied statistical decision theory.* Boston: Harvard University, Graduate School of Business Administration, Division of Research, 1961.

Savage, L. J., *et al. The foundations of statistical inference: A discussion.* New York: Wiley, 1962.

Schlaifer, R. *Probability and statistics for business decisions.* New York: McGraw-Hill, 1959.

Schlaifer, R. *Introduction to statistics for business decisions.* New York: McGraw-Hill, 1961.

Wilson, W. R. and Miller, H. A note on the inconclusiveness of accepting the null hypothesis. *Psychological Review*, 1964, **71**, 238–242.

23

much ado about the null hypothesis

Warner R. Wilson
Howard L. Miller
Jerold S. Lower[1,2]

Grant (1962) and Binder (1963) have clarified the fact that two strategies can be used in theory testing. First, one can identify the theory under test with the null hypothesis and claim support for the theory if the null hypothesis is accepted. The second, presumably more orthodox and traditional approach is to identify the theory under test with the alternative hypothesis and claim support for the theory if the null hypothesis is rejected. Binder has referred to these two approaches as acceptance support and rejection support strategies. In this paper, however, the authors will follow Edwards (1965) and speak of "identifying one's theory with the null hypothesis" and basing support on the acceptance of the null vs. "identifying with the alternative

From *Psychological Bulletin*, Vol. 67 (No. 3), 1967, pp. 188–196. Copyright 1967 by the American Psychological Association. Reproduced by permission.

1. The authors wish to express their thanks to Ward Edwards for his personal communications with them and for the patient forbearance he has demonstrated in attempting to help clarify the ideas that are discussed in this paper.

2. The order of authorship should not be interpreted as implying a greater contribution on the part of the senior author.

hypothesis" and basing support on the rejection of the null and, of course, the subsequent acceptance of the alternative.

Binder (1963) has ably pointed out that either strategy may be used effectively under some circumstances. Wilson and Miller (1964a, 1964b) have joined with Grant, however, in arguing that it is generally better to identify with the alternative and, hence, base support for a theory on the rejection of some null hypothesis. These writers pointed out that while the probability of *rejecting* the null hypothesis wrongly is held constant, for example, at the .05 level, the probability of *accepting* the null hypothesis wrongly varies with the precision of the experiment. To the extent that error is large, the study in question is biased for the null hypothesis and for any theories identified with it. According to this view, the conservative, cautious approach is to identify one's theory with the alternative hypothesis.

This essentially orthodox (Fisherian) view of classical statistical procedures has seemed so reasonable to the present authors that they were surprised to find Edwards, who identifies himself with Bayesian statistics, taking a dramatically opposed view. Edwards' article is only one of several considering the relative virtues of classical versus Bayesian statistics (see Binder, 1964, for an excellent review). Edwards' article seems especially important, however, due to the fact that it strongly urges changes in the tactics of the orthodox classical statistician—changes which might prove to be ill-advised in some cases and impossible in others. Edwards' (1965) paper seems to make or imply the following points: (a) Classical procedures, in fact, "are always violently biased against the null hypothesis [p. 400]." (b) The cautious, conservative approach, therefore, is to identify one's theory with the null hypothesis and, hence, base support for one's theory on the acceptance of the null hypothesis. (c) The ideal solution, however, is to compare the goodness of fit of several models to the same data, thus avoiding the whole problem of null hypothesis testing.

Edwards apparently believes that a Bayesian analysis is always feasible or that if it is not, the experiment in question is not worth doing. The present writers do not agree with this point. They do, however, find much that is admirable in Edwards' position and certainly agree that Bayesian procedures are to be preferred—when they can be used. The purpose of the present paper, therefore, is not to disagree with Edwards so much as to suggest clarification and qualification.

In connection with Point a, it is conceded that Edwards is commenting on differences between classical and Bayesian statistics that really exist. It is suggested, however, that the term "bias" is perhaps not the best way to sum up these differences. A Bayesian analysis typically assumes that the datum comes from a null distribution or from some other distribution. Classical statistics assumes that the datum comes from a null distribution or from some one of all other possible distributions. The assumption that the datum may come from *any* distribution does, indeed, always increase the apparent probability that it comes from some distribution other than the null. The difference lies in the nature of the alternatives which are to be taken into account. Classical procedures happen to assume that all possible alternatives must be taken into account. Granted this assumption, any bias for or against the null is then expressed by the probability level, which, even in the case of the .05 level, clearly favors the null.

In relation to Point b, it is suggested that the bias for theories identified with the null hypothesis in imprecise experiments, which Grant talked about, exists independently of and is logically distinct from the bias against the null hypothesis which Edwards talked about. Even when Edwards' bias *against* the null hypothesis exists, it does not imply the absence of Grant's bias *for* the null hypothesis. These considerations make the choice of tactics more complex than Edwards' article indicated. Edwards' (1965) tactical advice was that, "If classical procedures are to be used, a theory identified with a null hypothesis will have several strikes against it. . . . And the more thorough the experiment, the larger that bias becomes [p. 402]." An attempt will be made to show that this advice is valid only in experiments of extreme precision, a type presumably rare in psychology. As experiments become imprecise, just the opposite tactical advice becomes appropriate.

In relation to Point c, it is suggested that no matter how many models we may have, many people will still find null hypotheses which will seem to them to need testing.

*Is classical statistics
always biased against
the null hypothesis?*

Edwards' first point was that classical statistics is always violently biased against the acceptance of the null hypothesis. He argued persuasively for this point in several different ways. He presented, for one thing, the following example, which supposedly illustrates the bias. This example and other points made by Edwards will be considered here in hopes that the discussion will help clarify the circumstances under which classical procedures can and cannot meaningfully be said to be biased, and also give some indication of how often inappropriate rejections of the null hypothesis may, in fact, occur.

The following example gives the flavor of the argument, though it is extremely crude and makes no use of such tools as likelihood ratios. The boiling point of statistic acid is known to be exactly 50°C. [Presumably this number was intended to be 150°C.] You, an organic chemist, have attempted to synthesize statistic acid; in front of you is a beaker full of foul-smelling glop, and you would like to know whether or not it is indeed statistic acid. If it is not, it may be any of a large number of related compounds with boiling points diffusely (for the example, that means uniformly) distributed over the region from 130°C. to 170°C. By one of those happy accidents so common in statistical examples, your thermometer is known to be unbiased and to produce normally distributed errors with a standard deviation of 1°. So you measure the boiling point of the glop, once.

The example, of course, justifies the use of the classical critical ratio test with a standard deviation of 1°. Suppose that the glop really is statistic acid. What is the probability that the reading will be 151.96° or higher? Since 1.96 is the .05 level on a two-tailed critical ratio test, but we are here considering only the upper tail, that probability is .025. Similarly, the probability that the reading will be 152.58° or greater is .005. So the probability that the reading will fall between 151.96° and 152.58°, if the glop is really statistical acid, is .025 − .005 = .02.

What is the probability that the reading will fall in that interval if the glop is not statistic acid? The size of the interval is .62°. If the glop is not statistic acid, the boiling points of the other compounds that it might be instead are uniformly distributed over a 40° region. So the probability of any interval within that region is simply the width of the interval divided by the width of the region, .62/40 = .0155. So if the compound is statistic acid, the probability of a reading between 151.96° and 152.58° is .02, while if it is not statistic acid that probability is only .0155. Clearly the occurrence of a reading in that region, especially a reading near its lower end, would favor the null hypothesis, since a reading in that region is more likely if the null hypothesis is true than if it is false. And yet, any such reading would lead to a rejection of the null hypothesis at the .05 level by the critical ratio test [Edwards, 1965, p. 401].

If we follow the mode of analysis Edwards used, that of comparing an area of the null distribution to an area of the alternative distribution, we can note first that the probability of actually rejecting the null when the data in fact favor it is quite low, even in this contrived example. It would seem that we would reject the null when the data actually favor it when the observation falls in the interval 151.96–152.40. When the null is true, the data will fall in this interval, or in the corresponding lower interval, only about 3 % of the time.

In addition, the type of analysis Edwards used has two aspects that seem intuitively unappealing: (a) *All* outcomes have a low probability under the alternative hypotheses, and (b) this probability is equally low no matter where an observation occurs. For example, if a datum occurs at 150° the implied inference is that the probability of a hit in this segment of .62 is .62/40 or .0155; likewise, if a datum occurs at 169° the implied inference is that the probability of a hit in this segment of .62 is still .62/40 or .0155.

Another way of looking at this example avoids both of the aspects noted above. Suppose, for simplification, that 1.96 is rounded off to 2.00. The null hypothesis then implies that the observations should fall in a segment of 4° between 148° and 152° 95% of the time. Suppose the actual reading is 152°. The probability of a hit as far as 2° away from 150°, if the null is true, is only .05; therefore, the null is rejected. It would seem that in order to test the alternative hypothesis, one could ask, "What is the probability of a hit as close as 2° to 150° if the acid is not statistic?" The answer would seem to be 4/40 or .10. It would seem, then, that a reading of 151.96° or 152° is more probable if the null hypothesis is false, and rejection of the null would seem appropriate after all. Perhaps, then, the bias is not as prevalent as Edwards would lead us to believe. Indeed, if a person working at the .05 level of confidence is to run any danger of rejecting the null when the data actually support it, it would seem that the width of the distribution under the alternative hypothesis must be more than 80 standard deviations. The present authors will leave it up to Edwards to show that situations of this sort occur frequently enought to justify concern.

The reader may wish to note, however, that the apparent bias in classical procedures can be manipulated at will. If either a broad alternative distribution or a small error term is assumed, the bias will be increased.

Lindley (1957), another Bayesian, presumably had just such considerations in mind when he stated that data can always be invented that highly favor the null hypothesis yet lead to its rejection by a properly applied classical test. Although such data can be invented, it is still meaningful to ask whether such data are inevitable or even likely in reality. By assuming a wide enough alternative, a bias can be created; however, in reality the alternative distribution is supposedly based on some theoretical or empirical consideration, and its width cannot be set arbitrarily. Error terms, on the other hand, can be reduced, even in reality, by the expedient of collecting more cases. However, in order for a reduced error term to lead inevitably to a bias, it is necessary to assume that as the error term is reduced, the absolute deviation from chance becomes less, so that the probability of the deviation's occurrence remains constant. This convenient constancy of probability in the face of a shrinking error term cannot be expected in reality. Consider again the statistic acid example, assuming a deviation of 2° and an error term of 1°. As indicated above, the probability of a hit at 152° is .05 under the null and .10 under the alternative. In real life, any observation is more likely than not to be near the true value, so if data are collected until the error term becomes .1°, the mean value of all the observations may still be near 152°. Now the probability under the alternative would still be .10, but the probability under the null would have become far, far less, since the critical ratio would now be 20. Thus, although it is necessary to admit that data can always be invented which will make a classical test look biased, it is also possible to point out that such data are not necessarily obtainable in reality and that certainly it is also easy to invent data that make classical tests look unbiased.

The considerations up to this point seem to support the assertion that classical statistics if blindly applied will sometimes be biased against the null hypothesis. Support for the assertion that classical statistics is always biased seems lacking. Instead, it appears that the extent of such bias depends in great part on the width of the alternative distribution relative to the width of the null distribution.

In further exploring Edwards' position, it may be noted that Edwards conceded that the bias becomes less as the relative width of the alternative distribution decreases. He firmly insisted, however, that no matter how narrow the alternative distribution, the bias will persist. Edwards seems to have come to this conclusion through an inappropriate comparison of probability levels with likelihood ratios.

The likelihood ratio is the ratio of one probability density (at the point of the data) to another. In a case such as the acid example, the Bayesian would apparently rather base his conclusions on the likelihood ratio than on the probability level, and the present authors would have no objection so far as such cases are concerned. In commenting on the relation of likelihood ratios to classical significance tests, Edwards (1965) said:

Even a single-point alternative hypothesis located exactly where the data fall [the form of alternative distribution that most violently biases the likelihood ratio against the null hypothesis] cannot bias the likelihood ratio against the null hypothesis as severely as classical significance tests are biased [p. 401].

Whether we formally use likelihood ratios (ratios of ordinates) or simply other ratios of conditional probabilities (areas), what Edwards was saying seems to have a certain surface validity. If we consider only the probability (or probability density at a point) under one distribution, the null hypothesis, and do not take into consideration how likely this event might be under some specified alternative distribution, we are biasing ourselves against our null hypothesis by comparing it essentially to all possible alternatives instead of comparing it to just one. It seems to us that this is exactly what the classical statistician *intends* to do. If we have a clearly defined alternative, and we can say that "reality" must be one or the other, then we can justify a likelihood ratio or some similar procedure. If we do not have such alternative models, we cannot invent them to avoid a theoretical bias.

Edwards, Lindman, and Savage (1963) implied that in any inference based on statistics, the decision involved must be a joint function of a prior probability estimate (what you thought before about the likelihood of your hypothesis), the likelihood ratio, and the payoff matrix (the relative rewards and costs of being right and wrong about your hypothesis). Edwards seemed to imply that "classical statisticians" use no such considerations. It is doubtful that this is so. For one thing, a choice of significance level can, under some circumstances, be construed as a prior probability estimate—not the subjective one of the individual scientist but an admittedly arbitrary attempt to standardize a bias against alternative hypotheses (not altogether different from a bias for the null). It appears to be a deliberate attempt to offer a standardized, public method for objectifying an individual scientist's willingness to make an inference. An undisputed goal of science is objectivity—public reproducibility. To introduce, into inferential statistics, a methodology dependent on partially subjective estimates of probability would seem to undermine this goal.

It is apparently impossible to say whether the choice of low probability levels implies a low prior probability or a payoff matrix biased for retention of the null hypothesis, but one or both seem implicit. The natural tendency is for investigators to believe that their hypotheses are correct and that the world can ill afford to ignore them. If such subjective inclinations were allowed full sway, experimentation could become superfluous, and science might well degenerate into controversy. Classical statistics wisely resolves prior probability and payoff considerations in a conservative and standard rather than in a subjective and variable manner.

In answer to the obvious criticism concerning the subjectivity of invented alternative hypotheses, Edwards[3] stated essentially that a scientist always has some information regarding alternatives. Bayesian statistics considers this information; classical statistics does not.

---

3.   W. Edwards, personal communication, October 1966.

It seems that the bias that Edwards was discussing is a function of the failure to use (assume?) this additional information. In point of fact, the choice of one particular alternative distribution with which to compare the null excludes other possible alternatives. It is precisely this exclusion (which may be justifiable under some circumstances) which increases the probability that you will accept the null.

In this section we have attempted to discuss such questions as "Are classical procedures biased against the null hypothesis?" and "How often might such a bias result in rejections of the null when the data actually favor it or discredit it only weakly?" We see no reason to view classical procedures as biased against the null in any absolute sense—the opposite seems to be the case. We see no reason to view classical procedures as biased against the null hypothesis relative to Bayesian statistics since this comparison is at best unsatisfactory due to the difference in the procedures which are used and in the information which is assumed to be available. We can concede only that under special conditions, including presumably a specifiable alternative distribution, blind use of a classical analysis might result in a rejection of the null when a defensible Bayesian analysis, considering only the specifiable alternative, might show that the data actually support the null. We know of not one real-life instance in which the above has been demonstrated. It would seem to us that circumstances making such errors likely are not frequent, and it is suggested that the burden of proof is on those who think that such errors occur frequently —in the literature, as opposed to in the examples used in articles written by Bayesians.

*Should the scientific
conservative always
identify his theory with
the null hypothesis?*

Edwards' second main point was that if one does use classical statistics, the more conservative strategy is to identify one's theory *not* with the alternative hypothesis—as Wilson, Miller, and Grant advocated—but with the null hypothesis. This point, too, is apparently incorrect. What is more, even if the first point, about classical statistics being always biased, were correct, the second point would not necessarily follow. In order to see the actual independence of the two points, it is helpful to realize that if something is biased, it is biased relative to something else. Edwards presumably meant that classical statistics is always biased relative to Bayesian statistics.

On the other hand, when Grant, Wilson, and Miller said that an insensitive experiment is biased for the acceptance of the null hypothesis and any theory identified with it, they meant that an insensitive experiment is biased relative to a sensitive one. A classical analysis can be biased against the null in comparison to a Bayesian analysis, and an insensitive experiment can still be biased for the null in comparison to a sensitive experiment. The two biases exist independently. What is more, the bias for the null hypothesis in insensitive experiments is just as true with a Bayesian analysis as with a classical analysis.

The following example (see Table 1) is offered as an illustration of the bias in insensitive vs. sensitive experiments—a bias which, prior to the Edwards article, the present writers would have considered not in need of illustration. The example views experiments as perfectly sensitive or as completely insensitive; null hypotheses as true or false; and theories as identified with the alternative and supported if the null is rejected, or as identified with the null and supported if the null is not rejected.

Edwards said that if you are a conservative, that is, if you wish to minimize undeserved successes, you should always identify your theory with the null. Wilson, Miller, and Grant said that in the case of insensitive experiments, such as are common in psychology, just the opposite tactic is to be recommended to the conservative. Table 1 indicates the number of deserved and undeserved successes achieved by theorists depending on whether they do identify with the alternative or with the null. Overall, identification with the null clearly promotes success for one's theory, a total of 285 (out of 400) successes vs. 115

Table 1
Limits of deserved and undeserved successes assuming identification with the null versus the alternative in perfectly sensitive and insensitive experiments

	Identification of theory with the null		Identification of theory with the alternative	
	Percentage deserved successes	*Percentage undeserved successes*	*Percentage deserved successes*	*Percentage undeserved successes*
Sensitive experiments				
True null	95	0	0	5
False null	0	0	100	0
Insensitive experiments				
True null	95	0	0	5
False null	0	95	5	0

for those who identify with the alternative. The same is true in the case of total undeserved successes. Those who identify with the null get a total of 95 undeserved successes (out of 200) vs. 10 for those who identify with the alternative. The most dramatic difference occurs, of course, in the case of insensitive experiments. The score is 95 illegitimate successes for those who test their theories as null hypotheses and only 5 for those who test their theories as alternative hypotheses. Hopefully, no one will wish to attempt to reconcile these outcomes with Edwards' (1965) assertion: "The scientific conservative, eager to make sure that error is scotched at any cost, will therefore [always] prefer to test his theories as null hypotheses—to their detriment [p. 402]."

The authors would like to concede, however, that in recommending continued use of classical statistics combined with identification of theories with alternative hypotheses, they are operating on the basis of several beliefs which are not mathematically demonstrable.

Perhaps the most critical belief in this context is that most experiments in psychology are insensitive. It may be noted that a conservative would not favor identification with the alternative on the basis of Table 1 unless he held this belief. In a perfectly sensitive experiment, only identification with the alternative leads to accepting one's theory when it is false. This would occur because no matter how small the error, t's of 1.96 and greater will occur 5% of the time. These writers would point out, however, that in very sensitive experiments, specious deviations from chance, though technically significant, would be so small that they could hardly mislead anyone. It might also be argued that belief in ESP, for example, survives partly on just such deviations. Such a consideration might justify more concern about such errors, greater use of the .01 or .001 significance level, and greater interest in likelihood ratios when meaningful ones can be computed.

Although the good showing of "acceptance support" in sensitive experiments is in its favor, it should still be noted that, seemingly, grounds are seldom available for deciding if experiments are going to be sensitive. In the face of this inevitable equivocality, investigators are encouraged to identify their theories with the alternative and so put an upper limit on error of 5% rather than 95%. One is not justified, after all, in assuming that favorable circumstances—true theories and sensitive experiments—will occur generally. A sensible strategy must assume the possibility of unfavorable circumstances—false theories and insensitive experiments—and must provide protection against these unfavorable circumstances.

Intuitively, it might seem impossible to base any inference, or express any bias, on the basis of a completely insensitive experiment. This consideration, however, is just the point of the objection to identification with the null. Identification with the null allows one to base positive claims for theoretical confirmation on the acceptance of the null hypothesis, which is, of course, virtually assured ($p = .95$) in the completely insensitive experiment.

Yet another consideration relates to the fact that it makes relatively little difference which approach you use in precise experiments. With great precision, you cannot go too far wrong. As experiments become imprecise, however, the tactical choice makes an increasingly large difference. All the more reason, therefore, for the conservative to choose the tactic that protects him even when experiments are imprecise.

The second belief is that statistics can sometimes reveal facts worth knowing even if they are not apparent to the naked eye. The relationships between smoking and lung cancer and between obesity and heart disease are examples. It is true that statistics may lead one to be overly optimistic about the importance of effects that are more significant than important, and certainly this tendency is to be deplored. On the other hand, although the human observer, unbeguiled by statistics, may indeed discount many trivial effects, he may also infer strong effects when only a trivial effect or no effect at all is present. Many people are, in the opinion of these authors, overly optimistic about the existence of ESP and the efficacy of psychotherapy. This overoptimism exists, however, in spite of statistics, not because of them.

Those who favor the so-called interocular test should realize that situations in which effects are large relative to error will yield their secrets quickly. This consideration suggests that investigators will inevitably spend most of their time on ambiguous situations in which the effects of interest are small relative to the precision of measurement so far achieved. Statistics will be needed in such situations.

The third belief is that false positives are more damaging than false negatives. In the present context, this statement means that it is worse to view a false theory as already proved than to view a true theory as not yet proved. This belief is widespread (see, e.g., Campbell, 1959) and will not be belabored here. Granted the belief that false positives cause more trouble, identification of one's theory with the alternative is only natural. The traditional .05 significance level then limits the investigator to 5% error no matter how insensitive his experiments and no matter how false his hypotheses. When one identifies his theory with the null, however, the natural conservatism inherent in the traditional use of small probability levels works for, rather than against, hasty claims for support. Indeed, if an investigator identifies his theories with the null and if his theories are false, his number of false positives approaches not 5%, but 95%, as his experiments become increasingly imprecise.

The fourth belief is that many null hypotheses are worth testing. Edwards questioned this belief by suggesting that most null hypotheses are obviously false and that the testing of them is, therefore, meaningless. One of several possible replies is that the real question is frequently not whether the data deviate from the null, but whether the deviation is positive or negative. In such a case the testing of the null is obviously meaningful.

If the conservative investigator believes that false positives are the greater threat and that his experiment will be insensitive, he will surely choose to identify his theory with the null hypothesis. On the other hand, none of the beliefs discussed so far necessarily justifies a preference for probability levels over likelihood ratios, and likelihood ratios are, in fact, strongly recommended whenever it is possible to compute them. The last belief, however, is that in most psychological experiments it is not possible to use a Bayesian approach based on likelihood ratios. The calculation of a ratio requires at least one specifiable alternative distribution. In most psychology experiments, no grounds are available for arriving at such a distribution. In such cases, classical statistics appears to be the only alternative, and, under this condition, the possibility of classical statistics being biased relative to Bayesian statistics is a meaningless issue.

Naturally, classical statisticians as well as Bayesian statisticians should consider alternative distributions. The point is that such considerations may or may not yield enough information to clearly justify a Bayesian analysis. So long as such information is often, if not usually, lacking, Edwards' rejection of classical approaches seems premature.

Edwards implied, to be sure, that investigators using classical tests have often rejected true null hypotheses without real evidence even when Bayesian statistics were potentially available. Bayesians could perhaps make a definite contribution by analyzing a number of published experiments and pointing out instances in which classical statistics has led to null hypothesis rejection when a potentially available Bayesian analysis would not have. It seems entirely possible, however, that such examples might be hard to find. At least they seem to be conspicuously absent from Bayesian critiques. It is also suggested that it would be most instructive if Bayesians would supply a precise alternative distribution to accompany any of the following null hypotheses, which are presented as typical psychological problems: (a) partially reinforced subjects extinguish at the same rate as continuously reinforced subjects; (b) patients show no change on tests of adjustment as a function of counseling; (c) punishment does not influence response rate; and (d) students working with teaching machines learn no faster and no better than students reading ordinary textbooks. Furthermore, the likelihood ratio, even if available, is not likely to disagree with the classical test unless the alternative distribution is very broad. If the meaningful alternative is not uniform, as it was in the statistic acid example, but instead has a mode or modes somewhere in the neighborhood of the null value, the likelihood ratio and significance test are even more likely to point in the same direction.

Another tactical point that merits attention is the question of whether a null hypothesis rejection resulting from a sensitive experiment should always be viewed as a legitimate success. As Table 1 indicates, if a null hypothesis is false, a sufficiently sensitive experiment will always reject it, and theories identified with the alternative will always be supported. Table 1 views such successes as legitimate. The possibility always exists, however, that the difference, though real, may be so slight that recording it in the literature is a complete waste of effort. The present writers think that the indiscriminant cataloguing of trivial effects is, in fact, a major problem in psychology today, and they would certainly regret it if their position was in any way interpreted as encouraging this unfortunate practice. On the other hand, as Wilson and Miller have pointed out, one must weigh one problem against another. If investigators identify their theories with the alternative hypothesis, they may be tempted to run *many* subjects and report theories to be true, even though the thories have no predictive utility. On the other hand, if investigators identify their theories with the null hypothesis, they may be tempted to run *few* subjects and report theories to be true, even though they are completely false. The present writers find no difficulty in deciding that they would prefer to confront investigators with the first temptation rather than the second.

A consideration of the problem of accepting trivial effects does not, therefore, greatly modify this paper's inclination towards identification with the alternative hypothesis in combination with the use of classical tests. This strategy may not be the best imaginable, but it is still often the best available, and it is recommended to the scientific conservative.

In summing up this section, we wish to remind the reader that Edwards apparently recommended that investigators switch to Bayesian techniques altogether. He went on to say, however, that if one *does* use classical statistics, the more conservative tactic, that is, the tactic that minimizes erroneous claims for theoretical support, is identification with the null. Our perspective on this advice can be summed up very briefly: If a conservative is a person who wishes to adandon a tactic that puts a ceiling on error of 1 in 20 and adopt instead a tactic that puts a ceiling on error of 19 in 20, then this is excellent advice.

Does the development of
multiple models avoid the
need for null hypothesis
testing?

Edwards' last point was that the better tactic is to compare your data to several plausible models, and hence avoid null hypothesis testing altogether. Multiple models seem thoroughly desirable, and it seems worthwhile to note that in a traditional two-tailed test, classical statistics always implies three families of models: one predicting no difference, one predicting a positive difference, and one predicting a negative difference. On the other hand, it is hard to see how multiple models avoid the need for null hypothesis testing. Again an example from Edwards' (1965) paper may be helpful.

A man from Mars, asked whether or not your suit fits you, would have trouble answering. He could notice the discrepancies between its measurements and yours, and might answer no; he could notice that you did not trip over it, and might answer yes. But give him two suits and ask him which fits you better, and his task starts to make sense [p. 402].

But ask him if he's sure of his decision or if he might reverse it if he saw you model the suits again, and you have a null hypothesis to test. In other words, although on one occasion one model (suit) was judged to fit the data (you) better, one must still ask if the difference in fit is significant relative to the potential sources of error. However stated and however tested, this question still seems to constitute a null hypothesis. Bayesian statistics may offer a meaningful alternative to null hypothesis testing, but it will take more than this example to convince the present authors.

Are undefined alternative
hypotheses the fault of
classical statistics?

From the current vantage point, the classical bias against the null hypothesis does not appear as obvious as Edwards' bias against classical statistics. It is instructive to note one aspect of the rationale behind Edwards' (1965) bias: "The trouble is that in classical statistics the alternative hypothesis is essentially undefined, and so provides no standard by means of which to judge the congruence between datum and null hypothesis [p. 402]." Edwards seemed to see the absence of a specifiable alternative as a short-coming of classical procedure. It seems appropriate to point out that, in fact, the absence of a well-defined alternative is not a vice of classical statistics. The absence of a well-defined alternative is a problem, a problem which is unavoidable in many cases, a problem which Bayesian statistics presumably cannot handle, and also a problem which classical statistics is especially designed to avoid.

Summary

Some of the main points of the position of the present writers may be summed up as follows: (a) Identification with the alternative limits erroneous claim for theoretical support to 5%; identification with the null limits such errors to 95%. The conservative is, therefore, presumably better advised to identify with the alternative. (b) Classical procedures assume that only the null distribution can be specified, and ask if the data are from this distribution or some other. Bayesian procedures assume that two distributions can be specified, and ask if the data are from the null distribution or the alternative. Granted the difference in procedure and in the information assumed, discussion of a bias in one procedure relative to the other seems of dubious meaningfulness. (c) Granted the information assumed by classical procedures, they show an absolute bias in favor of the null hypothesis.

References

Binder, A. Further considerations on testing the null hypothesis and the strategy and tactics of investigating theoretical models. *Psychological Review*, 1963, **70**, 107–115.

Binder, A. Statistical theory. *Annual Review of Psychology*, 1964, **15**, 277–310.

Campbell, D. T. Methodological suggestions from a comparative psychology of knowledge processes. *Inquiry*, 1959, **2**, 152–182.

Edwards, W. Tactical note on the relation between scientific and statistical hypotheses. *Psychological Bulletin*, 1965, **63**, 400–402.

Edwards, W., Lindman, H., and Savage, L. J. Bayesian statistical inference for psychological research. *Psychological Review*, 1963, **70**, 193–242.

Grant, D. A. Testing the null hypothesis and the strategy and tactics of investigating theoretical models. *Psychological Review*, 1962, **69**, 54–61.

Lindley, D. V. A statistical paradox. *Biometrika*, 1957, **44**, 187–192.

Wilson, W. and Miller, H. The negative outlook. *Psychological Reports*, 1964, **15**, 977–978. (a)

Wilson, W. R. and Miller, H. A note on the inconclusiveness of accepting the null hypothesis. *Psychological Review*, 1964, **71**, 238–242. (b)